ANTICIPATING GOD'S NEW CREATION

Essays in Honor of Ted Peters

Carol Jacobson and Adam Pryor, Editors

Lutheran University Press
Minneapolis, Minnesota

Anticipating God's New Creation
Essays in Honor of Ted Peters
Carol Jacobson and Adam Pryor, Editors

Copyright © 2015 Lutheran University Press, an imprint of 1517 Media. All rights reserved. No part of this publication may be reproduced, stored in a retrieval system, or transmitted in any form or by any means, electronic, mechanical, photocopying, recording, or otherwise, without written permission of the publisher: 1517 Media Permissions, PO Box 1209, Minneapolis, MN 55440-1209, or copyright@1517.media.

ISBN 978-1-942304-12-8
eISBN 978-1-942304-41-8

Table of Contents

Introduction 7

THEOLOGICAL METHODOLOGY

What's Needed in Theology?
Worldview Construction, Retrieval, or . . . ? 13
Michael B. Aune

Methodological *Askēsis*: On Practicing a Theology of the Actual 28
Gaymon Bennett

Dialogue and Hospitality 60
David Ratke

What Kinds of Questions Are Explained in Theology? 69
Niels Henrik Gregersen

Method, Methodology, and Theology 79
Ted Peters

ESCHATOLOGY & RETROACTIVE ONTOLOGY

Will God Save the World or Not?
Prolepsis, Open Theism, and the World's Future 95
Carol Jacobson

Hummingbirds Make Stars Possible:
Exploring and Celebrating Ted Peters' Retroactive Ontology 105
Robert John Russell

Prolepsis and the Abolition of Hell: Why Hell Is Not Like Heaven 111
Kristin Johnston Largen

Apples and the Apocalypse 129
Jane E. Strohl

The Space between Us: Blessed Is Ted for He Is Timely Placed 140
Vitor Westhelle

A Retroactive Response to Retroactive Ontology 152
Ted Peters

THEOLOGY, CULTURE, & THE CROSS

Justification, Self-Justification, and Forgiveness:
Ted Peters on Sin and Its Overcoming 167
Derek Nelson

The Poetry of Gurram Joshua, GOD—the World's Future,
and Their Implications for Dalit Theology 178
Moses Penumaka

Jesus' Creation Theology and Multiethnic Practice 195
David L. Balch & Adam W. Pryor

"Happily Ever After":
An Approach for Novice Readers of Revelation 210
Wayne C. Kannaday

An Author-Character Match Made in Heaven:
Ted Peters and Leona Foxx 220
Jan-Olav Henriksen

The Theology of the Cross and Cultural Analysis 228
Ted Peters

THE EVOLUTION CONTROVERSY

Encountering Evolution:
Ted Peters on Darwin and Christian Theology 247
Martinez Hewlett

Human Origins: Present, Past, and Future 257
Ronald Cole-Turner

Sacramental Evolution: Emerging into the *Imago Dei* 267
Peter M.J. Hess

Animal Suffering, Animal Sin,
Theistic Evolution, and the Problem of Evil 280
Joshua M. Moritz

Evolution, Theodicy, and New Creation 294
Ted Peters

ASTROTHEOLOGY & ETHICS, BOTH HERE AND BEYOND
Stem Cells in Wonderland?
Proleptic Ethics and Stem Cell Research 307
Karen Lebacqz

The Dialogue between Worlds:
Ted Peters' Proleptic, Planetary Ethic 318
Whitney Bauman

Flying Saucers—No Laughing Matter!
Ted Peters and Astrotheology 328
Albert A. Harrison

Astrobiology, Theology, and Ethics 339
Brian Patrick Green

Terrestrial Ethics and Extraterrestrial Astrotheology 351
Ted Peters

Published Writings of Ted Peters 364

Index of Authors 385

Index of Subjects 388

Dr. Ted Peters

Introduction

It is a pleasure to offer these essays in recognition of the theology and scholarship of our colleague, Ted Peters. As an interdisciplinary academic and a faithful representative of the Lutheran tradition, Peters has influenced a generation of scholars, pastors, professors, and parishioners to realize that God's work in the world can be most fruitfully understood at the intersections between theology, science, and culture.

He has developed methods for theological inquiry that are born of and determined by his personal experiences, as well as by the political, historical, and scientific contexts in which he is living. Peters' scholarly acumen and theological curiosity have given rise to his many influential works—works on genetics, evolution, cosmology, and more—works that directly address the influences of a scientific worldview upon people's theological and secular self-understandings.

The essays here are organized into five sections, each representing those particular intersections between theology, science, and culture that are central to Peters' work. In the initial section, "Theological Methodology," authors engage Peters' work as a hermeneutical theologian and his uses of "critical realism" and "model-making" to ground his methodological approach to the work of the theologian. Believing that causal explanations and semantic explanations need to be consonant, but not identical, Peters argues for an engaging twist to the Tillichian method of correlation, stating that "when it comes to offering an explanation based upon natural causes, that's what we ask of the scientist. When it comes to offering the meaning of the world in which we live, that's what we ask of the theologian."

"Eschatology and Retroactive Ontology" contains essays by theologians, historians, and scientists alike, each of whom finds retroactive ontology fruitful for their own reflections on meaning-making. Peters himself identifies retroactive ontology as the "backbone of my theological worldview." But what exactly is retroactive ontology, and can it speak meaningfully outside a theologically trained audience? What does it mean to engage in the work of theology in an age of science believing that God promises a new creation—one that will transform the present creation and one that grounds all reality? Can it make sense to modern persons that the reality and meaning of the present moment is dependent upon its place in God's ultimate future? Is such a worldview exegetically sound? Is it explanatorily adequate?

In the most wide-ranging section, "Theology, Culture, and the Cross" discusses the dual mechanisms of self-justification and scapegoating that fuel the ever-present relativity of inhumanity and injustice in our world. In addition, the revelatory capacity of the cross of Jesus is highlighted as the only truth that can actually speak to the depths of sin. As Peters writes, "What is so difficult for the theologian of the cross is to untie the knots of political rhetoric so that the cross can do its job of revealing self-justification, hypocrisy, and exploitation." This exposing of the scapegoat mechanism is perhaps the most valuable "revelation" made by encountering the reality of the cross. But it reveals more as well, namely, that the Trinitarian God is fully present in the cross, and this means that the divine life is affected by the suffering of Jesus and the suffering of the world.

"The Evolution Controversy" details a long-standing theme in Peters' work. Each article addresses some of the intricacies of theistic evolution and the concomitant issue of theodicy that arises for theologians holding this position. In particular issues related to theological anthropology as it relates to forms of theistic evolution are addressed in depth as they strive to articulate critical features of an evolutionary account of evil.

Addressing ethical topics as small as stem cells and as vast as life in the span of the known universe, "Astrotheology and Ethics, Both Here and Beyond" is a testament to the scope of Peters' thinking. What each article reveals (whether in appreciation or critique) is Peters' deep concern for bringing together eschatology and ethics. The proleptic thrust so evident in the methodological analysis of section one is reprised in consideration of how to make the present world a better place. As Peters writes quite specifically, "The task of proleptic ethics, I believe, is to devise middle axioms that connect the grand eschatological vision of a new creation with our quite human responsibilities in the present time."

As editors of the volume what we have found revealed over and over in the diverse articles we received is that the emphasis Peters' work places on prolepsis cannot be overstated. He has consistently promulgated a theological vision for how God's action from the future is anticipated now. Moreover, it is clear from the tremendous enthusiasm and support we have received from contributors that Peters' thinking theologically about how God's future can become present to our world has shaped not only his own work but subsequent generations of scholars and professional colleagues.

No volume of this magnitude is completed without the help and support of many people and institutions. As the editors on the project we wanted to all too briefly acknowledge the hard work and support of all the authors who have contributed to the volume; Aaron Cooley, Emily Olsen, Sanna Reinholtzen, and Melissa Woeppel who have diligently worked on the editing and indexing of the volume; and Karen Walhof at Lutheran University Press for her enthusiastic willingness to publish this work. We are grateful to the editors of *Currents in Mission and Theology* who allowed us to retain the rights to re-publish a number of the articles that appear in this volume. We would also like to thank California Lutheran University, Pacific Lutheran Theological Seminary, and Bethany College for providing financial resources to support us in developing what began as a special issue of a journal into a far larger volume chronicling Peters' diverse work.

Finally, we would like to thank Ted Peters. His willingness and enthusiasm to respond to each of the articles has enriched this volume. Moreover though, he has been a wonderfully encouraging colleague and teacher for each of us (and so many others). Anyone who has spent time with him has experienced this support and can appreciate how his colloquial charm can offer clarifying insights into complex theological problems. We are grateful for the opportunity to honor Ted in a way that seems most appropriate for someone who has so actively contributed to theological scholarship throughout his career.

Carol R. Jacobson and Adam W. Pryor

THEOLOGICAL METHODOLOGY

What's Needed in Theology?

Worldview Construction, Retrieval, or . . . ?

Michael B. Aune

Introduction

When describing the current context in which theology is done, the term *postmodern* or a variant thereof is usually employed. Such a term, moreover, has enjoyed nearly canonical status for almost two-and-a-half decades. Seminarians invoke it with all the solemnity of liturgical prayer [if they actually believe such a thing exists anymore]. Colleagues employ the term to show other colleagues that they are hip to what's going on in academic circles and to show our friends across the street [as we often say in Berkeley to refer to the godless world of the University of California] that we can play *wissenschaftliche* hardball with the best of them.

Given this current scene, what is a Christian theologian to do? My colleague and friend Ted Peters—to whom this essay is dedicated—has responded to this question by articulating a systematic theology rooted in the traditional biblical symbols and yet in conversation with this postmodern time. Reviewers have hailed his *GOD—the World's Future* as an exemplary model of theological construction and depth that critically engages our current context because it shows how Christian faith is relevant and can contribute to humanity's, if not the entire universe's, future. This illustrates very well what one commentator on the newer projects in systematic theology calls the complementarity or "partnership of retrieval and recontextualization."[1]

This article was first published in *Currents in Theology and Mission*, volume 39, number 4 (August 2012): 268–278.

1 Gabriel Fackre, "The Surge in Systematics: A Commentary on Current Works," *The Journal of Religion* (1993): 234.

More recently, Peters has engaged what can only be called a belligerent atheism that angrily denies the existence of God in whom we place our faith. In a brief essay written for his Danish colleague Peter Widmann's *Festschrift*, entitled "The Systematic Theologian at Work in an Atheistic Context," he employs the major insights and contents of *GOD—the World's Future* to provide what I would call a "Cliff's notes" version of this larger work to address this atheistic challenge with its "trash talk" of theology as "a non-subject . . . vacuous . . . devoid of coherence and content."[2] Such a challenge confronts us with the question once again of the nature of the theological task. Peters' answer:

> Today's theologian is an intellectual carpenter whose business is worldview construction—that is, the theologian constructs a speculative picture of the whole of reality, within which everything is oriented toward the God of grace. Our day-to-day experience along with our secular knowledge of the magnificent world in which we live can be properly understood only in relationship to the God who created and redeems all things. And, furthermore, we Christians understand this God to be gracious.[3]

In what follows, I want to use Peters' essay to illustrate an understanding of a particular theological method—a correlational one (though he doesn't quite call it that, preferring instead the term hermeneutical, but the point or the dynamic is the same). It is to connect or correlate something in the past, whether message, faith, *kerygma*, the inherited tradition that confessed the Incarnation of God in Jesus Christ,[4] to its current setting by constructing a view of the world that is

---

[2] Richard Dawkins, "From the Other Side: Richard Dawkins Responds," *Science and Theology News* 6, no. 2 (October 2005): 38; cited in Ted Peters, "The Systematic Theologian at Work in an Atheistic Context," *Gudstankens aktualitet: Bidrag om teologiens opgave og indhold og protestantismens indre spaendinger. Festskrift til Peter Widmann*, Else Marie Wiberg Pederson, Bo Kristian Holm og Anders-Christian Jacobsen, Red (København: Forlaget ANIS, 2010), 55.

[3] Peters, "The Systematic Theologian," 55.

[4] Orthodox theologian John Behr gives us a helpful reminder about the Incarnation. He writes in his book *The Mystery of Christ* about seeing "a greater depth of meaning" in this term. It is "only in light of the Passion that we can even speak of 'Incarnation' so that the sense of this term is pregnant with a greater fertility.... our encounter is with the eschatological Lord, the Coming One, that is not just the second person of the Trinity born of the Virgin Mary but rather an interpretation made only in light of the Passion. In short, Incarnation refers to the entire saving event which, for Behr, is the Passion of Christ (*The Mystery of Christ: Life in Death* [Crestwood, New York: St. Vladimir's Seminary Press, 2006]), 16–18.

an understandable and believable portrayal of reality—of the world that is loved by a gracious God. Hence, my task in Part I is to summarize this essay so that in Part II I can provide a contrast to and a supplement to this approach to theology as worldview construction with one that is known as a "theology of retrieval" or a "theology of particularity."[5] Such theologies

> seek to give close attention to significant theologians of the past—particularly before modernity—in order to call into question and reframe the contemporary theological discussion. The point is not to repristinate these past theologies, but to read past theologians in a way which allows for them to call us into question.[6]

Moreover, these theologies give more singular attention to what the Germans call the *inhaltliche Bestimmtheit*[7]—"a precise and definite content" of this grace. This is theology's *Sollgehalt*—not "what you gotta believe" but what needs to be there—"the required content" of the Christian message that makes our theological talk identifiably Christian.[8] And such *Sollgehalt*, finally, takes its bearings from the ground of

---

5   Others might speak of a theology of "interruption" that seeks a more critical engagement with modernity and postmodernity. E.g., see Lieven Boeve, *God Interrupts History: Theology in a Time of Upheaval* (New York & London: Continuum, 2007). Like a theology of "retrieval," it is a mode of theological work that treats "pre-modern Christian theology as a resource rather than a problem" for recontextualization of the Christian message. John Webster, "Theologies of Retrieval," *The Oxford Handbook of Systematic Theology*, John Webster, Kathryn Tanner, Iain Torrance, eds. (Oxford & New York: Oxford University Press, 2007), 585.

6   Interview with J. Todd Billings discussing his new book, *Union with Christ: Reframing Theology and Ministry for the Church* (Grand Rapids, MI: Baker Academic, 2011). http://www.credomag.com/2012/01/17/interview-with-todd-billings-on-union-with-christ/. My emphases. Accessed March 25, 2012. See also Webster, "Theologies of Retrieval," 583–99.

7   See Matthias Wolfes, *Protestantische Theologie und moderne Welt: Studien zur Geschichte der liberalen Theologie nach 1918* (Berlin & New York: Walter de Gruyter, 1999), 573ff. Also, my "Discarding the Barthian Spectacle: Conclusion—Might We Be Liberals after All?" *Dialog* 46, no. 2 (Summer 2007): 153–65.

8   Edward H. Schroeder, "The Relationship between Dogmatics and Ethics in the Thought of Elert, Barth, and Troeltsch," *Concordia Theological Monthly* 36, no. 11 (December 1965): 744. In one of his "Thursday Theology" postings—June 8, 2006—on the topic of "The Trinitarian Dogma," Schroeder noted—"A 'dogma' (according to what the early church meant by the term) is NOT what you've 'gotta' believe in order to be a Christian, but what 'has to be' at the center of Christian preaching in order to make that proclamation 'gospel.' Werner Elert's simple '*fester Satz*' was '*Dogma ist das Sollgehalt des Kerygmas.*'" "*Fester Satz*," literally "a solid sentence," that Elert would dictate to his Erlangen students. The concern here is what can give us the best language for theological articulation and proclamation.

Christian belief itself, "expressed on the one hand by John 1:14 ("And the Word became flesh and made his dwelling among us") and on the other hand by the resurrection narratives...."[9]

Christian Theology as Worldview Construction

But let me proceed, first, with the heart of Peters' essay—worldview construction or "Worldview Construction as Indirect Apologetics."[10] As noted earlier, he presents his theological response to atheism's challenge and its denial "of the God in whom Christians believe." Such a response takes the form of "indirect apologetics" where the task is to draw a picture of reality "which includes the natural world studied by the scientist along with that of the creator's creator and redeemer." This portrayal, argues Peters, "must be more comprehensive if it is to depict a world loved by a gracious God. Moreover,

> what this means is that the response of the systematic theologian to the atheist denial of God is indirect rather than direct. The relative adequacy of the theologian's argument will be determined by its ability to illuminate a deeper and more comprehensive understanding of reality.[11]

Peters acknowledges here his indebtedness to Pannenberg's description of the theological task which states that the presentation of a systematic account of Christian doctrine—of God, creation, human history as a history of salvation—must possess an inner consistency but also a consonance with the biblical witness and a coherence with "all matters that have to be taken into account."[12] We are still in the realm of speculation and hypothesis-construction, however, because theological work remains under the eschatological proviso. It is admitting this provisionality of our theological statements, even though they are "strongly assertive . . . [a]s a condition of being taken seriously with their truth claims."[13]

What now remains is the task of identifying the principal cultural context to which the theologian presents his or her picture of reality.

---

9   Anthony J. Godzieba, "Incarnation, Theory, and Catholic Bodies: What Should Post-Postmodern Catholic Theology Look Like?" *Louvain Studies* 28 (2003): 225.
10 Peters, "The Systematic Theologian," 64ff.
11 Ibid., 64.
12 Wolfhart Pannenberg, *The Historicity of Nature: Essays on Science and Theology,* Niels Henrik Gregersen, ed. (West Conshohocken, PA: Templeton Foundation Press, 2008), 7.
13 Citing ibid., 8; Peters, "The Systematic Theologian," 64.

This modern or postmodern understanding of reality, for Peters, involves two hermeneutical questions. The first, which is well known to us at Pacific Lutheran Theological Seminary (PLTS), is:

> . . . how can the Christian faith, first experienced and symbolically articulated in an ancient culture now long out-of-date, speak meaningfully to human existence today as we experience it amid a worldview dominated by natural science, secular self-understanding, and the worldwide cry for freedom?"[14]

The second hermeneutical question for Peters is the "postmodern addendum":

> . . . how can the Christian faith be made intelligible amid an emerging postmodern consciousness that, although driven by a thirst for both individual and cosmic wholeness, still affirms and extends such modern themes as evolutionary progress, future consciousness, and individual freedom?[15]

Postmodernism, according to Peters, can either be "holistic" or "pluralistic." The former seeks to overcome the subject-object split and return to the whole. The "pluralists" [much too generous a name in my book] are characterized by deconstructionism, fragmentation, repudiation of "hegemonic meta-narratives," the cultural politics of difference, etc. Now, what is the theologian to do? S/he can go for the "modern" version of the world and an accompanying affirmation of a "single planetary reality united by reason, science, and technology."[16] A theologian who wishes to be "postmodern" will attend to the world's pluralism as a reality as well as an ideology—and perhaps its romanticism about "globalization."

Peters, however, is not particularly interested in embracing this pluralistic worldview or "supra-worldview."[17] He still wants to address the aggressive atheistic worldview that purportedly rests on scientific authority that has no room whatsoever for any religious or theological claim. "Theology," in the words of Sam Harris, "is now little more than a branch of human ignorance. Indeed, it is ignorance with wings."[18]

---

14 Peters, "The Systematic Theologian," 66.
15 Ibid.
16 Ibid., 67.
17 Ibid., 68.
18 Sam Harris, *The End of Faith: Religion, Terror, and the Future of Reason* (New York: W.W. Norton, 2004), 14.

In the midst of this belligerent talk of the denial of God's existence, Peters asks whether such an avowal of this so-called "God-Hypothesis" that rolls all of the deities into one is at all adequate. That is, does God provide a rational and scientific explanation of the natural world as the atheists aver? No. Rather, to affirm God's existence "expands our ability to explain the reality in which we live...." But such an affirmation is not the "product of scientific explanation."[19] Moreover, Peters argues, there is no need to invoke God in a specific scientific explanation of the natural world. But in the end, we do need an explanatory framework that provides us with a way of dealing with "ultimate reality in its most comprehensive scope conceivable."[20] This ultimate reality is the God of Israel, according to Peters.[21] Science cannot account for this. It cannot answer the questions of why the world exists at all or why is the human mind attuned to nature's laws.

But Christian theology can incorporate into its purview that world studied by natural science in order to provide that more comprehensive and more illuminating portrayal of reality in order to underscore the gracious God's creative and redemptive action. For Peters, this is much more expansive than the view of the world limited by material explanations.[22] This understanding of the natural world is to be incorporated into the work of the systematician because she is "seek[ing] a theology that allows for the full presence of God in, with, and for the world created by him, without reducing God to the world or to a consequence of the world."[23]

In the end, if the theologian is both to earn an honest living and continue to engage in the task of worldview construction, there will need to continue to be a respectful and mutual dialogue with scientists and readiness for both to expand their respective horizons of understanding. It comes down to this:

> ... the theologian should seek dialogue with laboratory scientists who pursue authentic scientific research, not atheists such as Dawkins who substitute materialist ideology for actual science. It is crucial for today's theologian to distinguish

---

19 Peters, "The Systematic Theologian," 72.
20 Ibid., 73.
21 Ibid.
22 Ibid.
23 Philip Clayton, *God and Contemporary Science* (Grand Rapids, Michigan: Wm. B. Eerdmans Publishing Co., 1997), 236; cited in Peters, 73.

sharply between authentic scientific research and the claims of materialist ideology. The former provides contextual meaning, while the latter requires theological engagement.[24]

Moreover, the systematic theologian needs to be hermeneutically astute—engaged in the interpretation of scripture and interpreting the reigning understanding of reality in the present. What makes this work distinctive is that his or her formulations about the world—"a world created by the God of grace and slated for ultimate transformation into a promised new creation"[25]—are to be as comprehensive in scope as possible

> describing reality at the highest level of generalization concomitant with its ultimate meaning—and consistent with one another so as to construct a single coherent worldview... [and] contextual[ing] historic faith commitments in light of the understandings which influence, if not dominate, the contemporary context....[26]

We see, then, the complementarity of "retrieval" and "contextualization" in offering "a comprehensive and integrated rendering of the classical doctrines of Christian faith responsive to historical context,"[27] but in "self-conscious opposition" to a Zeitgeist shaped by atheism. Hence, the Christian theologian is to construct "an intelligent and credible picture of reality that includes God's Trinitarian interaction with the world."[28] Such a portrayal is to meet the criteria of both explanatory adequacy that can give the community of faith its self-understanding and a point of departure for the apologetic task. In so proceeding, the theologian needs to know the difference between research science and atheistic materialism. Natural science, in providing material for the constructive work of theology through scientific discovery, can only enhance, if not strengthen, our appreciation of the work of God the creator who has made that world.

---

24 Peters, "The Systematic Theologian," 74.
25 Ibid.
26 Ibid., 74–75.
27 Fackre, 224.
28 Peters, "The Systematic Theologian," 75.

Now What? Questions of Theology's Method and Content

Most of the systematic theologians I know and read are concerned with context and that certainly exemplifies Ted Peters' work. Context is the watchword of today's theology and plays the decisive role as the theologian seeks to interpret Jesus' message in its original context and to formulate it anew in a particular cultural situation. Making the connection between these two is the so-called method of correlation and many, if not most, theologians operate with some version of it. We all learned from Paul Tillich, for example, that theology arises in the response of revelation to the questions of the situation and then "systematic theology . . . makes an analysis of the human situation out of which the existential questions arise, and it demonstrates that the symbols used in the Christian message are the answers to these questions."[29] Our late PLTS president, Timothy Lull, was always fond of saying that "the world sets the theological agenda." Peters, too, follows this method and the existential question emerging from the postmodern situation he is endeavoring to address is that of world and worldview—can they be of God and hence, oriented to the God of grace thus offering a counter-argument to the challenge posed by atheists?

The manner in which Peters addressed this question was to affirm that God is gracious and that a God of grace has created the world. This is the so-called "core" of Christian faith that can now be correlated with our modern/postmodern context. The assumption here is that there is some sort of continuity between the Christian message and the present context—an "intrinsic link between the significance of revelation, faith, church, and tradition, and the context in which they are given form."[30]

For example, "the modern strivings for rationality, human freedom, and social liberation are regarded as privileged *loci theologici* from which the recontextualization of the Christian faith in this God who is involved salvifically with human beings and their histories could take place."[31] Where human beings struggled for human dignity, God could not possibly be absent. "Secular culture was no longer considered to be alienated

---

29 Paul Tillich, *Systematic Theology, Vol. I* (Chicago: The University of Chicago Press, 1951), 62.
30 Boeve, *God Interrupts History*, 7.
31 My discussion here follows Boeve, 32ff, and also Boeve, "Beyond the Modern-Anti-Modern Dilemma: *Gaudium et Spes* and Theological Method in a Postmodern Context," *Horizons* 34, no. 2 (2007): 295ff.

from Christianity, but rather the place where God was actively present in the struggle for an authentic subjectivity and social justice."[32]

This has been a starting point for so-called "modern theologies." These strivings and principles thus are presumably continuous with modernity because there is the striving for rationality and emancipation, and Christian faith. What the theologian does, then, is to critically (cor)relate the saving message of Christian faith with this modern context. In seeking this consensus between culture and faith, a correlation theologian tends to assume that a Christian is "as modern as the average modern human being" and offers "even a surplus where modernity reached its limits (e.g., eschatologically correcting mere inner-worldly Utopian expectations)."[33]

This modern project of practice and theology is, hence, one in which nearly all Christians could participate, along with others of good will, and for good theological reasons because "the whole of created reality in which we live comes to us as grace in the ordinary things of everyday, in the faces of our fellow human beings and in the great aspirations of present-day humanity."[34] Here is that continuity between Christian faith and context, insofar as secular reason reaches truth, Christian faith cannot but comply with it.

In this case, faith adds to, or qualifies, what human beings know by secular reason alone, or faith makes visible and motivates what is already at work at the heart of the modern project—plausibility and rationality. And it can be communicated in a universally acknowledgeable language, because we have presumably learned the art of dialogue between faith and modernity. Yet all is not well in the land of correlationist theologies. As Neil Ormerod observed over fifteen years ago, with so an impressive pedigree of the method of correlation, what problems could there ever possibly be?[35] Should not it be obvious that this is the method—the preeminent theological method—that we should be employing? For how can God not be present in that modern project where we all participate together—with others of good will—for those great causes of rationality

---

32 Boeve, *Horizons*, 295.
33 Ibid. These are Boeve's emphases.
34 Edward Schillebeeckx, "Eindresulaat," in *Het Tweede Vaticaans Concile, Vol. 2* (Tielt/Den Haag: Lannoo, 1986), 69; cited in Erik Borgman, *Edward Schillebeeckx: A Theologian in His History,* John Bowden, trans. (London & New York: Continuum, 2003), 358 [Volume I: A Catholic Theology of Culture (1914–1965).
35 "Quarrels with the Method of Correlation," *Theological Studies* 57 (1996): 710.

and emancipation? There is somehow a universal truth simply residing deeply within us, ready to be activated.

Really? But that's the problem. Is it really true that there exists "a potential consensus between modern culture and Christianity when related to each other in a mutually critical manner?"[36] Is it true that "there should be no discrepancy between being a sincere modern human being and being an authentic Christian"?[37] But, why should we even think that we are to submit ourselves as theologians to some sort of ambivalent episode in human history for which we should be articulating the faith? Why should modernity or postmodernity or whatever we call this present time somehow be "the hidden *norma normans non normata* that decides what can and cannot be said and done in contemporary theology?"[38]

Is it not one of the theologian's tasks to critique modernity—the context in which he finds himself? Yes, it is. That critique can proceed in one of several ways. It can basically tell the current context to go to hell because it is un-redeemable anyway, and then present a totally anti-modern or anti-postmodern theology that challenges the so-called modern project at every turn, exposing its intellectual and moral bankruptcy.[39] Much more charitable, however, is an approach such as exemplified by John Behr in his book, *The Mystery of Christ*.[40] He appropriates a "pre-modern perspective in a cautious post-modern fashion...."[41] What that means is that one pursues theology that does not simply speak about God in the abstract, nor satisfy itself with a historical report about events in the past, but which contemplates the transforming power of God through the Cross."[42] It is here in this event, argues Behr, that we begin to find the theological method of the early church—a method that reaches

---

36 Boeve, *God Interrupts History*, 34.
37 Ibid., 34. My italics because, in my judgment, this expresses so well a general ethos here in the Graduate Theological Union.
38 Erik Borgman, "Retrieving God's Contemporary Presence: The Future of Edward Schillebeeckx's Theology of Cultures," *Edward Schillebeeckx and Contemporary Theology*, Frederiek Depoortere, Lieven Boeve, & Stephan Van Erp, eds. (London & New York: T & T Clark, 2010), 235. My ensuing discussion here depends on Borgman, 235ff.
39 Theologians need to read a work like Bruno Latour's, *We Have Never Been Modern* (Cambridge, Massachusetts: Harvard University Press, 1993) in order to rethink the definition and constitution of modernity itself. His work might also inspire us and instill in us the hope that postmodernism is not the only possibility at present.
40 John Behr, *The Mystery of Christ: Life in Death* (Yonkers, New York: St. Vladimir's Seminary Press, 2006).
41 Ibid., 19.
42 Ibid., 43.

backward and forward from the Passion for entering into the mystery of Christ. "The Christ of Christian faith," writes Behr, "revealed concretely in and through the apostolic proclamation of the crucified and risen Lord in accordance with the Scripture, is an eschatological figure, the Coming One."[43] More can be said about this way of doing theology but for now let it be this—"The reappropriation of a pre-modern perspective in a cautious post-modern fashion...might point a way out of the quandary in which theology has found itself in recent centuries, and forward to a space in which we can appreciate the integrity and unity of the discipline of theology and see anew its vision"—to place us once again in a position to recognize the eschatological Lord. So, here, a premodern theology—instead of being a problem—is a resource for our contemporary theological responsibility.

Or, the current context can be interrupted, intruded upon. Grace radically enters, intrudes into an existing context. Grace can also halt an existing understanding—for the sake of opening them up anew toward the reality of God in Jesus Christ. But for this interruption to actually work, in my estimation, it requires a retrieval of aspects of the Christian tradition that tend to be ignored or forgotten as theology became "modern" and now "postmodern."

However, these theologies of retrieval are not some direct form of theological conservatism, repristination, or even a neo-orthodoxy.[44] Rather, they seek to retrieve what is forgotten as a pre-condition to a fuller, more theological understanding of modernity or however we call our present time. This is no simple return from the fleshpots of the present to what might be considered a more authentic teaching from the past. Some may think that, but ultimately, theologians of retrieval are attempting to respond adequately to our situation—to seek what would be a true "orthodoxy" in the sense of here and now—where the subject matter of Christian theology is Christ—the one of whom Scripture has spoken and still speaks and who is recognized in the breaking of the bread. Failure to appreciate this leaves us in a kind of modern theology that can only be described as an odd mixture of metaphysics and mythology.

But to speak of orthodoxy does not at all imply that there is some unchanging substance. Rather, it has to be "re-invented" or, in the words

---

43 Ibid., 17.
44 Webster, "Theologies of Retrieval," 584ff.

of Lieven Boeve, "recontextualized"[45] because modern correlation theology suffers from too little recontextualization, not too much. Or, it has to be "retrieved" and, hence, seen as "a response to a self-bestowing divine reality which precedes and overcomes the limited reach of rational intention."[46] That is, there has not been enough questioning or challenging of the presupposition of continuity of Christian faith with the present. Nor have theologians realized their own hidden complicity with modernity, employing with particular aplomb, it seems, the epistemological and cultural values of the situation in which we find ourselves. As a result, such theology may seem too facile, too consensus-oriented, and too continuous with our liberal or conservative notions of truth and meaning.

We have forgotten that there is a particularity of Christian faith, and it is difficult to determine what that is if we are basing our work on human conceptual patterns derived from results of the social sciences or philosophy. We need to be reminded—as theologians of retrieval and of Christian particularity are wont to do—"There is no automatic link between the generally human and Christian particularity."[47]

Now, I think such a theology of retrieval or of particularity can shed further light on Peters' essay on "theology as worldview construction," as I stated in the introduction to this essay, by providing a more robust *inhaltliche Bestimmtheit*—"a precise and definite content" to his talk of a God of grace.[48] Though there he emphasizes "the God of grace" or a "gracious God" occurring about eight times during the course of his essay, I cannot help but notice that there is not much of a Christological actualization of that grace.[49] There is a brief mention of a "gracious Trin-

---

[45] Boeve, *God Interrupts History*, 37. In another essay, Boeve notes, "The concept of recontextualization . . . functions descriptively and normatively. As a descriptive category, it assists in the analysis of the ways in which tradition has been challenged by contextual change and novelty, to its uncritical embracing and adaptation." The normative function of this concept is to take the contextual challenges to Christian faith seriously "in order to come to a contemporary theological discourse which at the same time can claim theological validity and contextual plausibility." Cited in "Retrieving Augustine Today: Between Neo-Augustinianist Essentialism and Radical Hermeneutics," *Augustine and Postmodern Thought: A New Alliance against Modernity?*, L. Boeve, M. Lamberigts, M. Wisse, eds. (Leuven: Uitgeverij Peeters, 2009), 1.
[46] Webster, "Theologies of Retrieval," 584.
[47] Boeve, *God Interrupts History*, 38.
[48] See n. 6.
[49] I do realize that Peters devotes over 150 pages in *GOD—The World's Future* to Christology so I am quite curious why there is this Christological lack in this essay on theology as worldview construction.

itarian interaction with the world" but that is about all. The emphasis on "grace" and "gracious" not only here in the Peters essay but also in much "Lutheran-speak" these days feels flat, abstract, formulaic—without much *inhaltliche Bestimmtheit* or *Sollgehalt*.

I realize very well that there are contemporary Lutheran systematic theologians who are not really interested in whether their theology is somehow "Lutheran." Mark Mattes has observed in his review of *The Gift of Grace: The Future of Lutheran Theology*, for example, that many of the essayists in that volume "contend that Lutheran theology has a future, but only to the degree that it is not uniquely Lutheran."[50] Or, to be offering a Lutheran theology is to be offering no theology at all because theologians are to be serving the whole church. It is simply preaching to the choir as David Ratke has noted in his essay "Lutheran Systematic Theology: Where Is It Going?"[51]

But if we take the agenda of a theology of retrieval seriously then it cannot be some sort of "theology-in-general," broadly applicable to or interpretive of all Christian traditions. Liturgical theologians, for example, are just beginning to learn that there are particular forms, texts, styles of expression, sounds, words, beliefs—and not just one size fits all.[52] Hence, for theologians to say—Lutheran theologians, mind you—to say that offering a Lutheran theology is to be offering no theology at all is simplistic, if not totally naïve—comparable to the assertion I hear in my field that there is no such thing as "Lutheran liturgy." This may be a subtle ecumenical point as it is sometimes said, but the larger reality, if you will, is a pastoral—if not anthropological one. The reality is one of identity—of particularity.

And that brings us to the question of Christology—Christology comprises an entire section in his *GOD—the World's Future* of two significant parts—"the Person and Work of Jesus Christ" and "the Work and Person of Jesus Christ." In this discussion, Peters notes his problems with "Chalcedonian incarnationalism."[53] But to say that such a Christology makes it

---

50 [Review of] Niels Henrik Gregersen, Bo Holm, Ted Peters and Peter Widmann, eds., *The Gift of Grace: The Future of Lutheran Theology* (Minneapolis: Fortress Press, 2005), in *Scottish Journal of Theology* 62, no. 1 (2009): 97. Mattes also has published a much lengthier review in the *Lutheran Quarterly* 19, no. 4 (Winter 2005): 439–457.
51 David Ratke, "Lutheran Systematic Theology: Where Is It Going?" *Dialog* 40, no. 3 (Fall 2001): 217.
52 See my "The Current State of Liturgical Theology: A Plurality of Particularities," *St. Vladimir's Theological Quarterly* 53, no. 1–2 (2009): 209–229.
53 Peters, *GOD—the World's Future*, 231.

difficult to actually relate God to the world is not really true. It is exactly the opposite.⁵⁴ Moreover, we don't have access to "the originary experience of Jesus" anyway. But maybe we can get Peters off the hook with his notion of "prolepsis" for helping us make sense of "God with us."⁵⁵

A more adequate Christology will be substantially aided by a theology of retrieval or by the reappropriation of that "pre-modern" perspective now curiously "post-modern"—to move our understandings beyond the abstract and formulaic that I mentioned earlier. If the ground of our faith is to be found in Christology (John 1:14: "And the Word became flesh and dwelt among us") and the narratives of the resurrection (if our fundamental commitment is to the truth of God's incarnation in Christ), then we do need some assistance in making this revelatory particularity public and rationally accessible, because it still is the case, I would hope, that the real business of theology (while perhaps important to fend off the belligerent challengers to Christian faith) is still about learning how to deliver the gospel.⁵⁶

We can proceed even more boldly in our theological work, then, from the unique event of God's revelatory initiative—that paradigm of the incarnation that is concrete, particular, and historical—that radical particularity of "the Trinitarian God assuming human reality in the person of Jesus Christ as the Word truly made flesh."⁵⁷ This particularity of the Incarnation—and its retrieval—can "be the ground of a theological method that is accountable both to revelation and to the long tradition of practices and reflections" while also speaking to our contemporaries.⁵⁸

Other discussions of the centrality of grace—both as content and as charism—of our tradition are quite emphatic that the gracious God is, in

---

54 See John J. O'Keefe, "Impossible Suffering? Divine Passion and Fifth-Century Christology," *Theological Studies* 58 (1997): 39–60. O'Keefe argues that our perception of these Christological debates needs to be corrected by the larger and much more fundamental question of whether and where God contacts the world at all. He notes, "If we do not have a sufficiently incarnational Christology, we may even today complain with Cyril: 'they do not understand the economy.'" (60).
55 See "Will God Save the World or Not?" in this *Festschrift*.
56 Robert Kolb, "Lutheran Theology in Seventeenth Century Germany," *Lutheran Quarterly* 20 (2006): 455.
57 See my earlier note on a more expansive definition of the Incarnation (n.3).
58 Anthony J. Godzieba, Lieven Boeve, Michele Saracino, "Resurrection—Interruption—Transformation: Incarnation as a Hermeneutical Strategy: A Symposium," *Theological Studies* 67 (2006), 778.

the words of Robert W. Jenson, "an event, indeed a history."[59] Moreover, this event has a name—it is Jesus Christ—and his particular life and death—where "God is there for us and that this is favor and not disaster."[60] But to posit that it is this one who is God's act of grace to and for us brings us to what Jenson has termed "the notorious *communicatio idiomatum genus maiestaticum* (communication of the attributes of majesty) and indeed of *genus tapeinoticum* (of humility)."[61] Why notorious? Probably because Luther had made it so in the eucharistic controversy with Zwingli and Oecalampadius who just couldn't "get it" that the affirmation of God's turning toward us in grace—means we can say, "Here is God"—and that means, too, that we must also say, "Here is Christ the man."[62]

It is this retrieval of the communication of attributes "without reservation" that helps us to understand what a theology of grace is—"God favoring us with himself"—and to place it at the center of our practices and reflections. If our Lutheran theological tradition can remain faithful to this irreducible particularity of the Incarnation of the grace of God while continuing to incorporate other useful insights that have emerged in our history for the sake of the larger continuing theological enterprise of the whole church, then our colleague Ted Peters is right. He has reminded us of the foundation that is worthy of future theological construction—and, hence, of the future of our Lutheran theological tradition as well. And that is not necessarily a bad thing.

---

59 Robert W. Jenson, "Triune Grace," in *The Gift of Grace*, 23.
60 Ibid.
61 Ibid.
62 Ibid. We also see this in the controversies over the Lord's Supper and Christology where the Concordists used this *communicatio idiomatum* between Christ's divine and human natures on behalf of the doctrine of the presence of his body and blood in the Lord's Supper. See the "Catalogue of Testimonies." For a fine recent discussion, see Charles P. Arand, James A. Nestingen, & Robert Kolb, *The Lutheran Confessions: History and Theology of the Book of Concord* (Minneapolis: Fortress Press, 2012), 227–253 and 274–276.

Methodological *Askēsis*

On Practicing a Theology of the Actual

Gaymon Bennett

> This process [of inquiry] makes theology participatory because the questions we pose regarding God become simultaneously questions God poses to us. We ourselves become part of the questioned reality (Peters, 2002:31).

> ... we define spirituality as being the form of practices which postulate that, such as he is, the subject is not capable of the truth, but that, such as it is, the truth can transfigure and save the subject ... (Foucault, 2005:19).

Ted Peters' innovations in theological method constitute one of the most vital contributions of his work to systematic theology. Taking systematic theology as a lived practice, this essay sets out to show how Peters' contribution, though present in his formal methodological statements, is actually most vivid and powerful when viewed in terms of the overall trajectory and stakes of his work.

If the question of method begins with how work is done, then Peters' contribution only really can be appreciated by examining what he says about what he has done in relation to how he has actually done it. This perspective helps us see that Peters' method is not only appropriate to the specific projects he has carried out. More important, it constitutes a striking answer to the vexing question of what it means today, theologically, to think, and therein what it means, spiritually, to live the theological life.

Orienting Prologue: A Theology of the Actual

Peters' contributions to theological method are, on one level, straightforward: he incorporates empirical materials (consisting of interviews, fieldwork, analysis of contemporary events and specific claims) into the theology of culture developed by Paul Tillich and carried forward by Langdon Gilkey, and into the theology of history developed by Wolfhart Pannenberg.[1] In this way, Peters fashions theology proper into an ethical practice, which is to say, advances theology as an ethic and ethics as something more than a mere theological addendum. What this means, precisely, how he does this, and what this allows him to do, is both subtle and far-reaching, as I will show.

Incorporating the Actual

The assertion that Peters incorporates empirical materials should be taken in an etymologically serious sense. Peters does not merely add empirical data to the theologies of culture and history as received. He does not simply supplement Tillich's or Pannenberg's general insights and broad proposals with specific examples and proper nouns. Rather, by way of empirical materials Peters gives new form to theologies of culture and history. He gives theological form to culture and history in its empirical actuality.

This means that Peters does not simply pass through the empirical on his way to a deeper theological truth, one secretly hidden behind or underneath. When Tillich elaborates the existential structures of culture, revealing culture's religious depth, the specifics of any particular existence or culture disappear from thought.[2] Similarly, when Pannenberg insists that salvational history is nothing other than material history in the totality of its specificity, he does not actually tell us anything about that history in its specificity.[3] For Peters, by contrast, the empirical dimensions of existence and history are precisely that which need to be

---

[1] Given the richness of Peters' work and the constraints of a short article, my assessment of Peters' contributions to theological method is perforce selective and therefore partially exclusionary. I am focusing primarily on his turn to empirical inquiry as a key innovation. Equally important, and in a fashion connected to this turn, has been Peters' attention to the analysis of mythology and religion in the work of Huston Smith and others, as well as the ways in which the themes and structures of ancient religious traditions and practice become recapitulated in contemporary forms.

[2] See, esp., Paul Tillich, *Systematic Theology*, vol. 3 (Chicago: University of Chicago, 1963).

[3] See, esp., Wolfhart Pannenberg, *Systematic Theology*, vol. 1 (Grand Rapids, Michigan: Wm B Eerdmans Publishing Co., 1991).

brought into theological view and accounted for.

In sum, and to coin a term, one might say that by incorporating the empirical, Peters transforms a theology of culture and a theology of history into a theology of the actual.

A Very Short Excursus: Empirical + Actual

Before showing how Peters does this and why it matters, a very brief excursus is warranted. The terms empirical and actual have, in recent years, been the object of considerable philosophical and theological consternation. This is due in a large part to the continued influence of Gilles Deleuze, in whose work the empirical and the actual make several evocative appearances. What Deleuze actually intended by these terms is widely debated and not easy to grasp. What is clear—and without presuming to capture his full meaning—is that his use of the terms are helpful for thinking through Peters' project specifically, and for rethinking the critical task of theology more broadly.[4]

The Empirical

Generally speaking, the notion of the empirical carries a double sense. It distinguishes a mode of knowing based on observation, experiment, and experience. This mode is often opposed (sometimes polemically) to theory or to speculation. In a corollary fashion, the term names a certain kind of reality, one that can only be known through observation, experiment, and experience. This second, ontological sense of the term also implies a contrast; the "really real" is that which is known to experience.

Moving partially beyond these contrasts, while keeping them in view, Deleuze draws attention to the fact that, in experience, the empirical is always transactional. It is an artifact of a transaction between the thinker and the world. That transaction is carried out by way of conceptualization.[5] Conceptualization, the work of philosophy and theology, is a labor by way of which the empirical is actualized. As one of Deleuze's commentators has put it, concepts can "be seen as bridges that are always being

---

4 See Gilles Deleuze, "Contrôle et devenir," in *Pourparlers*, Paris: Les Éditions de Minuit (Orig. Futur antérieur, No. 1. printemps 90, entretien avec Tony Negri, 1997). Gilles Deleuze and Felix Guattari, *What Is Philosophy?* Graham Burchell, trans. (New York: Columbia University Press, 1996). Cf. Paul Rabinow on Deleuze and the critical work of thought in "Foucault's Untimely Struggle: Toward a Form of Spirituality," *Theory, Culture, Society* 26 (2009): 25, DOI: 10.1177/0263276409347699.

5 Nicholas Gane, "Concepts and the 'New' Empiricism," *European Journal of Social Theory* 12 (2009): 83.

assembled and re-assembled: on the one hand, they are forged out of a response to the immediacy of lived experience, while on the other they open the impossible challenge to present this world in thought."[6]

The Actual

The actual is equally knotty. In French as in English, the actual or actuality can simply mean "the present"—existing now. It can also mean "the real," as in "existing as a fact." Out of everything that might have been possible, the actual refers to that which has really happened. In French, however, the actual can also mean timely. It carries a sense of being suitable to an ethos or situation—opportune, of the moment. In this way the term carries a richer connotation: out of that which has become real, the actual designates that which is rightly part of a given ethos.

The actual, like the empirical, can thus be thought of as an artifactual and curative term. The actual does not simply refer to the vast sea of things "in the world" which one might possibly think about or attend to. It is, rather, those aspects of reality that are selected out as significant juncture points between the recent past and the near future, and attended to with conceptual care.[7]

To work on the actual is "to seize an event in its becoming."[8] The work of the history of thought since Kant, to offer a contrast, has typically consisted in seizing the past as the condition for the possibility of the present. That work involves moving from contingency to fixity. The work of thought on the actual moves in another direction. It consists in grasping the empirical in its relative stability so as to conceive it as the condition for a different possible future.

Put differently: at stake in thinking is not only the need for a clearer understanding of how reality has become what it is. Also at stake is the ability to think of reality as the material condition for the possibility of something else. To seize an event in its becoming is to seize it with an eye to helping make it that which it is not yet, and which it could not become without intervention. In this sense, the work of thought on the actual requires a double motion, simultaneously ontological and ethical: grasping the world as that which is given so as to test it to see what it might yet become.

---

6   Ibid.
7   Deleuze (1997) "*Contrôle et devenir.*"
8   Ibid.

From Prolepsis to Culture to the Actual: A First Practice

While a graduate student at the University of Chicago, Peters became a student and friend of Joseph Sittler. Sittler had pressed the case that theological ethics can be thought about as a practice of imagining and then working to actualize the future[9]—ethics as prolepsis, as Peters would later call it.[10]

The possibility of proleptic ethics as a theological possibility had catalytic effects, serving to connect and transform a number of themes that were already converging in Peters' work, especially his nascent and now-famous concern for the theological significance of the future. While his dissertation research took up the question of Pannenberg's theory of revelation-as-history in epistemological relation to hermeneutics, the stakes and question of his own project became how to imagine eschatology as the ethical structure of theological thought and practice.

Prolepsis and Theological Form-Giving

At the same time, and consonantly, Peters had become actively attentive to the question of ethics, modernity, and the global future, one he took to be resonant with the growing intellectual and political influence of the theologies of hope and liberation. In this light, proleptic ethics raised the question of theological form and thereby the question of theological form-giving. What did it mean for the practice of theology to say that eschatology was the ethical structure of theological thought? Minimally, it suggests that ethics cannot be imagined as a theological afterthought—an extra-discursive application of prior and more fundamental insights. Ethics, rather, must bear on the mode, form, and products of theological thought itself—theology as a practice in a strong sense.

The content and significance of theology, in other words, is bound up in the ability to think of God and the world as an active form of care—for others and for oneself. The question then was this: how to make proleptic ethics a properly theological practice.

---

9 See, e.g., Joseph Sittler, *The Structure of Christian Ethics*, reprinted ed. (Louisville: Westminster John Knox, 1998).

10 Ted Peters, *GOD—The World's Future: Systematic Theology for a New Era*, 2nd ed. (Minneapolis: Fortress Press, 2000).

Interpretations Are Cultural Facts

His first book, *UFOs—God's Chariots?* provided an initial answer, laying out lineaments that Peters would follow in his later works.[11] In a manner similar to his subsequent examinations of the New Age Movement,[12] Satanism,[13] and creationism,[14] in *UFOs* Peters gave thoroughgoing and serious theological consideration to a topic and to actors often merely derided or denounced by much of the academic world.

As Peters' points out in the book, the notion of UFOs and the cultural world of those who think about and claim to have experienced them were (and are) regularly ridiculed by scholarly elites. The scientific establishment was especially vitriolic, casting ufology as pseudo-science and those who "believe" in the objective reality of UFOs as, at best, "amateurs," and at worst, "kooks."[15]

But the question of the relevant scientific credibility of ufology, or of "whether or not people in fact see an objective reality that we can name a 'UFO'" is, Peters insisted, "almost irrelevant" for theology. The reason is that people's interpretations and understanding of what they take to be UFOs, as well as their articulated sense of why UFOs matter, are themselves objective realities. They are facts of the contemporary world in need of theological attention.

Cultural Theologies, Science, and This-Worldly Salvation

Peters begins his book by making two points, one phenomenological, the other hermeneutical. The first is that, however seemingly marginal, UFOs and thinking about UFOs had, by the mid-1970s become widespread. Eric von Daniken's 1973 book *Chariots of the Gods*, for example, had sold thirty-nine million copies. The second is that individuals who claim to have been contacted personally by UFOs, as well as those who report on such events, describe their experiences in religious terms.

---

11 Ted Peters, *UFOs—God's Chariots? Flying Saucers in Politics, Science, and Religion* (Louisville: John Knox Press, 1977).
12 Ted Peters, *The Cosmic Self: A Penetrating Look at Today's New Age Movements* (San Francisco: HarperSanFrancisco, 1991).
13 Ted Peters, *Sin: Radical Evil in Soul and Society* (Grand Rapids, Michigan: Wm. B. Eerdmans Publishing Co., 1994).
14 Ted Peters and Martinez Hewlett, *Evolution from Creation to New Creation: Conflict, Conversation, and Convergence* (Nashville: Abingdon Press, 2003).
15 Peters, *UFOs*, 79.

Drawing insight from Marcea Eliade's and Huston Smith's work on religion and mythology, Peters explains that interpretations of UFO experiences often involve a recasting of ancient symbols and sentiments in contemporary terms: the heavens, framed in terms from astronomy, are nonetheless considered holy; astronauts' experiences of the sublime in space are experiences of the divine; aliens are pitched as emissaries of utopian societies, seeking, through advanced technologies and evolutionary development, to deliver humans for a better world.

Analytically two things are clear. The first is that a distinctive UFO theology is developing. It is not just that individuals are having experiences in relation to which they express feelings usually associated with religion. These experiences and sentiments are being given systematic interpretation and articulation. These interpretations and articulations, in turn, are quite clearly theological. They are theological insofar as they are salvational. In a broadly consistent manner, individuals are interpreting their experiences of UFOs through structures of thought which, Peters shows, are consistent with the biblical promise of new creation: the good news that this world is not all there is and that all will be restored—a message of salvation.

The second analytic point is that the content of this salvational message is loosely, but undeniably, scientific. As Peters shows, for those who think about and claim to have experienced UFOs, salvational promise lies precisely in the possibility that natural creatures from other worlds—creatures which have advanced beyond humans both technically and morally—will provide humans with scientific insights and technological means sufficient to answering their deepest needs and remedying their most trenchant ills.[16] To this extent, however much the scientific establishment may be dismissive and derisory of it, ufology fits within a longer history of the scientific demystification of reality.

For Peters, a diagnostic conclusion follows. Scientific thinking is animated by the hope for and belief in this-worldly salvation. The structure of scientific thought is salvational. And this structure is an answer to humans' deepest inner needs.

Using language redolent of both Paul Tillich and Carl Jung, he writes: "We have a deep need to be assured that we are not alone, to be given courage in the face of anxiety over impending catastrophe, to be comforted that

---

16 Ibid., 19.

there is divine forgiveness and salvation for us even when we have sinned, and to know that the standards of right and wrong are not floating with whims of desire but are grounded in ultimate reality itself."[17]

It follows that theologians need to move beyond the question of the plausibility and objective reality of UFOs. In this way they will be able to attend to the more significant problem of how a growing fascination with UFOs reflects and shapes our shared cultural imagination. Whatever one makes of the relative seriousness of ufology, one needs to take seriously the fact that it gives particularly clear expression to current and widespread naturalized and scientized theologies of salvation.

From a Theology of Culture to a Theology of Cultural Theologies

On this diagnostic level, Peters' work reflects familiar aspects of the theology of culture, and is consistent with the previous efforts of both Tillich and Gilkey. Calling attention to the empirical surfaces of human experience, Peters indicates their religious depth. He then examines particular cultural forms as expressions of anthropological universals: salvational needs that, however specific in their historical manifestations, are nonetheless taken to be historically constant.

But here is where Peters moves beyond Tillich and Gilkey. Peters does not actually leave the surface behind. Peters' diagnostic claim that UFOs constitute an answer to a deeper human need is neither the point nor end of his analysis. It is, rather, the point of orientation and warrant for attending more carefully to the specific content and character of peoples' experiences, interpretations, and articulations. If UFOs are an expression of a deeper human need, it is that expression and not only that need that draws Peters' attention.

In practice, this means that Peters sets out to discover and make theological sense of what people are actually thinking, saying, and doing. Or, to put it in terms more often associated with anthropology than theology, Peters sets out to study and to make sense of a specific contemporary form of life in its specificity.

To this extent, it is perhaps not surprising—and far from incidental—that in the course of his work on UFOs Peters conducted hundreds of hours of interviews. The need for, and object of, these interviews was a theological assessment of the actual theologies that were being brought

---

17 Ibid., 149.

to articulation in relation, on the one hand, to a felt need for salvation, and on the other, to that felt need as one aspect of a scientized experience of late modernity.

What Peters gives us, in the end, is not only a theology of culture, but also a theological interpretation of cultural theologies. Or, in his words, he provides an understanding of how UFOs are understood.

From Theological Observation to Theology as Participant-Observation: A Second Practice

While working on UFOs, Peters was also completing his second book, *Futures—Human and Divine*.[18] Where UFOs provided an initial and tacit answer to the question of theology and proleptic ethics, *Futures* brought the question to systematic articulation. As such, alongside *UFOs*, *Futures* can be read as laying down programmatic elements that would define much of Peters' subsequent work.

In the early 1970s Peters began tracking the work of the Club of Rome and other organizations dedicated to thinking through, and making forecasts about, global ecological, economic, and political futures. In these efforts he followed, in part, indications offered by Huston Smith's analysis of futurology. In 1973, Peters became a member of the World Futures Society and in 1975 attended the WFS's Second General Assembly. By 1978 he had become an active and engaged member, pushing forward efforts (ultimately unsuccessfully) to constitute reflections on the future and religion as a formal and integrated section of WFS.

Peters' interests in the work of futurists turned precisely on the ethical structure of their enterprise. Their methods not only entailed running projections out from present trends and trying to calculate the likelihood of possible futures. Their methods also entailed thinking through which possible futures are preferable and what, if anything, can be done in the present—politically and techno-scientifically—to help actualize those preferred futures. This ethical structure seemed not only amenable to Christian thought, but a site of potential Christian participation in scientific thought.

In *UFOs* Peters had explicitly bracketed the question of the truth of the scientific claims made by ufologists and their critics. This bracketing allowed him to consider the significance of those claims per se as de-

---

18 Ted Peters, *Futures—Human and Divine* (Louisville: John Knox Press, 1978).

fining aspects of the contemporary situation. In this sense, analytically, Peters opened up a distinction between science as a cultural phenomenon characterized by salvational structures of thought, which one does not necessarily take seriously for oneself, and science as a truth practice, which one does.

Ultimately, the two sides of this analytic distinction need to be brought together. However much distance one strives to create in the name of analytic and phenomenological perspective, one cannot, in the end, live outside the world one studies. In the late modern world, the knowledge, capabilities, and institutions of establishment science are defining and dominant. Science needs to be taken seriously on its own terms, albeit in a manner which does not lose sight of its dimensions as a human practice.

With *Futures* Peters introduced the first of what would become multiple experiments to position theology in collaborative relationship with science as a truth practice.[19] These experiments would ultimately come to occupy the greater part of his reflections on science, especially in his several-decade position as a member of the Center for Theology and the Natural Sciences and in his institutionally situated work in bioethics.

In this light, the shift in intellectual emphasis from *UFOs* to *Futures* might be thought of as a shift in theological subject position: from the theological observation of science and culture to theology as a form of scientifically grounded participant-observation.

From Phenomenological Commonplaces to Hermeneutic Depth

Writing in the introduction to *Futures*, Peters proposes that the late twentieth century is characterized by "future consciousness." By future consciousness he means an acute and articulated sense that late industrial modernity is ramifying in such a way that the existential future of humanity is at stake.

Peters points out that future consciousness is shared by secular and religious individuals alike. In this sense, future consciousness constitutes what might be called a phenomenological commonplace between religious and non-religious culture.

---

19 Cf. Peters' *Playing God? Genetic Determinism and Human Freedom* (New York: Routledge, 2003), and Ted Peters, Karen Lebacqz, Gaymon Bennett, *Sacred Cells? Why Christians Should Support Stem Cell Research* (Lanham, Maryland: Rowman and Littlefield, 2008).

On both secular and religious fronts, for example, one finds a millennialist fascination: viz., that the year 2000 marks a *kairos* in human history. The major concern that sets that year apart as a turning point is that "the surface of our planet is exploding with science and technology, but it is a random and uncoordinated growth which lacks orientation and direction."[20] A salvational logic of planned and coordinated action is needed.

The twist is, although scientists and scientifically oriented futurists can forecast alternatives for the future, "someone must decide which future humans will have." Such a decision, Peters proposes, will ultimately turn on and be guided by a choice among values: "all seem to be in agreement on one point, namely, if we are to have a future at all, we must make a radical change in the values that orient the economic and social systems of the West. Our value system is now threatening humanity—through nuclear war, pollution of the biosphere, resource depletion, and starvation."[21]

From a Warrant to a Challenge

Phenomenological commonplaces alone provide a warrant for coordinated action between religious and non-religious communities. They do not, however, provide sufficient warrant to justify theological contribution to the labor of articulating a new set of values and possible plan of action. That warrant arises from a diagnosis and an interpretation.

Peters explains that for most involved, the trouble with "Western systems of value" in their broadly liberal and capitalist dimensions, is that they are marked by and turn on selfishness.[22] Whatever "value systems" actually refers to may not always be clear, but the vital point is that selfishness is not only taken to be a human reality to be contended with, but a reality, which, over time, will ultimately be vindicated in the world it ostensibly helps produce.

The problem with critiques of liberalism and the virtues of selfishness, on Peters' brief account, is that however much they seek to be counter- or post-modern, they ultimately lack a sufficient armature of conceptual tools to articulate an alternative understanding of the present and vision for the future. Religious traditions, by contrast, and the Christian tradition in particular, have long investigated selfishness as a root cause of human tragedy and self-destruction.

---

20 Ibid., 10.
21 Ibid., 11.
22 Ibid., 11ff.

The trouble with drawing on these theological traditions for engagement with futurist thinking is that much of futurology is marked by the modernist bias: namely, that the new must be valorized against the old. Christian theologians, therefore, are confronted with the difficult task of having to develop strategies for connecting the old and the new in such a way as to provide a pragmatic vision for a common human future that can be taken seriously in secular circles.

From Historical Consciousness to Hermeneutical Depth

Peters proposes two strategies for addressing these conceptual and political difficulties. The first turns on Paul Tillich's hermeneutic of culture. Conceived in the spirit of Heidegger's phenomenology, Tillich suggested that a core task of theology was to uncover the hidden religious dimensions of culture where those are covered over by seemingly non-religious forms of thought and practice. Defining religion "in the largest and most basic sense of the word" as that which deals with "ultimate concerns," Tillich proposed that theological interpretation was needed wherever human cultures express such concern.[23]

For Peters it follows that, insofar as future consciousness raises existentially ultimate questions—"Will the human race survive? If the human race does survive, will it still be human?"—it is properly religious and needs to be interpreted and responded to as such.[24]

In order to do this Peters identifies a bind at the heart of modern theology and seeks to cut through it. To provide an interpretation of future consciousness, theology must put present thinking about the future into critical perspective.[25] Traditionally, this critical perspective was achieved by appeal to past events, namely the life and career of Jesus of Nazareth, as a norm of critical reflection and institutional response. With the advent of historical-critical consciousness in the nineteenth century, however, any non-problematized attempt to draw direct connections between the modern present and the biblical past were foreclosed.

In a fashion consistent with other modern theologians (from the Neo-Orthodox theologians to many theologians of liberation), Tillich proposed to overcome the encumbrances of historical-critical consciousness by indexing theology to the effects of Christian faith in and on the

---

23 Ibid., 15.
24 Ibid.
25 Ibid., 16ff.

present and to do this in a manner more or less independent of historical reflection and the moorings of biblical authority. Such possible effects—and hence the worth and veracity of theology—could then be judged in existential and pragmatic terms. Operating in this mode, to pick one example, Tillich argued that it is a "biblical picture" of Christ, and not a real historical Jesus per se, that allows God to work in peoples' lives.

In short, in response to a modern ethos that valorizes the new against the old, modern theology did not so much overcome the historical-critical challenge as to try to move beyond its reach.

From Hermeneutical Depth to Historical Perspective

Modern theology effectively collapsed the future and the past into the present in the name of an interpretation and valorization of non-historical experience. The limitation with this approach, however, was that modern theology could not actually gain critical perspective on the present.[26] As Peters explains, for modern theology the relation with the past, including the biblical past, is only loosely comparative and in no way effectively normative; the relation with the future is similarly limited. It is a strictly figurative one in which eschatological hope can only be postulated and judged in terms of individual human experience and not in historical terms.

And yet the present-tense of experience, Peters shows, can only really be understood in light of a moving relation across and between the past and the future.[27] In order to follow that movement, the theologian must be willing to conduct inquiry.

This means that a first task for any theology striving to move beyond the limitations of the modern consists in rethinking and regaining the question of historical perspective. It does this by inquiring into the ways in which the past shapes the present, and how present problems cast genealogical light on the past. Equally important, and in some ways more difficult, it must also make sense of the dynamic relation between the present, as it has been actualized, and the future which is both made possible by, and reciprocally makes sense of, the present.

Quoting Pannenberg, Peters explains: theology must face up to the labor of "interpreting the transmitted material from the past in relation to the future, to the extent that the latter forms the horizon of present

---

26 Ibid.
27 Ibid., 18.

understanding, so that the importance of the past for the present with regard to its future becomes intelligible."[28]

Put in more exactingly Christian terms Peters writes:

> Christians need to go to the historical events of the death and resurrection of Jesus Christ, events that stand at the heart and center of God's revelation.... [T]he creation of the world was the necessary first act in God's continuing drama of salvation. The world in which we live is not merely a conglomeration of natural laws or puzzles.... It exists because it plays a part in the divine scenario of redemption. It is on the basis of what we know about the God who raised Jesus from the dead that Paul can perceive how creation has been "subjected to futility," that it "has been groaning in travail," and that God has furthermore "subjected it in hope" because it "will be set free from its bondage to decay and obtain the glorious liberty of the children of God."[29]

The challenge is neither to ignore, nor be over determined by, a modern sensibility or by the problem of hermeneutic distance implied in historical-critical consciousness. The challenge, rather, is to think of history in such a way that the present can be loosed from the past, and conceptually and pragmatically reworked as the material of a different possible future.[30] To do this, as *Futures* demonstrates, one has to return to history not merely in abstract or general terms but in the richness of its empirical detail.

From Ontic to Eschatological Seriousness

The work of theological inquiry, leading to the identification of significance, moves along and across what Nietzsche glossed as "the surface" of things historical. Because of this, the theologian must remain vigilantly hermeneutical, without thereby becoming confined in the depth-dimension entailed in the modern privileging of experience and the present. Or, to put it in terms familiar in phenomenological and hermeneutic circles: theology needs to remain sufficiently and steadfastly ontic.

Working in this mode, it would seem that theology might be in a better position to connect with the stakes and practices of a scientifically

---
28 Ibid.
29 Ibid., 26.
30 Ibid., 150ff.

informed futurology. And, on one level, it is. Futurology, after all, takes account of the present as the product of historical forces so as to seek to understand how those forces run forward under differential scenarios.

On another level, however, Christian theology conceives of the future in fundamentally different terms, ontologically and ethically. Futurology imagines the future as trends. The future is the present run forward. Peters designates this mode of imagining the future as *futurum*.[31] For Christian theology, by contrast, the future is not only the projection of the present. It is the hope of eschatological transformation. The future is imagined as salvational for the present and not just the present's unfolding. Peters designates this mode as *adventus*.[32]

And yet despite the disjuncture between *futurum* and *adventus*, it is precisely at this point that Peters identifies an opening for the possibility of a more productive engagement. Despite the fact that in the conduct of their analytic work futurists employ modes of reasoning appropriate to *futurum* (scenario planning, forecasting, projections, the calculation of probabilities and risks, etc.), that work itself is justified and carried out precisely under the sign of *adventus*. Futurists run trends against preferred futures and they do so in order to imagine and test the possibility of realizing those futures.

The future is thus a problem of possible transformations and actualizations, as much for the scientist as the theologian. The form and content of those transformations as well as the means of actualizing them might be quite different. But, as Peters recognizes, both kinds of thinkers are faced with the intellectual and ethical challenge of articulating values and providing accounts of reality in terms amenable to contributing, however modestly, to the work and hope of achieving an imagined future.

From Eschatological Realism to the Theological Dignity of the Actual: A Third Practice

Though Peters' dissertation research focused on the work of Wolfhart Pannenberg in its relation to mid-century hermeneutics, and though the presence of Pannenberg's conceptual reworking of the relation between history and revelation can be felt in Peters' early writings, it is not until Peters published his one-volume systematic theology that

---
31 Ibid., 20–27.
32 Ibid.

the full importance and creative potential of Pannenberg's thought for Peters' own project became evident.[33]

Shortly after the 1992 publication of the first edition of his systematics, Peters gave additional sharper articulation to his interest in and use of Pannenberg, especially for thinking about science and the theology of culture. In 1993, Peters edited an English-language collection of Pannenberg's essays on science and faith.[34] In the introduction to that volume Peters lays out in concise terms the elements of what can be read as the groundwork and warrant for theological inquiry as proleptic ethics.

What is crucial to Peters' summary of Pannenberg, as I explain below, is that he opens up methodological implications of Pannenberg's work, which Pannenberg himself never actually takes seriously in his own writing. As is true of any number of other twentieth-century philosophers—from Dewey to Heidegger to Wittgenstein—Pannenberg's assessment of the character and stakes of theology points the thinker back to the world in all its empirical detail and historical under-determination. And like those philosophers he does not actually go there.

The challenge for theology, which Peters takes up, consists in cultivating the intellectual prudence, courage, and repertoire of tools needed to return to the world in its actuality.

Theology as Science

Peters explains that for Pannenberg theology ought to be considered a science—the science of God.[35] It is a science because its claims can be made in such a way that their truth and falsity is susceptible to verification. In the first place, they are indirectly susceptible to verification because of the increased intelligibility they offer to an understanding of finite reality. In the second place, they are directly susceptible to verification because they are historical.[36]

For Pannenberg, and then for Peters, the scientificity of theology begins with a core claim about the hermeneutic character of all understanding: "Whether in the natural sciences or the humanities, interpreters of reality find themselves working intersubjectively in a

---

33 Peters, *GOD—The World's Future*, 1st ed. (Minneapolis: Fortress Press, 1992).
34 Wolfhart Pannenberg, *Towards a Theology of Nature: Essays on Science and Faith*, Ted Peters, ed. (Louisville: Westminster John Knox, 1993).
35 Peters, "Editor's Introduction: Pannenberg on Theology and Natural Science," in *Towards a Theology of Nature* (Louisville: Westminster John Knox, 1993).
36 Ibid., 6–9.

context of meaning, a context conditioned by one's semantic network and wider cultural setting."[37] Because God is thought of as an all-determining reality, Pannenberg hypothesizes that theology provides the widest possible context and hence carries implications for understanding the whole of finite reality.

What is critical is that for Pannenberg understanding works retroactively. An event cannot be adequately understood apart from its relevant contextual detail and its outcomes. Neither that detail nor those outcomes can be fully known except as part of the totality of finite reality. Meaning and significance are thus, per se, historical.

Finite reality, however, is not a totality.[38] At no point in history does it exist as a totality. This means that any appeal theology might make to a putatively all-encompassing context anchored in the reality of God can only be made as an act of anticipation and in the form of a hypothesis directed toward the possibility of eschatological wholeness.

What Peters suggests, and what he ultimately takes seriously for his own work, is that the historical character of knowledge means that theology in history can only be practiced as inquiry.[39] The thesis of faith is a hypothesis, which is either true or false. And apart from its eschatological vindication (or not) theology must proceed as a reflective discipline that looks to draw out "the implications of positive knowledge for an intelligible picture of the whole."[40] Theology may not be an empirical science, but it is obliged to understand how empirical science should be understood.

Revelation as History

This posture and approach is not merely or even primarily epistemological, despite the fact that it is determinative of the limits and style of theological knowing. It is, rather, primarily ontological and ethical.

Pannenberg's scientific view of theology follows from the core supposition of his oeuvre, namely that revelation needs to be understood as history. That supposition was worked out in the major collaborative project he undertook with biblical scholars Rolf Rendtorff, Trutz Rendtorff, and Ulrich Wilkens, *Revelation as History*, which put forward the terms

---
37   Ibid., 7.
38   Ibid., 8.
39   Ibid.
40   Ibid., 7.

of a fundamental break with Neo-Orthodox theology generally and with the theology of Karl Barth in particular.[41]

In the introduction to *Revelation as History*, Pannenberg asserted that since the rise to prominence of Neo-Orthodoxy the concept of revelation had come to be understood exclusively as God's self-revelation. Unlike earlier understandings, this meant that revelation is treated as consisting solely in the disclosure of God's being rather than, say, in the character of non-divine realities—religious experiences, events, subjectivity, history, etc.[42]

The notion of revelation as God's self-disclosure was further narrowed by the proposition that true revelation is always direct revelation. God's self-disclosure is God's direct self-disclosure. It is direct precisely because revelation is always revelation of God by God; God is taken to be the medium of God's self-disclosure.[43] Hegel's view of history as the dialectical unfolding of God's being coming to self-awareness epitomizes this view.

Against this view of revelation, and while accepting the idea that revelation must ultimately be revelation of the totality of God's being, Pannenberg and his colleagues argued that revelation should be understood in terms of the comprehensive whole of reality. The twist is that the whole of reality is not simply given. Revelation in history will therefore be indirect and mediated. Revelation "is a temporal process of a history that is not yet completed, but open to a future, which is anticipated in the teaching and personal history of Jesus."[44]

History as Vindication

Their warrant for this view was two-fold. The first was their rejection of the Neo-Orthodox use of the notion of the Word of God as the site and source of God's direct self-disclosure. They argued that such an understanding of God's word fails on biblical ground, that in scripture God's self-revelation is a reflex of God's action in history. These actions provide only partial disclosure of God's being. "The totality of God's speech and activity, the history brought about by God, shows who he is in an indirect way."[45]

---

41 Wolfhart Pannenberg, ed. *Revelation as History: A Proposal for a More Open, Less Authoritarian View of an Important Theological Concept*, David Granskou, trans. (New York: Collier-Macmillan, 1969).
42 Pannenberg, "Introduction," in *Revelation as History*.
43 Ibid., 4.
44 Ibid., 5.
45 Ibid., 13.

Second, and in connection with the first, they rejected the authoritarian style and posture implied in the Neo-Orthodox understanding of the Word. Placing the word of God in a more modest and subordinate role within the context of revelation as history they proposed to embrace "the open rationality of the Enlightenment" albeit in a fashion "combined with a concern for the substance of the Christian tradition."[46]

A central element in their understanding of revelation as history is their attention to the biblical notion of revelation as God's self-vindication.[47] Pannenberg points out that for the people of Israel, God's actions in history reveal and reassert God as truly divine by establishing justice. This means that in each historical act, and in history itself, God's full self-vindication and justice is anticipated. Revelation is vindicatory and historical.

History as Salvation and Salvation as History

For Pannenberg, then, revelation is linked with history, and full revelation is linked with the end of history.[48] These links follow from the indirect character of divine self-vindication in history, which Pannenberg proposes can only be complete with the close of history in its totality.

The linking of God and history thus in no way offers a more direct "way in" to knowledge of God. One cannot simply boot-strap from an experience of history to knowledge of God, as Schleiermacher arguably tried to do. The reason is that history as a totality is not open to theology as a self-contained unit.[49]

Even if this could be the case, if history could be approached as a totality, theology would effectively reduce the meaning of history to a single event and thereby contradict its historical character. This limitation presents a particular problem for Christian theology, which does in fact claim that a single event has absolute meaning and defines universal history: the life, death, and resurrection of Jesus Christ.[50]

Pannenberg concludes that Christian theologians must take the life and career of Jesus to be the revelation of the end, and in this sense an anticipation of events that will yet unfold. The life and career of Jesus, as

---

46 Ibid., 3.
47 Ibid., 128.
48 Ibid., 128ff.
49 Ibid., 131.
50 Ibid., 143.

revelation, is ontologically proleptic. It exists in history as the breaking in of the end.

This perspective is consistent, Pannenberg insists, with the biblical account of salvation in which God's vindication is an event in the future. Moreover, it reaffirms the view that the meaning of the present can only be understood in a mutually constitutive relationship between the past of Jesus and the future of full revelation. In the resurrection Jesus is the eschatological self-revelation of God. But it is history in its eschatological dimensions that allows for this to be actual for humankind.[51]

History is the actuality and the actualization of the eschatological. What this means is that theology cannot imagine the history of revelation and the history of salvation apart from the material history of the world in all its specificity. Revelation is not a drama played out on the stage of finite reality. Revelation must be thought of as the being of the world vindicated in its situated concreteness and embodied materiality.

Eschatological Realism and the Dignity of the Actual

If taken seriously, such a view entails what might be referred to as positional and affective consequences for the practice of theology. The subject position of the theologian becomes defined in part by a posture of eschatological realism. The present tense, taken up as a relation between the past and the future, is reworked as the material possibility of the eschaton and in the name of the eschaton becoming actual.

This does not mean that the significance of the present can be known in advance, as if its meanings were already settled by virtue of eschatological hope. Rather, as Peters puts it, this means that theology needs to explore interconnections among the empirical aspects of reality in view of the strong proposition that these aspects will be given redemptive form.[52] The subject position of the theologian is not one who has the answers in advance of inquiry. It is, rather, the subject position of one who conceptually moves through the past to the future in order to establish critical perspective on the present.

Eschatological realism names a theological relationship and disposition not an answer. It casts light on finite existence through a theological reworking of the actual.

---

51 Ibid., 142.
52 Peters, "Editors Introduction," 9.

An affective consequence follows. The details of everyday life, the heterogeneous non-totality of reality, can be approached as worthy of a certain respect, esteem, or honor. To steal a turn of phrase from the historian Michel Foucault, the theologian has no right to despise the present. The task and appropriate disposition, rather, is one that seeks to identify the worth and dignity of the actual in its relation to a possible future: to identify where change is necessary and where it is possible.

The Dignity of the Actual and the Ethical Practice of Theology

Early in his theological career Pannenberg turned to the question of anthropology,[53] a question indicated by his reading of revelation as history. His turn to anthropology, however, was conducted in the style and mode of nineteenth-century investigations of Man: the presumption and exploration of a trans-historical essence. His anthropology was the correlate of a philosophy of history.

In Peters' work there is a different sort of anthropological turn, one more consonant with what might be called the "fieldwork" tradition in American anthropology. While clearly taking seriously the philosophical and theological lessons of Pannenberg's work, Peters, in a fashion not unlike his reworking of the theology of culture, treats such lessons not as conclusions but as points of departure. The result is that theology can be pursued as an ethical vocation oriented to understanding the actual in its eschatological dignity.

Deleuze proposed, following Nietzsche, that historical contextualization could never be adequate to a philosophical vocation.[54] However necessary as a preliminary for the work of thought, it could never be adequate because it tends to give insight without invigorating or requiring action.

The test and trial of philosophy is thus precisely how to grasp the world in its specificity in order to participate in changing it. This, I submit, is precisely the test and trial to which Peters subjects his theological practice. History is neither the past that determines the present, nor is it the object of a universal theorizing. It is, rather, a domain of practice and of action in which the stakes of thought turn on the ability to discern and to pursue an eschatological possibility and to do so using the materials and substance of the historical situations inquired into.

---

53 Wolfhart Pannenberg, *Anthropology in Theological Perspective* (New York: Continuum, 2004).
54 Deleuze, "Control et devinir"; cf. Paul Rabinow, "Untimely Meditations."

The Difficult Pragmatics of Theological Life:
A Fourth Practice

To the extent that one takes seriously the proposition that the materials of everyday life are the actual materials of the eschaton, then the question of theological form and theological form-giving reasserts itself: one is confronted by the problem of how to relate and attend to the actual, intellectually, ethically, and methodologically. The question of theological method is not merely a matter of epistemological appropriateness, but of spiritual and vocational care.

Said differently, attention to the actual is an appropriate response to the concept of history as revelation. The question that remains is this: how to give form to a theological life appropriate to such a practice.

Subject Position One:
From First to Second Order and Back Again

Peters begins many of his books with quotes from popular publications. In the preface to *The Cosmic Self*, for example, Peters cites TV commercials (e.g., MasterCard's "Master Your Possibilities") and popular books (e.g., Shirley MacLaine's *Out on a Limb*). The quotes are not simply literary devices. They are included, rather, as examples of what Peters might call cultural consciousness.[55]

In selecting these quotes Peters accomplishes two things. First, he indicates places in the contemporary world where popular thinking seems to be moving against what he refers to as modern critical consciousness.[56] Modern consciousness is defined by secular doubt. It presumes that talk about God is only a human projection, that the only reality is a material one, and that contextualization leads inevitably to relativism.

Postmodern consciousness, on Peters' account, is characterized by a desire for reconstructive wholeness and movement away from what is perceived to be modern fragmentation and reductionism.[57] It is marked by the expectation that older notions of a cosmos can be reworked and that a more complex understanding of parts and wholes can be made part of the ethical work of addressing human ills.

---

55 See Peters on modern and postmodern consciousness in the introduction to the second edition of *GOD—The World's Future*.
56 Peters, *GOD—The World's Future*, 11.
57 Ibid., 16ff.

In this way—and this is the second thing he does with these quotes—Peters puts himself into what Niklas Luhmann has termed a "second-order" relationship with both modern as well as postmodern consciousness, making them available to theological inquiry.[58] As Luhmann defines it, second-order observation consists in "observing observers observing." Peters not only seeks to understand modern and postmodern consciousness as the objects and conditions for the possibility of theology, he also seeks to understand how modern and postmodern consciousness is being understood.

For Luhmann, the position of second-order observation consists in a certain kind of audit-posture.[59] The second-order observer can enter into a social situation and take account of how it is that the first-order actors in that situation are thinking and acting. This account can then be made part of the first-order world as a means of ameliorating the ability of first-order actors to realize their aims.

For Peters, however, the use and challenge of second-order observation does not turn on a metric of amelioration per se. It turns, rather, on the question and challenge of making theological judgments about the contemporary situation and about how theology might best contribute to the reconstruction of that situation.

In this way, Peters seeks to establish what might be called a postcritical subject position.[60] This subject position is a return to the first-order in the simple sense that, unlike the second-order observer, it no longer suspends judgments concerning normative questions of ends as well as courses of action. It makes those judgments, however, on the basis of what has been learned through second-order observation, including what has been learned about which problems and metrics should be prioritized. A postcritical subject position tries, as it were, to be third-order.

Subject Position Two: The Aporias of the Universal and Specific Intellectual

Given that it does not have a settled model and is not directly attached to material resources and thus institutional protection, Peters' proposed postcritical theological subject position is difficult to practice. It is particularly difficult in situations where the theologian wants to

---

58 Niklas Luhmann, *Observations on Modernity* (Palo Alto: Stanford University Press, 1998).
59 Ibid.
60 Ibid., 22ff.

practice theology as an active part of the situations into which she is conducting her inquiry.

To put it more concretely: Peters has conducted much of his work from the professional position of a university and seminary professor of theology. From this position, Peters has been more or less free to speak about what he wants to speak about in the fashion he wants to speak about it. However, from his early interactions with the World Futures Society and the Mutual UFO Network to his service on the bioethics advisory boards of biotech companies and government commissions, Peters has sought to experiment with the possibility of making a postcritical theology an integrated part of other contemporary venues.

Peters is obviously not the first theologian to undertake such experimentation. In the US, as in many other parts of the world, there is a relatively long tradition of theologians as public intellectuals. Moreover, Peters has conducted his experiment alongside several other colleagues who, like he, have confronted the question of what it means to speak theologically in situations where non-theological stakes are in play.

The current conditions for Peters' vocational experimentation, however, are distinctive and distinctively antagonistic. In the US, mid-century theologians such as Reinhold Niebuhr or even Paul Tillich were invited to speak publicly as theologians in the tradition of what Michel Foucault called "universal intellectuals."[61] Universal intellectuals, as the name implies, spoke in the name of Humanity or in the name of History in order give articulation to what were taken to be the deeper truths of common existence.

In the post-War period, however, the subject position of the universal intellectual, once occupied not only by theologians, but by philosophers, literary figures, and artists, began to be taken over by what Foucault called the "specific intellectual."[62] In the immediate post-War period these specific intellectuals consisted of atomic physicists. Later, biologists, doctors, and eventually social scientists were also included.

The specific intellectual is allowed to speak from a place of authority by the fact that she or he is an elite expert on a technical dimension of the modern world, particularly a dimension of political or economic consequence. The specific intellectual can offer pragmatic advice on how

---

61 Michel Foucault, "Truth and Power," in Faubion and Rabinow eds. *Michel Foucault: Power*, Essential Works of Foucault 1954-84 (New York: The New Press, 2000), 126ff.
62 Ibid., 127.

to act in a rationalized situation where instrumental goods are at stake.

The curious fact about the specific intellectual, as Foucault points out, is that having been included by virtue of technical virtuosity, the specific intellectual is often allowed to speak in the voice of the universal intellectual on matters of extra-technical consequence. The specific intellectual begins as something like Max Weber's "modern expert" who is only qualified to operationalize means-ends relationships and ends by being allowed to speak—and practice—authoritatively about which ends get to count.

In his efforts to constitute a mode of practice as a public theologian, particularly in his work in bioethics, Peters has had to face a dilemma. He is invited because he is a theologian and capable of speaking on matters of ultimate concern. Thus invited he is nonetheless expected to speak in the voice of a specific intellectual, and then only in a non-theological style.

The dilemma is a curious one. The theologian is invited to participate in bioethics precisely because it is assumed that science, such as it is, cannot tell us what ends we should pursue. It is further assumed that the theologian might be something of an expert on the question of ends. In public situations, however, the theologian is asked to speak about things that either can be "operationalized," or can be taken in the spirit of general admonition. This means, in effect, that the theologian must speak as a technical expert or secular sage, and never as a person of faith.

Expertise in this case can take one of two forms. The theologian can speak in the name of what "those traditions believe," thus providing a "religious perspective." Or, the theologian can speak formalistically as an expert on reasoning, i.e. the theologian, affecting a philosophical mode, can help "clarify issues." The theologian cannot, however, speak about God or about reality in light of the hypothesis of faith as if it were true.

Subject Position Three: From Modern Expert to Eschatological Reconstructionist

In his work *Reconstruction in Philosophy* John Dewey writes: "Reconstruction can be nothing less than the work of developing, of forming, of producing (in the literal sense of that word) the intellectual instrumentalities which will progressively direct inquiry into the deeply and inclusively human—that is to say, moral—facts of the present scene and situation."[63]

The modern expert, per se, cannot engage in the practice of recon-

---

[63] John Dewey, *Reconstruction in Philosophy* (New York, H. Holt and Company, 1920).

struction in anything like Dewey's sense of the term. Nor, really, can the universal intellectual. The theologian of the actual, however, would seem to be aptly placed to take up this work—if a subject position could be settled and a venue found willing to facilitate that subject position.

Until such time, Peters shows us that movement in this direction can be made through a certain work carried out on oneself—a labor of self-formation. Adapting distinctions from Paul Ricoeur, Peters proposes that theologians can become capable of their task by moving through and across "three stages along faith's way": Naive World-Construction, Critical Deconstruction, and Postcritical Reconstruction.[64]

Naive World-Construction, or "the first naiveté," is characterized by the cultivation of "an unbroken ecology of meaning in which everything fits together and makes sense." Critical Deconstruction, which Peters identifies with the modern ethos, is characterized by a presumption of alienation from the premodern world and by the deconstruction and relativizing of the symbols that made up that world. Postcritical Reconstruction, which in this series constitutes the highest theological virtue, is characterized by the cultivation of a life of faith and ethical meaning beyond, but in clear view of, the relativism and potential nihilism of critical deconstruction.

For Ricoeur this theological virtue takes the form of a wager: that the symbols of ancient religion can be hermeneutically reconstructed in order to offer new meaning in the contemporary world. Or, to borrow from Dewey, postcritical reconstruction consists of developing the intellectual instrumentalities needed to practice theology beyond either a naively integrated world or capitulation to modern alienation from the old in the name of the new.

Two features of postcritical reconstruction are especially crucial. First, postcritical reconstruction takes up religious symbols as points of orientation for inquiry. Peters describes them as "reality detectors."[65] The symbols are not treated as theological answers, but points of intellectual intervention. Second, taken up in this way, the symbols and concepts of Christian faith become equipment of participation in the situations under investigation. They allow one to enter into those situations and bring conceptual and hermeneutic order to aspects of reality otherwise marked by breakdown and fragmentation.

---

64 *God—the World's Future*, 22–32.
65 Ibid., 33.

The symbols become participatory in a second sense as well. Insofar as they allow us to enter into situations in a new analytic fashion and to give intellectual determination to those situations, they also allow us to put ourselves and our thinking in question as part of those situations. In other words—to cite the epigraph above—questions we pose about God and God's relation to finite reality "become simultaneously questions God poses to us. We ourselves become part of the questioned reality."[66]

The Making of Middle Axioms

In the conclusion to his systematic theology Peters proposes that the metric and test of the theological life is the life of beatitude. The proposal is not altogether new, as I note below. Beatification, after all, was the point and purpose of pursuing a relationship to truth for much of the ancient world. What is distinctive about Peters' proposal is that he connects the notion of a life of beatitude to the contemporary practice of theology.

The content of such a theological life consists in orientation to justice, mercy, wholeness, and peace.[67] The form of this life consists in proleptic ethics. Proleptic ethics, in turn, consists of conducting the inquiry necessary to be capable of characterizing the world today in relation to a possible eschatological future. This labor, carried to its end, facilitates the articulation of "middle axioms," that is, guides for practice. These guides are consistent with the challenge of grasping the actual as the condition for the possibility of the eschatological.[68]

The term "middle axiom" carries a particular significance. A middle axiom is simultaneously a descriptive, normative, and praxiological statement of truth. For the Stoics, who first tracked and catalogued them, *axia* (lit. worthy or weighty) were true statements of significance about reality.[69] These true statements could only be made as a result of careful and vigilant observation, observation oriented toward overcoming *doxa*, or mere opinion, and grasping reality in its actuality.

The Stoics held that these truth claims would have persuasive ethical effects. By confronting the ethical subject with a truth about the character of reality, the subject would be moved to desire right action. In

---

66 Ibid., 31.
67 Ibid., 372.
68 Ibid., 373.
69 Cf. Michel Foucault, *The Hermeneutics of the Subject: Lectures at the Collège de France 1981-82*, Gros et al., eds. (New York: Picador, 2005).

this sense, the power of *axia* turned on a relationship of truth and freedom oriented to the possibility of right conduct.

The Stoics also held that these truth claims, in their normativity, could be made the bases of practice or exercise (*askesis*) leading to the cultivation of ethical and spiritual capacity. It was not enough to know the truth; one needed to be bound to it. Such binding was achieved through exercise. In this way, in the face of life's complications and stultifications one might hold fast to truth and live well.

For Peters, theological inquiry enables the articulation of *axia* of a particular kind—middle *axia*. They are middle *axia* in a double sense. First, they are truth claims that enable ethical actions which stand between high principles and specific courses of action. In this sense they are something like "programs for action."

Second, and more profoundly, these *axia* are middle *axia* because they are brought to articulation at the conjunction of the present and the eschatological future in the form of the actual. In this way they function as equipment of mediation whereby the present tense can be taken up and worked over in the name of, and with a vision for, eschatological reconstruction.

Coda: Theology and Power

I close the main section of this essay with a brief word of critique. If there is one limitation to Peters' theological program, in my view, it is that he does not pay systematic attention to the material conditions of his own vocational striving as part of the explicit material of his theological analysis. Despite a feel for the actual, Peters only occasionally puts himself, and the venues in which he has sought to conduct his theological work, into explicit critical perspective as part of his theological narrative.

The reason this is a limitation is not because Peters is obliged to be more honest about his own "location in the world" or to come clean about the ostensible sociological sources of his biases. The reason, rather, has to do with the fact that theological attention to the actual needs to include careful attention to the question of power—a question which Peters, in practice, has encountered time and again through his experimental undertakings.

The practice of a theology of the actual in the mode that Peters has opened up is difficult precisely because we do not (yet?) live in a world suited to it. Peters' efforts to refuse a modern division of value spheres, and the energies he has subsequently spent opening up a place for theology in science and in bioethics, should be characterized as conceptual and pragmatic struggles. They are struggles precisely because relations of authority, careerism, and the persistent dominance of instrumental values continue to determine the limits of what can be said theologically where, to whom, and to what effect.

These power relations, in face of which Peters has conducted his work, are every bit as much a part of the modern world he has analyzed, and the postmodern consciousness he has tried to envision through UFOs, the Club of Rome, stem cells, or evolutionary biology. Making sense of these relations, and fostering theological practices appropriate to countering them, should be made an integral part of any theology worthy of the name.

Concluding Prolegomena: Rethinking the Problem of Method

In what would be one of the last series of lectures before his untimely death, Michel Foucault took up the question of method in terms of the relation between the pursuit of truth and modes of possible existence.[70] By way of a close reading of key antique texts, from Plato to Augustine to the Rule of Benedict and the Stoics, Foucault sought to make the case that prior to "the modern threshold in the relation between truth and the subject," the task and mandate of philosophy was not only "know thyself." That mandate, rather, was coupled to, and put in the service of, a second one: "care for thyself."[71]

This coupling, Foucault suggested, was warranted by a central and vitalizing postulate: "such as he is the subject is not capable of the truth."[72] The subject, located amidst the stultifying forces of life and left to him or herself, cannot have access to the truth. Access to the truth, rather, requires paying a certain price in terms of work on oneself, work undertaken at the level of one's very being.

This ontological work was cast as a matter of preparation, *paraskeuē*: making oneself ready, amidst life's uncertainties, to be grasped by the truth. Thus grasped one could hope to be transfigured, even beatified.

---

70 Ibid.
71 Ibid., 15ff.
72 Ibid., 15.

The truth itself, after all, was the author of a beatific life; the task of the philosopher was to prepare for such a life.

Method from Spirituality to Science

In the history of thought, this work-on-oneself required for access to the truth would ultimately be cast in terms of spiritual exercise—asceticism, *askēsis*, practice. Spirituality would be connected more to notions of religion and ethics than to philosophy or even theology. Philosophy and theology, in turn, would be reworked under the norm of science. And science would be cast precisely as that mode of truth production which did not require any changes at the level of one's being. Indeed, any mode of truth production which did require such changes was at best pseudo-science, at worst cultic.

Rather than work on one's being, access to the truth at "the modern threshold" required formalized methods. With the appropriate tools, training, and procedures truth could be forced to show itself. Reason, and therein truth, was exoteric. At the modern threshold, the question of the relation of truth and the subject, truth-making and a way of life, gave way to the question of the relation of truth to the object. The question of truth and the subject was reduced to epistemology and made a problem of theory not ethics. The question of the practices needed to access the truth was made procedurally discrete, if not mechanical and formalistic.

Modern Methods and Theology

Foucault did not locate the modern threshold at the rise of modern science—even if science would become its most famous exemplar. He located it, rather, in the fourteenth century controversies over the relations among theology, preaching, and the salvational worth of sacraments blessed by a priest in sin. These controversies sparked what would become a centuries-long struggle to construct theologies and theological institutions whose axis of truth and salvation would no longer turn on the state-of-grace of the theologian or priest, but on reason and the reasoned demonstration of dogma.

Put abstractly, this struggle consisted of an effort to bring into being a mode of theological practice wherein the theological subject, such as she is, would be capable of the truth. The hope and expectation was that the truth would nonetheless retain the power to save the subject. The first proposition ultimately found historical form in the sciences and the philosophical turn to certainty. The second, needless to say, did not.

Theology and the Possibility of Truth

The critique is not altogether original. Theologians will recognize in it reverberations of Karl Barth's founding critique of theological liberalism. Barth rejected theological liberalism insofar as it presumed humanity, such as it is, could discover truth about God through an examination of the contents of its own being.[73] Barth's theological program, by contrast, turned on the proposition that the human creature is defined by an anthropological bind: simultaneously called to proclaim God's truth, but on its own and without the Spirit's power in faith, unable to fulfill the terms of that call.

Barth's anti-liberal program, in turn, has been cast by several critics as anti-modern—a mere inversion of modernist takes on theological method and rationality.[74] For those hoping to advance beyond the modern, Barth could be dismissed twice over. Inverting modernity, he became its residual. As a residual, he could neither attain to modernity's better aspirations, nor escape its limitations.

On Wolfhart Pannenberg's account, Barth's critique of liberal theology entailed his giving up on reason itself and theology as a properly human and historical endeavor. As Pannenberg acidly proposed in *History as Revelation*, Barth's "authoritarian style of theological thought" needs to be given over in favor of "the open rationality of the Enlightenment," albeit one "combined with a concern for the substance of the Christian tradition."[75]

But Barth's theological program might be read differently. Barth can be understood as counter-modern rather than simply anti-modern. Barth did, in the end, affirm that the subject could be made capable of the truth. The catch and the requirement was that the subject could only speak the logos of *theos* in and through an event, namely an encounter with God: revelation as event. Redolent of Foucault's take on antique spirituality quoted in the epigraph at the start of this essay, Barth's theological subject, such as she is, may not be capable of the truth. But such as it is, the truth can transfigure and save the subject.

---

73 Karl Barth, *Church Dogmatics*, vol. 1, G.W. Bromiley and T.F. Torrance, trans. (Edinburgh: T. & T. Clark, 1936).

74 See Pannenberg, *History as Revelation*; see also John Milbank, *Theology and Social Theory: Beyond Secular Reason*, 2nd ed. (Oxford: Wiley-Blackwell, 2006).

75 Pannenberg, *Revelation as History*, ix.

Ted Peters and the Problem of Method

Peters' contributions to theological method are neither Foucauldian nor Barthian. Indeed, they are straightforwardly post-Barthian, following Pannenberg's return to history. They are nonetheless—I propose—counter-modern in the sense just suggested: they take seriously, and they confront directly, the problem of what one is to do, theologically, after the modern threshold.

For Pannenberg, the answer to the problem of theological method consists more in rethinking theology than in rethinking the modern. Rather than revelation being an event, it needs to be understood as history. It can thereby be made susceptible to public reason, albeit reason judged in eschatological perspective. For Peters—however much his work may resonate and depend on Pannenberg's formulations—things do not sit so easily. The relation between truth and the subject under the sign of modernity is an unsettled one, as the subtitle of Peters' systematic theology suggests.

The great University of Chicago instructor Richard McKeon suggested defining "method" in praxiological terms: a rule of practice by which a thinker brings things into conceptual relationship. The praxiological question, taken up in a counter-modern spirit is this: what work does one need to undertake on oneself in order to become capable of creating theological relationships worthy of the name?

The methodological question, in this sense, can be thought of more as a test of oneself by the truth, and less as a means by which one tests the truth. Theologically, this test consists in posing and reposing the question: to what extent does the rule by which I conduct myself as a thinker allow me to become capable of speaking a truth about God and, reciprocally, capable of the truth I speak? Or, to use Peters' terms, to what extent am I conducting myself in such a way that the questions I pose about God are simultaneously questions God poses about me?

Dialogue and Hospitality

David Ratke

The world is bigger than ever before, and the world is smaller than ever before. It is smaller because technology has made communication more immediate and available over larger distances than ever before in human history. It is possible to talk to nearly anybody nearly anywhere in the world at nearly any time. As I write this, I could check my smartphone or computer or other mobile device and see what the latest headlines are from all over the globe. In many cases, I can see live video from far-flung places like Afghanistan or China or Russia, the Middle East or Europe. The world is bigger, because this avalanche of information reminds us just how small and insignificant we are.

That we experience the world as both bigger and smaller points to two important elements of postmodernism: holism[1] and pluralism. I intend here to consider pluralism, although holism lurks in the background as a kind of subtext to the idea of hospitality, which I will shortly address. For now, it is enough to notice that holism is a kind of parallel to this notion that the world is smaller. It is possible (if we want) to see the similarities that unite humans. Humans everywhere seek meaning and value. They seek opportunity and belonging. That humans the world over are similar is not quite the same as holism. But it is a kind of parallel in that the whole is a way of making sense of the parts. Thinking about

---

This article was first published in *Currents in Theology and Mission*, volume 39, number 4 (August 2012): 306–11.

1   This has been a nearly constant refrain of Ted Peters; see, for example, *Anticipating Omega: Science, Faith, and Our Ultimate Future* (Religion, Theology, and Natural Science) (Göttingen: Vandenhoeck & Ruprecht, 2006), 79, 104–5; or *GOD—The World's Future: Systematic Theology for a New Era*, 2nd ed. (Minneapolis: Fortress Press, 2000), 17–8.

what unites humans is also a way of making sense of the parts, of making sense of all the differences between humans.

Pluralism is a feature of life in the twenty-first century. There is no shortage of literature that makes this point. Diana Eck made that case in 2001 with her study *A New Religious America: How a "Christian Country" Has Become the World's Most Religiously Diverse Nation*. Since then Stephen Prothero has accepted her basic conclusions and argued for more religious "literacy" in *Religious Literacy: What Every American Needs to Know—And Doesn't* in 2007. More recently and more germane to the pluralism argument, Prothero argued against Huston Smith in *God Is Not One: The Eight Rival Religions That Run the World* that all religions are not essentially the same.[2] Eboo Patel and the Interfaith Youth Core have developed a kind of "ministry" founded on the notion of plurality.[3] Pluralism is here to stay.

Hospitality and the "Other"

What does Christianity have to offer? The answer in a word is hospitality. Hospitality has been a feature of the Christian tradition from the very beginning—perhaps even before the beginning. When I was young I heard the story of the Tower of Babel and learned that it explained why there were so many languages and furthermore that the multiplicity of these languages was a curse placed on humans. More recently, I have come to see the account in Genesis 11 rather differently. The multiplicity of languages allows humans to say different things in many beautiful ways. The diversity of languages is a kind of blessing allowing us to appreciate the splendor of the variety of human expression. The Tower of Babel account pushes us to consider that God created different nations with different tongues. As such, if God created these different tongues, might we not consider that difference and diversity are good and blessed

---

2 Huston Smith is only one of the people that Prothero names as a proponent of the idea that all religions are the same. He is perhaps the best known representative for this idea which is central to *The World's Religions,* first published in 1958 under the title of *The Religions of Man*. Prothero, as is clear from the title of this more recent book, thinks that religions are unique, distinctive, and strive after different things. Prothero was not the first to make this argument. S. Mark Heim made a similar and more sophisticated and nuanced argument in *Salvations: Truth and Difference in Religion* (Maryknoll, New York: Orbis Books, 1995).
3 Eboo Patel, *Acts of Faith: The Story of an American Muslim, in the Struggle for the Soul of a Generation* (Boston: Beacon Press, 2007). See also the Interfaith Youth Core website at http://www.ifyc.org.

just as God is good and blessed? If this is the case, might we not then conclude that we ought to be open to others who are in some way different from us (whoever "us" might be)? And finally, does this not demand that we be hospitable to others, that we find ways to talk to one another and share with one another the richness and beauty of each other both individually and corporately?

The account of Abraham and Sarah receiving and welcoming strangers has been commented upon so often that I hardly need to remind us of that account. I will simply state here that whenever I hear this story (which is often as a part of the curriculum in a course I teach every semester), I find myself wondering what prompted Abraham and Sarah to welcome these interlopers in their neighborhood into their home. Might it not have been a conviction that they should open their home to strangers who might bless them even if in much more subtle ways than with a baby in their advanced years?

The story of Jonah is a story of a man called to reach out to a strange people. He ran away rather than talk to strangers. However God sought him, and Jonah was forced to meet some people with whom he would rather not have talked. God asked Jonah to speak to the Ninevites. Jonah did not want to and fled, but was compelled to do as God asked. When Jonah did and the Ninevites turned to God, Jonah was unhappy because God blessed that "conversation" (with the Ninevites) by having mercy on Ninevah. Jonah was angry with God because God had compassion for the enemy of Israel. Among the conclusions we might draw from this story is that God wants us to speak in love to our enemies. No matter how far we flee and no matter how carefully we hide, God will not be deterred from compelling us to speak to our enemies and to recognize them as children of God worthy of love, mercy, and compassion.

While there are important lessons to be drawn from Jonah's story, it is also true that it has its limitations. First, Jonah did not willingly speak to the Ninevites. Second, it was not a true exchange of ideas. At least it was not in the sense of Jonah hearing about Ninevite religion and culture. Nonetheless it does say something important about God's character and commitments. God told Jonah to go to the stranger. God hunted Jonah down to the ends of the earth so that the stranger would hear God's word. And finally, God changed God's mind about the Ninevites and had mercy upon them. That is, God listened to the Ninevites and did not simply see them as another people to add to God's collection of faithful nations.

A different kind of story is that of Ruth. Ruth was a foreigner in Israel who chose to stay with her mother-in-law even when it made much more sense to go back home. The opportunities for a good life for Ruth were better at home in Moab than they were for her in Israel. In Israel, she had very few rights as a woman without a husband and as a foreigner. Nonetheless she stayed in order to care for Naomi and to provide her with companionship and love. The story ends happily with Ruth marrying a well-placed Israelite with wealth and status. But the real point here is that a stranger, a woman of a different ethnicity (or nationality) and therefore a different religion, gave her "testimony." Ruth's love, compassion, and faithfulness to Naomi presented a kind of witness from a stranger to Israel's culture and religion. Ruth demonstrated that love, compassion, and faithfulness are not unique or limited to Israel.

In the New Testament there is no shortage of stories that describe encounters with people of other faiths or ethnicity. There is the parable of the Good Samaritan (Luke 10:25-37) in which the Samaritan shows by his actions what love, compassion, and mercy are. There is the account of the Syrophoenician woman who stands up to Jesus and challenges him to heal her daughter by arguing that even Gentiles deserve a measure of God's blessing and healing (Mark 7:24-30). There is the account of the encounter between Jesus and a Samaritan woman at a well in that land (John 4:3-26). Like the Syrophoenician woman, the Samaritan woman does not abide by the rules of engagement. Neither does Jesus for that matter. Jesus does most of the talking in this account. He tells the Samaritan woman that the Jews know better and that he is the source of never-ending water that forever will quench her thirst. The woman for her part listens and endeavors to represent her people and her religion well. The point here (and in the case of the Syrophoenician woman) is not so much that the woman wins (or loses) the argument, but rather that Jesus is talking to her. Jesus is talking to one who is not like him. How is she not like Jesus? First, she is a woman (and not a man). Second, she is a sinner (How many husbands has she had?!? And the man she is living with now is not even her lawful husband!) and Jesus is without sin. Finally, she is a Samaritan (who has presumably rejected the covenant and thereby God), whereas Jesus is Jewish (and consequently one of the chosen people). Their differences do not divide them. Their differences do not cause Jesus to run away in fear of strangers. Indeed he embraces these strangers (even if hesitantly sometimes).

The best example of outreach, conversation, and dialogue with strangers is the Acts of the Apostles. It is from beginning to end, from Pentecost to Paul's ministry in Rome, an account of Christians reaching out to others and often hearing and encountering those strangers on their own terms even while presenting the gospel of Jesus Christ. The account of the first Pentecost in Acts 2 could be read as a commissioning and blessing of the church to reach out and to truly meet others unlike us. The list of nationalities present at the first assembly reads like a United Nations roll call of the first century: Parthians, Medes, Elamites, Mesopotamians, Jews, Phrygians, Pamphylians, Egyptians, Libyans, Romans, Cretans, and Arabs. Is there anybody missing? Acts is often understood (rightly) to be an account of the expansion of the church and of the church's proclamation of the gospel in those first years. However, it is not a proclamation that is unaware or disinterested in the lives, the culture, and the convictions of its hearers.

The story of Peter and Cornelius is among the most compelling narratives on this theme in Acts. Cornelius really has nothing going for him. He is an officer in the Roman army that occupies Palestine. He must have been despised as a representative of a hated occupier. Nonetheless, Luke recounts, Cornelius "was a devout man who feared God . . . ; he gave alms generously to the people and prayed constantly to God" (Acts 10:2; see also 10:22). The center of this account is Peter's vision in which he was told, "What God has made clean, you must not call profane" (10:15). The Spirit, Luke tells us, made the meaning of this puzzling statement clear to Peter when he met Cornelius: "the gift of the Holy Spirit had been poured out even on the Gentiles" (10:45). Christians are called, like Peter, to welcome the "other" and to know them. One thing that is striking in this passage is that nothing is said about Cornelius having to make himself into something he is not. Cornelius is not asked or told to give up his Roman identity. Indeed, Luke seems to suggest that his identity has been made clean. It is no longer profane.

The account of the council of Jerusalem in Acts 15 confirms this. Luke reports that there were some who were gathered that insisted that the Gentiles become Jewish: "It is necessary for them [the Gentiles] to be circumcised and ordered to keep the law of Moses" (15:5, also 15:1). Peter disagreed. He said that God has given them the Holy Spirit, cleansed their hearts, and "made no distinction between them and us" (15:9). In fact, the conversion of the Gentiles (presumably of their hearts and not their ethnicity) "brought great joy" (15:3). People who are not like us are not to be feared or avoided. In fact, people who are not like us but have the Spirit are to be rejoiced over because they have the Spirit.

One of the important narrative strands in the Bible is the ongoing growth of the people of God. God's chosen people, at the very beginning, are two people. They are an old man and his wife (Abraham and Sarah) who are well past child-bearing age. Even at the end of Genesis, God's chosen people cannot number more than a few dozen: Jacob and his wives and their twelve sons along with their wives and children. In Exodus, hospitality and inclusion—of a sort—are extended to sojourners, aliens, and others who live in the midst of the Israelites. In the New Testament, Paul and Peter challenge the church to open the doors to everybody who "confesses that Jesus is Lord" and have presumably received the Holy Spirit. All are included. All are to be welcomed. The church is radically inclusive and radically relational.

A Relational God

One reason, perhaps, that the church is inclusive and relational is because God is inclusive and relational. This is a, if not the, primary meaning or significance of the doctrine of the Trinity. It is, as Peters likes to say, not a problem of arithmetic.[4] How can $1 + 1 + 1 = 1$? This kind of question misses the point. The point is that the Trinity is a way of talking about the relational character of God.

The examination of the Bible passages above should already alert us that God seeks relationships with all humans—and arguably all creatures—in the world. This is the economic Trinity. This is God in the world, the Trinitarian God active in the world. The term "economic" here has to do with its Greek root: oikos or "household." The world is God's "house." As such God is sovereign and cares for the world. The clearest and most succinct expression of this economic Trinity is the Apostles' Creed.

The first article of the creed confesses that God is the "creator of heaven and earth." This article establishes the sovereignty or authority of God. At the same time it establishes a relationship to the world. The first person of the Trinity is relational.

The second article of the creed confesses that Jesus has "ascended into heaven" and judges the "living and the dead." The divinity of Jesus,

---

4   Ted Peters, *God as Trinity: Relationality and Temporality in Divine Life* (Louisville: Westminster John Knox Press, 1993), 17–18; see also Peters, *GOD—The World's Future*, 99.

or at least the authority of Jesus, is hereby asserted. Less apparent is that Jesus cares. And yet, this article reminds us that Jesus was "born of the virgin Mary, suffered under Pontius Pilate, was crucified, died, and was buried." That Jesus was born and suffered reminds us that he was human. It is reasonable to suppose that Jesus became human in order to be like us. God became human so as to better understand and to identify with us. Did God need to do that? Probably not. However perhaps we need to be reminded that God cares about us and creation, and that God understands and identifies with us.

Finally, the third article does not explicitly say anything about the activity of God the Spirit. However, the church, the resurrection of the body, and life everlasting are all mentioned in the same breath. This suggests that God the Spirit is somehow connected to these earthly realities. The force of the creed is to establish the authority and, arguably, the divinity of the three persons of the godhead, but also to establish the relationship between the three persons of the godhead and the world. God creates, rules over, redeems, sustains, and sanctifies the world.

A Relational Doctrine of the Trinity

The Apostles' Creed does not say much about the relationship between each of the three persons of the Trinity. How is the Father related to the Son? To the Holy Spirit? And how is the Spirit related to Jesus the Christ? This is the subject of the teaching of the immanent Trinity. Christians have almost always declared that the three persons of the Trinity are in relationship with one another. More recently some theologians have become preoccupied with how three persons can be one God. This matter, as I have already mentioned, is the wrong question. What do the relationships between the three persons of the Trinity tell us about God? This is the proper question.

One thing that we already know is that God is relational. Scripture is clear about this as I have already demonstrated. That this is so is apparent from the Trinity itself. Whatever we mean by "persons" when speaking about the Trinity, it is clear that at the heart of the Trinity we are talking about relationships. William Placher notes that if we begin our thinking about the Trinity by asking how the one God is three persons, it is difficult to get to that reality of community and relationality. However, this "is not the logic of Trinitarian thought. Rather, Christians begin with three, and the doctrine of the Trinity is the explanation of their oneness."⁵ Christopher Morse makes a similar point in a statement evocative of Peters' comment that we ought to leave arithmetic out of it: "The oneness of God is not to be thought of as a quantitative numerical unit but as a relational unity."⁶ So far, the key words are relational, unity, and persons.

What does "person" mean in this context? This is not as straightforward as we might think. If we think of "person" in the same sense that you are or I am a person, this does not quite seem to be what is intended. After all, since the Enlightenment we have an inclination to think of each of us as a more or less autonomous and isolated individual.⁷ This image has two difficulties. The first is that it almost necessarily leads to a kind of tritheism. The second is that this image of an aloof entity is at odds with the active, engaged, and involved God that Christianity asserts. Indeed, one might argue that the entire witness of Scripture is to say that God is involved in the history of Israel and the church and all of creation. This Trinity business seems to be a complicated affair. It is difficult to be sure what we mean when we say that there are three persons in the Trinity; what exactly is a "person" is in this context?

Placher, following Aquinas, suggests that whatever we might say about "person," it is inextricably tied with "relation." In fact, "persons are relations."⁸ His point is affirmed by Elizabeth Johnson (and others) before him. Johnson says, "[A]s the outcome of theological reflection on the Christian experience of relationship to God, [the Trinity] is a symbol that indirectly points to God's relationality, at first with reference to the world and then with reference to God's own mystery."⁹ Catherine Mowry LaCugna is even more emphatic:

> The doctrine of the Trinity is ultimately... a teaching not about the abstract nature of God, nor about God in isolation from everything other than God, but a teaching about God's life with us and our life with each other. Trinitarian theology could be described as par excellence a theology of relationship, which explores the mysteries of love, relationship,

---

5 William C. Placher, *The Triune God: An Essay in Postliberal Theology* (Louisville: Westminster John Knox Press, 2007), 136, also 119–21.
6 Christopher Morse, *Not Every Spirit: A Dogmatics of Christian Disbelief*, 2nd ed. (New York: Continuum, 2009), 136.
7 Placher, *The Triune God*, 129; also Elizabeth A. Johnson, *She Who Is: The Mystery of God in Feminist Theological Discourse* (New York: Crossroad, 1992), 203.
8 Placher, *The Triune God*, 143.
9 Johnson, *She Who Is*, 204–5, also 216.

personhood, and communion within the framework of God's self-revelation in the person of Christ and the activity of the Spirit.[10]

A good number of theologians agree that an important feature of the doctrine of the Trinity is that it embeds relationality in the very being of God.

The argument I have been pushing toward is that God is inherently relational. Scripture witnesses to the relational nature of God. The doctrine of the Trinity is an expression of that scripture witness to God's relational nature.

If we are to take seriously the notion in Genesis 1:26–27 that humans are created in the image of God, I think it is reasonable to assume that we are relational because God is relational. I think that it is also reasonable to conclude that God has taken pains to push Israel and the people of God to reach out to others in mutual dialogue and be "mutually encouraged by each other's faith" (Romans 1:12). This history of the people of God has been one where they have been compelled to ever expand their own self-identity to include others, whoever those "others" might be. It is not just simply a matter of expanding our self-identity. Central to this endeavor has been the encounter or the conversation. It is not entirely an accident that Christ is the "Word." Conversation and dialogue are not possible without words. That Christ is the Word suggests that it is in Christ that God "talks" to us who are "other" to God. In like manner, we might use our words (and actions) to talk to those who are "other" to us, and, like we are, "other" to God. Scripture is an account of, if you will, God's hospitality. God does not have to communicate with us, but God does. God does not have to share the work of creation with us, but God does. God does not have to share the hope of a future of justice and peace, but God does. Hospitality and relationality are, I think, essentially the same thing. More than that, hospitality and relationality are not just about sharing ourselves and our gifts with others, but also about receiving others and their gifts.

---

10 Catherine Mowry LaCugna, *God for Us: The Trinity and Christian Life* (San Francisco: HarperSanFrancisco, 1991), 1.

What Kinds of Questions Are Explained in Theology?

Niels Henrik Gregersen

Ted Peters' engagement in the field of science-religion has been lifelong, wide-ranging, deep, and influential. It is therefore necessary for me to focus on only one theme in this essay, the question of explanation in theology. Already in his systematic theology, *GOD—The World's Future: Systematic Theology for a New Era*, Peters lists "seven principles of evangelical explication," the final of which is what he calls explanatory adequacy:

> The explication of Christian symbols sets as its goal the construction of the most adequate explanation of reality possible. There is a way in which the Christian explanation is measured against competing visions of reality offered by secular philosophers and other religious traditions. We must ask: does the Christian vision offer a more comprehensive accounting or more fruitful illumination of the human experience with oneself, the world, and God?[1]

More precisely, according to Peters, there should be "instances of actual contemporary experience to which theology should apply" in order for theology to "make sense," or even "more sense."[2] Alongside this principle of applicability, there is also the more difficult principle of comprehensiveness. This implies the claim that "there are no significant realities that in principle are not interpretable and explainable according to the theological scheme." Any theological exposition will, of course, be finite in scope, but Peters argues that the texture of theology should be "porous so as to admit new experiences with honest and

---

1 Ted Peters, *GOD—The World's Future: Systematic Theology for a New Era*, 2nd ed., (Minneapolis: Fortress Press, 2000), 78.
2 Ibid., 79.

meaningful incorporation."[3] The dilemma here is, as aptly formulated by Peters, that theology needs to recognize the human thirst and desire for truth, which urges "an understanding of a single whole of reality," while also acknowledging that we, empirically speaking, always have to start out in the midst of things, from the given experiences which involve a vast variety of partially conflicting symbolizations of the human experience."[4] To these principles of external adequacy, as I would dub them, Peters also adds the internal coherence whereby the various aspects of a theology complement one another: "To cohere, they need to presuppose one another and to imply one another."[5]

From Grand-Scale Explanations to Empirical Explanations

Obviously Peters is here speaking about how to cope with grand-scale symbolizations in theology and philosophy, and he is adopting for theology the criteria of explanatory adequacy that Alfred North Whitehead formulated for a suitable metaphysics.[6]

Now what then about the interruptions coming from the sciences to such claims of systematic order? What if we, using Occam's razor, make an intellectual preference for minimal explanation of particular facts, identifiable natural capacities, and resilient structures and processes of nature, thus searching for a maximal consensus based on a minimalist economy of explanatory concepts, while discarding all religious, semi-religious, or secular "symbolizations," giving up the aspiration of developing a "system"? We here face the challenge of empiricism to theology. This is, for example, the challenge of Richard Dawkins who exactly treats the hypothesis of God's existence as a scientific theory like any other, just a clumsy and abysmally stupid one.[7]

The problem here is what we might say about the idea of explanation, what my compatriot Søren Kierkegaard allegedly said about the Latin word *res*, or thing: "It can mean just anything but buttonhooks." Ted Peters himself has already responded to many particular aspects of this

---

3   Ibid.
4   Ibid.
5   Ibid., 80.
6   Ibid., 79, n. 32, with reference to A. N. Whitehead, *Process and Reality*, corrected version, David Ray Griffin and Donald W. Sherburne, eds. (New York: Free Press, 1978), 3–4.
7   Richard Dawkins, *The God Delusion* (Boston, New York: Houghton Mifflin Company, 2006), 50 and 61.

scientific challenge, especially from proponents of ideological forms of Darwinism, or "Darwinicisms." More programmatically he has endorsed Ernan McMullin's notion of the ideal of a consonance between science and theology. The idea of a "hypothetical consonance" thus comes up in several of his methodological writings.[8] "If there be one God and one creation, then what natural scientists study is the same cosmos that God has created. We should expect in the long run, then that knowledge gained from empirical research and knowledge gained from special revelation will be consonant."[9]

Hypothetical Consonance and Critical Realism

Hypothetical consonance is indeed an attractive model and serves well in articulating an ideal view of the relation between science and theology. The model presupposes, however, the view of critical realism, meaning that science and theology are referring to the same world, hence must be consonant, although their perspectives and epistemic resources may differ. As Peters himself acknowledges, the model of hypothetical consonance hereby aims to redeem the elements of truth in the two-language theory that only knows how to separate theological from scientific language. "[H]ypothetical consonance is the name I give to the negotiations that carry the two-language theory beyond truce to a fuller cooperation."[10] For again, there must be a correspondence between what scientists say about the world of nature, and what the Abrahamic traditions refer to as God's creation. Peters admits that strong consonance, in the sense of accord or harmony, may still be wanting, and suggests that we work with "consonance in a weak sense—that is, by identifying common domains of question asking. The advances in physics, especially thermodynamics and quantum theory in relation to Big Bang cosmology, have in their own way raised questions about transcendent reality."[11] And with reference to Paul Davies, it is suggested that also the God question may be raised from the perspective of science. "Theologians and

---

8   Ted Peters, ed., *Cosmos as Creation: Theology and Science in Consonance* (Nashville: Abington Press), 13–17; Ted Peters, ed., *Science and Theology: The New Consonance* (Boulder, Colorado: Westview Press, 1998); Ted Peters, "Science and Faith: From Warfare to Consonance," in *God, Life, and the Cosmos: Christian and Islamic Perspectives*, Ted Peters, Muzzafar Iqbal, and Syed Nomanul Haq, eds. (Aldershot, United Kingdom: Ashgate, 2002), 77–99.
9   Peters, "Science and Faith," 79.
10 Ibid., 86.
11 Ibid., 86–87.

scientists may now be sharing a common subject matter, and the idea of hypothetical consonance encourages further cooperation."[12]

While I share with Peters his search for bridges between science and theology, especially on specific topical areas, I have myself become somewhat more critical of critical realism as a consensus position in the field of science and religion—not because I do not agree with the view just expressed by Peters, but because I see critical realism as a presumption more than as something that can easily be achieved. The idea of critical realism in science and religion has several independent theses built into it. Science and theology are seen as cousins or comrades searching for the same sort of reality (the epistemic thesis of similarity between science and theology). This view, however, may fail to acknowledge the different kinds of quests for explanation in science and religion, and the asymmetry between science and theology. Secondly, even if classic-minded scientists and classic-minded theologians (like Peters and myself) agree that there is something "real" to speak about (what Stathis Psillos called metaphysical realism) as well as semantic realism, this does not mean that theology can be seen as explanatory in the same sense as the sciences do (what Psillos called theoretical-explanatory realism). Neither does it mean that the eventual progress of the sciences (in the few domains where one may dare speak about an "approximation to truth") in any way guarantees, or even makes it probable, that an analogous progress can be warranted within theology (say, in terms of an approximation towards the ultimate reality of God).[13]

This brings me to my second reservation, which is a challenge to my own theology as well. It might well be the case (at least this is the challenge to be met) that theological explanations of reality are so to speak parasitic on scientific developments, so that we theologians take in what we can from scientific explanations, but give nothing in return to the sciences. Insofar as this is the case, there is not really a mutual, critical interaction going on between science and theology (as most of us, who have learned from Arthur Peacocke and Robert John Russell, would like to have it), but a one-sided transport of scientific explanations into theology, without theology ever being on the sponsoring side.

---

12 Ibid., 87.
13 Niels Henrik Gregersen, "Critical Realism and Other Realisms," in *Fifty Years in Science and Theology: Ian G. Barbour and His Legacy*, Robert John Russell, ed. (Aldershot, United Kingdom: Ashgate, 2002), 77–96 (90–92).

Three Steps of Concretization

So we are back where we started: How to make a case for a theoretical-explanatory realism, within theology? I see three ways to make such a case. (Observe here that while my overt ambitions appear to be a bit weaker than expressed by Peters, my step-wise suggestions are meant to point in the direction of Peters' more ambitious claims.)

The first step is to admit that "explanation," as a matter of fact, means something different from one discipline to another discipline within the sciences, and so much more between the sciences and philosophies. There are here two ways to go. Either one can make a sort of hermeneutical also-you argument to practicing sciences, following for example Stephen Toulmin, who argues also that scientific explanations do nothing more than "making sense" of observables. Toulmin thus argued already in the early 1960s that the explanatory techniques of science must not only be, as phrased by Copernicus, "consistent with the numerical records" but also be acceptable to the human community, "pleasing to the mind."[14] In *Explanation from Physics to Theology*, our colleague Philip Clayton followed this path, arguing for a "contextual shift from formalism to hermeneutics" in the sciences, relativizing explanation as just "an element within the broader hermeneutical task that is science."[15] This view has the advantage of expressing a continuum from science to philosophy and theology, but has the disadvantage of not attending to the specificities of explanation in, say, the search for fundamental laws in physics, the explanation of resilient structures and causal capacities (beyond laws) in chemistry and biology, the role of statistics in economy, the concrete case-studies in sociology and psychology, etc. When observing such disunities within the sciences, it would be curious to expect that theological explanation should somehow be like physics. The point here is to keep in mind the pragmatic question: What do you want to know about?

The second step is to emphasize that theology, in some rare cases, is in a position to explain, in a meta-scientific explanation, natural states that the sciences themselves either discover, or presuppose. Why, for example, are the mathematical models of reality "unreasonably effective"

---

14 Stephen Toulmin, *Foresight and Understanding: An Inquiry into the Aims Science* (Bloomington: University of Indiana Press, 1961), 115.
15 Philip Clayton, *Explanation from Physics to Theology: An Essay in Rationality and Religion*, (New Haven, Connecticuit: London, 1989), 39 (italized by author).

(Eugene Wigner), pointing to a mathematical order in the universe itself? Whence this order? Or, why are the fundamental laws of nature fine-tuned for the emergence of life and meaning? Why this fine-tuning? Or, more generally, why is the physical matter as bio-friendly as it actually is, hosting even emotions and rational beings, when matter itself, according to our best scientific theories, is neither alive nor conscious?

My third step takes up a challenge that Ted Peters has raised to me and consists of the distinction between causal and semantic explanations. In which sense can one make sense of the divine action in and through the self-organizing capacities of natural processes? In what sense may we talk about God's involvement in, with, and under biological processes of natural selection?[16] In both cases I will argue that theology should not present an explanation other than those offered by the sciences. The role of theology here is to offer a richer semantic redescription of processes already described (sometimes tightly, sometimes more loosely) and explained by the sciences. Though theology here may not offer a causal explanation of the specific processes of self-organization and selection, theology may offer a sense-making explanation—what I call a semantic explanation.

Here I follow the lead of Wentzel van Huysteen, who early on made the case that the kinds of questions raised by religious reflection are not the same as those raised by the sciences: "Accepting that different kinds of rationality are involved in the practices of science and theology and that neither can provide the content of the other's knowledge does not mean that they do not inform the context in which their perspective is to be constructed."[17] Starting out from the pragmatic perspective of who are asking the questions of explanation, and for what purpose, belongs to the very nature of inquiry, and should not be seen as something purely extrinsic to the task of explaining, neither do such pragmatic conditions imply that theology does not make cognitive claims—claims expressed in language understandable also for open-minded rational inquirers not convinced by the theological explanation. Here the semantics of explanation precede the more difficult question of the justification of an explanatory claim. As a matter of fact, there always exist more candi-

---

[16] See Ted Peters, "Happy Danes and Deep Incarnation," *Dialog: A Journal of Theology* 52:3 (September 2013), and my response in the same issue.

[17] J. Wentzel van Huyssteen, "Experience and Explanation: The Justification of Cognitive Claims in Theology," in *Essays on Postfoundationalist Theology* (Grand Rapids, Michigan: Wm. B. Eerdmans Publishing Co., 1997), 162–179 (163).

dates for explanation than explanations finding full assent. Moreover, often we are left with explanatory sketches for a certain domain, without being able to fully identify the scope and boundaries of explanations, and of the relationship between one type of explanation and another. Also in the sciences, comprehensiveness and global applicability are an ideal more than a *fait-accompli*.

Who Asks for an Explanation, and for What Purpose?

Already in 1980, in "The Pragmatic Theory of Explanation," Bas van Fraassen developed a pragmatic view of what it means to seek an explanation. As he points out, "An explanation is not the same as a proposition, or an argument, or list of propositions; it is an answer. . . . An explanation is an answer to a why-question. So, a theory of explanation must be a theory of why-questions."[18] In the view of van Fraassen, scientific explanations are simply those "which draw upon science for the adduced information." But as he immediately adds, "That is not always what the questioner wants."[19]

So there are other sorts of explanation, which adduce information from resources other than science, for example, based on experience or well-winnowed traditions. Moreover, van Fraassen's so-called semantic theory of scientific explanation is, as he himself acknowledges, not dependent on his non-realist view of science, but can be embraced by proponents of realism of one or another sort (like Peters and myself). Philip Kitcher makes a similar point by reminding us that even the most substantive explanations are the result of a conditioned explanatory quest: "The most obvious way in which to categorize explanation is to view it as an activity. In this activity we answer the actual or anticipated questions of an actual or anticipated audience. We do so by presenting reasons. We draw on the beliefs we hold, frequently using or adapting arguments furnished to us by the sciences."[20] Moreover, Kitcher argues that scientific explanation only seldom takes the form of a subsumption of particular sequences of event under general laws plus antecedent conditions, as in Hempel and Oppenheimer's famous nomothetic-deductive model of scientific explanation. More often, Kitcher

---

18 Bas van Frasssen, *The Scientific Image* (Oxford: Oxford University Press, 1980), ch. 5.
19 Bas van Fraassen, *Laws and Symmetry* (Oxford: Oxfrod University Press, 1989), ch. 8.
20 Philip Kitcher, "Explanatory Unification," in *Theories of Explanation*, Joseph C. Pitt, ed. (New York, Oxford: Oxford University Press, 1988), 168. The following references to this article.

says, explanation takes the form of a theoretical unification of hitherto disparate phenomena. His main example is Darwin who offered a variety of "explanation-sketches" that exhibited a more general "pattern of argument," able to unify a host of biological phenomena[21] under the perspective of natural selection and variegated circumstances, such as fossil records, diversity of groups within species, embryological homologies between species, similarities of building platforms, etc. The question is, of course, whether or not theological explanations are of this sort: an attempt at answering religious why-questions by offering explanatory sketches close to human experience, while unifying the information coming from such first-hand experiences with information coming from self-reflective, religious traditions as well as from other resources such as the sciences. Kitcher foresees such applications and wants to protect his model of explanatory unification within the sciences from what he calls "spurious unifications" as, for example,[22]

God wants it to be the case that "a"...
What God wants to be the case is the case.
Therefore "a" is the case...

The problem here is that "patterns of self-derivation and the type of pattern exemplified in the example of the theological community merely provide trivial, omnipresent connections, and, in consequence, the unification they offer is spurious."[23] In order to avoid such generalities, Kitcher adds the additional criterion, "the unification achieved [must not be] by patterns which adapt themselves to any conclusion and by patterns which accidentally restrict such universally hospitable patterns."[24] The two-fold danger, in other words, is vacuous generality ("God wants all that happens to happen."), or ad-hoc restrictions ("God wants the sun to shine on me, not the rain to fall.").

Kitcher shows that theological explanations of general scope cannot be treated as theoretical unifications in a scientific sense. But his pragmatic point of departure leaves open other ways by which theology may be said to provide explanations of a general sort. One can argue, as Mikael Stenmark has done, that regarding life-view orientations other types of questions may be raised. "How can I live in accordance with

---

21 Ibid., 172.
22 Ibid., 183.
23 Ibid.
24 Ibid., 184.

nature?" "How can I live a flourishing life?" Or even, "How can I live as a Christian?" The explanatory answers to be given would in all three cases include information from resources outside of, as well as inside, the sciences: "You should do this, because x, y, z," where the concrete information of the latter sentence would include the content qualifiers, the "arguments," for why I should live so or so. Rather than seeing such "life-view beliefs" as either irrational (contrary to reason) or as a-rational (outside the domain of exact reasoning), one could also argue with Stenmark that "we can make a rational choice between different views of life, but the standards and the reasons are somewhat different from the ones used in science."[25]

Now, of course, giving a reason does not *eo ipso* mean offering a theoretical explanation. But I would argue that insofar as information about reality is part of the reasoning, and the information is neither vacuous in its generality nor purely ad hoc, theology does offer explanations (that is, offers answers to why-questions) both in the form of compressed "explanatory sketches" or eye-opening examples and as comprehensive views of reality (as in Wisdom traditions, for example). Yet we are still a far cry away from scientific explanations. And theological explanations of this kind belong to the family of explanations that are to explicate experiences in a qualitative sense, to order experiences within a wider setting, to understand the potential meanings of traditions, and to orientate one's life in accord with a comprehensive world view, into which scientific information may well be built.

Conclusion

It seems to me that theology has the two-fold task of explicating religious traditions (in the case of Christian systematic theology, the living Christian traditions) and of offering explanations of otherwise known facts, from first-hand experience, from philosophical reflection, or from the repertoires of sciences, from the natural sciences to the social and human sciences. Theology does not usually make predictions, but neither are theological explanations simply ad hoc-explanations, since they do explain (that is, make sense of) persistent features of the universe. And theological theory can be said to be progressive by being able to

---

[25] Mikael Stenmark, *Rationality in Science, Religion, and Everyday Life: A Critical Examination of Four Models of Rationality* (Notre Dame, Indiana: University of Notre Dame Press, 1995), 274.

use existing evidence (not least from the sciences) for answering pragmatically important theological why-questions.[26] At this level, however, it seems to me that theological explanations normally take the form of a semantic explanation by offering a coherent picture about how things relate to one another (without necessarily being able to explain the causal route from the creative power of God to the particulars of the created world). It seems to me that the difference between causal and semantic explanations has not always been made sufficiently clear in science-religion discussions on explanation, maybe because of the fuzziness of the very term "explanation" in the English language.

Theology asks for answers to pertinent questions such as the following, "How can you speak of an omnipotent God in the midst of evolutionarily induced suffering?" It seems to me that it is to such pertinent questions that Ted Peters always has been responding—not only in his capacities as a leading systematic theologian but also in his deep and extremely well-informed interaction with the biological sciences—from genetics to macroevolutionary theory. Sense-making is what makes sense.

---

[26] Still inspiring here is the bold work of Nancey Murphy, *Theology in an Age of Scientific Reasoning* (Ithaca, New York: Cornell University Press, 1990). My own appreciative critique of Murphy's concept of theology as an empirical research program is found in Niels Henrik Gregersen and J. Wentzel van Huyssteen, eds., *Rethinking Theology and Science* (Grand Rapids, Michigan: Wm. B. Eerdmans Publishing Co., 1998), 205–212.

Method, Methodology, and Theology

Ted Peters

While studying at the Ruprecht-Karl University in Heidelberg, I had an American friend named Gus Johansson. Repeatedly over a cup of coffee Johansson would fume about what would be said in his doctoral seminar. "They always talk about *Methode*. What the hell is a *Methode*?" We discussed the matter. It was unclear to any of us English speakers just what the German scholars meant by *die Methode*.

"Next seminar meeting, I have to deliver a *Referat*," whined Johansson on one occasion. "They'll all ask me about my *Methode*. What should I do?"

"Just do your best with the subject matter, the *Inhalt*," we advised Johansson.

The day following his seminar, we met again for coffee. "How'd your seminar presentation go?" I asked Johansson.

"Just great!" he answered with a smile. "And the students and the professor all said I had a great *Methode*. But, I still don't know what a *Methode* is." Obviously, Johansson's theological intuition constructed his *Methode* to the satisfaction if not the admiration of his colleagues.

After departing Heidelberg to finish my doctorate at the University of Chicago, I figured it out. What the Germans had called *die Methode* the Americans were calling *methodology*. Actually, to be precise, *methodology* is the philosophical exploration into epistemology and related preparatory concerns that lead up to theological reflection. *Methodology* explores options. Once one has explored the options and elected one single method, then the word changes. Now, instead of *methodology*, the theologian is pursuing theology with a *method*. Whew. Did you get that?

Roman Catholics call methodology *fundamental theology*. I found this out because my *Doktorvater* at the University of Chicago was a Catholic priest, David Tracy. Whether we refer to this work as methodology or fundamental theology, Tracy was and perhaps is the world's expert.[1] For each methodological assertion Tracy makes, he supports it with a number of footnotes equal to the stars in the Milky Way.

When decades ago I set out to write my systematic theology, *GOD—The World's Future*, I prefaced the treatment of doctrine with multiple chapters on methodology. An early draft included so many footnotes even Tracy would have been aghast. Then I took a hatchet to the text and chopped off as many footnotes in the surviving two chapters as I could in good conscience discard. The result is a tightly organized set of road signs to guide the reader through doctrinal discussions.

My approach is hermeneutical. That is to say, I see theology as a form of interpretation. I begin with primary discourse: the symbolic and multivalent language of Scripture. Then, I rise up through directed interpretation to the level of secondary discourse. Theology is secondary discourse based upon rational reflection on the more fundamental symbolic discourse of the Bible, liturgy, prayer, hymnody, and even art. The systematic theologian is rational, seeking to turn equivocal symbolic meaning into univocal propositions that fit together coherently with one another. Even though systematic theology leaves its biblical home to provide rational explanations of reality, it never forgets where it came from. Biblical symbols always say more than the theological interpreter can say.

As a hermeneutical theologian I interpret Scripture. I also interpret culture. I find myself returning again and again to Langdon Gilkey, who learned his method for interpreting culture from Paul Tillich and Reinhold Niebuhr. Gilkey referred to his own method as a *hermeneutic of secular experience,* which attempts "to see what religious dimensions there may be ... in ordinary life ... which will uncover what is normally hidden and forgotten."[2] Gilkey adds, "What it seeks to uncover ... are those aspects of daily experience which the secular mood has overlooked ... there are levels latent in secular life of which our age is undoubtedly aware but about which it is unable to speak or to think intelligibly. These

---

[1] Roman Catholic fundamental theology overlaps with Protestant philosophical theology or methodology. But, fundamental theology has absolutely nothing in common with Protestant fundamentalist theology.

[2] Langdon Gilkey, *Naming the Whirlwind: The Renewal of God-Language* (Indianapolis and New York: Bobbs-Merrill, 1969), 234.

elements are the dimension of ultimacy presupposed in all our interaction with the relative world, and the presence of ambiguity within our freedom and our creativity, of the demonic and the despairing in life as well as the joyful, with both of which secular experience is suffused."[3] With this interpretive method, I look for hidden religious or spiritual yearnings coming to oblique or disguised expression in science, politics, art, and other manifestations of secular self-understanding.

This attempt to structure a theological method and to provide methodological justification is the focus of other writers in this *Festschrift*. It is illuminating for me to read what others write about my work. It is also challenging. I would like to rise to this challenge in what follows.

The Method of Correlation: Michael Aune on Retrieval

My first theological love was the work of Paul Tillich. Even though my intellectual flirtations have included innumerable other alluring schools of thought, I've never sought a divorce from Tillich's method of correlation. "The method of correlation explains the contents of the Christian faith through existential questions and theological answers in mutual interdependence."[4] Tracy modified Tillich's correlation model with his *mutually critical* correlation model: "the revisionist model can perhaps be best described as a critical reformulation of both the meanings manifested by our common human experience and the meanings manifested by an interpretation of the central motifs of the Christian tradition."[5] That is to say, biblically based theological claims can engage contemporary experience and contemporary culture critically, and contemporary philosophical thought can engage traditional Christian answers with critical proposals for revision. In short, theologians must listen as well as speak.

It is the workings of this method of correlation that prompt Michael Aune to ruminate in his *Festschrift* chapter, "What's Needed in Theology? World-view Construction, Retrieval, or . . .? A correlation method such as we find in Tillich or Tracy or even my own method will require a component of retrieval. After all, if we are going to answer contemporary existential questions with classic Christian answers, we will have to retrieve these answers from Scripture or tradition. How should such a retrieval take place? This is Aune's concern.

---

3   Ibid., 260.
4   Paul Tillich, *Systematic Theology*, 3 volumes (Chicago: University of Chicago Press, 1951–1963), 1:60.
5   Aune alludes to Tracy, *Blessed Rage for Order*, 34.

Actually, Aune issues a warning when we wish to retrieve our classical Christian roots: There is no purity back there in time. We must recognize that our contemporary perspective influences what we retrieve. And it should.

Theologies of retrieval are not some direct form of theological conservatism, repristination, or even a neo-orthodoxy. Rather, they seek to retrieve what is forgotten as a pre-condition to a fuller, more theological understanding of modernity or however we call our present time. This is no simple return from the fleshpots of the present to what might be considered a more authentic teaching from the past. Some may think that, but ultimately, theologians of retrieval are attempting to respond adequately to our situation—to seek what would be a true "orthodoxy" in the sense of here and now—where the subject matter of Christian theology is Christ—the one of whom Scripture has spoken and still speaks and who is recognized in the breaking of the bread. Failure to appreciate this leaves us in a kind of modern theology "that can only be described as an odd mixture of metaphysics and mythology."[6]

Or, to say it Tracy's way, our retrieval of the Christian answer to today's existential question includes in the very retrieving, an adaptation to the present situation.

The Atheist Challenge: Michael Aune on Grace

Turning to the other pole in the correlation—existential questions arising out of the present situation—the topic of atheism arises. When reviewing my own project of speaking apologetically to the contemporary situation characterized in large part by the influence of the new aggressive atheists, Aune registers concern that my Christology might be too weak. "I cannot help but notice that there is not much of a Christological actualization of that grace. There is a brief mention of a gracious Trinitarian interaction with the world, but that is about all." My vague allusion to the God of grace is not specific enough, not particular enough. Aune writes:

> We can proceed even more boldly in our theological work, then, from the unique event of God's revelatory initiative—that paradigm of the incarnation that is concrete, particular, and historical—that radical particularity of "the Trinitarian God assuming human reality in the person of Jesus Christ as

---

6 Aune, 23.

the Word truly made flesh." This particularity of the Incarnation—and its retrieval—can "be the ground of a theological method that is accountable both to revelation and to the long tradition of practices and reflections" while also speaking to our contemporaries.[7]

To this I need to formulate a response. When addressing atheist arguments, I begin with their arguments. They frequently take the form of a *God hypothesis*, mimicking what they think goes on in science. The question of God's existence becomes a scientific problem to be researched, they demand. Upon researching the God hypothesis, they conclude that God most likely does not exist.

This demand that proof for the existence or non-existence of the deity becomes a scientific hypothesis is like a demand by the San Francisco Forty-Niners that the San Francisco Giants play on their own field, the football field. The baseball players would have to play by football rules. Home runs will no longer count. No wonder the Forty-Niners could boast of a quick victory over their baseball rivals.

Perhaps the most rapacious among the demanders is Richard Dawkins. Dawkins is the Oxford professor of science education who gave us the concept of the *selfish gene*, and who is known for championing the field of sociobiology.[8] The question of God is a scientific question, he avers. Dawkins raises the God hypothesis and then finds it falsifiable. We note that scientists can only speak in probabilities, not absolutes. So, curiously, Dawkins reports that it is his considered scientific judgment that, most probably, God does not exist.

I wish to ask: Just what kind of God does Dawkins repudiate the existence of? After all, quite a diversity of ideas of God abound among the world's religions, and even within single religious traditions. So, just which idea of God is Dawkins combatting? Dawkins, thankfully, is quite clear. He says he is not attacking any specific divine figure such as Yahweh, Jesus, Allah, Baal, Zeus, or Wotan. Rather, he is attacking all of them at once. All belief in such divinities can be swept up into a single "God Hypothesis," which Dawkins attempts to falsify. "I shall define the God Hypothesis more defensibly: *there exists a super-human, supernatural intel-*

---

7 Aune here cites Anthony J. Godzieba, Lieven Boeve, Michele Saracino, "Resurrection-Interruption–Transformation: Incarnation as a Hermeneutical Strategy: A Symposium," *Theological Studies* 67 (2006): 778.

8 Richard Dawkins, *The Selfish Gene* (Oxford and New York: Oxford University Press, 1979, 1989).

ligence who deliberately designed and created the universe and everything in it, including us."⁹ No such deity can be demonstrated by science to exist, he concludes.

Again: what kind of deity is being disproven by the God-hypothesis? The kind of God Dawkins rejects is the kind of God who provides an explanation for a scientific description of the natural world. Well, I ask: how much of a stake does a Christian theologian have in this kind of deity? A celestial engineer? An intelligent designer? A formulator of natural laws? An overmind who thinks mathematically? Are these the divine attributes I would go to the mat to defend?

No. My concern is whether or not God is gracious. In fact, I am so concerned about this, that I think the question of divine grace ranks above the question of divine existence. If a deity exists but is not gracious, who cares? Not just any ol' deity will do. I want a gracious God, or none at all.

What we find significant in the atheist discussion of our era is the question of God being raised in secular circles. What we need to do is respond to this question. However, the God-hypothesis misplaces the question. There is no room in the way the God-hypothesis is formulated to ask about grace. The theologian needs to re-ask the secular question so that the claim that God is gracious can appear on the questioner's horizon. Question and answer must be mutually critical.

This means that I invest my theological energies in explicating the biblical claim that the God of creation and redemption is a God of grace. And this retrieval of the classic Christian claim must *critically* appropriate today's question of God to make the Christian answer plausible and credible. The matter of divine grace is what is decisive, in my judgment. So, in conversation with the atheists, I try to make this point and only this point.

Michael Aune's complaint is that by generalizing about some undefined deity who is gracious, I fail to witness to my particularity as a committed believer in Jesus Christ. Now, Aune is certainly correct in adding that we learn about divine graciousness primarily through the revelation that comes to us through Jesus Christ. Yes, indeed!

---

9 Richard Dawkins, *The God Delusion* (Boston and New York: Houghton Mifflin Company, 2006), 31. Dawkins's italics.

Public Theology: Gaymon Bennett on Bioethics

Gaymon Bennett formulates an issue regarding Christian particularity that looks somewhat like that posed by Aune. The context here is not atheism. Rather, it is medical research accompanied by bioethics. Bennett and I along with Karen Lebacqz and other colleagues have spent considerable time in research laboratories, focusing our theological resources on codifying moral guidelines for genomics, stem cells, reproduction, and related areas. Yanked out of the church setting, we are put down in a secular and scientific setting and, like monkeys in a circus, asked to perform. What happens? We confront a dilemma.

The dilemma is a curious one. The theologian is invited to participate in bioethics precisely because it is assumed that science, such as it is, cannot tell us what ends we should pursue. It is further assumed that the theologian might be something of an expert on the question of ends. In public situations, however, the theologian is asked to speak about things which either can be operationalized, or can be taken in the spirit of general admonition. This means, in effect, that the theologian must speak as a technical expert or secular sage, and never as a person of faith.

That's what Bennett says in his *Festschrift* chapter, "Methodological *Askēsis*: On Practicing a Theology of the Actual."

It is the theological sophistication and critical thinking that accompanies this sophistication that prepares us to make a contribution to public policy considerations. Because science is allegedly value free, it takes the value-orientation of a theologian or someone like a theologian to codify ethical principles. Yet, we dare not footnote these principles with reference to our particular belief in God. Bennett is right, "the dilemma is a curious one." Yet, it is the reality a theologian faces when speaking within a secular context.

This concern with particularity gives rise to a related matter, namely, the issue of social location viewed through the lenses of deconstructionist postmodernism. This leads Bennett to a criticism of my work. "If there is one limitation to Peters' theological program, in my view, it is that he does not pay systematic attention to the material conditions of his own vocational striving as part of the explicit material of his theological analysis. Despite a feel for the actual, Peters only occasionally puts himself, and the venues in which he has sought to conduct his theological work, into explicit critical perspective as part of his theological narrative." What has become *de rigor* in the methodology of many postmodern theorists is the indispensable acknowledgement of the social location of the theoretician. Barely visible vested interests and even power relations can become visible when the protagonist's social location is subjected to critical review. Bennett finds my own method lacking because of a lack of transparency.

> The reason this is a limitation is not because Peters is obliged to be more honest about his own location in the world or to come clean about the ostensible sociological sources of his biases. The reason, rather, has to do with the fact that theological attention to the actual needs to include careful attention to the question of power—a question which Peters, in practice, has encountered time and again through his experimental undertakings . . . Peters' efforts to refuse a modern division of value spheres, and the energies he has subsequently spent opening up a place for theology in science and in bioethics, should be characterized as conceptual and pragmatic struggles. They are struggles precisely because relations of authority, careerism, and the persistent dominance of instrumental values continue to determine the limits of what can be said theologically where, to whom, and to what effect. . . . These power relations, in face of which Peters has conducted his work, are every bit as much a part of the modern world he has analyzed, and the postmodern consciousness he has tried to envision through UFOs, the Club of Rome, stem cells, or evolutionary biology. Making sense of these relations, and fostering theological practices appropriate to countering them, should be made an integral part of any theology worthy of the name.[10]

The need for transparency is not due to my hiding vested interests, according to Bennett. Rather, transparency is required by the modern and emerging postmodern context within which the theologian must work. "Relations of authority, careerism, and the persistent dominance of instrumental values" are co-present to every intellectual and ethical enterprise, and they must become acknowledged factors in our theological and moral reasoning. Good advice.

---

10 Bennett, 55-56.

Critical Realism in Science and Theology: The Demure of Niels Henrik Gregersen

When I first made my swan dive into the bottomless pool of science and religion, I swam immediately to a fetching buoy, critical realism. According to the late Ian G. Barbour, "*critical realism* must acknowledge both the creativity of man's mind, and the existence of patterns in events that are not created by man's mind . . . scientific language does not provide a replica of nature but a symbolic system that is abstract and selective and deals with limited aspects of the situation for particular purposes."[11] Theoretical scientists are not literalists. They do not speak univocally about reality. Rather, they imaginatively construct conceptual models of the reality they describe. The world the scientist studies is assumed to be real; yet the scientist still constructs imaginary models of that reality. It is the imaginary construction part that warrants the label "critical."

Critical realism in action requires the creation of conceptual models, frequently mathematical models, to assess data and organize measurements. Physical cosmologist Stephen Hawking refers to model construction as *model-dependent realism*. "The naive view of reality therefore is not compatible with modern physics. . . we shall adopt an approach that we call model-dependent realism."[12] Hawking contends that "a physical theory or world picture is a model (generally of a mathematical nature) and a set of rules that connect the elements of the model to observations."[13] Hawking's model-making is dependent upon the assumptions of *critical realism.* "Models, on this reading, are to be taken seriously but not literally."[14] By plugging empirically derived facts into the model, the researcher hopes to generate fertile new directions to take his or her research. The model method permits research to press forward when the naive option or literal option is unavailable.

I like this. Could we build a bridge between science and theology here? It appears to me that both research scientists and research theolo-

---

11 Ian G. Barbour, *Issues in Science and Religion* (Englewood Cliffs, New Jersey: Prentice Hall, 1966), 172. See also Ted Peters and Carl Peterson, "The Higgs Boson: An Adventure in Critical Realism" *Theology and Science* 11, no. 3 (2013): 185–207.
12 Stephen Hawking and Leonard Mlodinow, *The Grand Design* (New York: Bantam Books, 2010) 7.
13 Ibid., 43.
14 Ian G. Barbour, *Religion in an Age of Science*, Gifford Lectures 1989–1991, vol. 1 (New York: Harper, 1990), 43. See *New World Encyclopedia*, "Critical Realism," http://www.newworldencyclopedia.org/entry/Critical_realism.

gians together employ critical realism and model-making. God, the object of theological inquiry, cannot be seen. Yet, we judge that God is there. Even though God is real, no literal appellations apply to God. God cannot be conceived. The best St. Anselm could do was tell us that God is that than which nothing greater can be conceived. So, without univocal reference to theological assertions, we must engage in indirect conceptual reasoning and circumlocutionary discourse. We presume that God is real, yet our conceptual discourse relies upon imaginative constructions. These imaginative constructions become theological models. I like this buoy, because it appears to me that critical realism provides a bridge on which traffic can travel between theological method and scientific method.

Niels Henrik Gregersen is less sanguine than I am about critical realism. In his *Festschrift* essay, "What Kinds of Questions Are Explained in Theology?" he registers his doubts. "While I share with Peters his search for bridges between science and theology, especially on specific topical areas, I have myself somewhat become a little more critical of critical realism (CR) as a consensus position in the field of science and religion . . . because I see critical realism as a presumption more than as something that can easily be achieved." What's the problem? According to Gregersen, even though theologians and scientists employ CR in a similar fashion, the types of explanations they seek differ. My view "may fail to acknowledge the different kinds of quests for explanation in science and religion, and the asymmetry between science and theology."

Gregersen continues his demure. "Even if classic-minded scientists and classic-minded theologians (like Peters and myself) agree that there is something real to speak about . . . this does not mean that theology can be seen as explanatory in the same sense as the sciences."[15] Gregersen's concern here is not with thumbs up or thumbs down on CR. Rather, his concern is with the premature assumption that theologians and scientists are sisters in method. Neighbors, maybe. But not family.

Where should we go from here? Gregersen recommends we take three steps. "The first step is to admit that *explanation,* as a matter of fact, means something different from one discipline to another discipline within the sciences, and so much more between the sciences and philosophies." Just within the sciences, explanations look different from

---

15 See Niels Henrik Gregersen, "Critical Realism and Other Realisms," in *Fifty Years in Science and Religion: Ian G. Barbour and His Legacy*, Robert John Russell, ed. (Aldershot, United Kingdom: Ashgate 2002), 77-96 (90-92). BL241. F57

discipline to discipline. We find "the search for fundamental laws in physics, the explanation of resilient structures and causal capacities (beyond laws) in chemistry and biology, the role of statistics in economy, the concrete case-studies in sociology and psychology, etc. When observing such disunities within the sciences, it would be curious to expect that theological explanation should somehow be like physics. The point here is to keep in mind the pragmatic question: What do you want to know about?"[16] In short, it is too much to ask for identity between theological method and scientific method even if both rely in part on CR assumptions.

"The second step," says Gregersen, "is to emphasize that theology, in some rare cases, is in a position to explain, in a meta-scientific explanation, natural states that the sciences themselves either discover, or presuppose."[16] It would seem to me that philosophically constituted theological constructions regarding the whole of reality—the reality involving God and the entire creation—would provide an example. We would not expect any scientific discipline to pursue such a construction, but it certainly pops up on the theologian's agenda after reciting the creed: "I believe in God the Father Almighty, creator of heaven and earth." This begs for an explanatory conceptual model.

Gregersen goes on to map the path. "My third step takes up a challenge that Peters has raised to me, and consists of the distinction between causal and semantic explanations. In which sense can one make sense of the divine action in and through the self-organizing capacities of natural processes? In what sense may we talk about God's involvement in, with, and under biological processes of natural selection?"[17] I just love Gregersen's use of "in, with, and under" here. But, he goes on. "In both cases, I will argue, that theology should not present another explanation than those offered by the sciences. The role of theology here is to offer a richer semantic re-description of processes already described and (sometimes tightly, sometimes more loosely) explained by the sciences. Though theology here may not offer a causal explanation of the specific processes of self-organization and selection, theology may offer a sense-making explanation, what I call a semantic explanation." This is an insightful step Gregersen is taking. When it comes to offering an ex-

---

16 Gregersen, 73.

17 See Ted Peters, "Happy Danes and Deep Incarnation," *Dialog: A Journal of Theology* 52, no. 3 (September 2013), and my response in the same issue.

planation based upon natural causes, that is what we ask of the scientist. When it comes to offering the meaning of the world in which we live, that is what we ask of the theologian. Causal explanations and semantic explanations should be consonant, but not identical.

Explanations in Science and Theology: A Response to Niels Henrik Gregersen

Let me strengthen Gregersen's contention that explanation in science differs from explanation in theology. I extend Gregersen's question this way: just how do the two types of explanation differ and how should the theologian adapt?

Let me turn for a moment to a philosopher of science, Thomas Nagel. Nagel is asking for a new naturalism that better explains how the conscious mind has arisen from within a universe governed by physical laws. The current reigning form of naturalism is reductionist materialism, which misleadingly reduces centered subjectivity to objective natural law. Nagel's argument against reductionist materialism, though interesting in itself, is not my concern here. My concern is this: what passes for scientific explanation? Nagel says, "Explanation, unlike causation, is not just of an event, but of an event under a description. An explanation must show why it was likely that an event *of that type* occurred."[18] Or, to say it another way, a scientific explanation requires a comprehensive theory with principles that can actually predict what will happen. In this case, Nagel wants a naturalistic theory that would predict the rise of human consciousness and mental states.

What criteria does Nagel invoke to evaluate any such proposed theory? The new explanatory theory he seeks must, like the materialism he rejects, remain strictly naturalistic. It must rely on a closed universe. All the laws of nature must be accounted for internally to the closed cosmic domain.

This implies something important for the theologian: it rules out any appeal to God as an explanatory factor. "The essential character of such an understanding would be to explain the appearance of life, consciousness, reason, and knowledge neither as accidental side effects of the physical laws of nature [against materialism] nor as the result of intentional intervention in nature from without [against theism] but as an unsurprising if not inevitable consequence of the order that governs the

---

18 Thomas Nagel, *Mind and Cosmos: Why the Materialist Neo-Darwinian Conception of Nature Is Almost Certainly False* (Oxford: Oxford University Press, 2012), 47. Nagel's italics.

natural world from within . . . and I suspect it will have to include teleological elements."[19] Nagel's new naturalism would remain atheistic, but it would avoid the materialist variant of atheism.

First, I note that this exclusion of the divine from scientific explanation is based not upon evidence but on an a priori assumption that natural explanations rely on a closed natural system. Second, Nagel assumes that the only way to envision divine action in the natural world is from an external or supra-natural position that requires intervention into nature. Nagel is opposed to divine interventionism. What Nagel does not consider is a theology that sees God at work in nature in a non-interventionism manner. Theistic evolutionists such as Niels Henrik Gregersen, for example, see God working in, with, and under natural processes.

Third, Gregersen is correct: I need to take this into account when developing my own principle of explanatory adequacy. As Gregersen already cited, I judge a theological explanation to be more or less adequate on four criteria: applicability, comprehensiveness, logic, and coherence.[20] Of particular interest here is the criterion of comprehensiveness, because this is already decisive for Nagel in seeking a new and improved naturalism. Because the Christian speaks of God as creator of all things, I should think the Christian theologian is ready and willing to lift up a conceptual model inclusive of all reality. The theologian is in the comprehensive explanation business, so to speak.

Yet, the theologian dare not confine a theological explanation to a closed causal cosmos as Nagel and as materialists do. The whole of physical and conscious reality, from a theological point of view, must vector from the reality of God. If Gregersen would describe the theologian's explanation as semantic and inclusive of the causal explanation we expect from the natural scientist, I believe I could work with this.

Although Gregersen comes closer to the two-language model for relating Science & Religion than I do, I can agree with Gregersen on the following: "It seems to me that theological explanations normally take the form of a semantic explanation by offering a coherent picture about how things relate to one another (without necessarily being able to explain the causal route from the creative power of God to the particulars of the created world)."[21]

---

19 Ibid., 32–33.
20 Peters, *GOD—The World's Future*, 78–80.
21 Radke, 68.

Dialogue and Hospitality: David Ratke

Since publishing my book, *God as Trinity: Relationality and Temporality in Divine Life,* in 1993, I've joined the club of new Trinitarian theologians who incorporate the history of creation into the perichoresis between Father, Son, and Holy Spirit. I had not thought of this in terms of hospitality. But, David Ratke has. "Hospitality and relationality are, I think, essentially the same thing,"[22] he writes. "More than that, hospitality and relationality are not just about sharing ourselves and our gifts with others, but also receiving others and their gifts." Well said.

---

22 Ratke, 68.

ESCHATOLOGY & RETROACTIVE ONTOLOGY

Will God Save the World or Not?

Prolepsis, Open Theism, and the World's Future

Carol R. Jacobson

Anticipating Omega

As Søren Kierkegaard astutely observed, "life can only be understood backwards; but it must be lived forwards."[1] Not only in life, but also in Christian eschatology, his insight holds true. Not unlike Kierkegaard, Ted Peters employs what he calls a "retroactive ontology"[2] when it comes to thinking theologically about the future. At the center of this retroactive ontology is the assertion that who we are today, as well as who we have been, is both "determined by, and defined by, our future."[3] In other words, we can only understand our past existence, or our existence today, if we look backwards at it from the perspective of God's promised future. Thus, Peters says, "God creates from the future, not the past,"[4] and moreover, "the first thing God did for the cosmos [at its creation] was to give it a future."[5]

This article was first published in *Currents in Theology and Mission*, volume 39, number 4 (August 2012): 290–96.

1 Søren Kierkegaard, cited in *Søren Kierkegaard's Journals and Papers*, vol. 1, A–E, Howard V. Hong and Edna H. Hong, eds. & trans. (Bloomington & London: Indiana University Press, 1967–1978). Throughout his collected journals and papers, Kierkegaard gives expression to this in several entries. See especially entries 1025 and 1030.
2 See Ted Peters, *Anticipating Omega: Science, Faith, and Our Ultimate Future* (Göttingen: Vandenhoeck and Ruprecht, 2006), 12ff.
3 Ibid., 12.
4 Ibid.
5 Ibid., 13.

This retroactive ontological relationship between God and the world should not be understood as slavish or deterministic, however. Peters' retroactive ontology includes the possibility of genuine openness and novelty. "Contrary to common sense," he writes, "past causes do not hold the present moment [and so not the future either] in the grip of absolute determinism."[6] Rather,

> The first thing God did was provide nascent reality with an open future. Since then, God has continued this double relationship to the created order, negatively releasing the grip of the past while positively offering being and openness to a future of new possibilities. ... God opens up an array of potentials that await actualization.[7]

God opens up an array of potentials that await actualization. God's gift of a future—given to the world at its creation—makes both contingency and freedom in present existence, and in the future, genuinely possible.

God's gift of a future to the created order functions in a twofold way according to Peters. Not only is it the ground of contingency and freedom, but it also contains within it God's offer of a final future, an ultimate future, a fulfilling future. "At omega" Peters writes, "creation will be complete."[8] Thus, the creation of the cosmos is God's ongoing eschatological act—an ongoing act grounded in the future, not the past.

> This eschatological action by God will include the incorporation into the divine life of our cosmic reality. The creation will be absorbed into God, and God's presence will imbue the creation as a whole and in all its parts.... The entirety of past history will be taken up into eschatological eternity.... God's creative activity will attain its completion. God will be able to take that Sabbath rest described in Genesis 2:2.... That seventh day is tomorrow, the day that will conclude all of God's creative work. When it is redeemed, our world will be created.[9]

Elsewhere Peters says, when God's creative work is redeemed, it will at last be the new heaven and the new earth promised in Revelation 21:1.

To further underscore the ontological priority of the future, Peters advocates a way of thinking theologically that is proleptic: a theologi-

---

6 Ibid.
7 Ibid., 13–14.
8 Ibid., 14.
9 Ibid., 18.

cal method that emphasizes the "ontological weight of anticipation."[10] For Peters, the definitive example of prolepsis, which he defines as "an embodied anticipation,"[11] is the incarnation and resurrection of Jesus. Thus, to think eschatologically in a proleptic way means to consider, among other things of course, the ontological weight of the relationship between God's promised resurrection of the cosmos and its proleptic anticipation in the incarnation and resurrection of Jesus. "What happened to Jesus on the first Easter was a prolepsis of the new creation, an anticipation of the final resurrection that will include you and me."[12]

Constrained By Love

At first glance, Peters' retroactive ontology and proleptic method appear compatible with central tenets of "open theism."[13] Generally identified as "a version of historic free will theism which posits God as granting to human beings significant freedom to cooperate with or to resist the will of God for their lives,"[14] open theism unfolds a doctrine of creation with the understanding that "God's goal is to make possible relationships of mutual love between God and creatures and therefore set up a dynamic give and take situation in which God can even be said to risk failure to the degree permitted by the overall plan."[15]

Open theism is "a relational and Trinitarian doctrine with an emphasis on God as personal and interactive."[16] It is considered "open" in the sense that there is more than one possible future for creation. That is, not everything that happens in creation is either ordained or pre-ordained by God at creation. In order to guarantee genuine openness in creation, God cannot possess exhaustive definite foreknowledge (EDF) with regard to the future. Open theists understand God as limiting God's

---

10 Ibid., 27.
11 Ibid.
12 Ibid.
13 Open theism (sometimes referred to as openview theism) is a theological school of thought generally thought to have arisen in 1994 by a group of respected Evangelical scholars, led by Clark H. Pinnock, in a book entitled *The Openness of God*. I am grateful to Pastor Wes Telyea for introducing me to this contemporary theological movement and its eschatological perspectives.
14 Clark H. Pinnock, "Open Theism: An Answer to My Critics," *Dialog: A Journal of Theology* 44, no. 3 (Fall 2005): 237.
15 Ibid.
16 Ibid. Peters appreciates the relational foundations of open theism. For example, see Peters, *Anticipating Omega*, 152.

own self—giving up exhaustive definite foreknowledge for the sake of granting genuine freedom to the whole creation and to every individual.

Thus, God takes risks in creating a free cosmos and free creatures. The nature and seriousness of the risk becomes apparent when we consider that, according to open theists, in a genuinely free cosmos God gives up the power to coerce creatures for the sake of achieving divine purposes either in the present or in the future.

> Openview theists deny that God can both grant individuals freedom and control its use. Rather, to the extent that God grants individual freedom, he gives up complete control over the decisions that are made. Consequently, openview theism denies a compatibilist view of freedom, endorsing instead libertarian freedom.[17]

Furthermore, to some degree, God cannot even know the future of the world in its totality.

> Our model affirms omniscience but denies exhaustive definite foreknowledge. It grants that God knows everything that can be known but holds that the future free actions of creatures, including even God's own future actions, are not yet actual and, therefore, cannot be known with complete certainty.[18]

While many may be receptive to open theism's commitment to genuine human freedom, the corollary assertion that God does not have exhaustive definite foreknowledge regarding the future has proven to be one of the most controversial and contested positions it holds.

According to open theists, God's self-limiting with regard to knowledge of the future ensures that present and future human actions have real consequences for the future and can effect both God's future and the world's. Most important, God does it for the sake of love.

> God surrenders power because he does not want to squelch the creature; God is moved by love to restrain the divine power, temporarily and voluntarily, out of respect for the integrity of creatures, even creatures whose activities fall short of God's purposes.[19]

---

17 Michael Robinson, "Why Divine Foreknowledge," *Religious Studies* 36, no. 3 (September 2000): 252.
18 Pinnock, "Open Theism," 240.
19 Clark H. Pinnock, "Constrained by Love," *Perspectives in Religious Studies* 34, no. 2 (Summer 2007): 150.

God's surrender of freedom is for the sake of giving us true freedom. Additionally, God's self-limiting safeguards the possibility of genuine novelty in the future. Real freedom means that the future of the world cannot be exhaustively known by anyone, not even by God.

Causation, Coercion, and Power

Like Peters, open theists affirm a triune God of love who created everything that exists. And again like Peters, at the heart of open theism is the triune relationality of God, a perichoretic Trinity characterized by responsiveness, pathos, and risk-taking for the sake of love. Moreover, genuine openness and meaningful historical novelty are important in both approaches. When it comes to speaking specifically about the world's future, however, significant differences in their eschatological thinking clearly emerge.

To begin, Peters and open theists have different ontological emphases and divergent theological agendas. Open theism, with its ontology of freedom very much concerned with a future that cannot be known, adopts a forward facing temporal trajectory in its theological system. We could say that open theists give ontological priority to exercising freedom in the "life lived forwards." In so doing they simultaneously seek to avoid problems of divine coercion often implicit in ontologies that try to "understand backwards." As we have seen already, Peters prefers to employ a retroactive ontological approach. But what does this difference matter to understanding the world's future and God's knowledge of it?

In order to answer this question, I suggest that we take notice of the different notions of causation operative in the two approaches. Seeking to preserve an understanding of the future of the world as a "whole," both approaches grapple to understand the nature of causation. Peters' retroactive ontology employs a downward understanding of causation, while open theism seems to make use of an upward one. Peters explains that "in upward causation the parts alter one another and the whole; in downward causation the whole alters the parts by incorporating their participation in the dynamics of the whole."[20] That is, upward causation prioritizes the parts that can and do change the resultant "whole"; whereas downward causation prioritizes the "whole" which changes and incorporates its parts into the ongoing realization of itself. In contrast to open theism where a free future "whole" will be the sum of its present and past free "parts," Pe-

---
20 Peters, *Anticipating Omega*, 15.

ters prefers to "think of God acting on the whole of creation and, thereby, reorienting and redefining all of the parts within."[21]

As we have observed, open theism emphasizes the ways in which the whole creation presently existing (and realities and persons yet to exist) change each other and the future in ways that nobody—not even God—can know exhaustively, hence, open theism's rejection of God's exhaustive, definitive foreknowledge we examined earlier. However, the downward causation employed by Peters' retroactive ontology emphasizes the "whole"—the promised future that God realizes at omega—which has transfigured and continues to transfigure the present and the future into the realization of its own fulfillment. Retroactive ontology's downward analysis of causation allows us to speak eschatologically about freedom (both present and future) from within a larger framework: God's final future, given to the whole cosmos at its creation. "All of God's current works are parts of a single, comprehensive act of creating the world."[22]

In addition, open theism's understanding of causation employs a quantitative analysis when it comes to thinking about the relationship between divine power and human freedom. For open theists, God's power plus creation's freedom cannot exceed a total of 100 percent. Thus if God is more powerful, the creation must be somehow less free. Open theism's rejection of exhaustive definite foreknowledge is necessitated by this kind of quantitative analysis, since "total knowledge of the future would imply a fixity of events. Nothing in the future would need to be decided. It also would imply that human freedom is an illusion, that we make no difference and are not responsible."[23] In order to provide for the creation's genuine freedom, open theism insists upon a limitation of God's own freedom, divinely self-imposed for the sake of love.

The problem with this approach, Peters says, is that "it presumes a fixed pie of power, according to which God must take a smaller slice in order for the world to get a larger slice." He continues,

> In contrast to this view, I believe it is the exercise of God's power that empowers the world. God exercises this power duratively, faithfully maintaining the world in existence

---
21 Ibid.
22 Peters, *Anticipating Omega*, 15.
23 Clark H. Pinnock, "Systematic Theology," in *The Openness of God: A Biblical Challenge to the Traditional Understanding of God*, Clark H. Pinnock, et. al., ed. (Downers Grove: InterVarsity Press: 1994), 123.

while granting partial release from the mechanistic grip of the past nexus of efficient causation. It is the exercise of God's power upon the world that makes contingency in nature and freedom for humanity possible.[24]

Here we find Peters employing a durative rather than a quantitative analysis of the relationship between divine power and human freedom. In this way of thinking, it is God's power and freedom that make genuine human and natural freedom possible in the first place, rather than somehow limiting it or rendering it merely illusory.

Yet, if God's future is indeed the world's future—and further, if God has already given this future to the whole cosmos—then in what sense does God's act of power make human beings free? If the whole creation is moving toward God's future, how can it be said that it is genuinely free? According to Peters, the answer to this question begins with the recognition that "we will not become who God intends us to be until we ourselves share in the resurrection at omega."[25] Once raised, Peters continues, "we will look back over our biographies and over the evolutionary biography of the entire human race and understand who we are in our totality."[26] At the present time, according to Peters, we exist in-between God's first creative act and that final creative act at omega. We who are alive now are living on the road toward omega. We are still becoming, free to become more and more what God created us to be. Our actions matter and our evolution toward becoming more and more human is not illusory. How can Peters suggest that this is the case? By looking to the incarnation and resurrection of Jesus of Nazareth, the Son of God, the revelation of God's future redemption of the entire cosmos.

Proleptic Particularity

While open theism and retroactive ontology both emphasize the centrality of the future in their systematic theology, we can now begin to understand why Peters' approach offers a more cogent framework for thinking eschatologically—one that, like open theism rejects divine coercion and historical determinism, but one that does not deny the power and promise of God to both know and accomplish the future given to the whole creation at its beginning. Peters' retroactive ontology recognizes

---

24 Peters, *Anticipating Omega*, 21–22.
25 Ibid., 22–23.
26 Ibid.

both the importance of understanding our future by looking backwards from God's future, and the importance of living forward into that future proleptically. In addition, once we begin to think both retroactively and proleptically about the world's future, we not only escape the trap of determinism, but we also avoid empty relativism which cannot claim any lasting significance for history, experience or the present moment. As we have seen, Peters suggests that God is saving the world by granting it a future and simultaneously bringing that future into present existence more and more by empowering human freedom, not by overriding it. But at least one more important thing must be emphasized about Peters' understanding of God's creative and redeeming act of creation. God gives the world a particular kind of future: one that has already been proleptically anticipated within time and history.

Recall that retroactive ontology gives theological weight to anticipation in its system. It looks for anticipations of God's future in time and history and expects to find them there. For Peters, Jesus of Nazareth, incarnate, crucified, and risen, is the paradigmatic anticipation and revelation of God's future in time, space, and history. Jesus Christ truly is, in Tertullian's words, "the hinge of salvation"[27] and the true revelation of what being human will truly become at omega. Jesus the Christ shows forth God's future for all humanity ahead of omega in his own flesh and bones. "When Jesus Christ—whom the New Testament describes as the true image of God, the *eikon tou theou* or *imago dei*—rose from the dead on Easter, this introduced resurrection into the definition of what a human being is."[28]

So, ever since Easter morning, and precisely because of the resurrection of Jesus, the nature of what it means to be truly human has been and is continuing to be transfigured. Resurrection has indeed been introduced into the definition of being human. That is why Peters goes on to say that "the future new reality has arrived ahead of time, so to speak, in the singular event of Easter. What was true for Jesus on the first Easter will become true for all of physical reality at the advent of the eschaton."[29] In this way, Peters' retroactive ontology both grounds and safeguards newness and innovation simultaneously, not as the result of free choices by free agents, but rather as a result of God's own anticipation of the future's fulfillment ahead of time in history. "Anticipation

---

27 "Caro cardo salutis"—"The flesh is the hinge of salvation." Cited by Karl Rahner in "A Faith That Loves the Earth," in *Everyday Faith* (New York: Herder and Herder, 1968), 83.
28 Peters, *Anticipating Omega*, 22.
29 Ibid., 41.

of omega [in Jesus Christ] incarnates the future ahead of time. Our life of hope is based upon God's promise to provide eschatological confirmation of what we now anticipate."[30] God's promise for all creation is revealed in Jesus' resurrection, and "in the Lord's resurrection God has shown that he has taken the earth to himself forever."[31] God's gift of an ultimate future at the creation of the cosmos, when understood as both retroactive and proleptically potent, assures the eternal significance of present and future actions, assures and does not threaten them.

> Not only does Jesus' resurrection encourage us to make a "forward glance" and ask about our ultimate destiny, both individual and corporate (familiar to us from Paul's discussion in 1 Corinthians 15), but to make the "backward glance" as well, and ask this: what kind of body is it that can have the capacity to accept and sustain the eschatological transformation experienced by Christ?[32]

However, as we know well, our bodies are not presently capable of resurrection from the dead. So, what exactly will resurrected life look like, not only for ourselves but for the whole creation?[33] Peters reminds us that "according to present laws of physics, resurrected life is impossible."[34] Thus, in order to have the God-given future realized in history, it seems the very laws of nature will have to be transformed.[35] Just how this will occur, we do not know. That it will occur, we believe because of the resurrection of Jesus on the first Easter morning. Jesus Christ, incarnated, crucified, and risen, grounds eschatological hope in the midst of space and history.

Open theism has a much more difficult time finding a ground for eschatological hope. As Richard Rice observes, "for God to will something . . . does not make its occurrence inevitable. Factors can arise that hinder or prevent its realization. Consequently, God may reformulate his plans, or alter his intentions, in response to developments."[36]

---

30 Ibid., 199.
31 Rahner, "A Faith That Loves the Earth," 82–83.
32 Anthony J. Godzieba, "Stay With Us . . .: Incarnation, Eschatology, and Theology's Sweet Predicament," *Theological Studies* 67 (2006): 788.
33 For a discussion of Peters' understanding of proleptic ethics, see Balch and Pryor in this volume.
34 Peters, *Anticipating Omega*, 41.
35 For a discussion of transforming natural laws, see Russell in this volume.
36 Richard Rice, "Biblical Support for a New Perspective," in *The Openness of God: A Biblical Challenge to the Traditional Understanding of God*, Clark Pinnock, et al., eds. (Downers Grove, Illinois: InterVarsity Press, 1994), 26.

For Peters, however, "the end is proleptically present and operative beforehand, rehearsing the qualities of the eschatological kingdom—peace, love, joy, freedom, equality, unity—in the course of history's forward movement."[37] In the life, death, and resurrection of Jesus, the Triune God has promised that a new heaven and a new earth, where resurrection awaits us all, is at hand. This, Peters says, "provides the source of our vision of a transformed future" and calls us "to live in hope today out of the power of tomorrow's reality."[38] However, God's ultimate future, the one given to the whole cosmos at its creation, depends upon ongoing action on God's part: what Peters calls "an ultimate transformation that only God can deliver."[39]

I began this essay by asking "Will God save the world, or not?" For open theism, I think, the answer must be "perhaps." For Peters, however, the answer is an enthusiastic "Yes!" Indeed, the incarnation and resurrection of Jesus teach us this above all else—Easter is not a past event, but rather the beginning of God's ongoing revelation of the world's ultimate future. Will God save the world? Of course! God has already promised the world a redeemed future. In the meantime, Peters says, "Our ethical mandate is to live in hope today out of the power of tomorrow's reality."[40] When we do, "we participate proleptically in the eschatological consummation yet to come in its fullness."[41]

---

[37] Carl E. Braaten, *Eschatology and Ethics* (Minneapolis: Augsburg, 1974), 121.
[38] Peters, *Anticipating Omega*, 200.
[39] Ibid.
[40] Ibid.
[41] Ibid.

Hummingbirds Make Stars Possible

Exploring and Celebrating Ted Peters' Retroactive Ontology

Robert John Russell

I am very grateful to the organizers of this publication for inviting me to contribute an essay, even if it is far too brief and schematic, which reflects, even only in part, my immense gratitude to Ted Peters. Peters and I have interacted for nearly three decades, both verbally and in writing, through Center for Theology and Natural Science programs and conferences and in the numerous courses that we co-taught. Through it all, I have learned a tremendous amount about theology from this seasoned and immensely reasonable scholar, I have reveled in his unique interaction between theology and science in such areas as theistic evolution, stem cell research, and Extra Terrestrial Intelligence/astrobiology, and I have gained a glistening perspective and a keen sense of wisdom about what is truly important in theology from him. For this and many more things I owe Ted an immense sense of gratitude and joy.

Here, within the confines of a short essay, I wish to lift up and examine one of Peters' most important concepts as a form of praise to him. In a complex, dense and scintillating discussion, Peters tells us about this remarkable concept, "retroactive ontology," in his splendid anthology, *Anticipating Omega*.[1] According to Peters,

> Our final future will retroactively transform who we are today. It will determine who we had been as we anticipat-

---

This article was first published in *Currents in Theology and Mission*, volume 39, number 4 (August 2012): 312–15.

1 Ted Peters, *Anticipating Omega: Science, Faith, and Our Ultimate Future* (Göttingen: Vandenhoeck & Ruprecht, 2006).

ed who we would become. I would like to call this line of thinking *retroactive ontology*. The fundamental insight is that our being is determined by, and defined by, our future. The transformed reality promised by God is the ground for all our reality that anticipates it.... The meaning and even being of the past is contingent on its future. God's omega redefines—actually defines—all that has gone before. Who we are now is dependent on who we will be at omega.[2]

Here we find several interwoven claims both in this paragraph and its surrounding text. I will highlight them before focusing on one in this paper.

First, the "future" Peters has in mind is really two distinct futures, the proximate and the ultimate future, and both are effective in the present. The crucial point is that they "are not separated into a short time and a long time. Rather, both are almost present, almost but not quite fully here now. Both are as close to us as is the next moment."[3] Next is the fundamental importance of this double future. According to Peters, God's creation of the present moment is to give it a future. "To be is to have a future . . . the way God gives being is to give a future. . . . God is moment to moment giving to all of reality its future."[4] Third, God has what Peters calls a "double relationship to the created order," one which is both positive and negative. God's positive relation to time and the created order is that God upholds and supports all that is as its ground of being. Without God's positive relation to the created order, all that is would simply cease to be. God's negative relation to time is that "by giving [it] a new future God releases the present from the grip of the past. . . . Past causes do not hold the present moment in the grip of absolute determinism. The present moment is open to change, open to what is new."[5] Finally Peters recognizes that while past causes may inform the present moment, "God opens up an array of potentials [in the present]

---

2 Ibid., 12
3 Ibid., 14.
4 Ibid., 13.
5 Ibid. Below I will suggest that the case needed to support Peters' claim is harder if nature is deterministic at all levels, and I will suggest that, in fact, nature is indeterministic at most, if not all, levels.

that await actualization [in the future]. The way the creatures within the world behave determines which potentials become actualized."[6]

In light of this rich array of insights and directions for conversation, I want to focus, in this short article, on Peters' central notion of "retroactive ontology." By this term Peters means God's causality from the immediate future on the present. I will separate this out from Peters notion of "prolepsis," the manifestation and appearance in history (at the original Easter) of the eschatological Risen Lord of the New Creation. Prolepsis deserves its own distinctive discussion at a later time.

Let the reader note: for the purposes of this paper, I will make the perhaps unexpected assumption, given one reading of my previous work, that the natural world is "open" at many, if not all, levels of complexity such as from quarks to brain states.[7] The problem is that, for the professional field of theology and science, one must restrict oneself to interpreting well-proven theories in science, not speculating on what one hopes may be true to the world as such. Only quantum mechanics gives us the opportunity to interpret the world in such an open and indeterministic character.[8] Nevertheless, I will here make the bold leap of faith and assume that the world is open to divine action at every level of complexity (whether or not the *current* sciences of these levels warrants

---

[6] Ibid., 13–14. Here determining factors come from the behavior of creatures rather than entirely from the underlying physical causes, suggesting again that the physical world is indeterministic.

[7] I write "unexpected" because many who have commented on my writings have assumed that since my writings tend to deal with quantum mechanics when it comes to the "open" character of nature (i.e., its ontological indeterminacy), I only believe that nature is open at the subatomic level. This is a false assumption, as I have suggested several times in writing. I happen to believe, theologically, that nature is open at many, perhaps all, levels to non-interventionist divine action. However, the field of theology and science must rely on proven theories in science if it is to interpret them philosophically (do they portray nature as open or closed?) and then use this interpretation for a theology of divine action. Here it is problematic to claim that other sciences besides quantum mechanics (and perhaps those involved in the mind-brain problem) portray the world as ontologically indeterministic, hence, the "unexpectedness" of my present assumption. In short I am relying here more on my belief in the openness of nature on many, perhaps all, levels of complexity than on its track record in the sciences of the macroscopic world.

[8] My arguments against the claims for such ontological openness by John Polkinghorne (referring to chaos theory) and Arthur Peacocke (referring to the "universe-as-a-whole") are well known. See for example, Robert John Russell, *Cosmology from Alpha to Omega: The Creative Mutual Interaction of Theology and Science* (Fortress Press, 2008), chaps. 4–5.

such an assumption).⁹ I think that this assumption is required if we are to appreciate and extend Peters' position in a creative way. Conversely it might be much harder to do so if the world were one of Newtonian mechanism—which it is clearly not.

With this in mind, I would like to compare what can be called the "ordinary open ontology" of nature to Peters' view of retroactive ontology. According to the ordinary view of an open ontology, the present, time t, contains a set of future possibilities, time t+T, and nature or God or both actualizes one of them to make a specific future real. For example, according to this ontology, some stars such as our sun contain futures in which hummingbirds are possible given the right evolutionary conditions on the right planet, etc., and nature or God or both actualizes that future, thus creating hummingbirds in the future out of the possibilities of the present. A standard example of this approach is theistic evolution in which God works "in, with, and under" natural processes, to use Arthur Peacocke's beautiful phrase, to bring about biological complexity and ultimately sentient life from the past inorganic world.

Now we can see the truly distinctive claim Peters makes about nature and divine action. According to his "retroactive ontology," since hummingbirds are real now at time t+T, stars of a certain kind must have been possible in the past at a time t, namely those such as our sun and its predecessor star in which the future of our sun, and the far future of its predecessor star, contains hummingbirds. So time t+T when hummingbirds are real requires that at a time t stars such as our sun and its predecessor must have been real because they have within their future possibilities the reality of hummingbirds. So the reality of hummingbirds requires that certain kinds of stars existed in the past.

We can put this in a simplified grammar. Suppose state A is the present state at time t (e.g., stars) and state B is the future state at time t+T (eg., stars plus planets and hummingbirds). Then:

> state A at time t in the present = the actual present + its multiple potential futures including state B at time t+T

---

9 The word "current" is meant to acknowledge John Polkinghorne's visionary agenda that, if we believe God and humans act without intervention in the world, the world must be indeterministic even at the macroscopic level. Thus, in turn, we should search for new theories of the science of chaos in which indeterminism would be favored over current theories which are obviously deterministic. He refers to such new theories as "holistic chaos." See John Polkinghorne, *Faith of a Physicist* (Philadelphia: Augsburg Fortress, 1996), chaps. 1 & 4.

state B at time t+T in the future = the actual future chosen or realized from among the multiple potential futures of state A at time t

With this in place we can compare the ordinary ontology we typically assume with Peters' idea of retroactive ontology.

Ordinary ontology: t leads to t+T from the possibilities of t, A precedes B

Retroactive ontology: t+T leads to t in which t+T is possible, B precedes A

This is truly a revolutionary concept!

Another way to describe the relation between ordinary and retroactive ontology is this: *From the ordinary perspective*, today there are many possible futures; tomorrow there is only one. So God narrows the range of possibilities in the present as it leads to the future. *From the retroactive perspective*, there is only one tomorrow that God wants, so God ensures that the possibility that that tomorrow is at least one of several possibilities today which include that future state, tomorrow, in order that it becomes the actual future.

Now let's spell this out in more detail. From Peters' perspective on retroactive ontology, God both sustains ("protects") the entire history of nature in being and releases the determining factors of the past, opening the past to many new future possibilities. As before, this requires two assumptions.[10] The first, already noted above, is that natural causality (i.e., the efficient causal factors in nature that physics describes) are predispositional, not deterministic. By predispositional, I mean more than the kind of "mere chance" which signals our epistemic ignorance of what are in fact real underlying deterministic causes. I mean instead genuine ontological indeterminism at many, perhaps all, levels of complexity (but note that whether science supports this is a question for ongoing research).[11] The second is novel: I want to combine such indeterministic efficient causality (the past affects the present) with Peters' retroactive causality (the future affects the present). Here then causality works in both directions in time.

---

10 Actually this scheme might work in a deterministic world, such as the Newtonian mechanistic one, but it would rely on an interventionist theory of divine agency. For related details, see Russell, *Cosmology from Alpha to Omega*, chaps. 4–5.
11 See the Vatican Observatory / CTNS series on "scientific perspectives on divine action," summaries of which are available at: http://www.ctns.org/books.html.

With this we arrive at a model of retroactive causality in its full bloom. Following Peters it includes four ideas:

1. God *eliminates* some predispostional factors in the present that might, working together, have completely shaped the future from the present set of possible futures.
2. God *leaves* in place some predispositional factors that tend to shape the future which God desires from the present set of possible futures.[12]
3. God *creates* new predispositional factors in the present that shape the future to be different from the present and lead to the future which God desires.
4. God does all three of these from "the immediate future."

It is the fourth idea in conjunction with the first three which, in my opinion, most sharply distinguishes Peters' view from others working on this problem, and to which we most clearly owe Peters a debt of gratitude.

I will end this brief essay by pointing to new areas in research physics which one might explore if one started from Peters' view as described above. This would primarily include an assessment of formulations in physics in which causality in nature works both from the future and from the past, the so-called "time symmetric" formulations of physics. Although it might seem unlikely, we actually find such formulations for both classical electromagnetism and quantum mechanics.[13] These provide evidence for the fertility of the idea of retroactive ontology, and in turn a fitting tribute to Ted Peters' lifelong work on this topic.

---

12 The first two lines of thinking are vaguely reminiscent of Whitehead, who includes not allowing all the effect of the causes of the past to affect the future (cf. Whitehead's "negative prehension") and allowing those causes of the past which do partially affect the future (cf. his "positive prehension").

13 See also Robert John Russell, *Time in Eternity: Pannenberg, Physics, and Cosmology in Creative Mutual Interaction* (University of Notre Dame: University of Notre Dame Press, 2012), chap. 6.

Prolepsis and the Abolition of Hell

Why Hell Is Not Like Heaven

Kristin Johnston Largen

The Concept of Prolepsis.

Anyone who has read Ted Peters' theology knows that the concept of prolepsis is a fundamental organizing principle, a central axis around which the doctrine of God, understanding of creation, and interpretation of the life, death, and resurrection of Jesus Christ revolve. The ramifications of his use and interpretation of this concept are far-reaching, and they often take the reader in surprising, exciting directions. One example of this can be found in Peters' treatment of "our final destinies"—specifically in his discussion of hell. The conclusions he reaches in *GOD—The World's Future*, including though not limited to his version of the ancient doctrine of *apokatastasis*, the ultimate restoration of all things to God, are, in my view, both powerful and compelling.

In Chapter 11 of *GOD—The World's Future*, Peters discusses the doctrine of hell in the context of a debate between two mutually exclusive options he calls "double destiny" and "universal salvation." In the course of his argument, he notes the diversity and ambiguity in the New Testament witness on this question, but nonetheless goes on to argue for an "evangelical explication" that leads him to argue the following two hypotheses: "First, salvation will be universal—that is, it has been given in Christ and will be applied to all human beings regardless of their sinful behavior on earth. Second, hell, if it does exist now, cannot last forever. Only God's kingdom is everlasting."[1] In what follows, then, I would like to pick up on Peters' insights in this area, focusing specifically on the doctrine of hell.

---
1 Ted Peters, *GOD—The World's Future*, 2nd ed. (Minneapolis: Fortress Press, 2000), 368.

In particular, what I propose is to use Peters' concept of prolepsis as a lens and to draw out more fully and in more detail the consequences such a perspective entails regarding a Christian understanding of hell. Specifically, I want to endorse and emphasize Peters' conclusion that "hell, if it does exist now, cannot last forever" by making the argument that the concept of hell is fundamentally and inherently different from the concept of heaven; that is, they are not best understood as simply parallel, though opposing, destinations. There are three primary reasons for this, all of which follow from the doctrine of prolepsis: first, heaven is governed by the future while hell is governed by the past; second, heaven is of God's creation, while hell is created by humanity itself; and finally, heaven is eternal—it belongs to *kairos* time, while hell remains bound to *chronos*, chronological time, and will thus ultimately come to an end.

Before I begin my analysis, let me offer one qualification. While I am arguing for the abolition of hell, I am not arguing for the doctrine of universal salvation, even though one might assume that the first logically implies the second. This is not because I believe in the eternal damnation of some, but rather because I believe in the possibility of a variety of religious ends, not all of which necessarily can be subsumed under the Christian understanding of salvation. While as a Christian, I hope for eternal life in communion with God in Jesus Christ, I also know that my Buddhist friends do not hope for such an end, and it seems both narrow-minded and overbearing to demand for them an end that they do not aspire to for themselves—indeed, an end that does not even make sense in the context of their own religious beliefs and practices. Mark Heim's work in this area, particularly his two books, *Salvations* and *the Depth of the Riches*, articulates this possibility eloquently and persuasively.[2]

Futurum, Adventus, Venturum

As early as 1977, in his book, *Futures Human and Divine*, Peters wrote, "*Futurum* is human, *adventus* divine."[3] This statement must be interpreted within the larger context of the definitions Peters gives for each word. He argues that *futurum* points to "the future actualization of potential-

---

2   S. Mark Heim, *Salvations* (Maryknoll: Orbis Books, 1995), and *The Depth of the Riches* (Grand Rapids: Wm. B. Eerdmans Publishing Co., 2000).
3   Ted Peters, *Futures Human and Divine* (Atlanta: John Knox Press, 1977), 70.

ities already existing within things,"⁴ like an oak tree growing from an acorn. By contrast, he argues that *adventus* describes "the appearance of something new. . . . It is a future that can be anticipated or hoped for, but its arrival is not dependent only upon present potentialities. It cannot be understood through projections based upon present trends."⁵ In *GOD—The World's Future*, Peters builds upon these two understandings of the future by adding a third, *venturum*, which, he argues, "gives us the sense of prolepsis, the invasion of the present by the power of what is yet to come."⁶

In the section that follows, I want to draw out the ramifications of the distinction between the first two ways of understanding the future: *futurum*, and *adventus*. This distinction points to an important difference in the way in which heaven and hell relate to the present, and it also gives some insight into how they are radically different.

Heaven Is Governed by the Future

I want to acknowledge at the beginning of this section the passages in Scripture that seem to indicate that heaven, like hell, is governed by the past, and is a reward for what one has done cumulatively in the span of one's lifetime. Let me give what are perhaps the two most well-known examples of this interpretation. First, the sheep and the goats passage from Matthew 25: after judging the nations based on what they have or have not done to the last and the least, the Son of Man says to the sheep at his right hand, "Come, you that are blessed by my Father, inherit the kingdom prepared for you from the foundation of the world . . ." and then he says to the goats at his left hand, "You that are accursed, depart from me into the eternal fire prepared for the devil and his angels. . . ." Second, the Dives and Lazarus passage in Luke 16: Jesus tells the Pharisees, "who were lovers of money," the parable of the rich man and Lazarus—"The poor man died and was carried away by the angels to be with Abraham. The rich man also died and was buried. In Hades, where he was being tormented, he looked up and saw Abraham far away with Lazarus by his side. . . ."

While there are many problematic aspects of this parallelism, as I hope to show, there is one important feature of this supposition of con-

---

4   Ibid., 20.
5   Ibid., 21.
6   Peters, *GOD—The World's Future*, 320–21.

trasting destinations, each based on one's deeds and beliefs in this life, and that is the connection it upholds between one's past and one's future. While there are many uncertain aspects about the kingdom of God and life after death, one thing the Christian tradition has always maintained is that who we are here and now—the life that we lead and the choices we make—matters; the way in which we live our lives makes a difference. It is not irrelevant or unimportant how we treat our families, our neighbors, indeed, the whole of creation, and the idea that, in fact, our present lives have ultimate significance, reinforces that.

However, the main problem with such an interpretation is that it makes the past normative for determining the future; that is, it makes both heaven and hell *futurum*, the logical result of the consequences of past actions. The difficulty with this assumption, as it relates to heaven, is that heaven is in no way governed by our "logical" interpretation of how things should be—this is what Jesus was getting at in his parable of the laborers in the vineyard who all received the same wage, even though some worked only an hour and some worked all day. Instead, heaven, rightly understood, is the expression of something totally new from God's hand, breaking in upon us from the future, to great surprise and rejoicing. That is, while it is certainly true that neither Scripture nor Christian tradition are univocal on this point, there is a dominant strand of interpretation in both those sources of wisdom that affirms that heaven is, and will be, in the end, something heretofore unforeseen, something that is not the result of past actions or efforts, but something that comes to us unexpected, unearned, and unanticipated. This is what Peters is pointing to in his idea of *adventus*. Let me offer just one example.

While there are different places one finds this idea in Scripture, perhaps the most obvious example comes in Paul's description of "spiritual bodies" in 1 Corinthians 15. There he writes, "So it is with the resurrection of the dead. What is sown is perishable, what is raised is imperishable. It is sown in dishonor, it is raised in glory. It is sown in weakness, it is raised in power. It is sown a physical body, it is raised a spiritual body. . . . For this perishable body must put on imperishability, and this mortal body must put on immortality." Here, Paul is pointing to the reality that in the resurrection, we will be radically different from who we are today, and that the body we will be given by God is like nothing that we have seen or experienced before. Thus, Paul must create a new image—"spiritual body," which literally doesn't make sense, in order to convey the reality that awaits us in the future.

Thus, while many theologians over the course of the last 21 centuries have speculated on the nature of heaven, with visions of varying degrees of continuity and discontinuity from their contemporary societies, a degree of mystery to the whole thing always remained. It has always been clear that, when speaking of these sorts of "last things," humans can only speculate. It is God and God alone who knows the details of what awaits us, and while we can trust in the goodness and joy of that future, because of who God has revealed Godself to be in Jesus Christ, we must admit, in the end, that all our well-crafted theories and persuasive images will fade in the face of the great reality that only God can properly see or imagine.

There are two important corollaries of this interpretation of heaven: first, the affirmation that it is the future that determines the past, not vice-versa, and second, the affirmation that our past does not define us. Let me say more about each of these.

First, when we say that the future determines the past, we are affirming the truth that a life can only be evaluated at the end: it is from the resurrection that we judge the crucifixion; it is from the perspective of the new Adam that we judge the old; it is from the rainbow that we make sense of the flood.

Even in our own lives, often it is impossible to know whether or not a specific choice was the right one until we live into it—sometimes for days, sometimes for months, sometimes for years. We only find the true meaning of our lives by looking back on our past from the vantage point of the future; only from there are we truly able to judge the good from the bad, the right from the wrong. This is because it is only in the future that the whole finally is complete, and the parts can be seen in their larger, proper context. Only in the future do we see where all the roads were leading all along; only in the future can we connect all the dots. Until that time, we never know which parts of our past will prove central and which will prove peripheral.

Second, this understanding of heaven as belonging to *adventus* reminds us of a central piece of the gospel message that affirms the conviction that our past sins and mistakes do not define us—not now, and certainly not forever, and that we are called to see ourselves as God sees us, through Jesus Christ, as we will be when we are perfected in the kingdom. One of the key manifestations of human sinfulness is the way in which we refuse both to forgive and to be forgiven. We hold grudges, we let wounds fester, and we continue to see people through the lens of their cruelty, callousness, indifference, and malice—even when they themselves have moved beyond such sinful behavior and regret it. We cease to see people as they are, and can only see them as they were, sometimes even until the very end of their lives. And this is not all. Even when we are on the other side, the ones in need of forgiveness, we are often too ashamed of who we were to either ask for forgiveness or to accept it. We become paralyzed and cannot live into a new reality for ourselves because we are stuck playing back frightful images of wrongs we committed, things done and left undone. In both of these cases, we allow the past to determine the future, and we carry it around on our backs until it shapes our entire being.

Contrary to this, however, is the gospel of forgiveness, grace, and mercy, which reminds us that in baptism our slate has been wiped clean, and the past has no more power over us. It is this freedom from past shame that Jesus grants when he says to the woman caught in adultery, "Go your way, and from now on do not sin again." It is this freedom from past disgrace that God bestows when Elizabeth conceives; it is this freedom from past sins that Saul receives when Jesus sends the Holy Spirit upon him to renew his sight and to change his life. Over and over again in the lives of our biblical foremothers and forefathers, we see God at work, forgiving their past mistakes, idolatries, and transgressions, and opening up to them a new future they never could have lived into on their own. So also is God at work in our lives; thus we, too, daily, experience the power of the future over the past, the power of heaven over earth. In *Playing God?* Peters writes, "It is not from nature that we seek liberation. What we seek liberation from is the past, and we do so on behalf of an openness toward the future."[7] It is this openness that the metaphor and destination of heaven represent.

Hell Is Governed by the Past

By contrast, in the Christian tradition, hell has always been thought of as the accumulation of one's past—the result of past deeds. Thus, the metaphor and destination of hell clearly belongs to the realm of *futurum*: it is wholly governed by the past. The clearest proof of this comes in the primary symbolism that has been used to describe it for centuries. Hell is a place of judgment for the wicked. It is a place where people are pun-

---

7 Ted Peters, *Playing God?* (New York: Routledge, 1997), 162.

ished in proportion to their misdeeds here on earth; it is a place where evildoers finally are paid-back for the wrongs they committed to others.

Alan Bernstein, in *The Formation of Hell*, notes that in the New Testament, there are three views about what happens to those who fall outside the parameters of the "saved." He argues that the possibility we see in Paul's letters and the Gospel of John is "'mere' death"—that is, those dying outside Christ's saving grace would simply "remain in their graves, decompose, and pass into nothingness. That would be natural or simple death, or what the New Testament calls destruction."[8] However, other biblical texts, particularly those in the Synoptic Gospels, advocate a different possibility. Bernstein writes, "A second view holds that simple death does not suffice: justice demands retribution. Those who reject the Christian message will also be resurrected, but then they will be sent to a fate separate from, and worse than, that of the blessed. The damned will suffer 'wrath' or 'evil,' either temporally or unendingly in eternal damnation."[9] Finally, the third possibility follows from the idea that punishment will not be eternal, and argues that, even if there is a time of punishment, ultimately, God will draw all things to God's self in a final, universal restoration.

In all possibilities, however, what is noteworthy is the way it is assumed that hell is the logical end of a continuum that proceeds from start to finish along a person's life. This interpretation fits perfectly with our traditional understanding of the way time works. Peters describes it this way: "Our commonly accepted idea of temporality is that time consists of a linear one-way passage from the past, through the present, toward the future. And, when it comes to causality, we are *archonic*. We assume that the power of being comes from the past. We assume that everything that exists is due to a past cause and a present effect. The power of being, it is commonly assumed, comes in the form of a push from the past."[10]

Regarding hell, one of the most well-known depictions of this understanding of eternal cause and effect is found in Dante's *Inferno*. As is well known, the *Inferno* details an elaborate system of circular hells, spiraling downward, peopled with sinners who are being punished according to their deeds, beginning with the mildest and culminating with the most se-

---

8   Alan Bernstein, *The Formation of Hell* (Ithaca: Cornell University Press, 1993), 206–07.
9   Ibid., 207.
10 Ted Peters, *Science, Theology, and Ethics* (Burlington: Ashgate Publishing, 2003), 85.

vere. Thus, the first circle of hell is "Limbo," where the unbaptized and the "virtuous pagans" suffer the relatively mild punishment of eternal longing for the divine, as they recognize their separation from God, but cannot do anything to correct it. The succeeding circles punish the lustful, the gluttonous, the greedy, the wrathful, and the violent, ending with those whom Dante believes deserve the most severe punishment, the treacherous and the traitors. There, in the very center of the cold pit of hell, Dante places Satan, whom he depicts as having three different faces—yellow, red, and black—and great wings whose flapping fills the pit with icy winds. With each different mouth, Satan gnaws on a prominent sinner: Cassius and Brutus, traitors to Julius Caesar; and of course, Judas Iscariot, who bears the greatest punishment of any sinner in hell, as his head is entirely in Satan's mouth, and his back is eternally skinned by Satan's claws.[11]

A great body of literature has been written about how Dante's depictions reflect his own biases against certain individuals, and how they enabled him to, metaphorically at least, punish those whom he believed were responsible for his downfall and exile from Florence. *The Inferno* is an extreme example, to be sure, but it serves well as an illustration of how, in some ways, hell is always a projection of our past onto the future, an imposition of our concepts of payment, penalty, and retribution onto God's future. This fact alone should stand as a caution to us to be more circumspect and modest in our predictions not only of our own, but especially of another's future. In light of what has already been said about the power of God that resides in the future, it is theologically questionable how far we can or should go in making one's past normative for one's entire existence, and how strongly we can or should assert that the past will have the last word over the future.

By Whose Hand?
Heaven Has Its Origin in the Creative Work and Being of God

Many times in Scripture, Jesus begins a parable with the words, "The kingdom of heaven is like. . . ." In Matthew 13 alone, Jesus compares the kingdom of heaven to a prodigal sower, a mustard seed, a measure of yeast, a hidden treasure, a merchant searching for a fine pearl, and a net that catches every kind of fish. In one place, Jesus says that all must become like little children to enter the kingdom; in another, that everyone must

---

11 Dante Alighieri, *The Inferno*, Robert Hollander and Jean Hollander, trans. (New York: Random House, 2000), 629-31.

be born of water and the Spirit to enter it. Further, he proclaims that it is easier for a camel to go through the eye of a needle than for the rich to enter the kingdom, and he shocks the chief priests and elders by telling them that the prostitutes and tax collectors will enter into the kingdom before they will. What's more, in Luke 17, Jesus tells the confused Pharisees that the kingdom of God is within them. What conclusions are we to draw about heaven from this vast and varied treasury of images?

First, heaven will surprise us. One of the main functions of Jesus' various kingdom of heaven parables is to throw his hearers off guard and to unsettle their preconceived notions about what heaven will be like. It is clear from many of Jesus' examples that the kingdom will not be anything like they imagine it will be; in fact, in many ways, it will come as a prophetic reality that stands over and against all of their expectations. Second, heaven will be like nothing we can imagine. Jesus chooses the strangest images to embody heaven, surely none of which his hearers would have suggested as suitable representations. It is clear, then, that the kingdom of heaven is, at least to some degree, discontinuous with what has come before; instead of confirming human probabilities, it will inaugurate some wonderful new work of God. Finally, heaven will not follow the patterns of social intercourse established by human society. Jesus is insistent that there will be a dramatic reversal of fortunes in heaven, with the children leading the way, and the prostitutes and tax collectors following at their heels. Those who imagine themselves righteous and deserving are given a rude awakening in Jesus' many parables, and it is clear that the heavenly banqueting table will be comprised of quite a motley assortment of diners—not at all like the exclusive supper club some of the Pharisees seem to be anticipating.

All of this serves as an important reminder about who the composer of heaven is—whose hands shaped it, whose love generated it, and whose word brought it into being. Regardless of how much we might enjoy speculating about heaven, we are entirely on the receiving end of this work of God: we cannot and do not mold it according to our wishes or transform it according to our labors. God and God alone is the author of heaven, and as humans, our task is to receive it gratefully as a gift when God determines the time is right to grant it.

Heaven, then, is in some ways both the culmination of and the justification for the creation of the cosmos as a whole; the very existence of heaven is intimately bound up with the existence of the world. Both are interrelated pieces of one whole divine, creative work, which occurs both at the beginning of the world, and also on a continual, day-to-day basis sustaining all life. God's creative activity, to be fully revealed at the end of time, in the coming of the kingdom of heaven, is the same creative activity out of which all life springs; thus, it is only in heaven that the relationship between all the divergent parts, the meaning of all existence, will be fulfilled.

Hell Has Its Origin in Human Sinfulness and Estrangement from God

Contrast this understanding of heaven's divine agency with the origin of hell. Alice Turner, in her book, *The History of Hell*, notes that some form of what Christians call "hell" can be found all the way back on baked clay tablets from Sumer societies, who lived almost 4,000 years ago in what is now Iraq.[12] In fact, in cultures all over the world, perhaps in all times and all places, evidence for some doctrine of "hell" can be found, whether it be in the context of dying-god vegetation myths, the stories of great heroes on a quest, such as Gilgamesh or Orpheus, or passing through a hall of justice to enter some form of life after death, as in Egypt. As most Christians are aware, the Jews also had a concept of a place of the dead; in Scripture, this is typically called Sheol, a shadowy pit of death, or Gehenna, a waste dump that, according to Turner, "served as a metaphor for an unpleasant place and also as a curse, for death in such a place would have indicated a life far removed from the laws of Yahweh."[13] It is fair to say, then, that many, if not most human societies have operated with some concept of a place after death where at least the possibility of suffering is present. Why is this so?

Obviously, such a broad question goes far beyond the limits of this chapter; however, certainly the question can be asked specifically with regard to Christianity. Turner notes that "it is on the Gospel of Matthew that much of the Christian proof of Hell's existence and purpose depends."[14] Certainly, there are more direct references and more explicit descriptions of hell in that particular Gospel than any other single book in the New Testament. Matthew seems to have two purposes in mind in his writings on hell: first, to hammer home the point that salvation comes only through Jesus Christ; and second, bad things will happen to you if you are not saved. In essence, Matthew is emphasizing that hu-

---

12 Alice K. Turner, *The History of Hell* (New York: Harcourt Brace and Company, 1993), 5.
13 Ibid., 41.
14 Ibid., 53.

manity needs saving, and in his descriptions of hell, he provides strong incentive to procure that salvation through belief in Jesus Christ. So, looking only at Matthew, then, we might conclude that hell exists to punish those who do not believe; it is the consequence of refusing to become a disciple of Jesus.

Augustine, however, takes this idea in a slightly different direction, in some ways, increasing the stakes for everyone involved. It is well known that Augustine's view of sin—particularly original sin—was extraordinarily influential in the succeeding development of Christian theology; indeed, the weight of his authority still can be felt today. For Augustine, the roots of sin are deep and strong, and no human being can possibly escape their tangle of evil. In fact, Augustine believed that all humans deserved punishment for their sins; it was only by the grace of God—and more than we rightly could expect—that God would chose to save even a few sinners. In Augustine's eyes, the condemnation of many only made God's deliverance of some more merciful. For Augustine, then, the fires of hell were entirely fitting to humanity's rebelliousness and deceit; the existence of hell was clearly warranted by original sin.

Much more could be said, of course, but I hope this is enough to suggest that for Christians, the reason hell exists is human sinfulness and evil. Hell was not created by God, and it certainly was not part of God's original plan for creation. Hell is the result of humanity's fundamental turn away from God; it comes from our choice to serve ourselves rather than God, and to poison all our relationships with hatred, greed, anger, and lust. Hans Urs Von Balthasar writes, "[I]t is clear, for one thing, that we cannot say that God has 'created hell'; no one but man [sic] can be blamed for its existence."[15]

There are, I think, two important manifestations of this connection between hell and human sinfulness, two ways in which we can see clearly that hell is indeed impossible without human sin and draws its power from it. First is the fact that throughout Christian history people have taken great and perverse delight in describing in vivid, excruciating detail the torments of hell. This ghoulish pleasure is perhaps most obvious in the visual arts: Hieronymus Bosch's "Garden of Earthly Delights," for example, in which more sheer physical tortures and abasements are depicted than can possibly be described; Fra Angelico's "Last Judgment,"

---

15 Hans Urs von Balthasar, *Dare We Hope 'That All Men Be Saved?* David Kipp, trans. (San Francisco: Ignatius Press, 1988), 53–54.

depicting a ravenous Satan in the middle of boiling cauldron [being stirred by devils], devouring bodies as fast as he can shove them into his mouth; and Jan Van Eyck's "Last Judgment," portraying hell as a gaping pit, over which Death stretches his skeletal arms, and into which the damned fall headlong, where they are eaten alive by a motley assortment of demons. These are not isolated examples. It is a sign of how pervasive human sinfulness really is when we take such pains to envision and describe such agonizing tortures for our neighbors, whom, as we know, Christ commands us to love. One might well argue that the very existence of such descriptions is a sign that we ourselves already are closer to hell than we may imagine.

The second manifestation of the connection between hell and human sinfulness is the persistence of speculation that God and the saints in heaven enjoy the suffering of the damned. This is both theologically and ethically troubling, to say the least. This sort of speculation is nothing more than a projection that attempts to justify our worst and basest impulses by attributing them to the divine. Philip Almond, in his study of the ideas of both heaven and hell during the period of the English Enlightenment, notes that in the seventeenth century, the physical, sensual torments of hell were often vividly described. However, as a part of the explicit description of these horrors, the writers also included the merciless laughter by God and the saints as they were rejoicing over the suffering in hell. Almond writes, "The inaptly named Puritan Christopher Love similarly rejoiced in the prospect of the laughter of God at the sufferings of the damned: 'when thou art scorching in thy flames, when thou art howling in thy torments, then shall God laugh at thy destruction, and then the Saints of God shall sing and rejoyce [sic], that thou art a vessel of his justice, and so his power and wrath are made known in thee.'"[16] Almond notes how this "abominable fancy" can also be found in Augustine, Tertullian, Aquinas, and Peter of Lombard.[17]

It is one thing to admit that we ourselves secretly, or not so secretly, enjoy the prospect of others' suffering. It is another thing entirely, I argue, to assume that God enjoys such suffering. In light of everything Christians believe about Jesus Christ—his care for the outcast and the excluded, his ministry of healing and forgiveness, the love of God incar-

---

16 Philip C. Almond, *Heaven and Hell in Enlightenment England* (Cambridge: Cambridge University Press, 1994), 83.

17 Ibid., 97. Almond argues that this interpretation—that is, the rejoicing of the saved over the condemned—had ended roughly by the nineteenth century.

nated in his very flesh, and the death he died to conquer the power of death forever—make it impossible to justify the idea that God somehow rejoices in the face of suffering. The same God that sought out the one lost sheep, the one lost coin, and the one lost son would certainly not celebrate the permanent loss of any part of God's beloved creation. The construction of hell and its prominent place in Christian theology has been at the hands of humanity, not God, and as we will see in the final section of this chapter, something that has mere human origin is not and can never be eternal.

Temporary or Permanent?

Hell Is Temporal

In *GOD—The World's Future*, Peters argues that "If hell were to remain forever, it would also remain as a constant reminder that God's will is not completely done, that God's power is less than complete. Unless God's kingdom is universal and all-inclusive, God is not all-powerful. Therefore, hell, if it exists, must be temporary, and once it passes out of existence all will be taken into the consummate kingdom of God."[18] Peters here is relying on one of the classic arguments, used by different theologians through the centuries, to explain the final abolition of hell—that is, the scriptural witness that promises in the end, God will be all and all. It is this argument I want to focus on here.

Hans Küng notes that the doctrine of "eternal punishment with the devil" was established definitively by the Catholic Church first at the Synod of Constantinople in 543, and then later at the Fourth Lateran Council in 1215.[19] However, this fact has not kept theologians both before and after these dates from speculating on the ultimate abolition of hell. There are two primary places in Scripture that have been used to defend this argument: In Philippians 2:1-11, we read ". . . at the name of Jesus every knee should bend, in heaven and on earth and under the earth, and every tongue should confess that Jesus Christ is Lord, to the glory of God the Father"; likewise, from 1 Corinthians 15:

> . . . for as all die in Adam, so all will be made alive in Christ. But each in his own order: Christ the first fruits, then at his coming those who belong to Christ. Then comes the end, when he hands over the kingdom to God the Father, after he

---
18 Peters, *GOD—The World's Future*, 368.
19 Hans Küng, *Eternal Life?* Edwards Quinn, trans. (New York: Crossroad, 1991), 130.

has destroyed every ruler and every authority and power. For he must reign until he has put all his enemies under his feet. The last enemy to be destroyed is death. For 'God has put all things in subjection under his feet.' But when it says, 'All things are put in subjection,' it is plain that this does not include the one who put all things in subjection under him. When all things are subjected to him, then the Son himself will also be subjected to the one who put all things in subjection under him, so that God may be all in all (vv. 22–28).

Certainly, these are not the only texts that can be marshaled in defense of the final annihilation of hell—the number varies depending on how literally one interprets the "all" in such passages—but these two have been used most consistently in the tradition over time.

It is believed that Clement of Alexandria was the first Christian writer to suggest, albeit hesitantly, that the fires of hell would, eventually, be extinguished. Clement used the Philippians passage quoted above, among others, to argue that in Christ, God has saved the whole world, and ultimately, the whole world will come to serve God and worship God. This includes, of course, those in hell. Thus, for Clement, the whole purpose of hell was for purification, and once that function was complete, hell would come to an end. He used medical imagery, and compared the "discerning fire" of eschatological punishment with various types of curative surgery performed on a diseased arm or leg, such as amputation, and the removal of diseased tissue by a surgeon. Further, Clement argued for five specific characteristics of the punishment that occurred in hell, all of which supported his conclusion that hell itself finally would come to an end: punishment after death is redemptive in nature and limited in duration; punishment is pedagogical; punishment is medicinal; punishment is discerning—that is, it is appropriate to the person, not identical for each individual; and punishment is consistent with the character of God.

Certainly Clement was not the only one to make this argument. Most famously, perhaps, it is found in the writings of Origen, who focused on the 1 Corinthians text cited above, and reasoned from those verses that ultimately, all God's enemies would be subjected to God and would worship God. For Origen, evil—and consequently hell—ultimately would be excluded from God's harmonious universe. Gregory of Nyssa should also be mentioned here, as he, too, argued for the final destruction of hell, but using a different logic. For Gregory, evil did not have true existence;

only what comes from God's hand has permanent, genuine existence—evil lives only as a parasite on the good. Thus, God had no part in either creating or willing the existence of evil [and, by extension, hell]. Gregory, too, believed in the purification process inherent in punishment; he argued that once the evil was burned off, the individual would be left with a purely good will, and would, then, freely choose to be with God. Over time, everyone who needed it would go through this process, and thus hell would cease to exist.

Another line of argumentation for the ultimate demise of hell comes not from God's lordship, but rather from God's love. Romans 8:38–39 reads, "For I am convinced that neither death, nor life, nor angels, nor rulers, nor things present, nor things to come, nor powers, nor height, nor depth, or anything else in all creation, will be able to separate us from the love of God in Christ Jesus our Lord." Many theologians do not interpret the "anything else in all creation" as including hell or Satan, or both, but again, from what Scripture tells us about who God is in Jesus Christ, there does seem to be warrant for at least considering the possibility that Paul did, in fact, mean to be genuinely all-inclusive. Read this way, this passage (and others like it), points to the reality that separation from God is never permanent; because God is eternal, and because it is in God's nature to reach out to humanity, so also is God's hand eternally extended in love and grace. Continually and everlastingly God reaches out across every gap that would separate humanity from God; ultimately, God's loving desire for all creation will be accomplished.

One final line of argumentation for this position is based on a particular theological analysis of Christ's descent into hell. This event was not for one moment only; rather, it has eternal and everlasting significance. It is a key part of the crucifixion/resurrection event that forever defines God's relationship with humanity and the world. While certainly not everyone has interpreted the "harrowing of hell" as comprehensive—perhaps it is meant only to point to those Dante put in Limbo, the righteous patriarchs, matriarchs, and prophets from the Old Testament, for example—certainly it is possible to see this act of love by Jesus Christ as filling the most god-forsaken place one could ever imagine or inhabit, thereby destroying it forever. After all, what is hell except the complete and utter absence of God? If Christ has gone even there, to the deepest pit of existence, what of "hell" is left?

Let me close this section with a quote from Hans Küng, who in his analysis of purgatory and hell, returns in many ways to the arguments of the church fathers mentioned above. In *Eternal Life?* he writes, "But however the scriptural texts are interpreted in detail, the 'eternity' of the punishment of hell may never be regarded as absolute. It remains subject to God, to his will and his grace. And individual texts suggest—in contrast to others—a reconciliation of all, an act of universal mercy."[20] In both Scripture and the tradition we see variations of this theme over and over: while God is eternal, hell is not; somehow, in some way, God's gracious will and God's love for creation will have the last and final word.

Heaven Is Eternal

The permanence of heaven is hardly ever questioned and, thus, needs only a few sentences of elaboration. Both Scripture and Christian tradition have consistently witnessed to the fact that while human life here is marked with suffering, sin, impermanence, and loss, it will not always be that way. God has prepared a future for us where we will be restored, and our reconciliation with God will be perfect and permanent. There will be no more crying, no more death, no more mourning; God will dwell eternally with God's people in perfect peace. This is the meaning of the symbol "Alpha and Omega" used for Jesus Christ—he was there at the beginning of creation and will be there at its consummation; when he comes again in glory he will reign eternally without end. This also is the meaning of the symbol in Isaiah of the lion lying down with the lamb. In the kingdom of heaven, there will be no more predation and no more enemies; all will share in sisterly love and friendship.

This reality is also witnessed to in the Christian sacraments of Baptism and Holy Communion. In baptism, Christians die a death like Christ in order to share in his resurrection and eternal life. In communion, Christians experience a "foretaste of the feast to come," a small appetizer to the great meal that awaits at the heavenly banqueting table. Thus, sometimes in the church, the language of one's "heavenly birthday" is used at a funeral, to indicate that the day of one's mortal death on earth is also the first day of her eternal life in heaven. When it is said that one has "joined the church triumphant," this language, too, points to this same reality.

One of the main functions of the doctrine of eschatology, then, is to elaborate a Christian vision for the end time that is grounded in God's great love and mercy for the world, and proleptically glimpsed in the

---

20 Ibid., 140.

life, death, and resurrection of Jesus Christ. In this vision, Christians see the culmination of God's act of creation; in Jesus Christ, we get to jump ahead and read the last few pages of the book so we know how it all turns out. In *God as Trinity*, Peters writes, "The Christian notion of eschatology points to a future event initiated by God that will not simply put an end to temporal history; it will unify it and fulfill it. The theological vision seems to warrant a principle of cosmic holism."[21]

In light of this principle of holism, then, heaven promises the permanent righting of all wrongs, the permanent uniting of all that is divided, and the permanent healing of all that is broken; creation will be perfected and live eternally in perfect harmony with God. Thus, heaven is a symbol of cosmic redemption, and in some ways, encompasses the whole of the Christian message in its imagery. For this reason, Wolfhart Pannenberg can write, "eschatology is not just the subject of a single chapter in dogmatics; it determines the perspective of Christian doctrine as a whole."[22] This holistic vision of the coming of God's final, perfect kingdom, in which the glory of God fills creation, and every eye is dried, every heart mended, is the eschatological promise foreshadowed in Jesus Christ, and hell has no part in it.

Conclusion

I recognize that some, if not many, will disagree with me at many points in the above argument. The existence and nature of hell has been heatedly debated (no pun intended) for thousands of years, and that debate certainly shows no sign of cooling down. However, I would like to give the final word in this chapter to Hans Urs von Balthasar who writes that it is, in the end, impossible to state definitively whether or not all people will be reconciled to God and hell finally will be abolished. It is only God who judges, and only God who knows.

Nonetheless, von Balthasar argues that Christians should not be indifferent about this matter, and that it is actually incumbent upon us to desire a certain outcome. He writes, "But love *hopes all things* (1 Corinthians 13:7). It cannot do otherwise than to hope for the reconciliation of all men [sic] in Christ. Such unlimited hope is, from the Christian standpoint,

---

21 Ted Peters, *God as Trinity* (Louisville: Westminister/John Knox Press, 1993), 173.
22 Wolfhart Pannenberg, *Systematic Theology, vol. 3*, Geoffrey W. Bromiley, trans. (Grand Rapids: Wm. B. Eerdmans Publishing Co., 1998), 531.

not only permitted, but *commanded*."[23] He goes on to quote Catherine of Sienna, who wrote, "How could I ever reconcile myself, Lord, to the prospect that a single one of those whom, like me, you have created in your image and likeness should become lost and slip from your hands? No, in absolutely no case do I want to see a single one of my brethren [sic] meet with ruin, not a single one of those, who, through their like birth, are one with me by nature and by grace. I want them all to be wrested from the grasp of the ancient enemy, so that they all become yours to the honor and great glorification of your name."[24]

Maybe hell will be abolished, and maybe it will not. Until we experience that final reality for ourselves, only God knows for sure. However, and this is no small thing, in the meantime, can we not hope and pray that it is so? Would it not be a cause for rejoicing if it were true? And, if for whatever reason we cannot or will not hope and pray for such a thing, I am afraid we are already perilously close to the edge of the pit, and in grave danger of toppling in ourselves.

---

[23] Hans Urs von Balthasar, *Dare We Hope 'That All Men Be Saved'?* David Kipp, trans. (San Francisco: Ignatius Press, 1988), 213. Author's emphasis.
[24] Ibid., 214–15.

Apples and the Apocalypse

Jane E. Strohl

Several years ago I was part of a three-person panel doing an entrance interview for a candidate for ordained ministry. When asked about his call, the candidate told us that he felt compelled to carry the news of judgment to people and make them mindful of the end of the world, which was bearing down upon us all. He was thankful, he said, that none of his relationships with women had ever worked out, because now he would not have to agonize over the fate of spouse and children. The man knew these were hard words for people to hear, especially for those with families, but they could not be ignored any longer. The world went its foolish, sinful way as if God were indifferent. This man feared it was too late, but nonetheless he must try to bring people to repentance. One of the members of the committee asked the man where the gospel of God's freely given grace to sinners fit into his theology. He confirmed that good news ardently, but he did not seem concerned about integrating it with his apocalyptic convictions. The committee was in shock. We sent him off for a cup of coffee and deliberated. As troubling as we found his focus on the end times and the judgment of God, we had to admit that it had biblical warrant as well as confessional support.

In all of the Synoptic Gospels Jesus forewarns his hearers of the cosmic disaster destined to befall the earth, a cataclysm he expects them to endure in their lifetime (Matthew 24; Mark 13; Luke 21).

> Pray that it may not happen in winter. For in those days there will be such tribulation as has not been from the beginning of the creation which God created until now, and never will be. And if the Lord had not shortened the days, no human being would be saved; but for the sake of the elect, whom he chose, he shortened the days. And then if any one says to you, "Look, here is the Christ!" or "Look, there he is!" do

not believe it. False Christs and false prophets will arise and show sign and wonders, to lead astray, if possible, the elect. But take heed; I have told you all things beforehand.

But in those days, after that tribulation, the sun will be darken, and the moon will not give its light and the stars will be falling from heaven, and the powers in the heavens will be shaken. And then they will see the Son of man coming in clouds with great power and glory. And then he will send out the angels, and gather his elect from the four winds, from the end of the earth to the ends of heaven (Mark 13:18–27).

Article XVII of the Augsburg Confession echoes and affirms this expectation of a majestic, and for some, horrific end.

They also teach that at the consummation of the world Christ will appear for judgment and will bring to life all the dead. He will give eternal life and endless joy to the righteous and elect, but he will condemn the ungodly and the devils to endless torment (Latin text).

Article XVII of the Apology is quite brief:

The opponents accept article seventeen without qualification. In it we confess that Christ will appear at the consummation of the world and will raise up all the dead, giving eternal life and eternal joys to the godly but condemning the ungodly to endless torment with the devil.

For a younger generation of believers, theologians, and pastors, this doctrine, readily accepted by both sides in the religious debates at the Diet of Augsburg, is often very problematic. The theo-logic of the evangelical gospel points to universalism. After all, when every human being is *simul iustus et peccator*, how could God weed out the ungodly from the godly? Moreover, if first and foremost the God of our Lord Jesus Christ is gracious, why would God want to do such a thing? When the concept of eschatology enters the theological conversation, it will usually be as realized eschatology. How is the power of the resurrection active in us today? How is the Spirit guiding us into the ways of justice and peace? This is what matters here and now. The Spirit may well also be driving us to the *eschaton*, but what's a Christian to do about that? It is a bit like the posture of northern Californians. The "big one," the earthquake that will rupture gas lines and create a conflagration, put seismic retrofitting to the ultimate test, and undoubtedly be an agent of death, could come anytime (soon, according to seismologists, is getting sooner now that we have entered a new century). The most you can do is stockpile supplies in your garage. Then you go on with a non-earthquake-centered life, hoping you will remember periodically to replace the items with an expiration date in your emergency collection.

"If I knew the world were going to end tomorrow, I would go out and plant an apple tree today." Although never verified in his works, this saying has long been attributed to Luther. If it is not genuine Luther, it is *echt lutherisch*. It reflects his confident, down-to-earth sense of discipleship. It is God's will that we live our lives in the world and for the world. Everyone carries multiple vocations—in the workplace, in the family, in the community. Some days the best you can do is put one foot in front of another. Other times the mundane becomes transcendent. For Luther, anticipating the heavenly kingdom to come with some sort of warm-up practice on earth is wholly unnecessary. As he tartly observes, there is no need to design one's own crosses to bear—such as the monastic requirements of poverty, chastity and obedience—when one can count on life to bring more than enough such heuristic devices along the way. Moreover, the experience of redemption manifests itself in the seemingly inglorious, in the ability of the mother, the teacher, the restaurant manager, the assembly line worker to reach beyond her or his own self-love and love the neighbor with true generosity. It is in the planting of apple trees—visiting the sick, staving off foreclosures, protecting abused animals, cleaning polluted waters—that the kingdom of God is made known here and now.

Luther argues that the real challenge is living in the world without becoming of it, not one-upping the world from the outset by withdrawing into a realm of allegedly superior righteousness. After all, how was your neighbor well served by your vow of chastity, especially when it had been extorted from you at an age when you simply did not know yourself well enough to make such a commitment? What merit was there for anyone if you sat in your monastery knowing that though circumstances insured that you would keep that vow in deed, in your heart you broke it daily? This situation was, for Luther, one of the signs of the impending end. Something was fatally amiss when the church, the self-proclaimed body of Christ, became the instrument of violating consciences and did so with indifference. Here is the heart of Luther's intense apocalyptic expectation. The pope shamelessly revealed himself as the Antichrist, the church was his whore, and the gospel, the Spirit's legitimate offspring, hadn't a prayer.

Luther's argument was a kind of Occupy Movement of the faith. Luther called for faithful pastors to preach and teach; he was convinced that the Word would do it all. He summoned the faithful to step up to the plate and to confess the true faith both by the way they worshipped and by the way they lived lives of unexceptional discipleship. God and the angels look down from heaven, see a father changing a diaper, and laugh with delight because they know he does this unappetizing task in faith. In later years that father faithfully attends science fairs and band concerts. He stands outside Target to get signatures on petitions supporting school bonds and opposing the closure of the local hospital. A whole community of children becomes his concern. And the angels keep laughing. Luther's doctrine of vocation has been an extraordinary gift to the church in its ability to dignify difficult, sometimes tedious tasks without romanticizing them. Toilet training your offspring, tending to a mentally addled relative, sorting out a difficult marriage, coping with a narcissistic boss—these are not such stuff as dreams are made of, but they are the stuff of Christian discipleship. We do not get to pick our relatives; we do not get to pick our neighbors either. By the grace of Christ we learn to serve them as they need to be served and to be at peace with it. One could argue that this rigorous schooling in the discipline of generosity is the very presence of Christ's kingdom among us. That is the "apple tree" side of Luther. We are not called to look over our shoulders to make sure that we have secured God's favor. We are not called to look ahead, wondering if we are definitely in God's "keeper" category to be saved for eternity. We are called to keep our noses to the ground of the world that we know and to live our lives so that others may see our good works and give glory to our Father who is in heaven.

Yet there was another side to Luther's vision of the world as well. He did not always sit back contentedly to face the creation's future with an act of gardening. There is urgency in his preaching when he talks about the imminent arrival of *den jungsten Tag* and a surging fury that will ultimately render the world and its affairs irrelevant. Indeed, he regularly exhorts his hearers to pray fervently for the arrival of the Last Day. For Christians it should be the object of eager, joyous anticipation, despite the misery it will bring for much of humankind. This is the moment when the prayers of one's lifetime are fulfilled: "Thy kingdom come, thy will be done on earth as it is in heaven." "Lead us not into temptation, but deliver us from evil." On the other side of the grave and judgment lie safety and rest. There need be no more daily trips to the drowning waters so that the old Adam may die and the new Adam may confidently emerge. There need be no more exhausting vigilance against the snares of the evil one and the insidiousness of sin. But for the Christian in this life the level of the danger of terrorism is code red every day. Luther shrewdly pointed out that temptation did not usually make a full frontal attack. If we were told flat out to commit adultery or murder, to steal from our neighbor, or to tell God to kiss off, we would know exactly what and whom we were up against. We could just say no, turn our backs, and get on with our discipleship. But most of the time we play the devil's fool. The entrance of original sin into the world sets the pattern.

In his Lectures on Genesis Luther portrays Eve as naïve and careless rather than corrupt and scheming. She wanders the garden, respecting the command concerning the tree of the knowledge of good and evil. (It is interesting that the first liturgical act of our first ancestors consisted of a not-doing: Do not touch that tree!) Luther speculates that the serpent did not look like a serpent as we know them, but rather was appealing in appearance, perhaps something like a little puppy dog. How was Eve to know? She hadn't been around the block a time or two, because at that point in the history of our race there was no block, no accumulated wisdom to learn from. So she enters into conversation with her fellow creature, who poses questions that she answers thoughtfully. And then the wily animal slips her one, a kind of theological roofie, which seduces her. "You will not die. For God knows that when you eat of it your eyes will be opened, and you will be like God, knowing good and evil" (Genesis 3:4–5). Eve ends up positioned over against God, standing in judgment of God's intentions. "So when the woman saw that the tree was good for food, and that it was a delight to the eyes, and that the tree was to be desired to make one wise, she took of its fruit and ate. . ." (Genesis 3:5). For Luther this is the beginning of the end. This first ding in the windshield quickly spreads to shatter the whole expanse of glass. Eve eats of the fruit; Adam eats of the fruit. They recognize their nakedness as something shameful, which may be the beginning of humanity's age-old suspicion of the flesh. They hide from God; they lie to God. They play the blame game, Adam going so far as to suggest that none of this would even have happened if God had not brought Eve into the picture.

There is the etiology of original sin: a moment of unwitting foolishness leads to an entrenched inability to fear, love and trust God. Then follows a rapacious self-centeredness—*incurvatus in se*—that has no heart for the neighbor's need when its own advantage is at stake. Yet even in the midst of this tragedy there are unmistakable seeds of hope. Although God had told Adam and Eve that they would die if they ate the fruit of the tree, God spares their lives. They can no longer remain in the garden; they cannot return to their state of vulnerable innocence. God metes out punishment, but it is important to note what God does not impose. Adam and Eve do not lose the companionship of each other. They are not forced to face the sadly altered future alone. Indeed, one finds here the root of Luther's extraordinary enthusiasm for marriage. The fact that it did not remain a sacrament in Lutheran churches in no way implied a diminishment of its status in Lutheran theology. Sacraments are God's gift to believers to seal before their very eyes and upon their mortal flesh the forgiveness of their sins and the promise of the life to come for Christ's sake. Marriage is not designed to do that. It originated before the fall, when God presented Eve to Adam, and the man recognized her as "bone of my bone." Marriage is part of the foundation of creation, the necessary precursor to God's desire that creatures be fruitful and multiply. It by no means pertains exclusively to Christians; people of all tribes and nations have some form of marriage, and it does not communicate the forgiveness of sins for Christ's sake.

In his commentary on the fall story, Luther indulges in a little imaginative supposition. He finds it likely that Eve comforts the downcast Adam with a kind of glass half-full analysis of God's judgment upon them. Rather than lament the bitter loss they will suffer, she sees instead the surprising generosity of God towards the couple. She focuses on the issue of progeny. God has not taken from them the power to procreate. Indeed, God has promised that from their seed shall come the one who will avenge them by bruising the serpent's head. Here one sees the two rivers of Luther's eschatological thought rising from the same headwaters. There is the ongoing daily discipline of family life. Sustaining a marriage is never easy. Luther is keenly aware of the vulnerabilities afflicting husband and wife at the very heart of their relationship. Add to that the responsibility for children, and the challenge of one's discipleship becomes clear. Communicating clearly and remaining faithful on the one hand, raising godly children and preparing them for useful vocations on the other—this is the work that Adam and Eve take up when they leave paradise. It has remained the divine charge given to humanity ever since. So the cultural patterns of mating and family life take shape, and no matter how imminent the end times may seem, communities still make provision for the education of the young and their appropriate, publicly recognized mating.

At the same time it is this very coupling that brings to pass the salvation that triumphs over the old age of sinfulness and inaugurates the eternal kingdom of God. Contrary to their expectations, Adam and Eve did not bring the seed of redemption into the world, but they began the generations of life that would finally end in the birth of Jesus. It is for this reason that fertility is of such paramount concern throughout the patriarchal and matriarchal narratives. The issue is not that women must be able to drop babies in order to be included in God saving work. Rather, it is a sign of the everyday nature of God's work among us that birthing babies, something that generally does come naturally, serves as the means of divine action. Sarah is not only the quiet helpmate who modestly remains in the kitchen, preparing a meal for Abraham and his three mysterious guests. She is also the prophetess who reminds her tenderhearted husband that God's promise was given to Isaac, their son, the one she bore in her old age after suffering the contempt of Hagar and Abraham's illegitimate son, Ishmael. She does not rest until her husband gets rid of the threat they pose.

The matriarchs fiercely defend the right to participate in bearing the line of sons, through which God fulfills the promise first made to Abraham. This is brazenly clear in the story of Tamar. She has the misfortune of being mated to Judah's firstborn, an impious miscreant whom God strikes dead. Judah then betroths her to his second son, the notorious Onan, who inflicts upon Tamar an act of heinous *coitus interruptus*. God strikes Onan down for having made a mockery of God's command to be fruitful and multiply. Luther also castigates the deceased for his appalling abuse of Tamar. Playing fast and loose with a woman at the peak of her sexual desire is not good care of the neighbor.

The perpetuation of family life from generation to generation does not seem fraught with eschatological desperation. It is the most business-as-usual of human experiences. Its necessity remains—"Be fruitful and multiply" is a standing order—but its urgency fades. While Eve or Sarah may have thought the fulfillment of God's promise was as close as the maturation of her son, they both learn otherwise. The women of Israel do not give up. They continue faithfully bearing offspring, but in some way the birth of a child is paradoxical. One is always hoping that this is the one who will save Israel, that is, bring in God's kingdom. At the same time a child is welcomed as an agent of continuity, of the enduring of things as they are. Consequently, they need to be socialized, educated, and married off.

The apocalypse and the apple tree—for Luther, they represent the two poles of the believer's life from the time of the fall through each successive chapter of God's story of salvation. Such a paradox cannot be resolved; it needs to be managed. Over time the arc of movement favors one pole and then the other, moving back and forth as needed to re-establish the balance. The "now" and the "not yet," so essential to Paul's understanding of the gospel, are foundational for Luther's as well. The key doctrines of his theology—simultaneously saint and sinner, living in two kingdoms, knowing fully by the light of glory what is now ours only by the light of faith, the duality of God's Word as law and gospel—generate tensions in the life of the believer that function as strategies for redemption but are not the goal. The internal conflicts of individual believers and faith communities cry out for release, which can come only with the passing of the old order and the establishment of the new. Then the Christian will no longer be saint and sinner but wholly saint. She will not hear the Word of God as law and gospel but solely as the joyous proclamation of God's love, for there will be no further need for the second use of the law that drives the sinner to repentance and opens him to mercy. God will reign directly, no longer requiring the cover of masks to act in the kingdom of the left hand. What has been seen through a glass darkly will become clear, even radiant, as the hidden God reveals Godself as unequivocally our champion, keeping faith with the Son and with us that not one whom the Father has given the Son will be lost.

The struggle to remain faithful in this life is fierce. Temptations great and small can cast us down at any moment. Moreover, the neighbors around us whom we are called to serve with unending generosity, are often hard to be in the same room with, less lay down our lives for. At heart, human beings act like unholy narcissists, and such a person is not easy on one's own sanity. The life of the believer, the simultaneously saint and sinner, is unsustainable over the long haul. It is the life of a cat on a hot tin roof, lifting one paw after the other to avoid being burned and hoping in vain to jump down. Only God can provide the means of escape. No wonder the believer prays fervently, "Thy kingdom come," and now would be the perfect time.

Finally, there is the opaqueness of God's, and even Christ's, work in the world. There is so much in our experience that urges doubt, if not unbelief, upon us. From personal tragedy to cultural genocide to environmental cataclysm, it does not seem that God loves all that God has made after all. And yet we are commanded to soldier on as if all matter of things will be well. One of the most striking traits of Luther's new Adam and Eve is their feistiness in prayer. On the one hand Luther urges the believer to cast the promise of God into the teeth of the tempter when he threatens and cajoles. "This word is true for me," I can say, "but not for you, so just get off my back." At the same time Luther admonishes the Christian to get into God's face with this very same promise. It is as if by faith we now have a debt to call in. God cannot change God's mind because we can hold God to the promise. Now that God has by God's own doing become our God, we are in danger of giving our *incurvatus in se* nature a new lease on life, locking God into position in our warped field of vision.

The apocalyptic cast of Luther's thought is also rooted in his interpretation of the historical events of his day. According to the theology of the cross, it should not be possible to read the final judgments of God from the vicissitudes of history. However, for Luther the world had entered the last times, and the veil was lifting between the kingdom of this world and the kingdom of God. Riddled with arrogant sinning and contempt for God, the world practically taunted God into inflicting punishment. The gospel had emerged with a clarity unparalleled since the time of the Apostles. It revealed to Luther the brazen arrival of the Antichrist in the abomination of the papal office. Any man who occupied the throne of St. Peter participated in its corruption, even if he were not himself corrupt. The pope was the architect of the overthrow of the gospel, putting a price on grace for the faithful that Christ had already paid. The church itself, the mother of the faithful, proved to be anything but. Moreover, the problem was not just the Roman Church. The list of betrayers kept growing. The false practice and teaching and the pastorally criminal intent of Rome, the *Schwaermer*, Zwingli, the Anabaptists, and the Jews turned them into ultimate enemies. They made a mockery of the gospel; they refused to be corrected; they robbed countless souls of the true forgiveness and comfort given in Christ Jesus. To behave this way was for Luther the devil's work, and consequently he regarded them as the devil's agents. In some sense this made them both more and less than human—able to do eternal harm, no longer able to claim the true (evangelical) gospel as pro me, and deserving of no quarter from their opponents (as Luther's polemics make dramatically clear).

Unlike some of his contemporaries (and ours), Luther did not determine a specific date for the Lord's arrival and chastised those who did. Yet his expectation of the end as imminent and devastating for those who played fast and loose with the gospel was unequivocal. He did not live to see it, anymore than St. Paul did, or we have. Such apocalyptic views are part of the very structure of Christianity and arise repeatedly. They are not so much a conclusion drawn from the present reality as they are a lens brought to the interpretation of what one sees. Their failure to materialize does not discredit them but rather simply defers them. Luther's sixteenth-century vision of the approaching Last Day may be of historical interest to contemporary Lutherans, but our own eschatological projections will be peopled very differently.

Not long ago Peters had prepared a survey that he made available to the seminary community. The subject was the possible arrival of aliens on our planet and the implications that would have for the Christian faith as we have defined it. I told my teenage daughter about the questionnaire, and she was once again impressed by "Uncle Ted's" beat-of-a-different-drummer mind. She in turn told her erstwhile boyfriend, a young man who, for all I could tell, had never been touched by the possibilities of Christian faith, or any faith for that matter. He had recently made an award-winning film on zombies; other life or semi-life forms were his passion. The idea that the church would care about the possibility of extraterrestrial beings impressed him greatly. So much so that when I was scheduled to deliver the annual Luther lecture, he asked my daughter if he might go with her. Alas, hoping to encounter Ted Peters and a PowerPoint presentation on our possible neighbors in the galaxy, he got me instead, speaking at length on Luther's understanding of suffering and then preaching a sound sermon on justifying faith. He was polite but clearly mystified. Where was the guy who spoke his language?!?

A number of us at the seminary joked about Peters' questionnaire and created some goofy additions. That, of course, is because it is more than our minds can, or want, to comprehend. The Lutheran Confessions (Augsburg Confession, Article II) describe original sin as the inability to fear, love, and trust God, that is, to be so turned in on ourselves that we cannot see God or our neighbor apart from our own self-concern. The whole process of redemption is to free us from this bondage so that we can look up and really see our neighbor, not insofar as they are a useful reflection of us but as beloved creatures of God in their own right. Who better to capture our attention than an alien! Who better to free us from our relentless self-centeredness than a being literally outside of our own orbit? Who better to challenge our assumption that we are the apple of God's eye, that the one and only purpose of God's action in Jesus Christ is saving us from sin and death? It would be humbling and freeing. The end would come not with a cataclysm but with the arrival of unexpected company. The same challenge would be there: to let go of ourselves and to live the life God is calling us to live, to love as God loves. When the kingdom to come is grounded in hospitality, God's graciousness to us, and our consequent openness to one another, it makes sense to plant an apple tree today.

The Space between Us

Blessed Is Ted for He Is Timely Placed

Vítor Westhelle

> I could stand here forever, she thinks. She could occupy this spot that's neither land nor water, wait here until the sky and the sea uncouple their dark, intertwined limbs and separate again in the light of a new day.
>
> Thrity Umrigar, The Space between Us[1]

> *But they will teach us that Eternity is the Standing still of the Present Time, a* Nunc-stans *(as the schools call it); which neither they, nor any else understand, no more than they would a* Hic-stans *for an Infinite greatness of Place.*
>
> Hobbes, Leviathan[2]

I have known Ted Peters before I ever met him. This is obviously a trade of renown. At a banquet that I was attending a couple of decades ago, I was seated at a table with a celebrated church historian who asked me about my credentials. After telling him what my trade and position were, he said: "I never heard of you. In U.S. Lutheranism today, the systematician that counts," he continued, "is Ted Peters." I could think of a number of others at the time that I thought "counted." But I got the point; it was not I. So much for my ego, but it lifted up the significance of Professor Ted Peters.

I have enjoyed the presence and graciousness of Peters on a number of occasions since then. And recently he sent me a critique he wrote

---

1 Thrity Umrigar, *The Space between Us* (New York: Harper Perennial, 2007), 320.
2 Hobbes, *Leviathan*, IV, 46, 22.

of my book, *Eschatology and Space*, suggesting to me that this *Festschrift* would be a venue for me to respond to him.[3] That I shall do.

I was honored while puzzled by his reading of my text. But then I was infiltrating a *space*, the "doctrine of the last things," that has long been acclaimed territory, if "last things" can be acclaimed a territory. His argument is rather simple, and I paraphrase: "Westhelle hates time and lifts up space. Although he has a point, he overcompensates in his plea and misses the proleptic structure of the beatitudes in which the present-tense blessedness is buttressed by the future-tense promise, as in: 'Blessed *are* the meek, for they *will* inherit the earth'" (Matthew 5:5). Thus he goes on to propose a "beatitudinal eschatology." Peters is careful enough not to generalize and miss the point that the first beatitude is rendered in the present tense, therefore precluding his proleptic approach: "Blessed *are* the poor in spirit, for theirs *is* the kingdom of heaven" (Matthew 5:3).

I don't think that Peters has given a fair reading of my text (and I do not presume to claim that it deserves it), for I do not hate time nor do I eulogize space. I am neither a Platonic gnostic nor an Eckardian mystic, or even a Tillichian existentialist for that matter, calling for a *hic et nunc aeternum* to solve the problem of time and space. Peters goes to the core of the issue even claiming that "God is not immune to time; rather God is eminently timely."[4] Yet I wonder if he could also say, on account of his incarnational theology, that God is not immune to space, and is eminently material—and thus spatial.

I speak with a deferential voice in these words that I wish could be etched to the memorabilia of a professor and inspirer of generations of pastors and theologians. Nevertheless, I still recognize a space between us, which might turn out to be a wonderful playground or just a gap. We do play when all our efforts are directed to figuring out things immeasurable and end up in laughter saying: "Well, that was not it now, was it?"

For Peters, my senior colleague, I offer these reflections about space *and time* hoping to keep the conversation going, while the friendship is taken for granted. The space between us is real, but I know that the atonement between the place he is in and my place has taken place already. While Peters has tried so hard to bring together the sciences and

---

[3] Peters' text is now available as "Beatitudinal Eschatology: In Space or Time?" in *Churrasco: A Theological Feast in Honor of Vítor Westhelle*, Mary Philip, John Arthur Nunes, and Charles M. Collier, eds. (Eugene, Oregon: Pickwick, 2013), 29–37.

[4] Ted Peters, *God as Trinity* (Louisville: Westminster/John Knox, 1993), 149.

their grammar to a common vocabulary, defying Babel, he is bordering the unbridgeable ditch between science and faith, that which you are expected to do and that which is done to, or for, you. And I know that Peters has long been attempting to jump over that ditch, or as I prefer to phrase it, a lacuna, a gap in the matter that matters.

Of course, Peters is wrong when he said that I despise time in favor of space. My only claim is one that he knows better than I do: time and space are relative to each other.[5] It has been the failure of Western theology to celebrate history and time dissociated from or even against space. If I run the risk of ideologizing space, it is because I care about time, in the same way as those who ideologize time cares about space. As de Certeau has shown, convincingly to me, the former is represented by the hegemonic group in a society, the latter by the subaltern.[6] And there is indeed a space between the two.

Peters claims that I overemphasize space, yet his proposal of a third option, "beatitudinal eschatology," is not a *tertium datur* as he suggests, but the reinstatement of a disembodied future in the Augustinian "one-after-the-otherness of events in succession" only tamed by being proleptically enunciated. My apparent overemphasis of the spatial dimension clearly was not enough to persuade Peters of its importance. The fact that theology has not gotten this, namely, the incarnation as a time-space event, a located and situated occurrence of the unbound eternal circumscribed in time and space, should not keep us from pursuing a better language to express it. It is all about situated-ness—where one situates oneself to do theology. Between Peters and me there is gap, a space, that is unavoidable, and it may be a garden—not a ditch—in which we have met on occasions. These meeting places are the points in which time and space come together, possibly in a chalice of pinot noir in the Carnero Valley!

The way space is used in my rendition of eschatology works in a literal sense of geographical site with its borders, but also metonymically to denote materiality in general, and metaphorically to signify psychological and epistemological domains. The space, or rather the gap between Peters and me can best be described metaphorically in the epistemo-

---

5   See his informed discussion of special and general relativity in *God as Trinity*, 155ff.
6   Michel de Certau, *The Practice of Everyday Life*, Steven Rendall, trans. (Berkeley: California University Press, 1984), 35–37. See also Vítor Westhelle, *Eschatology and Space: The Lost Dimension in Theology Past and Present* (New York: Palgrave/Macmillan, 2012), 119–22.

logical sense that allows for God-talk when rationality and science itself breaks down, and the indefinite that surfaces is a cypher of the infinite. Time, as *chronos*, can be expanded without limit only to find its completion in eternity itself as I think Peters would maintain. Yet space, as *topos*, literally or metaphorically, is broken by limits, borders, edges, and margins. What lies beyond these limits can indeed be proleptically and poetically envisaged, but most often cannot be anticipated. It takes faith to trust the crossing, for, in it lies danger, or as Hölderlin phrases it in a poem properly entitled "Patmos": "Near and difficult to grasp, the God, but where danger threatens that which saves from it also grows."[7] So the space between us is the gap in knowledge itself that Peters, as a maestro, turns but into a strident movement that blends itself into a countless, timely, infinite melody. But it so happens that I am interested in the gap, the raucous and indomitable interruption that cyphers a presence of the divine in disguise, the only way God's presence is available to us.

Allow me to lay out why spatial thinking in many of its dimensions is decisively important for eschatology. Here I will be primarily using space metaphorically to speak about epistemic limits.

Revisiting the God of the Gaps

Theologian and phenomenologist of religion, Rudolf Otto, commenting on the famous thesis of Johannes Weiss and Albert Schweitzer that the message of Jesus, according to the New Testament, was fundamentally eschatological, calls attention to an apparent contradiction. In his book *The Kingdom of God and the Son of Man* he registers the curious apposition between a "consistent" eschatological vision and that which Schweitzer called "the marvelous ethics" of Jesus. And thus argues Otto:

> In so doing he seems to me not to notice that when these two expressions are brought together, there would be an inconsistency if one did not pay regard to the peculiar irrationality which essentially inheres in a genuine eschatology. For without this irrationality an ethic, just in as far as it is marvelous, and even as an "interim-ethic," would be inherently inconsistent with teaching that the end is at hand.[8]

---

7   Friedrich Hölderlin, *Poems and Fragments*, Michael Hamburger, trans. (London: Anvil, 2005), 551.
8   Rudolf Otto, *The Kingdom of God and the Son of Man: A Study in the History of Religion*, Floyd Filson and Bertram Lee-Woolf, trans. (London: Lutterworth, 1943), 59.

More than anyone else of his time, Otto perceived the irreconcilable nature of the question of God, of the numinous, with Kantian rationality that rescues religion to the inner limits of practical reason. If the scientific thought, morality, or even aesthetics can be regimented by reason, as Kant has argued, religious experience that fascinates and quivers (*fascinans et tremendum*) escapes from these limits and evades the domain of science unless it is reduced to the scientific operations that can be controlled by reason alone. To phrase the question that is implicit in Otto's struggle with his Kantianism, it is the limit, the *limen* itself, that demarcates the adjacency of the religious experience. And this is the issue that Peters has been involved in as a major spokesperson in the religion and science debate in theology today.

But if I am not mistaken, I am reasoning myself into a fallacy here. I am reasoning because that is what language is about. But then in my own reasoning I am suggesting that there is something beyond reason itself. This is certainly a sophistry, namely, to start with apparently valid premises to reach absurd results. But this is what happens when we approach limit-questions, the issues that inhabit the very contours of the limits of rationality itself. To these belong an array of experiences that defy the definite, that which can be said with the evidence of the tactile phenomena that the rational commands. Hence I am here apparently confusing the infinite with the indefinite, which in Greek may be rendered by the same noun: *apeiron*. But this is precisely my point: when the rational breaks down, there is the place in which the infinite breaks in.

Jorge Luis Borges has a short story entitled "Aleph," which may help me to make my point. It describes the experience of the author who has seen in a single quantum moment all there is in space and in time. So he proceeds to narrate his experience:

> I arrive now at the ineffable core of my story. And here begins my despair as a writer. All language is a set of symbols whose use among its speakers assumes a shared past. How, then, can I translate into words the limitless Aleph, which my floundering mind can scarcely encompass? Mystics, faced with the same problem, fall back on symbols: to signify the godhead, one Persian speaks of a bird that somehow is all birds; Alanus de Insulis, of a sphere whose center is everywhere and circumference is nowhere; Ezekiel, of a four-faced angel who at one and the same time moves east and west,

north and south. (Not in vain do I recall these inconceivable analogies; they bear some relation to the Aleph.) Perhaps the gods might grant me a similar metaphor, but then this account would become contaminated by literature, by fiction. Really, what I want to do is impossible, for any listing of an endless series is doomed to be infinitesimal. In that single, gigantic instant I saw millions of acts both delightful and awful; not one of them occupied the same point in space, without overlapping or transparency. What my eyes beheld was simultaneous, but what I shall now write down will be successive, because language is successive. Nonetheless, I'll try to recollect what I can.[9]

This text suggests, or rather detects our aim at encompassing all of time into eternity itself, but reveals the self-contradictory nature of the enterprise, the limits of expressing even the mystical *hic et nunc*, the here and now of the infinite itself. The infinite cannot be inscribed without being at the same time negated. What is called the "postmodern" (which ironically has been in fashion, that is, "in mode") is not the superation of modernity, but the demonstration of its limits. In theological terms what modernity has pursued is the dream of a prelapsarian language, an Esperanto that would revert the representation of the fall into language that we find mythically expressed in the story of the Tower of Babel. Borges laments the unfulfilled desire of representing the unrepresentable presence in the midst of the wild profusion of all that in time and space exists. The postmodern flags the conscience that what we inscribe or enunciate replicates the finite structure of our experience of reality. Against it militates our desire to yoke the knowledge of the eternal (or positive theology) with our "scientific" reasoning and conquer the edges and limits of our noetic enterprise. In other words we want to cover the gap and expel the gods that inhabit it. But these gods of the gap are resilient. If one gap is covered many others will be open because that is the nature of our own way or reasoning. It is because of these gaps that theology thrives as a marginal discourse, a discourse still possible even after the last things, even when it pretends to be a discourse about continuities, knowledge, systems that are adapted to an acceptable regime of truth. This happens even with religious fundamentalisms, which are to science what a computer operational system is to another (say, Microsoft or Apple). They

---

9   Jorge Luis Borges, *El Aleph (Buenos Aires: Emecé, 1974)*, 174.

don't share the same platform, but they presuppose the very same binary system of digital modern computers. What I am suggesting is something different. It is something that is beyond the limit of any platform and the binary system on which they rely, to stay with the analogy.

What has been called science is what has made the exercise of knowledge also to be an exercise of power. Richard Rorty, the North American neo-pragmatist, said once that "worries about 'cognitive status' and 'objectivity' are characteristic of a secularized society in which the scientist replaces the priest. The scientist is now seen as the person who keeps humanity in touch with something beyond itself."[10] The comment is interesting because it also points to the difference between the so-called human sciences and hard sciences given that the latter are the ones that point to something beyond the human reality. But it is necessary to partially correct Rorty's statement. What is true in it is that science is indeed able to underscore the division between the subject and the "external" nature through the practice of inscription, the scientist thus becoming the mediator between the two poles. But the word "priest" in Rorty's text can at most be taken as a figure of speech for it is an improper analogy. In the religious sense of the term, the priest is the one who situates herself between the irreducible separation of the infinite and the finite, while the scientist tries to shorten the gap between the indefinite and the definition, between presence and representation.

"The only way to define the world," observed Georges Bataille with irony, "is to reduce it to our measurements and then, with laughter, to discover that it is beyond our measurings."[11] This is the laughter that distinguishes the priest from the scientist. The latter despises the beyond and believes in sequestering the world into inscription. The scientist is always taciturn. Laughter is a concession to madness when the very limits and borders of the canons of rationality run into the undefined, resiliently defying its reduction to inscription. What lies outside, beyond the limits of rationality, does not inherit the kingdom of knowledge. Bataille's laughter is that which moves us from the picture to the frame, from the quotidian to the *eschaton*.

Science, however, is neither intrinsically demonic and perverse, nor inherently virtuous and benevolent, but it is always genuinely linked to power in both senses: the obvious one, of having control over the object

---

10 Richard Rorty, *Objectivity, Relativism, and Truth: Philosophical Papers: Volume I.* (Cambridge: Cambridge Univ Press, 1991), 35.
11 George Bataille, *The Impossible* (San Francisco: City Lights Books, 1991), 99.

under investigation, and also the one that pertains to the conditions by which objects can be investigated at all. Power is not only to be located in the technological result of the use of dispositives, but in the very constitutions of science itself. With this observation I shift the discussion from judging science and technology for what they produce and bring to the fore the limits, the *eschata,* that science creates to determine what fits and what does not into the canons of rationality and inscription. The obvious ones are celebrated as victories: Why has chemistry replaced alchemy, and astronomy supplanted astrology? The answer is that the former has inscriptional consistency that the latter does not. But when we enter into human psychology and try to establish with the same inscriptional precision the difference between an apparition and an actual event, dream and reality, hope and calamity, the divide is infinitely expanded and at the same time blurred.

Representations

This is the basic reason for me to postulate that eschatology is a teaching of Christian theology that is both subversively apocalyptic and equally subversively Gnostic. Subversively apocalyptic because it renders the Armageddon immanent, and subversively Gnostic because it is about the wisdom of the limits of knowledge itself. Figuratively speaking it is a proto-theology (or *theologia prima*) that just tells us that epistemologically the frame has a picture and the picture has a frame. In the Lutheran jargon that Peters often sponsors, it is the difference between the God revealed and preached, and the unpreached God who is hidden, more precisely, the stance in between the two.

How is this eschatological feature to be rendered in day-to-day experience? A suggestive answer is offered by Anthony Giddens with his notion of "sequestered experiences."[12] He points out institutional contexts of everyday life that mimic what science does with representation and language.[13] Through internalized referential systems of knowledge and power (what can or cannot be said) we separate everyday life from disturbing issues as infirmity, madness, criminality, death, and sexuality. This sequestering spares us from problematizing these issues as part of our quotidian experience because they raise the level of anxiety. In other words, these issues raise the level of *angst* and cause discomfort because

---

12 Anthony Giddens, *Modernity and Self-Identity: Self and Society in the Late Modern Age* (Stanford: Stanford Univ Press, 1991), 144–80.
13 Ibid., 155–56.

they interfere into the accepted referential systems that have to deal with power and knowledge. They produce the inconvenient laughter of Bataille. This laughter is a disruption of the order of things exactly at the point in which they break down. Laughter and panic are twin offspring of eschatological experiences.

Foucault has a similar approach to the *eschaton* when he refers to the *"insurrection of subjugated knowledges . . . beneath the required level of cognition and scientificity . . . through [which] criticism performs its work."*[14] In his list of such "knowledges" ajar he includes the psychiatric patient, the infirm, the delinquent, and others that he leaves undefined. However Foucault goes a step further than Giddens in calling for an "anti-sciences."[15]

> It is not that they [anti-sciences] are concerned to deny knowledge or that they esteem the virtues...that escapes encapsulation in knowledge....We are concerned, rather with the insurrection of knowledges that are opposed primarily not to the contents, methods, or concepts of science, but to the effect of the centralizing powers which are linked to the institution and functioning of an organized scientific discourse within a society such as ours.[16]

Instead of an irrationalist appeal, Foucault defends "the union of erudite knowledge and local memories which allow us to establish a historical knowledge of struggles and to make use of this knowledge tactically today."[17]

What is obvious in both lists of sequestered or subjugated experiences is the absence of religious experiences, rites and myths, even though they may be included in Foucault's local memories with considerable erudition or internal referenciality in Giddens. In a more general outlook of what happened to theology during the time in which the scientific discourse of modernity formed itself, it is arguable that theology has taken the characteristics of an anti-science, even as it has struggled hard to hide the fact that it has been increasingly marginalized from the "institution and functioning of an organized scientific discourse."

---

14 Michel Foucault, *Power/Knowledge: Selected Interviews and Other Writings: 1972-1977*, Colin Gordon, ed. (New York: Pantheon Books, 1980), 81–82.
15 Ibid., 83.
16 Ibid., 84.
17 Ibid., 83. This union of local memories and erudition is what Foucault names "genealogy," a less hyperbolic expression than "anti-science." See *The Foucault Reader*, Paul Rabinow, ed. (New York, Pantheon, 1984), 76–97.

Modern science, or rationality, created a paradox: in attempting to comprehend the extended object in its discourse, it created or invented this object pretending it to be more really present in its concept or its representation, the more absent it is in reality itself. In doing so, this form of rationality becomes self-referential. In other words, in proposing the re-presentation to be the real thing it justifies itself insofar as it is able to build allegiances in the scientific community. The only issue is whether this paradox is made explicit or not. It is exactly the task of criticism to make explicit the gap between presence and the scientific *re-presentation*.

Theology on the other hand is a form of knowledge that presupposes the paradox and its task is to make it explicit. It is in this sense, at the surface level of the representational practice that theology works differently than the hegemonic scientific inscription. The latter works with the practice of representation in two different but often confused levels. The objective reality not at hand is represented as in a picture. This is the most acclaimed level of representation. Diagrams, equations, maps are examples of how the "absent" object is (re-) presented (in the sense of *Darstellung*). But there is also a second sense of representation that must be distinguished from the first. It is representation in the sense of proxy, as in the political and judicial sense of representation (*Vertretung*). This is not so obvious, but much of the scientific work is spent in recruiting faithful allies in order to "thicken" a research program, defending a theory, or developing a hypothesis for which subsidies and grants must be amassed in order to make it viable. Much of the scientific work is spent on developing projects that in order to be subsidized depend on the astuteness in expounding this second sense of representation. It is important to acknowledge this difference. But what they have in common as "representation" is that they both postulate and defend something that is in fact not present.

Religion, however, presents a different story even when theology borrows the two types of representation (as described above) from the established sciences. It is about eschatological "presence," a word loaded with theological meaning. Etymologically it comes from the Latin *prae-esse*, that which is by or in the adjacency of essence. In Greek we have a word with the same etymology that abounds in the New Testament: *parousia* from *para-ousia*. In theology this word has often been associated with the "second" coming or advent of Christ. Even if in the New

Testament in some passages it alludes to Christ being present again, the expression *deutera parousia* ("second coming") never occurs. The expression comes from the second century (with Justin the Apologist) who uses it to point to a second visitation, or a second presence, or literally a representation. Since then theology has learned to dodge presence and settle for its representation, postponing presence and having it only proleptically anticipated. But *parousia* is about presence, about a present, a gift, grace.

Eschatology, or the Story of the Gap

I come back to my original quest: eschatology insofar as it pertains to the limits of epistemic domains or knowledges. Obviously I am stepping into the territory surveyed and mined uniquely by Ted Peters. In more than one way it is his signature *locus*. For our theologian it is about the "Aleph" of Borges that comes in a fragment of time, a *kairos*, that exposes us to presence, the unexpected *parousia*.

But where is real presence? It is anticipatory, proleptic presence as in the signing of a contract, or writing a testament. One anticipates the aim the contract or the testament point to, but one does not have it yet. Meanwhile, as time unfolds, one has to ponder and negotiate how to keep business going while presence is delayed and only rhetorically available by prolepsis. But the real thing, the *eschaton* as presence is precisely there in the unavailing and otiose gaps that don't compute, do not deny leisure, the *otium*, that don't engage in negotiation (*nec-otium*). The point is that presence is in the adjacency of that which escapes utility; it plays, laughs, cries. Presence is vagabond; it is an idle rogue; it is to play without purpose just for the sake of playing, as children do or that which makes us a child. The references to children in the sayings of Jesus as those able to *receive* the gift, the Kingdom (e.g., Mark 10:13; Matthew 18:3) make explicit this connection between being otiose and the gift. Children, Rudolf Bultmann once observed, know how to receive a gift without negotiating; therefore, theirs is the Kingdom. Bultmann's observation is pertinent for while so many studies (from Marcel Mauss to Jacques Derrida) about the gift and its impossibility have been issued and reissued, they still operate with the accepted canons of rationality that control the *oeconomia*. But it is in the moment this rationality breaks down that the gift insurges as a "happy exchange," nothing for all, all for nothing, as Luther expressed what presence meant. That can be told as stories, but it cannot be registered as history for they defy the protocols and attires of what is admitted into the domain of knowledge. Presence, once more, is only when it breaks through as a gift that only a child or a vagabond knows how to receive.

In his book *Works of Love*, Søren Kierkegaard surmises that the purest gesture of love, because it escapes the rules of exchange, is the one done for someone who has passed away, for there is no possibility of an exchange, a negotiation. It is an eschatological gesture; it is otiose. But we need to change the perspective from that of the Dane. It is about looking at the gift from the "point of view" of the receiver, the one who is dead. In other words, one needs to be "dead," radically otiose, to receive a gift. This is the eschatological event, when all is received and not even an embrace can be given in return—for the hands have been nailed into a pathetic, receptive gesture.

Bertold Brecht has a parable about the Buddha. The Buddha has a crowd by him who keep asking him about Nirvana—what it looks like, how does it feel being there, and so forth. The Buddha did not offer any answer to the inquiring curious folk. Later when the crowd was gone his closest disciples asked him why he had not given any answers to the ones who inquired him about Nirvana. The Buddha looked with care to them and told them: "On one occasion I was going on my way, and I passed a house that was burning. I noticed that many inhabitants were still inside. I came to the doorstep and cried out for them to leave the house. Some came to the window and with flames up to their eyebrows were asking me: How is it outside? Is it windy? Is it cold? Is it raining? Then in silence I went my way. These people deserve to burn."[18] The *eschaton* was announcing itself by the door, but negotiation prevented a child-like attitude of just leaving the house and its rules (*oikonomia*) behind.

---

18 Bertold Brecht, *Gedichte und Lieder,* Peter Suhrkamp, ed. (Berlin: Suhrkamp, n.d.), 135f.

A Retroactive Response to Retroactive Ontology

Ted Peters

That my colleagues would deem my theological program worthy of avouchment and analysis evokes in me surprise, honor, and gratitude. My appreciation for this collegial cooperation and fraternity is heartfelt; yet, I am even more deeply moved by the earnestness and thoroughness of the scholarly engagement. This *Festschrift* provides a gridiron, so to speak, on which to scrimmage over the viability of proleptic eschatology.

If I were to wear a hat, I would take it off in respect to Carol Jacobson and Adam Pryor. I can recall them when just beginning their doctorates and now they have matured into ranking scholars, teachers, and leaders. Their stature as well as their zeal does me honor. I am genuinely thankful for what they and this volume's authors have brought forth.

In this response to the *Festschrift's* academic essays, I need to assess criticisms and emendations to the backbone of my theological worldview, namely, retroactive ontology. The Christian gospel, I believe, includes God's promise of a new creation that will transform the present creation, and it is the fulfillment of this promise that grounds reality. The reality and meaning of the present moment is dependent upon its place in God's ultimate future. Now, I need to test this hypothesis. Is it exegetically sound? Is it coherent? Is it outmatched by a more comprehensive construction? Is it explanatorily adequate?

What Is Retroactive Ontology?

The cardinal insight of *retroactive ontology* is that our being is determined by and defined by, our future. The transformed reality promised by God is the ground for all other reality that anticipates it. One important implication is this: creation is contingent on transformation. The meaning and even being of the past is contingent on its future. God's final future redefines—actually defines—all that has gone before. Who we are now is dependent on who we will be at that final future, at omega.

Contrary to what passes for common sense, I contend that God creates from the future, not from the past. Common sense suggests that causes belong to the past and effects belong to the present. As we look at the car sitting in our driveway, we recognize that it was manufactured. Should we investigate, we could find out where and when in time that car came into existence. Before that time, there was no car. The engineering, manufacturing, and distribution are causes, while the car sitting in our driveway is the effect. So, common sense would place the creation of all present things in the past. What we see daily is the result of past creativity.

Common sense places the cause in the past and the effect in the present. When we think of the creation of the world, then, we look to the past. We look to the *arche*, to the beginning, to the point of origin. We look backwards to alpha. What we find back at alpha we call *genesis*. Common sense places creation at genesis.

But I ask us to look once again, a bit more closely. Just what does it mean to be? What does it mean to have existence? Can we exist without a future? No. Without a future, we are not. Without a minimal future such as the next moment, the car in the driveway would not exist in the present. If someone takes away our future, we drop from existence into non-existence. This is what death is, the loss of our future.

To be is to have a future. If this is the case, then the way God gives being is to give a future. Each moment, God gives the cosmos the next moment. God is moment by moment giving to all corporeality its future. Without this future-giving on the part of God, all of our world would freeze up and cease. God "gives life to the dead and calls into existence the things that do not exist" (NRS, Romans 4:17b). God's calling us into existence is a moment by moment activity, an ongoing or continuing form of divine action.

Let us return for a moment to alpha, the moment our cosmos originated. Perhaps we could say this: *the first thing God did for the cosmos was to give it a future.* By calling it from nothing into something, God bestowed a future that set reality on the course of historical becoming. By *creation*, we refer to God's gracious gift of futurity. And moment by moment with unceasing faithfulness God continues to bestow a future.

The concept of retroactive ontology includes a dynamic relationship between God the future-giver and the creation which receives this gift. This dynamic interaction includes another important element, namely, openness. By this I mean: openness to what is new. This means that God's future-giving is both positive and negative. It is positive in that God is the ground of being, the one who protects what exists now from ceasing to be. God's work is negative, as well, in that by giving a new future God releases the present from the grip of the past. Contrary to common sense, past causes do not hold the present moment in the grip of total determinism. The present moment is open to change, open to what is new. This is because God liberates the present from the oppression of the past. New things can happen because God prevents the past from over determining the present.

Back to that car in our driveway. Such cars did not exist back at the Big Bang. They did not exist when the Declaration of Independence was signed in 1776. The very concept of an automobile is new. And the specific car in our driveway is the product of specific human creativity: engineering, manufacturing, and the institutions that deliver it. If the ancient past were totally determinate, then new things could not come into existence. By relieving the present moment from the vice grip of past causes, God liberates each moment for creaturely creativity and the advent of new things. God did not design the car, but God made an opening in being that could be filled by human creativity. This liberation from the complete determination of the past is what God offers our creation each and every moment. God is a future-giver.

Let's go back again to the very beginning. Whether we call it *genesis* or *Big Bang* or *alpha*, God provided nascent reality with an open future. Since then, God has continued this double relationship to the created order, negatively releasing the grip of the past while positively offering being an openness to a future replete with new possibilities. Yes, past causes may set the parameters that give specific form to the finitude of each present moment. Still, within these parameters, God opens up an array of potentials that await actualization. The way creatures within the world behave determines which potentials become actualized.

According to retroactive ontology, God's future-giving is what makes both contingency and freedom possible. The course of natural events is subject to contingency—that is, events in nature are not predictable. Despite the determinism of the laws of nature, natural history does not operate like a machine. New and unpredictable events happen. Then, when we turn to the course of human events, we take a giant step beyond contingency. Human actions are not predictable; this is because they are freely determined. The human situation adds a subjective self that envisions the array of potentials and then makes a conscious decision to actualize some and not others. The openness of the future is the condition that makes freedom possible.

Let me add a distinction. We should distinguish between the proximate and ultimate futures. What we have just described is the proximate future, the effect on the present moment of God's future-giving. In addition, God offers an ultimate future. The ultimate future is omega. God promises a final future, a fulfilling future, a moment when all reality will attain its full quality. At omega, the now-becoming creation will be complete.

Actually, this distinction between the proximate and ultimate futures is a matter of perspective. They are not ontologically separate. The proximate and ultimate futures are not separated into a short time and a long time. Rather, both are almost present, almost but not quite fully here now. Both are as close to us as is the next moment. It is God's vision of the ultimate future that draws the present moment out of the nonbeing of the past toward the fullness of omega being. Omega, to this point in history, has allowed and encouraged each moment to engage freely in self-definition and self-actualization. The ultimacy of God's destiny is only a moment away, practically present. In the twinkling of an eye, it could arrive in its fullness.

It is God's promise that all things will be transformed at omega. If this is our expectation, then just what is the ontological status of all things right now? Whatever things are now, they will not remain as they are. Perhaps we can say that nothing in our present reality has attained its final state. Nothing has attained its final definition. Everything is subject to routine process and modification, and everything is subject to total redefinition at the coming of omega. Omega, then, becomes that which determines reality, that which retroactively defines who we are and what all things are. We can expect omega to provide transformation, salvation, and eternal definition. The meaning of our existence and self-understanding today is contingent on our transformation in the future. Our final future will retroactively transform who we are today. It will determine who we had been as we anticipated who we would become.

Carol Jacobson: Can Creaturely Freedom Everlastingly Frustrate God?

I like the way Carol Jacobson outlines the overlap between my own view of retroactive ontology with the principal concerns taken up by the open theists. In her *Festschrift* chapter, "Will God Save the World or Not? Prolepsis, Open Theism, and the World's Future," Jacobson shows how Clark Pinnock develops "a version of historic free will theism which posits God as granting to human beings significant freedom to cooperate with or to resist the will of God for their lives."[1] Central to open theism or openview theism is the emphasis on human freedom, even if that freedom retards and frustrates God's will. God has self-restricted, so to speak, in order to make room for the self-defining accomplishments of human free action. God's omnipotence is compromised, so to speak, by a divine self-constriction that makes room for human potency. One implication, which open theists themselves draw out, is that God cannot exercise omniscience regarding future events. Because future events are contingent upon creaturely freedom, they cannot be known in advance by God. In sum, open theists offer an ontology according to which creaturely contingency and freedom trump divine action.

As one might expect, I sense a partial kinship between my own position and that proffered by open theists. Like process theologians, I along with open theists affirm that God can know everything that can be known, but God cannot know which creaturely potentials will be actualized before the actualization takes place. God can know the Godself—God can know his own character and his own promise to establish a new creation and redeem all reality—but as divine self-knowledge it differs from predicting an unknowable creaturely future. God knows that eschatological fulfillment of the divine promise is coming in the future, but God knows this not as a soothsayer but as one who has self-confidence in his own promise keeping. My position overlaps in part with that of open theists and process theologians on this point: the future yet to be known is an as yet undetermined future.

As Jacobson astutely points out, the priority given to creaturely freedom by the open theists undermines their own ability to affirm an eschatological consummation. Like process theology, open theism undercuts God's capacity to fulfill the divine will for creation. As

---

1 Clark H. Pinnock, "Open Theism: An Answer to My Critics," *Dialog: A Journal of Theology* 44, no. 3 (Fall 2005): 237.

non-compatibilists, open theists believe human freedom and divine power are in competition [incompatible], and human freedom could win in this contest. God may find the divine self everlastingly frustrated by a creation that stubbornly refuses to cooperate.

Jacobson accurately shows how my position differs. I apply downward causation—downward causation in the form of whole-part causation—to resolve the delicate dialectic between divine power and creaturely freedom. God's transformative power exerted as whole-part causation respects creaturely actualization of potential; yet, God redefines creaturely action by divinely defining the more inclusive context. The most inclusive context is the eschatological kingdom of God, the new creation. Whereas, according to Carol, "open theists give ontological priority to exercising freedom in the life lived forwards," I give priority to a retroactively effective ontology. I give ontological priority to omega applied to the whole of reality and show how this provides for both daily human freedom as well as God's eschatological fulfillment.

Will God save the world or not? For open theism, Jacobson surmises the answer must be "Perhaps." For me, in contrast, I answer with an enthusiastic "Yes!" It appears to me that Jacobson has this just right.

Robert John Russell: Is Nature Open at All Levels of Complexity?

One of the salient differences between my own approach to divine action and that of Bob Russell is this: my approach relies primarily on top-down causation, whereas Russell adds bottom-up causation. That is, for Russell, God's action impacts sub-atomic activity, and, because atoms are everywhere, God's providential action impacts nature everywhere. So, it does not surprise me that in his *Festschrift* chapter, "Hummingbirds Make Stars Possible: Exploring and Celebrating Ted Peters' *Retroactive Ontology*," Russell would pose the challenging question: how can we conceive of ontological indeterminism at many or even all levels of complexity?

It might appear that my reliance upon top-down causation—more precisely, whole-part causation beginning with the eschatological omega as the whole that retroactively defines all parts through all time—has completely abandoned past and present nature to efficient causation. With the politesse of the classic "gentleman and scholar," Russell courteously tenders a proposal to "appreciate and extend Peters' position in a creative way."

Before addressing directly Russell's proposed emendation, let me remind the reader of Russell's own position. Here's the back story, so to speak. Russell affectionately calls his position QM-NIODA, an acronym for *non-interventionist objective divine action,* in this case, at the subatomic level where *quantum mechanics* prevails.² Within the framework of the indeterminist interpretation of quantum mechanics, Russell can describe how God acts in a deterministic fashion such that this deterministic action avoids any intervention that would conflict with a law of nature. If nature is already indeterminate, then God's action can be non-interventionist and still be considered action. In my judgment, this is the most ingenious insight to arise out of the last half century of interaction between theologians and scientists. Russell has provided an intelligible model that accounts for ubiquitous divine action in the natural world that avoids any breaking of identified natural laws. In addition, we note that it is a bottom-up approach to God's action in the created world.

With this as the back story, let's now turn to Russell's proposal here in this *Festschrift*. His proposed emendation to my retroactive ontology sets up the issue this way: "there is only one tomorrow that God wants, so God ensures that the possibility that that tomorrow is at least one of several possibilities today which include that future state, tomorrow, in order that it becomes the actual future." Note what Russell wants to account for, namely, divine determination within the indeterminate world. Russell wants me to account for divine determination of the promised eschatological new creation. Let me offer an observation: what Russell wants applies to what I have dubbed the ultimate future. It does not apply to the proximate future.

When it comes to the proximate future, the theory of retroactive ontology accounts for the indeterminism we experience in nature; it accounts for contingency and freedom. I submit that it is God's liberating action that frees the present moment from the oppressive grip of past efficient causes. It is God's action that makes indeterminism possible. Russell's agenda, in contrast, presupposes the framework of an already existing indeterminism. With QM-NIODA, what Russell wishes to account for is God's action within a world already replete with contingency and freedom. Whereas Russell accounts for God's action within an already indeterministic world, I account for God's action to bring about this indeterministic world. In both cases, we are addressing the proximate future.

---

2 Robert John Russell, *Cosmology from Alpha to Omega: The Creative Mutual Interaction of Theology and Science* (Minneapolis: Fortress Press, 2008), 19.

When it comes to the ultimate future—the eschatological consummation and fulfillment of creation's destiny in the New Creation—Russell's proposal could be illuminating. Without stressing it, he is developing here the concept of prolepsis. He comes close to saying: God's new creation cannot come to pass unless the possibility for new creation was already present within the old creation, within the present creation. To be present ahead of time is what we dub *prolepsis,* although in this case Russell uses *possibility.* The difference is that *possibility* has to do with open potential, whereas *prolepsis* refers to a pre-actualization of the potential in anticipation of the final actualization. However, this distinction between possibility and prolepsis need not divert us from dealing with Russell's focus here, namely, God must act now to cultivate a potential that can be actualized later.

I must pause to consider this. Both Russell and I have agreed that the Easter resurrection of Jesus Christ provides us with a prolepsis, a pre-actualization in the person of Jesus of the eschatological new creation applied to the whole of creation. So, just what is Russell now recommending? Is he recommending that we add on the possibility for prolepsis prior to the prolepsis? For the prolepsis to become a pre-actualization, must the prolepsis already be the actualization of a prior potential? Could this be what he is recommending? Or, does the prolepsis itself constitute the possibility Russell is recommending? If the latter, it is already present within my model of retroactive ontology.

But, perhaps Russell is asking for more than a prolepsis in Christ. Perhaps he is asking for the presence in every physical moment of at least one possibility among others that counts as a prolepsis, that counts as an anticipation of God's new creation. If so, then I would need to ask: would such a present possibility result from a bottom-up determinative action by God? Does God determine possibility from bottom-up activity that eventually becomes actualized at the global or holistic level? Does God first create the potential for a redeemed creation and then actualize this potential?

I wonder if we should shave with Occam's razor here. That is, would it be simpler to say that what Russell is asking for is already accomplished in the Easter event as prolepsis? What would we gain by adding the pre-creation of a pre-possibility for the Easter event?

Jane Strohl and Kristin Johnston Largen: Should We Plant an Apple Tree in Hell?

According to her *Festschrift* essay, "Apples and the Apocalypse," Reformation historian Jane Strohl says the apple tree and the apocalypse represent two poles of the believer's life from the time of the fall through each successive chapter of God's story of salvation. On the one hand, in the face of the apocalypse, we might abandon this world to perdition and ready ourselves for the new life in the post-apocalyptic world. On the other hand, we might affirm our love for this passing world and let God be the one to determine what is preserved and what is canceled. The latter option is what Luther elected. "If I knew the world were going to end tomorrow, I would go out and plant an apple tree today." Now, we are not completely sure that Luther said this. Yet, avers Jane Strohl, even if it is not genuine Luther, it is *echt lutherisch*, true to Luther.

Beyond the apocalypse we expect to confront heaven and hell. But, will we actually get what we expect? In her *Festschrift* chapter, "Prolepsis and the Abolition of Hell: Why Hell Is Not Like Heaven," Kristin Johnston Largen, indefatigable editor-in-chief of *Dialog: A Journal of Theology*, argues for the abolition of hell. Yet, her argument *against* the existence of hell is not an argument *for* the doctrine of universal salvation, even though one might assume that the first logically implies the second. As Largen and Strohl both know, I find arguments within systematic theology that support this proposition: If hell exists, it will not exist forever. I draw this speculation from our combined commitments to God's omnipotence and God's grace: If our gracious God has the power to forgive and redeem, then finally all creatures will be redeemed. Or, if our gracious and omnipotent God desires the redemption of the entire creation, then universal salvation follows.

The problem as both Strohl and Largen acknowledge is that this is not exactly what the Bible says. "And the devil who had deceived them was thrown into the lake of fire and sulfur, where the beast and the false prophet were, and they will be tormented day and night forever and ever.... Then Death and Hades were thrown into the lake of fire" (Revelation 20:10, 14b). If the burning sulfur in the lake of fire is everlasting, then universal salvation seems precluded. If the burning lake metaphorically represents the destruction of evil, then universal salvation seems to be God's promise to us.

Despite the apocalyptic threat, we have faith that God's grace will ultimately prevail. Despite the apocalyptic warning, we believe the children of light will triumph over the children of darkness. Beyond the triumph, only light and salvation will remain in God's renewed creation. No burning sulfur. If this is what we believe, then I have a recommendation. I recommend we walk right into that lake of fire with our trowel, fertilizer, and a bucket of water. Right there, in the lake of fire, I recommend we plant an apple tree.

Vitor Westhelle: How Should We Think about Eschatology in Time and Space?

I had found my aisle seat on a United flight from Chicago to Sao Paulo. As the plane took off, I dozed. When awakened by the flight attendant delivering our first drink order, I noticed the dapper man sitting next to me had ordered a single malt Scotch, neat. After his first sip, he turned to me and posed a question, "Whom do you believe is the theologian that counts—I mean, really counts—in both North American and Latin American theology?"

I took a swig of my Coors Lite while considering a judicious answer. "Vitor Westhelle," I trumpeted. "To read Westhelle is to feast on savory style, exquisite exegesis, meaty metaphor, flavorful faith, sapid soteriology, and, of course, gustatory grace. This is why his international fan club has produced *Churrasco: A Theological Feast in Honor of Vitor Westhelle*."[3]

The gentleman next to me finished his Scotch in a single gulp.

Westhelle is one of the most conceptually creative among our theological colleagues; he shocks routine scholarship with post-colonial stun guns. When we focus on linear time and a consummate eschatology, argues Westhelle, we marginalize and render something invisible, namely, space. In particular, we render invisible the separate spaces of marginalized peoples. By turning our attention away from time and toward space, Westhelle says our gaze will suddenly include the separate territories where meaningful events happen in the lives of peoples left out of the picture drawn by linear history and a single encompassing eschatology. This sends my mind spinning. I ask: Is Westhelle talking about the ontology of time and space? Or, metaphorically, is he trying to draw our attention to the conceptual isolation that a dominant metanarrative

---

[3] Mary Philip, John Arthur Nunes, and Charles M. Collier, eds., *Churrasco: A Theological Feast in Honor of Vitor Westhelle* (Eugene, Oregon: Pickwick, 2013).

exacts on those who live within it? If the latter, then I must ask: does what passes as universal Christian eschatology actually present a Western European ideology, an exclusivist ideology? Just what is the shock Westhelle is prodding for?

My response to Vitor Westhelle has been to produce a classification (classifying is a disease afflicting systematic theologians). Imagine three boxes, each with its own eschatology: *linear eschatology, spatial eschatology*, and *beatitudinal eschatology*. I place Westhelle in the second box and myself in the third. But like a slinking cat, Westhelle crawls out of his box and into the linear one. "Time and space are relative to each other," he writes. "It has been the failure of Western theology to celebrate history and time dissociated from or even against space. If I run the risk of ideologizing space it is because I care about time, in the same way as those who ideologize time care about space."[4]

I thought I was comfortable in my box, until I read what Westhelle writes. "Peters' 'beatitudinal eschatology' is not a *tertium datur* as he suggests, but the reinstatement of a disembodied future in the Augustinian 'one-after-the-otherness of events in succession' only tamed by being proleptically enunciated."[5] Yes, I do think of beatitudinal eschatology as "proleptically enunciated." When we read one of Jesus' beatitudes—such as Matthew 5:7, "Blessed are the merciful, for they will receive mercy"—I think the word *prolepsis* helps to illuminate what this means. Westhelle counters by picking out the first of the beatitudes—Matthew 5:3, "Blessed are the poor in spirit, for theirs is the kingdom of heaven"—which is in the present tense. As if in a shoot out on the streets of Tombstone, Arizona, Vitor Westhelle and I fire Bible passages at one another. I'm wounded. Does the presence of the present in Matthew 5:3 eliminate prolepsis? Does it eliminate eschatology altogether?

Now, I'm feeling claustrophobic in my box. I wonder if I should slink over into the other two boxes. Or, instead of slinking, should I fire back with a question: Is Westhelle's spatial eschatology ontological or metaphorical? He answers: It is metaphor plus.

> The way space is used in my rendition of eschatology works in a literal sense of a geographical site with its borders, but also metonymically to denote materiality in general, and metaphorically to signify psychological and epistemological

---

4 Westhelle, 142-3.
5 Westhelle, 142.

domains.... Time, as *chronos*, can be expanded without limit only to find its completion in eternity itself as I think Peters would maintain. Yet space, as *topos*, literally or metaphorically, is broken by limits, borders, edges, and margins. What lies beyond these limits can indeed be proleptically and poetically envisaged, but most often cannot be anticipated.[6]

While time can be expanded, space can be broken. I think this is what Westhelle is saying. If the eschatological new creation that God has promised us includes healing as well as "completion," then I think this healing would include reconnecting those broken spaces. Redemption is holistic, both temporally and spatially. Temporal healing would be lost to abstraction unless it applies to the very spaces that belong to its history. On this count, I suddenly find myself in the spatial eschatology box.

Westhelle registers concern about the hegemony of established science over knowledge systems found in other spaces, ignored or subjugated spaces. He cites Michel Foucault who is on the lookout for the "*insurrection of subjugated knowledges . . .* beneath the required level of cognition and scientificity . . . through [which] criticism performs its work."[7] Does the linear eschatology box include in it the hegemonic metanarrative of modern science? If so, is this the reason Westhelle stuns us with a discharge from spatial eschatology?

Westhelle wants to shock us with a shot from the margins, and from religious insight as well. When referring to scientific rationality, he is frustrated by the fence dividing the finite from the infinite. "What lies outside, beyond the limits of rationality, does not inherit the kingdom of knowledge." What I would expect from Westhelle at this point is a bow in the direction of the neo-orthodox theologians—such as Karl Barth, Karl Rahner, Paul Tillich, Rudolph Bultmann—for whom the very revelation of God is the revelation of mystery. Whereas scientific reasoning turns mystery into knowledge, divine revelation turns knowledge into mystery. God reveals Godself as mysterious, infinitely mysterious, yet still present.

Mysterious yet present. Might we think of the present mystery proleptically? As an anticipation of what is to come yet in the future? "As time unfolds," writes Westhelle, "one has to ponder and negotiate how to keep business going while presence is delayed and only rhetorically available by

---

6   Westhelle, 150.
7   Michel Foucault, *Power/Knowledge: Selected Interviews and Other Writings: 1972-1977*, Colin Gordon, ed. (New York, Pantheon Books, 1980), 81–82.

prolepsis. But the real thing, the eschaton as presence is precisely there in the unavailing and otiose gaps that do not compute, do not deny leisure, the *otium*, that do not engage in negotiation (*nec-otium*). The point is that presence is in the adjacency of that which escapes utility; it plays, laughs, cries. Presence is vagabond, it is an idle rogue, it is to play without purpose just for the sake of playing, as children do or that which makes us a child."[8] Here the spaces are the gaps, the hiatuses, the disconnections. Today's gaps provide the spaces for anticipating tomorrow's linear future.

The merit of Westhelle's spatial eschatology is that it honors what is local, geographically or territorially discreet, separate, humble, and in need of respect and dignity. His moral motive here is to destabilize the metanarrative of linear eschatology. By taking time away and substituting space, linear eschatologists—if there is such a group—are left empty handed. They have lost their time because Westhelle has replaced it with his space. Due to a change in the recipe, Westhelle's eschatological desert will emit multiple tastes for multiple taste buds. More important than the conceptual change here is the moral shift, that is, drawing our attention to the *other* who had previously been marginalized. No longer is eschatology a metaphysical or conceptual matter; it is now a moral matter.

The moral dimension is what I find in the box with beatitudinal eschatology. What comes next? On the one hand, beatitudinal eschatology begins with universal history and a single eschatological fulfillment for all of creation. I must confess: it is a metanarrative. On the other hand, it treasures the purity of heart among the humble in their specific time and place. It is spatial, in Westhelle's sense of spatiality. Like the widow's mite, beatitudinal eschatology treasures the small while glorifying the magnificent.

Conclusion: Beatitudinal Eschatology

The beatitudinal version of proleptic eschatology begins by recognizing that God has promised an apocalyptic-scale transformation of the present creation into the new creation. Further, it recognizes that this transformation is cosmic in scope, embracing all creation of all time and all places. The eschatological event is not local only; it is universal and total and whole and complete. Still further, the time of the consummate *eschaton* is not located on the calendar. It is almost, but not quite fully, present. It is imminent without being consummate. The totality of transformation is as close to us right now as the next moment is. In fact, it is the next moment emitting power and grace and transformation into the present moment.

---

8 Westhelle, 150.

THEOLOGY, CULTURE, & THE CROSS

Justification, Self-Justification, and Forgiveness

Ted Peters on Sin and Its Overcoming

Derek R. Nelson

My first book begins with a dedication to three people, one of whom is Ted Peters. It reads, "May they know that when I think about sin, I think about them."[1] Now, that is supposed to be kind of funny, but it is not only a joke. Peters, in his subtle and yet expansive treatment of the doctrines of sin and grace, has in fact influenced me and countless others. One of his main achievements has been to help rescue the doctrine of sin from a kind of moralistic, legalistic navel-gazing and transform it into a form of analysis of human subjectivity that can actually improve people's lives here and now. There are implications for an understanding of sin and grace that transcend the here-and-now, of course. But what I wish to focus on in this essay is how Peters' theological interpretation of sin can actually enrich human life in its personal, social, and even political dimensions this side of heaven.

Theology is a humanistic enterprise, because its key element is *interpretation*. The humanities have been in decline in our colleges and universities for a long time, for a variety of factors. Our nation's emphasis on science and technology is one component, and a changing conception of higher education as being less like personal, human development and more like job training is another. But there are signs that the academy and the culture at large may be seeing the value of humanistic traditions, including theology, once again. Books like *Nudge: Improving*

---

1 Derek R. Nelson, *What's Wrong with Sin: Sin in Social and Individual Perspective from Schleiermacher to Theologies of Liberation* (New York: Continuum, 2009), vi.

Decisions in Health, Wealth, and Happiness[2] and *Thinking, Fast and Slow*[3] have become bestsellers by asserting that a richer understanding of human nature is necessary for the disciplines of economics and psychology to flourish. By extension, theorists like these are saying that economists and psychologists have too simplistic a view of human *desire*; therefore, their attempts at explaining the connections between desires and behaviors come up short. Could it be that theology could help here? Peters would loudly say, "Yes."

Theology, especially but certainly not limited to neo-orthodox theology and its rich legacy, can provide an analysis of human desire and human action that is richer than one finds in any other discipline. And one need not share its assumptions or even its conclusions to benefit from its analysis. This essay will proceed in three parts to try to show that this is the case. In the first part, I describe what Peters' basic position is on the *theological difference* that talking about sin makes for understanding human nature. In the second part, I present a précis of Peters' understanding of the overcoming of sin (though this is limited to the doctrine of justification). And in the third part, I revisit a classic (and now perhaps seemingly forgotten) text of one of Peters' teachers to show how this all might make a difference for contemporary life today: *Shantung Compound* by Langdon Gilkey.

Peters on Sin: Sin as Self-Justification and Scapegoating

Needing a twelve-step program only about half as much as some people, Peters follows a seven-step program in analyzing the concrete forms sin takes in human life. His book, *Sin: Radical Evil in Soul and Society*, argues that sin has its roots in anxiety, and then has six additional moments.[4] The person who is anxious, who experiences the world as threat, and who fears the undoing of his existence, consequently *disbelieves* the promises of God, and then replaces belief with *pride*. Unbelief denies God, and pride makes oneself into a god. When one thinks of oneself as the center of the universe, it follows that one thinks one should have whatever one wants. This is the next step: *concupiscence*. Our insatiable and disordered desires of concupiscent sin cannot be satisfied, because we

---

2   Richard H. Thaler and Cass R. Sunstein, *Nudge: Improving Decisions in Health, Wealth, and Happiness* (New York: Penguin, 2013).
3   Daniel Kahneman, *Thinking, Fast and Slow* (New York: Farrar, Strauss and Giroux, 2011).
4   Ted Peters, *Sin: Radical Evil in Soul and Society* (Grand Rapids: Wm. B. Eerdmans Publishing Co., 1994).

desire an infinite amount of a finite thing (pleasure, money, status, power, and so on).

The fact of the scarcity of the objects of our desires leads to their frustration. What happens when we want more power or more prestige, but there isn't enough to go around? Then comes the key point—the fulcrum—of Peters' doctrine of sin. We try to *justify ourselves while scapegoating others*. We tell ourselves a lie. "My needs must be met, and it is the fault of X that they aren't being met." We justify our own unrighteousness and blame someone else for it. We draw a line of rectitude in the sand, conveniently placing ourselves on the side of justice and X on the other side. Once the world is neatly divided into the righteous and unrighteous, we feel that we may do whatever we want to the unrighteous, and so the fifth step is *cruelty*. To decide who is righteous and who is not, placing oneself in the position of God, robbing God of God's divinity, and co-opting the power of divine symbols, is the last stage, *blasphemy*.

The reason that justifying oneself while scapegoating another is the centerpiece of this theory is because it is the most critical for the formation of the self. It is at that particular point, when I place myself on the right side of the line and my chosen scapegoat on the other that my self-righteous sense of who I am is cemented. If I can convince myself that it is the Republicans' fault that the country is going to pieces, then I will feel even more strongly like a Democrat. If I see that one neighbor is not doing his part to keep the sidewalk shoveled, I will know that I am a "good person" when I shovel my part of the walk. It feels good to feel right. It feels so good, in fact, that we will distort and misremember reality in virtually any imaginable way to make ourselves stand in the "right."

Psychologist Fred Luskin calls this phenomenon a *grievance story*.[5] We tend to assemble events from our memories into a narrative that supports our instinct that others are in the wrong and we are in the right. So when the evening news shows a photo of a crime suspect who looks a certain way, subconsciously we say, "That figures." Or, to go a bit deeper, we might say, "Oh, great. That is going to confirm the stereotypes of a lot of biased, bigoted people out there. Thank goodness I'm so enlightened that I don't do that kind of thing." Either way, we are assembling a storyline in our minds that puts others at fault and makes us right. Not only does this make forgiveness difficult (which is Luskin's main point),

---

5 Fred Luskin, *Forgive for Good: A Proven Prescription for Health and Happiness* (San Francisco: Harper, 2002), especially 33–41.

this makes our sense of self both rigid and unyielding. It threatens to make our sinful self the only self we have, by co-opting our memories and shaping the script by which we live our lives.

Research on memory from many neuroscientists suggests that the act of remembering is not merely the retrieval of some static "thing" that is somehow "in there" in the mind. It is also a process of *reconstruction*. We tend to believe that our identities are stable and so think that when we tell a story we are simply taking objects from some dark corner of our mind and shedding light on them. But psychologist Charles Fernyhough, in his book *Pieces of Light*, insists that viewing memories as physical things is misleading. "Memories are not possessions that you either have or do not have. They are mental constructions, created in the present moment, according to the demands of the present moment."[6]

Memories are therefore not any more stable than the selfhood of the person remembering them. A memory is not like a favorite decoration we take out of the closet on holidays. Instead, as Fernyhough puts it, "a memory is more like a *habit*, a process of constructing something from its parts, in similar but subtly changing ways each time."[7] The fragmentary threads that our memories weave and reweave are located in our bodies and in the stories and practices that communities of people have shared over time.

This is another way of putting an issue that has been called by another of Peters' mentors, Paul Ricoeur, the problem of the "narrative self."[8] We literally *become* the stories we tell about ourselves and our world.[9] If I remember one event from my past over and over again, and I tell the story as though I was the victim of another's evil deed, then eventually it does not matter what the truth about that remembered incident is: I have made myself the victim by the power of my memory.

So when you consider the fact that human action stems from human identity, and human identity comes, in large part, from the stories humans tell about themselves and their world, Peters' identification of

---

6 Charles Fernyhough, *Pieces of Light: How the New Science of Memory Illuminates the Stories We Tell about Our Pasts* (New York: Harper, 2013), 6.

7 Ibid., 7.

8 Paul Ricoeur, *Oneself as Another*, Kathleen Blamey, trans. (Chicago: University of Chicago Press, 1992), 113–68.

9 Ted Peters and I, along with our colleague Joshua M. Moritz, have reflected on the intersection between theology and one's life story in our book, *Theologians in Their Own Words* (Minneapolis: Fortress, 2013).

self-justification and scapegoating as the centerpiece of sin takes on special significance. In experiencing other people and new situations, I bring to my experience ready-made categories by which I can draw lines in the sand. I can incorporate each new person into my old constructions. I can say, "Oh, he's just like the rest of them." Or, "If only everyone else were more like me...."

The construction of the self, then, is radically and fearfully open to the influence of other, already-sinfully-constructed selves. This is a version of a doctrine of original sin. Surrounded by self-justifying scapegoaters, we learn habits of self-justifying scapegoating. It feels "natural" to us, despite the fact, known only to faith, that sin is profoundly unnatural.

One question that haunts Peters' work here, and that remains still in need of an answer, I think, is the way this fits into an evolutionary framework. Peters co-directed a multi-year, interdisciplinary investigation called "Theodicy, Evolution and Genocide," in which I was pleased to participate.[10] The project addressed a worry. That worry can be stated something like this. If evolution favors those genes that survive from one generation to the next, and an eradication of some kinds of genes (a genocide) means that violence might be evolutionarily favorable, then if God in some sense directs natural history, is not God therefore somehow responsible for genocide?

Put another way, there seems to be a kind of conflation of so-called "natural evil" and "moral evil," whereas the grand theological tradition has wanted to distinguish between the two.[11] Human subjectivity is shaped by our place in the long history of the natural world, including evolutionary history. And yet human sin, as I understand it, is qualitatively different from anything else in the natural world. Human beings act counter to their created nature, not in accord with their *telos*, in a way that nothing else in the world does.[12] And so it seems that greater care is needed in explaining what it is about sin that has roots in evo-

---

10 The main publication of this project is Gaymon Bennett, Martinez J. Hewlett, Ted Peters, and Robert John Russell, eds., *The Evolution of Evil* (Göttingen: Vandenhoeck and Ruprecht, 2008).
11 The distinction may have some value, but I see problems with it. If human economic activity changes global weather patterns, is the suffering that stems from subsequent hurricanes the result of "natural" or "moral" evil? The overlap is so significant as to render the distinction artificial. Perhaps the same is true with evil when viewed from an evolutionary perspective.
12 The *locus classicus* here is Holmes Rolston, III, "Does Nature Need to Be Redeemed?" in *Zygon* 29 (1994), 205–29.

lutionary history, but is not reducible to or explainable in terms of that history.[13]

This brief reservation aside, I hope it is clear that Peters' development of the doctrine of sin has great value in helping contemporary people (not just Christians!) interpret the human condition. His writings are peppered with evocative anecdotes from personal life that take on much greater depth when analyzed with the lens of a doctrine of sin. Readers are invited to understand their own lives better by seeing the world through a theologian's lens for a time. After their encounter with the doctrine of sin, they may even be pushed toward a hope for grace.

Peters on Grace: God's Justifying Word and Faithful, Bold Sinning

Peters' understanding of sin is deeply indebted to the work of Rene Girard. Girard is Roman Catholic but writes not from the perspective of theology, but rather from his longstanding fascination with the great texts of ancient mythology and modern literature. In an expansive oeuvre, Girard finds *imitative desire*, or *mimesis*, to be at the core of human life and great writings about human life. We desire things according to the desire of another, Girard says. I want the latest fashion because I see that others want it. I am not sure that I want to buy a particular house until I learn that someone else has put in an offer on it, and then I have to have it for myself. The tension that comes from the scarcity of available goods is "solved" (disastrously and temporarily) by identifying a scapegoat.

Girard's work has been rightly hailed by people from all different disciplines, from sociology to philosophy to biology. There is even a website for preachers that interprets the texts of the revised common lectionary from a Girardian point of view.[14] Yet one thing has always seemed dissatisfying about Girard's work, acknowledged even by those theologians who use Girardian analysis in their writings on sin.[15] There is a kind of

---

13 Peters has raised questions along these lines in publications like "Evolution and Evil" in *The Evolution of Evil*, 19–52, and in Ted Peters and Martinez Hewlett, *Evolution from Creation to New Creation* (Nashville: Abingdon, 2003), 115–82.
14 www.girardianlectionary.net
15 Besides Ted Peters, the two theologians who have most successfully placed Girard in the contemporary theological discussions of sin are James Alison, especially in *Raising Abel: The Recovery of the Eschatological Imagination* (London: SCM, 1996) and *The Joy of Being Wrong: Original Sin through Easter Eyes* (New York: Crossroad, 1998), and Gil Bailie, *Violence Unveiled: Humanity at the Crossroads* (New York: Crossroad, 1996).

latent gnosticism that lurks behind Girard's assumptions about human behavior. Girard seems to think that once people realize that they cope with their frustrated mimetic desires by scapegoating innocent victims, they will stop doing so. That is, the knowledge of their true intentions is so compelling that it will "save" them from their sin. Now, neither Girard nor his students, Gil Bailie, James Alison, or S. Mark Heim, would ever claim such a thing forthrightly.[16] Yet there lingers a sense for me when reading these works that it is not enough simply to *know* that one is in need of salvation. One needs to be saved, *extra nos*, from the situation of sin and self-justification.

Here Peters' work on the doctrine of justification comes into play. Unlike Heim, Bailie, and Alison, Peters pairs his understanding of sin-as-self-justification with a rich notion of divine grace, and faith, therein, that can actually speak to the depths of sin. Sin is bad enough that we cannot save ourselves from it. We need another. We need Jesus. In his book *Sin Boldly!* Peters provides the sequel to his work on sin and the need for justification from without.[17] Again he works with a multi-step framework, but the steps do not correlate with the stages of sin. In *Sin Boldly!* Peters argues that: 1) faith responds to God's Word; 2) faith recognizes that God is gracious; 3) faith believes; 4) faith trusts; 5) faith experiences the risen Jesus Christ dwelling in one's soul; 6) faith sins boldly in love; and finally, 7) faith seeks understanding.

It would be a delight to engage all seven of those steps, but I cannot do so here. What I wish to focus on especially is the step that seems to me to be the most needful one for our culture to hear, the one that speaks most powerfully to all people today, not just Christians. And that is the sixth step, "Faith sins boldly in love."

Of course, Peters takes this phrase "sin boldly" from Martin Luther's letter to Philip Melanchthon of August 1, 1521.[18] Melanchthon was being overly scrupulous with excessive hand-wringing. He worried too much about his paltry sins and therefore was too timid in taking on the great tasks that fell to him while Luther was imprisoned in Wartburg

---

16 William C. Placher was one of the few theologians to notice this tendency in the Girardian camp. See his review of S. Mark Heim's book, *Saved from Sacrifice: A Theology of the Cross*, in the article, "Why the Cross?" in *Christian Century*, December 12, 2006, 39.
17 Ted Peters, *Sin Boldly! Justifying Faith for Fragile Souls and Broken Souls* (Minneapolis: Fortress, 2015).
18 The Latin is *pecca fortiter*, which might be better translated "sin bravely," i.e., with fortitude. The emphasis is on courage, not brashness. LW 48:281-2.

Castle. To jar his friend from his fence-sitting, Luther had to re-orient Melanchthon's thinking about sin. Allow me to grossly over-simplify a complicated theological history. The theology of the later Middle Ages tended to say that certain kinds of acts, performed in certain ways with certain motives, were sinful and vicious, and other acts, performed in certain ways with certain motives, were virtuous. Picture a menu with two columns. Column A has healthy options, and Column B has unhealthy ones. The purpose of grace is to assist the chooser in having the strength to choose from Column A. But Luther, picking up on a long tradition going back through Peter Lombard, St. Augustine, and further, conceives of sin differently. Rather than seeing it as a feature of some acts rather than others, Luther sees it as a dimension of all acts.[19] Even our virtues are as sinful as our vices, as Gerhard Forde used to say.[20] Virtually anything that we do, no matter how self-giving and pure-minded, is somehow tainted by the stain of sin. For example, my desire to give to charity is a good desire, yet there lurks beneath my motive a desire to be recognized for my generosity, or at least not to feel guilty for not giving. Therefore grace comes to people who realize that they bear a "true and not a fictitious sin." Cheap legalism be damned. Literally.

In a culture that is bent either on perfectionism or antinomianism, as our modern world seems to display, Luther's insight, and Peters' development thereof, that sinfulness remains the life-situation of every person, can come as a relief. This does not excuse moral sloth, nor does it impede spiritual growth. Indeed, the person who suffers from, say, writer's block would hear it as great news if he were told that the next sentence he wrote did not have to be perfect on the first try. Marriages will not be perfect. Children will not be perfect, and should not be expected to be. To grasp this is to be freed to act as well as one can, trusting in the hope that God will provide in lieu of our shortcomings.

When Rowan Williams announced his retirement from the post of archbishop of Canterbury, one commentator reflected on Williams' courage in leading the Church of England through some of its rockiest waters. According to the commentator, Williams did so with grace because he understood sin. "Williams knows he will fail. He signed up to that when he signed up to Christianity because Christianity recognises that failure

---

19 See the excellent essay by Piotr Malysz, "Sin between Law and Gospel" in *Lutheran Quarterly* 28, no. 2 (2014): 149–78.
20 Gerhard Forde, "Christian Life," in *Christian Dogmatics,* Carl E. Braaten and Robert W. Jenson, eds. (Minneapolis: Fortress, 1984) II:449.

is what human beings do. And yet, that recognition is not humiliating but liberating because it delivers us from aspiring to mythic goals of absolute human control over human destiny."[21] Anything worth doing is worth doing well, as everyone knows. But what is often missed is the truth that anything worth doing is also worth doing poorly. Obviously one should try to do it well. But it is better to try and fail than not to try simply because one knows one may fail.

To sum up this section, consider a somewhat shocking epigram from another theologian. In his lovely book, *A History of Sin*, John Portmann concludes by making the assertion that sin is "the best we can do."[22] It is liberating, Portmann argues, to be rescued from the expectation that everything we do can and should be done perfectly, and that others owe their duty to us to be perfect, as well. One can and should have high expectations of others and oneself, but also must know that one's faults are permanent and deep, and that therefore grace must abound as well. Not just people in Christian churches, but also employers, voters, parents, neighbors, and friends can benefit from thinking about our shared life together along these lines.[23]

Why It Matters: Sin and Grace in Contemporary Theology, but Not for Theology

So sin-talk is not just the stuff of smug Christian piety or navel-gazing. It is a vital contribution that Christians can make to the wider culture. Let me conclude by resurrecting an old classic from this genre, a book that spoke to the culture about sin yet almost never used the term.

One of the classics of neo-orthodox theology on the doctrine of sin is a book called *Shantung Compound*, written by one of Ted Peters' teachers, Langdon Gilkey.[24] This is rather ironic, because Gilkey is not really a neo-Orthodox theologian and *Shantung Compound* is not a book of doctrine. Instead, it is a memoir of Gilkey's time spent as a prisoner of war in the 1940s in China, incarcerated at an internment camp run by the

---

21 Mark Vernon, "Rowan Williams, We'll Miss You," in *The Guardian*, September 12, 2012, A6.
22 John Portmann, *A History of Sin: How Evil Changes but Never Goes Away* (Lanham, Maryland: Rowman and Littlefield, 2007), 177–98.
23 One attempt to apply this line of thinking to our political thinking is Mark Ellingsen, *Blessed Are the Cynical: How Original Sin Can Make America a Better Place* (Grand Rapids: Brazos, 2003).
24 Langdon Gilkey, *Shantung Compound: The Story of Men and Women under Pressure* (New York: Harper and Row, 1966).

Japanese army. But it is not just a memoir. It functions also as an interpretation of the human condition, and powerfully implies (but does not argue) that a robust doctrine of sin is, practically speaking, necessary for the health of society. After leaving the compound at the conclusion of the war, Gilkey studied with Reinhold Niebuhr and Paul Tillich, internalizing their profound sense of the shape of sin and adding his own touches to their pioneering work.[25]

The one scene that has stuck with me from Gilkey's powerful memoir is the surprise that struck him as he reflected on his time in the camp. The camp was completely self-contained and operated with virtually no intervention from the Japanese soldiers, who mostly just guarded the camp from atop its outer walls and ensured that no one would escape. So the camp became a little experimental community, a microcosm of society that needed to provide for its own needs. Gilkey recalled worrying at the outset that the demographics of the camp's population did not look promising. As he looked around those first few days at the people he would live with, he was hoping to see more carpenters, bakers, masons, and farmers. He wanted people with skills that would make camp life better. Yet he realized in retrospect that he was prioritizing the wrong thing. Gilkey writes, "During our stay there, the problem of *politics*, of our own self-government and self-direction, remained to me the most subtle, the most frustrating and baffling issue we had to face. It was also the most fascinating, as I discovered early."[26]

Gilkey goes on to state that in fact it was a *spiritual* crisis that haunted the people at Shantung Compound, not a *practical* one. And he does not mean "spiritual" in a kind of touchy-feely religious way, but rather that the human spirit was not accounted for in camp life. Spiritual goods like trust, cooperation, and forgiveness of each other for their shortcomings was in shorter supply than the ability to plant vegetables or cook bread. Gilkey noticed other things about human nature, as well. Social stratification remained in place for a short time, but quickly people began to throw away status reserved for those who were wealthy or sophisticated, and those who were virtuous or pleasant took their places. Gilkey remembers, "The laziest man on my cooking shift was an executive from a shipping company with 'fine blood' and a privileged education. Bored with every-

---

25 One of the very best introductions available on Gilkey's work comes from none other than Ted Peters, "Langdon Gilkey: In Memoriam," in *Dialog: A Journal of Theology* 44, no. 1 (2005): 69–80.

26 Gilkey, *Shantung Compound*, 24.

thing in his life in camp, he was neither cooperative nor charming and so of little use to anyone. Perhaps the greatest value of this [Shantung] experience . . . was that we worked our way through the false barriers of the world at large to reach our common humanity. In time, we were able to see our neighbors for what they were, rather than what they had."[27]

Crisis followed close on the heels of crisis. A black market economy created even greater shortages of necessities as some hoarded and hid while others starved. An aid association from one nation was able to airlift supplies into the compound, but the internees could not find a way to distribute the goods equitably, and so many goods were spoiled and destroyed in the melee that ensued. Theft and malingering could not be punished, nor barely even policed, because the spiritual and interpersonal "capital" that was needed for such a thing was the good in shortest supply.

In coming to understand what had happened to him at Shantung Compound, Gilkey found that what would have served him best behind the camp walls—what would have been eminently practical—was a theology of human nature, of sin and its overcoming by grace.

What strikes me about that insight is that, in fact, many totally secular colleges could learn from this. As the pressure mounts for higher education simply to be job training, college administrators and seminaries—whose students rush to the supposedly practical skills of preaching and church administration and often shy away from the supposedly impractical disciplines of theology, languages, and philosophy—would do well to remind the world of the practicality of the spiritual. For the most practical thing in the world is a good theory! The wider world outside of the church and its theology has not learned all that it can from these insights into fallen and redeemed human nature, and one of the voices to which it would most profitably listen is, as I hope I have shown, Ted Peters.

---

27 Ibid., 27.

The Poetry of Gurram Joshua, GOD—*The World's Future*, and Their Implications for Dalit Theology

Moses Penumaka

> Where freedom freely strolls in fields
> yielding not to the rule of hardened heart,
> Prefers to be poor to being a tongue-less tool,
> Where people love orphans more than their own children
> Kindly tell me where it is: I want to meet those brothers.
>
> Gurram Joshua in *Gabbilam*

Theodore Frank Peters is a systematic and philosophical theologian, a scientist, a teacher, a pastor, a mentor, and most of all a simple human being with honesty and integrity in the church, the academy, the world, and the universe. Peters' theology is centered in God's grace and hope revealed through Christ's suffering, death, cross, and resurrection. "The grace of God working through Jesus Christ is total, complete, and sufficient to accomplish our salvation."[1]

Peters maintains the integrity of various theological, philosophical, and scientific disciplines while conducting cultural investigation accompanied by theological analysis. As a systematic and philosophi-

---

This article was first published in *Currents in Theology and Mission*, volume 39, number 4 (August 2012): 297–305, entitled "The Suffering Reality of the Oppressed in *GOD—The World's Future* and Its Implications for Dalit Theology."

1 Ted Peters, *GOD—The World's Future*, rev. ed. (Minneapolis: Fortress Press, 2000) 257.

cal theologian, he is deeply committed to Christian doctrinal reflection. With the mind of a scientist, he is passionate about scientific imagination and exploration. As a scholar, he offers an apologetic for Christian belief in a global culture shot through with secular self-understanding, scientific thinking, and *"the worldwide cry for freedom."*[2] Peters has been cultivating theological skills among seminarians and doctoral students for nearly four decades, influencing our pastors and our professors with his research method and doctrinal insights. I had the privilege of working with him as a student, colleague, and friend. I consider it a great honor to be one of the contributors to this *Festschrift*.

Peters' investigations into the interaction between theology and science might seem far beyond comprehension for some, but for the theological and scientific reader, they provide humor, deep insights, and creative imagination. For example, in *The Evolution of Terrestrial and Extraterrestrial Life,* Peters raises a perennial theological and existential question and responds in a scientifically analytical and theologically hermeneutical way. In one of the lectures Peters states:

> Beginning with the cross one might ask: can what we have learned about God's love and grace through divine revelation in the cross apply to our expanding knowledge of nature's evolutionary history? Because the story of Jesus is the story of God's incarnation entailing the taking up of the human experience of injustice and suffering into divine life, would it follow that in nature God identifies with the victims of unfitness? Would it follow from Jesus' Easter resurrection that we have reason to believe the future will be different from the past, that eschatologically the lion will lie down with the lamb? Yes.[3]

Of course Peters says, *Yes.* Yet, I would like to point out that such a future-oriented theology has value for domains other than the dialogue between theology and science. The divine promise of eschatological transformation announces the breaking of chains with the past, and it provides divine grounding for the hope that guides and inspires liberation theology.

---

2 Ibid., 7; author's emphasis.
3 Ted Peters, *The Evolution of Terrestrial and Extraterrestrial Life,* Proceedings of the Seventh Annual Goshen Conference on Religion and Science, Carl S. Helrich, ed. (Kitchener, Ontario: Pandora Press, 2008), 93.

The question *how* such eschatological "difference" becomes reality always remains hypothetical unless and until we hear the voices from the margins, the voices of the victims, the women, the dalits, the aboriginals, the homeless, and the underclass in the social hierarchy. How can the future of those presently marginalized be different? This chapter attempts to address the question of *how* from an Indian *dalit* theological perspective.

Into dialogue with Peters I will place a Telugu poet, Gurram Joshua (1895–1971). Joshua has lifted up the voices of the countless outcastes, untouchables, and marginalized in Indian society so that these voices can be heard, so that we can hear "the worldwide cry for freedom."

Orthodoxy Versus Liberation Theology

Liberation and other contextual theologies emerged as a response to the inappropriateness of the dominant religious orthodoxy and lacuna created and perpetuated by such orthodoxy. Liberation theologians reflected on praxis, resistance, spirituality, mysticism, and contemplation in light of the Scriptures and of the struggles within their own contexts. Personal struggles, stories, and experiences of being dalit, crucified, wounded, oppressed, poor, victim, and marginalized became the loci and impetus for liberation theology. The two most important aspects that liberation theology addresses are *poverty and praxis*. In my Indian context, there are various dalit liberation movements and theologies developed and led by many outstanding leaders, thinkers, and poets. Gurram Joshua is one such radical thinker who used poetry to critique dominant and oppressive culture in India. As a rare and outstanding poet, emerging from the dalit (meaning oppressed, broken, or marginalized) social background, Gurram Joshua developed a radical social and theological critique of dominant culture of Hinduism in Andhra Pradesh, India. Joshua's pioneering contextual and dalit theology challenged orthodoxy in Andhra Pradesh, and became a call for rethinking orthopraxis, political activism, and social liberation and transformation with an emphasis on changing the minds of the dominant and changing the conditions of the downtrodden.

The Emergence of Dalit Theology

A detailed analysis of the nature and history of religions reveals that religious experience is dependent on the human condition and the relation of that condition to the situation that surrounds it. Explicating human nature in terms of *homo religiosis* (the human being as religious), Mercia Eliade explains that religious human beings live only in an open world but desire to be at a center. At the center of one's life-world is where there is the possibility of communicating or relating with gods. At the center, we humans can live "in communication with the gods" and share in the "sanctity of the world."[4]

Centering is important to self-understanding. Dalit theology includes the affirmation of being at the center; it leads a resistance movement against caste oppression that pushes lower caste people to the margins. Dalit theology offers a critical reflection on dominant tradition, culture, and faith that cause the suffering and oppression of people. It critiques the fundamental principles of human society on behalf of equality and justice over against hierarchy and injustice. Further, dalit theology transcends the pitfall of drawing the dualistic line between bipolar categories in reality such as God and creation, matter and spirit, rich and poor, oppressor and oppressed, and exploiter and exploited. Dalit theology places the suffering reality and the liberating experience of the untouchables, the poor, the oppressed, the exploited, the victims, the wounded, and the crucified in the "center" of theology.

Dharma or Adharma: Sanatana or Varnashrama

Hindu philosophy supports *Varnashrama Dharma* (an order based on color/complexion and vocation) to complement *Sanatana Dharma*, which in Sanskrit means eternal justice or order. An ideal order of justice ought to provide impetus to actualize this justice in society. But, this actualization of the ideal fails. It misses the mark. What gets actualized is a social hierarchy based upon skin color. A person's color, *varna*, determines his or her caste.

Thomas Thangaraj describes Hinduism as "geo-piety" and "bio-piety." "Geo-piety," according to Thangaraj, indicates that Hinduism can be defined by its geographical location, rather than by a founder or a

---

4   Mircea Eliade, *The Sacred and the Profane, the Nature of Religion*, Willard R. Trask, trans. (New York: Harper & Row, 1957), 173. Peters relies heavily on Eliade's phenomenology of religion when developing the notion of religious sensibilities, such as the symbolic connection between sky and earth and the "ontological thirst" that propels human consciousness to ask the question of God. For example, see Ted Peters, *UFOs: God's Chariots? Spirituality, Ancient Aliens, and Religious Yearnings in the Age of Extraterrestrials* (Pompton Plains, New Jersey: New Page, 2014) 181, 192.

set of doctrines or creeds. In this case, Hinduism and its particular piety is defined by its location. Of course, *advaitins* (disciples of *advaita* or non-dualistic philosophy) may challenge this *autochthony* (identification of people with land) on the basis that the naming of ultimate reality as Brahman, the non-dualistic Reality, transcends time and space,[5] even the space, or land, where one lives.

The *advaita*, or non-dualistic view of ultimate reality, and its designation of "world" as *maya* could posit an ontological unity by simply relativizing one's local geographical region. While this is true in theory, in practice many Hindus attach themselves to their geography. They cultivate a sense that they belong to the land where they live. They become autochthonous, even if autochthony is inconsistent with Hinduism's fundamental metaphysical commitment to an overarching nongeographic unity of all things in one thing.

"Bio-piety," as Thangaraj describes it, is *Sanatana Dharma* (the eternal order) of Hinduism, that is, the caste system based on the biological history of an individual. Also known as *Varnashrama Dharma*, the caste system is based on the caste (color) and profession determined by birth. The caste system is believed to be eternal order for human flourishing. It emerged from creator *Brahma*. From the head of *Brahma* came the *brahmins* or the priestly caste; from the shoulders came the *kshatriyas* or the warrior caste; from the bosom came the *Vaishyas* or the trader caste; and from the feet came the *shudra* or the artisan and crafts castes. The native Indians are kept outside the caste system and treated as polluted and untouchable.

The British called them *panchamas*, the fifth caste or outcaste. The outcastes do not belong to the body of Brahma. They do not fit into the house-cosmos-body homology. They are outside the system. Today panchamas or the untouchables are known as *dalits*. Dal in Sanskrit means broken, empty, weak insignificant. The caste system is an unjust, atrocious, and unequal categorization giving certain privileges to a few people based on the caste of their birth. The system denies even basic privileges to lower castes. The outcastes are completely disowned; yet the social demands on them are for total servitude and surrender. Gurram Joshua grew up in Indian society when there were severe caste

---

5 M. Thomas Thangaraj, "Hinduism and Globalization, a Christian Theological Approach," in *God and Globalization, vol. 3, Christ and the Dominations of Civilization*, Max L. Stackhouse and Diane B. Obenchain, eds. (Harrisburg, Pennsylvania: Trinity Press International, 2002), 213–38.

restrictions, total dehumanization, and discrimination. Sadly, the same situation or environment exists today. A social, cultural, and theological analysis will help us understand the exploitation of the dalits and the challenge for repentance and transformation.

Origins of Christianity in India

The origins of Christianity in India can be traced to the arrival of St. Thomas in the first century. The Marthoma Christians—the followers of St. Thomas—claim the background of this tradition. One church in Chennai claims to have been founded in 54 CE, prior to the compilation of the New Testament. The foundations for Christian witness in India were laid down very early indeed.

During the sixteenth century, the Jesuits Francis Xavier and Robert de Nobili arrived and with their approach of inculturation[6] were able to convert some caste Hindus to Christianity. In the late nineteenth and early twentieth centuries, Protestant missionaries from Europe and America came to India with their variant of the gospel of Jesus Christ. These missionaries attempted to bring the gospel to the entire nation. Philosophically, Hinduism is tolerant and respectful of any other religious traditions. However, Christianity condemned caste discrimination within Hinduism, and this criticism of social and cultural injustice was not well received.

Upper caste Hindus were less open to the Christian message than lower caste Hindus and outcastes. Even though the missionaries tried to preach the gospel starting from Brahmins and to everyone in India, the dalits converted in large numbers leading to mass movements. The dalits could find meaning in the suffering of Christ similar to their own suffering. They embraced Christ for a new social identity and human dignity. They could recognize a God who identifies with the dalits, suffers with the dehumanized, and liberates the oppressed. Gurram Joshua affirmed the faith and identity of dalits, expressing both powerfully in Telugu poetry, which he used as a potent hermeneutical tool. Gurram Joshua developed a unique, radical, social, religious, and cultural critique.

India reclaimed its independence from British rule through non-violence and Satyagraha led by the Mahatma Gandhi. The Indian masses in large numbers responded to the call of the Mahatma with their dreams

---

6   Inculturation is the practice of evangelization through respect for and use of the local culture.

and hope for a free India. In the formation of *Swaraj*, self-rule, the masses who participated in the freedom fight, were beaten with batons, went to prison, and were left behind without recognition.

India's national congress struggled to find a suitable model that would bring justice to all people. The first option was banking, which allowed Indians to carry on with the high standard, material culture of the West, consisting of science, technology, and passion for progress. Gandhi proposed to break with the western model of civilization based on division of labor and the centralized modern state. Gandhi's ideal for Hindu *swaraj* as a true *swaraj* was political, economic, and moral independence, based on far-reaching decentralization. Gandhi's ideal of Ramarajya was to shift from the urban market to village based production and rule (*Kutiraparisrama* and *Grameena Panchayathi*). But Prime Minister Jawaharlal Nehru sought a sovereign, national state, with the possibility of developing a socialist state free from the West and dependency on its model of development. B.R. Ambedkar, the only strong voice for the masses, feared the reinforcement of the caste structure through political decentralization. Therefore, he was a strong proponent for political decentralization. He supported a modern state after western models and ensured that many of those principles were incorporated into the Indian constitution.

The Indian constitution, designed by Ambedkar, was adopted on January 26, 1948. In the Ambedkar's proposed constitution, Article 17 abolishes "untouchability," the caste system. Unfortunately, the final form of the constitution does not contain an article or a directing principle regarding abolishing the caste system.[7] Ambedkar's draft for Article 17 stated that, "any privilege or disability arising out of rank, birth, person, family, religion, or religious usage and custom is abolished." But this article was not accepted by the parliament.[8] G. Shah concludes: "the constitution envisages building an egalitarian society within the capitalist framework without uprooting the caste system."[9] Such insulation and insensitivity to the issues of injustice and discrimination show that the dalits were left to their own "fate," even in modern India.

---

[7] Gabriela Dietrich & Bas Wielenga, *Towards Understanding Indian Society* (Arasaradi, Madurai: Center for Social Analysis, 1977), 142.
[8] Ibid.
[9] B. Ambedkar, *Writings and Speeches*, vol. 2, (1982) as quoted by Gabriela Dietrich & Bas Wielenga, *Towards Understanding Indian Society*, 142.

The Problem of Untouchability

Untouchability in India is not just the problem of dalits. The Indian caste system continues to perpetuate inequality at all levels. Sadly, there is a great reluctance among non-dalit movements to be inclusive and to make the struggle against practices of untouchability part of their agenda. Gabriela Dietrich states that such movements fail to see the urgency of this problem for dalits. Also they hesitate for fear that taking up the issue may place too much of a burden on their organization. Any struggle for a new, just society in which there is equality, must confront untouchability as a major obstacle. "It is an atrocious form of exclusivity and segregation which prevents true solidarity and sows the seeds of bitterness and confrontation which the vested interests will be using for their divide and rule policies."[10] Therefore, untouchability remains an issue addressed only on superficial levels. Gurram Joshua struggled in India under the severe caste discrimination of his times.

Preferential option for the poor became the central tenant of liberation theology as it developed in Latin America and spread to other contexts where it resonated with those experiencing class or racial oppression. Liberation theologians attacked many conventional dualisms such as the poor and the rich, or the oppressed and the oppressors, for misleading social consciousness. When reality is presented as built upon such dualisms, the poor and the oppressed will too easily accept their fate. What liberation theologians cultivate is a transformation of consciousness, a consciousness-raising that leads to a self-raising among marginalized peoples. The power to inspire such self-raising comes from the gospel of Jesus Christ, the message that in the eyes of a gracious God, the poor and the rich are equal in dignity.

What I see in Ted Peters' proleptic ontology is the grounding of a social and political ethic that begins with a vision of the future that will be different from today. In God's coming kingdom, present inequalities will be replaced with a dignity that is experienced by everyone. "In terms of ethics," he writes, "this means that as citizens of the eschatological polis, we are called to support just political structures in the present and to transform those structures when they fail to embody and enhance justice."[11] Proleptic eschatology provides the basic vision that guides liberation ethics and offers renewed confidence in God's plan for the poor, a

---

10 Dietrich and Wielenga, *Towards Understanding Indian Society*, 228.
11 Peters, *GOD—The World's Future*, 376.

plan that includes the kind of reversal seen in Jesus' parables and promises. "Once we apprehend God's will for the consummate future, we seek to incarnate that future proleptically in present human action."[12]

The Christian church in India as well as in every clime on our globe is responsible for lifting up the vision of a transformed future. In India, the possibility and viability of the church taking a stand for transformation raises two important issues. First, with which group does the church identify? And, does not taking sides with one group mean siding against the other? The second, valid only if the ultimate goal of liberation is forgotten and a new humanity is desired, all persons must be moved to a new position. Therefore, not only are the oppressed liberated from their obvious oppression, but oppressors are also liberated from their more subtle, though no less real, oppression.[13] Liberation theology places the poor in the center as opposed to the privileged side. The poor become the good news; the poor become the bearers of salvation. The poor and the crucified remind us that liberation is complete only when there is no separation of rich and poor or oppressors and oppressed. As Salvadorian Jesuit Jon Sobrino states: "There can be no civilization on the basis of unreality, of what we have called Docetism. Reality offers us redemption from unreality, and the poor offer us redemption from social and ecclesial Docetism. To put it more modestly, they invite us to come close to them, to be real."[14]

Therefore, in coming close to the reality, the reality of suffering and being crucified, we experience God. Our partisanship with the poor and the suffering liberates us. The point of departure for dalit theology is the suffering reality of the dalits. For the experience of the struggles of dalits becomes central to God, a locus to theological discourse; it also becomes the sign for the liberation experience. Reality can never be unreal for dalits.

Daridranarayana of Gurram Joshua Kavi

Gurram Joshua known as *"navayuga kavi cakravarti"* (emperor of modern poetry) was one of the great Telugu poets of the twentieth century. Joshua wrote many Kannda Kaavyaalu (a type of Telugu poetry based on a particular meter) with a profound sense of social consciousness and theological critique. Joshua, born in a dalit Christian family, found mean-

---
12 Ibid., 379.
13 Dietrich and Wielenga, *Towards Understanding Indian Society*, 8.
14 Jon Sobrino, *Where Is God? Earthquake, Terrorism, Barbarity, and Hope*, Margaret Wilde, trans. (Maryknoll, New York: Orbis Books, 2004), 101.

ing, identity, and inspiration in the gospel of Jesus Christ. He developed a theological and social critique of the dominant Hinduism by using poetic literature that is considered to be the personification of Saraswathi, goddess of wisdom and knowledge. Gurram Joshua's social and theological critique is unique and radical. Through his powerful poetic literature, Joshua critiqued the social oppression and cultural bondage of *daridranarayanudu*, the one wedded to suffering and misery, the untouchable in Indian society.

Biographical Sketch and Works

Gurram Joshua (1895–1971) was born in Vinukonda, a remote village in the country side in Guntur District of Andhra Pradesh, South India. Veerayya, his father, was a convert to Christianity from *Jadav*, a shepherd community. Lingamamba, his mother, was a dalit girl from the mission hostel. From his childhood, Joshua affirmed his identity as a human being with self-respect, identity, and human dignity. Unfortunately he suffered humiliation and discrimination along with millions of dalits. Gurram Joshua resisted this humiliation and used poetry as a hermeneutical tool.

Joshua became a well-known poet with rare distinction among leading poets of his time. Though he was awarded titles as *Kavi Samrat* (emperor of poetry), *Padma Shri* (one who is wedded with the goddess of wisdom, *Saraswathi*), *Kavi kokila* (cuckoo of poetry), *Kavitha Visaratha, Kavidiggaja, Mathura Srinadha,* and *Visvakavi Samrat*, he was deliberately humiliated many times by the so-called upper caste poets. People used to admire his oratory and poetic talent, only to abandon and even humiliate him once they learned about his social background. Joshua's scholarship became a difficult talent to bear. However, he used Telugu poetic literature as a tool to resist oppression and to bring conscientization to both the oppressive, high-caste Hindus as well as to the dalit victims.

Initially Joshua's choice of Telugu poetry was not welcomed by Christian converts from Hinduism, who also experienced the dominant Hindu religious belief as excluding them from social privileges and denying them their self-identity and human dignity. Joshua's fellow Christians later realized his passion for liberation and his powerful critique against the dominant Hinduism. In Guntur, Andhra Pradesh, the Central Literary Academy awarded him for his writing of *Life of Jesus Christ*. Joshua served as an elected civil servant, a member to the State Assembly. The Andhra University, one of the premier educational institutions, conferred *Kalaprapurna* (Scholar of Arts) title on him. Gurram Joshua Kavi died on July 24, 1971.[15]

Gabbilam: The Bat

Joshua wrote thirty volumes of creative, critical, and challenging poetry. Among his works, *Gabbilam*, which means "bat," is an outstanding piece. Joshua wrote the kannda kavyam inspired by the epic Kalidas's *meghasandesham*. In *meghasandesham* a lover sends his message of love to his beloved through a cloud. In *Gabbilam,* Joshua uses a bat, a powerful representative symbol of the dalits, to bring to Shiva the reality of the pain and agony of the dalits. In India, in Hindu temples, bats live in the *sanctum sanctorum*—the holy of the holies, the *Gharbhagudi*—hanging upside down. Dalits are denied entry to the temples in India, but the bat goes into the most sacred of places.[16] Through the hero of his poem, Joshua requests that the bat tell of the plight of the dalits when it is hanging upside down, close to the ears of Shiva.

Gabbilam is an epic poem and a revolutionary masterpiece with high aesthetics and a searing attack on untouchability. The bat, a nocturnal mammal, has the characteristics of a bird, in that it flies, as well as those of a mammal, in that it has hair and suckles its young. When the bat comes out during the daytime, it is treated with hostility by both birds and mammals. It is isolated as an "outcaste" by birds similar to the discrimination of dalits by the upper caste people. Neither a bird nor a mammal, this lonely creature is considered a bad omen in India. The so called "untouchables," or dalits, are considered neither human beings nor creatures, but rather as total infidels and invalid ones in the society. Joshua chooses a bat as a most suitable, appropriate, and powerful representative symbol of dalits to speak with Lord Shiva in the temple and to inform him of the pain and agony that the "untouchables" endure because of the caste system. Joshua sees the bat as the only one who could understand his own experience of being humiliated, dehumanized, and distorted.

---

15 Gurram Joshua, *Gabbilam* (Vijayawarda, India: Joshua Foundation, Vijaya Graphics, 1996), 77.

16 Since Independence, untouchability has been abolished and entry into temples is permitted. However, there are many places where dalits are still restricted from entering the temples.

In the poem, Gurram Joshua describes the beauty of the land, the pride of the nation, the contribution the untouchables make in serving the nation and the plight they receive in exchange:

> In this fatted, arrogant world,
> Who are friends and relatives to the poor?
> Except, worms and creatures of anthills?

or

> Who will talk to the low, except
> A bird or a bat or a rat

Here Joshua is expressing the social discrimination and the feeling of being lonely in a land of millions of people. Furthermore, Joshua explains the pain and agony of the outcaste son of *Arundhati* (a dalit woman whom a *Brahmin* married) as follows:

> Even if his life were doomed, his caste degraded
> Destined to poverty and lowly labor by cruel fate
> He gladly covers the feet of *Bharat's* [India's] people with sandals
> The land is indebted to him, the poor cobbler! Indeed.
> Without his hand's labor
> Crops hesitate to ripen
> By his sweat he folds the land
> But himself, he has little to eat.
> Yet, the heavenly Ganges refuses
> To wash away the dirt heaped on his head
> Snakes fed on milk and ants on sugar
> In this blessed land of *Karma*
> But the Goddess of Justice is startled
> By the poor cobbler's despised presence
> He has iron fetters from mother's arms
> His blood is drained by the land
> The four-hooded [four castes] *Hindu nagaraja* [king cobra]
>   hisses aloud
> Touched by his smell carried by the breeze
> And One day,
> Having waved farewell to the setting sun
> He sat down to eat his meager meal of gruel
> At the end of a long day's back-breaking toil
> And stretched on a cot, resting his weary limbs

It was then that a bat flew into the hut, a small, black, furry ball with a face and nose. Fluttering across his hut, it struck the flame of the castor-oil lamp and put it out, spreading the darkness of the night. Instead of getting angry at the bat for blowing out the lamp, listening to the thuds and bumps of the shuttling bat, the son of *Arundathi's* thoughts began racing. He was reminded of the darkness in the lives of his fellow dalits, their shame and misery, their hunger and pain, their lack of homes and friends, their unremitting hardship and unrewarding labor. Seeing a friend in the bat, he warmly welcomes it, saying:

> Welcome Queen of Bats, residing in sacred shrines,
> Enjoying honor we lowly people cannot have,
> Convey our greetings to your kinfolk too
> Meditating head down in the awnings of temple towers

He then breaks out explaining his tale of woe, tears rolling down his cheeks, and pleads with the bat to represent his life-story to Shiva. The poem continues that the bat is able to get close to the ears of Lord Shiva when the bat goes to rest, hanging upside down in the *gharbagudi* in the holy sanctuary, unlike him, an untouchable who is denied access to the *dharshan*—presence—of gods and silenced by the law of karma. He asks the bat to find out why the gods take revenge on him and his fellow dalits. He warns the bat to be careful to narrate his story to Shiva only when the *Poojaris* (priests) are out. For if the priests hear her, they will cast her out also for having visited the forbidden house of an outcaste, and thus deny her forever the privileges of dining on the *Prasad*—food—offered to gods.

Regarding the plight of the untouchables, Joshua goes on to say that it is a heartless society, in which thousands of rupees are spent on the marrying of the idols, and fresh milk is fed to idols, but not to the poor and destitute. He profusely thanks the bat for daring to visit him and exhorts her to be courageous when representing his story to Shiva because:

> Justice has never been a coward
> Truth cannot be put to death
> There is no need of fear for
> A Creature to speak to the Creator

Joshua takes courage to resist his social situation by justifying his self-authentication to send a message directly to the god, crossing over all sanctions and barriers. Joshua gives call to his fellow dalits not to be afraid to claim their rights.

In the concluding part of the poem, with his commitment and yearning for human dignity, equality, justice, and unity of all people across caste and creed towards a one human family, Joshua visualizes liberation as a journey, a destination, and a dwelling place.

> O, hermit bat, kindly tell me whether you saw a place
> Where the poor do not meet to envy a rich man's face,
> Where knowledge grows against the foolish customs of society
> Where the child of art grows to youth ignoring caste decrees
> Where freedom freely strolls in fields yielding not to the rule
> Of hardened heart, prefers to be poor to being a tongue-less tool,
> Where people love orphans more than their own children,
> Kindly tell me where it is: I want to meet those brothers
>
> The place where mother tongue is honored well in lore,
> Where mutts, religions rival not as in days of yore,
> Where voices of saintly poets sound without fear
> Where parents do not teach hatred to their children dear
> Where footprints of venomous hypocrites appear not to the eye,
> Such a palace, be it a bat's abode, is happy under the sky.

As exemplified in "The Bat," Joshua's agony over the suffering of the *Daridranarayana*, and his vision for a renewed society with freedom, justice, human dignity, and also religious harmony are powerfully expressed in all of his writings.

Gurram Joshua's Theological Methodology

Joshua's poetry as a literary composition conveys the sufferings and hopes, the dilemmas and dreams of dalits and their struggles for a new and renewed society. In Joshua's poetry, one can see the efforts to relate faith to the dalit reality of brokenness, oppression, and alienation, and catch glimpses of spirituality in struggle, transcendence in suffering, aspirations and hopes for freedom—all of which constitute the roots of dalit liberation in the early twentieth century.[17]

---

[17] M.E. Prabhakar, "In Search of Roots—Dalit Aspirations and the Christian Dalit Question: Perceptions of the Telugu Poet Laureate, Joshua," in *Religion and Society*, 41, no. 1 (March 1994): 2.

Joshua's dalit consciousness was shaped by his own dalit experience of shame and suffering. Instead of surrendering to such an oppressive system, he rebelled at being discriminated against in the name of caste. Joshua's poetry is filled with social content that shook the complacency and insensitivity of classical Telugu literary traditions, which exclusively extolled the art, aesthetic, and transcendentalism of the dominant high-caste poets. Joshua's poetry became challenging, inspiring, and thought-provoking dalit literature, because he presented dalit life from a dalit point of view with dalit insights that formulated a vision of dalit liberation. Speaking to his daughter Hemalatha Lavanam about his life and work, Joshua said, "I have learnt many lessons in life, under two gurus: poverty and caste-creed discrimination. The first taught me patience and the second taught me to protest against remaining a bonded slave. I decided to break myself free from the shackles of poverty and caste. I took up my sword to fight them. My sword was my poetry. My hatred is not against society, but I hate its life-patterns."[18] Joshua used poetry as the tool to analyze and critique the dominant Hindu ideology.

Joshua's poetry expresses life. One day, during his childhood, a few upper-caste people drew back in haste on seeing him, which made him so furious that he hit four of them and ran away to his mother to complain. He narrates this event and his mother's response in the following verses:

> Crying I told her of the incident,
> Hugging me to her breast and kissing me
> She said, "Son, this is an awful country,
> But don't complain of caste discrimination;
> You'll lose your food, as a *Panchama*
> You have no claim to human rights on your life.[19]
>
> These gods here won't grant their favors
> They will not accept a *Panchama's* worship
> The Lord Jesus Christ alone is your refuge
> Adore him, he'll be merciful.[20]

---

18 Hemalatha Lavanam in her biography, *My Father*, 10, as quoted by M.E. Prabhakar, 3.
19 P. Swarnalata Ranjan, "Christian Dalit Aspirations as Expressed by Joshua Kavi in Gabbilum (Bat)," *Religion and Society*, 34, no. 3 (September 1987): 53ff. Quoted from Gurram Joshua, *My Story*, cf. stanza 116.
20 Ibid., stanza 117.

The power of this poem is felt more in Telugu than the above translation (with due respect to the translator). Joshua's talent to describe the social problems and injustice are very powerfully articulated with imagery, symbolism, and scholarship in Telugu literature. Through symbolic characters and Telugu poetic literature, Joshua analyses the social reality of caste oppression and demands justice, human dignity, and identity for all people. Gurram Joshua challenges Hindu social values and restriction for the dalits and demands that justice be restored to everyone. His theology is based on an interfaith dialogue and critique that is inspired by Jesus Christ who embraces the untouchables, leads them to the temple, challenges the oppressive structures, and ultimately suffers in the same way the dalits suffer. His theological methodology therefore is unique and can be described as a contextual, liberationist, and dialogical method.

Critique of Joshua

Joshua used Telugu (one of the south Indian languages) poetic literature as an aesthetic to highlight the injustice, oppression, and marginalization done to fellow human beings by the dominant religious system. Joshua's critique of Hinduism and his imagery of a nocturnal bat that represents his sufferings to the god have deep theological insights. Joshua chose the bat, an animal that lives in the holiest of the holies in the central temple, because dalits, who are viewed as polluted and untouchable, are restricted from entering a Hindu temple. Similarly, the bat with its nocturnal habits and liminal status is considered a bad omen in India. So first, Joshua picked a representative who can understand his state of suffering. Second, Joshua used Lord Shiva, though he was aware of many other deities in the Indian context. Shiva is the god of destruction and an *arthanareeshvara* (half male and half female). Shiva also is a *Neelakahanta*, whose throat is bluish because he swallowed poison and saved the world. Through these symbolic characters, Joshua analyses caste oppression and demands. His theological methodology therefore can be described as contextual and liberationist.

Theological Implications of *Dalit* Theology

In the perspectives briefly discussed above, discrimination, suffering, pain, misery, poverty, and oppression are the experience of the activists as well as the people for whom they are advocating. From the dalit perspective, their suffering is their actual reality, and that reality, in which each of them finds inner strength, gives them hope for liberation. In these perspectives, the suffering reality becomes a liberating reality. In other words, their suffering becomes central to the Godhead, not detached or indifferent. Any system that ignores, denies, or cannot experience the suffering reality is therefore irrelevant and does not have any soteriological value. In post-colonial approaches to theology, we remember the future. We remember a future that is open, and we remember a past that is unstable and changing because it is subject to transformation. The suffering experience of the dalits is temporal and temporary, not eternal.

This means that our future—God's future—will include a great reversal. The marginalized will become centered. The low will be raised. The untouchables will be touched by God's grace. "In the Easter resurrection of Jesus, God has given us a prolepsis of what is to come, a pre-actualization of the eschatological wholeness that will imbue all things."[21]

When we look to God as the world's future, the suffering reality of creation's history is remembered through the cross, through the painful experience of the victims in the past. God experiences this pain, and so God too remembers it. The suffering of the dalits has been experienced by God in the suffering of Jesus on the cross in the abiding presence of God's Holy Spirit within dalit daily life. In addition, in the raising of Jesus on that first Easter, this suffering was transformed. This same transformation is promised to us as well, dalits especially. The power of Jesus' Easter resurrection imbues the vision of liberation that the Christian witness lifts up, and it inspires the political and cultural action required to transform India's past into a more just future.

---

21 Peters, *GOD—The World's Future*, 392.

Jesus' Creation Theology and Multiethnic Practice

David L. Balch & Adam Pryor

Reading studies of the historical Jesus, it is surprising that his crossing the ethnic border into Samaria has not been more emphasized.[1] This *Festschrift* chapter suggests that one source of this socially provocative action was Jesus' Jewish reading of Genesis, Leviticus, and deutero-Isaiah, that is, creation theology in Torah, developed in the context of Roman imperial colonization of Judea. We will first note some texts in which Jesus appeals to God as Creator, and second, connect this with his integration of ethnic others, in particular Samaritans, among his disciples. Third, we will examine how Jesus' provocative act of ethnic boundary crossing implies a political/theological friendship ethic different from Aristotle's.

Retracing this ethnic border crossing by Jesus has ramifications for contemporary theology, ethics, and the responsibility of the Christian church in a pluralistic global society. In his eschatological vision mediating the future to the present, Ted Peters looks ahead to the Kingdom of God and to universal human dignity. Anticipating such a future, we today should lift up a moral vision of a world "organized socially so that dignity and freedom are respected and protected in every quarter."[2] This vision combined with political and cultural transformation functions to confer dignity on those who dwell on the margins of the dominant

---

This article was first published in *Currents in Theology and Mission*, volume 39, number 4 (August 2012): 279-89.

1 Ethnicity and race are extraordinarily difficult to define. See Eric D. Barreto, *Ethnic Negotiations: The Function of Race and Ethnicity in Acts 16* (WUNT 2.294; Tübingen: Mohr Siebeck, 2010), chaps. 1-2, who surveys scholarship, cautioning against essentializing; ethnicities are socially constructed but nevertheless powerful categories.
2 Ted Peters, *GOD—The World's Future*, 2nd ed. (Minneapolis: Fortress Press, 2000), 381.

society. Christian ministry consists of the conferral of dignity on those without dignity. Our conferral of dignity across ethnic lines proleptically anticipates the eschatological kingdom of God.

Even though what follows is largely a historical study, what we learn should have an impact on our Christian mission today. Just as Jesus' interethnic dialogue was steeped in protological and eschatological commitments, we must, as with Peters, realize the proleptic ramifications of opening ourselves to diverse others. If we confer dignity in interethnic dialogue, we incarnate today what will become reality at the advent of the Kingdom of God

Jesus' Creation Theology

Israel's confession of one, unique God responsible for history, creation, and salvation is central to Jesus' thinking and preaching. These themes are developed especially with regard to how he understands the kingdom of God. His understanding is most akin to the post-exilic writing of deutero-Isaiah, which emphasizes the eschatological features of this confession (Isaiah 40:3-4; 41:4, 21-29; 43:10-13; 45:5-7). Much as the prophet announced salvation with the cry, "Your God reigns" (Isaiah 52:7), so too did Jesus (Mark 1:14-15).[3] However, Jesus is not alone in this process of reinterpretation. For example, while we find Jesus proclaimed the gospel of deutero-Isaiah to beggars, as with "Blessed are the poor" (Q/Luke 6:20b, alluding to Isaiah 61:1), Kloppenborg-Verbin[4] identifies a Qumran text with the same allusion, "For the heavens and the earth shall listen to his Messiah. . . . For He shall heal the critically wounded, He shall revive the dead, He shall send good news to the afflicted (Isaiah 61:1), He shall satisfy the poor . . . , He shall make the hungry rich. . . ." (4Q521, Abegg, trans. [AcCordance]). Jesus' blessing of the poor is part of a wider search in Judea in a colonial context for how to interpret these scriptures. What then might we highlight as notable themes in Jesus' acts of reinterpretation?

We suggest two critical and related features. First, protology, the original will of God at creation, and eschatology correspond in Jesus' sayings and deeds. Creation and salvation are not disparate concepts with a radical break between them; instead, salvation stands as the end

---

3   Udo Schnelle, *Theology of the New Testament* (Grand Rapids: Baker, 2009), 81, 88.
4   John S. Kloppenborg-Verbin, *Excavating Q: The History and Setting of the Sayings Gospel* (Minneapolis: Fortress Press, 2000), 123.

towards which creation moves. This paradigm is not without precedent. Leo Perdue, in his form-critical analysis of the wisdom sayings of Jesus, distinguishes between an older wisdom, as a "paradigm of order," and a newer wisdom, as a "paradigm of conflict."[5] The connection of protology and eschatology we find in Jesus' sayings and deeds fits neatly within this newer paradigm: the saving act of God's *eschaton* is already in motion within this world in conflict with and working to overcome the evil of this world. Second, we do not stand idly by in the midst of this in-breaking of the Kingdom of God. The connection of protology and eschatology implements a wisdom tradition theology of creation with definite ethical ramifications. Jesus implements a wisdom theology of creation (akin to Perdue's newer paradigm) that is saturated with a radical prophetic ethics of the present. The kingdom of God implements the original will of God as it unfolds a new reality with a distinctive ethical structure by which we participate in the new reality.[6] To draw a hard distinction between the protological and eschatological features of Jesus' theology of creation would be inauthentic; they form a fluid unity rooting his ethical developments.

This context sheds important light on how we can read the threefold command to love that is so central to interpretations of Jesus' ethics: love of neighbor, love of enemy, and love of God.[7] Love of enemies is particularly important because the absolute demand to love enemies (Q/Luke 6:27a; Matthew 5:44a) is grounded in a distinctive Jesuanic protological/eschatological creation theology: "But I say to you, Love your enemies and pray for those who persecute you, so that you may be children of your Father in heaven; for he makes his sun rise on the evil and on the good, and sends rain on the righteous and on the unrighteous" (Q/Luke 6:35; Matthew 5:45). The ethic of love is tied to our recognition of being part of the wide breadth of God's creation, with a duty to inculcate the kingdom of God in the world through our way of being with one another. These love commands and the grounding in creation theology press the adherent beyond any confining nationalism.

Two examples regarding foreigners help bring the implications of this insight into sharper perspective. First, keeping with themes devel-

---

5 Kloppenborg-Verbin, *Excavating Q*, 382, n. 40, citing J. Gammie and L. Perdue, *The Sage in Israel and the Ancient Near East* (Winona Lake: Eisenbrauns, 1990), 457–78; compare Perdue, "The Wisdom Sayings of Jesus," *Forum* 2, no. 3 (September 1986): 3–35.
6 Schnelle, *Theology*, 108–114.
7 Ibid., 118–121.

oped out of Isaiah, we find other authentic Q and Markan texts referring not to the poor of Isaiah, but rather to foreigners. "Then people will come from east and west, [from north and south,] and will eat in the kingdom of God." (Q/Luke 13:28; Matthew 8:11).[8] Not only Jesus, but both apocalyptic and other Jews were reflecting on the relation between Israel and the peoples of the world—those to the east and west—as well. Decisively, Jesus' saying in Q/Luke 13:28-29 includes ethnic others from east and west eating in the kingdom of God. Conflicts within contemporary Judaisms as well as conflicts within Jewish Christianities and Gentile Christianities show that table fellowship was a decisive issue. Jesus emphasizes the praxis of this eating in the eschatological promise by choosing table fellowship with those who had been excluded—a praxis with traces in all the sources.[9] Linking table fellowship to this eschatological procession of Gentiles to Jerusalem, Jesus' table fellowship with the unclean in Galilean villages signals through ethical praxis the inbreaking of God's kingdom that forms his theology of creation and eschatology.

Second, Jesus' typical activities of healing and exorcism involved both Judeans and ethnic others. In Capernaum, he healed the centurion's slave/servant, remarking, "not even in Israel have I found such faith" (Q/Luke 7:9). Jesus breathes "woe" on the Galilean towns of Chorazin and Bethsaida, "For if the deeds of power done in you had been done in Tyre and Sidon [Syria], they would have repented long ago...." (Q/Luke 10:13). Further, he exorcized a demon from the daughter of a Gentile woman, a Syrophoenician (Mark 7:26-28; compare Matthew 15:21-23 [a Canaanite woman]), after she famously debated him on the meaning of their ethnic and gender differences. These three authentic sayings from Q all assume some tension between Judeans and others: a Roman centurion, Tyre and Sidon, as well as a Syrophoenician. The Gospel of Thomas 53 is similar, although available only in Coptic translation, not in the earlier Greek texts. Both the a) multiple attestation and b) their coherence suggest that these miracle/exorcism stories correspond to Jesus' Isaianic hope for the eschatological pilgrimage of Gentiles to Jerusalem.

---

8   As editor, Luke added "from north and south," seen again in the story of the southern Ethiopian/African (Acts 8:26-40).
9   Schnelle, *Theology*, 107-08.

Social Consequences of Jesus' Theology of Creation: Crossing the Ethnic Frontier into Samaria

Given the connection between an ethic of love and an eschatologically driven creation theology, it behooves us to look more closely at the implications of those instances where Jesus advocates crossing ethnic/nationalistic borders, since these instances overflow with meaning as we attempt to understand what it is to live into the kingdom of God today. On this point, Josephus is helpful as he is specific about conflicts between (some) Judeans and (some) Samaritans. We briefly recount two of his stories, which illustrate these tensions and their ethnic symbols. Alexander the Great approached Jerusalem (narrative time: fourth century BCE) and was shown the book of Daniel (Antiquities 11.227), which declares that a Greek should destroy the Persians. He supposed this Greek to be himself, Josephus tells us, and so he granted Jews in Jerusalem and those in Babylon the right to live by their own laws (11.338). He then visited the Samaritans and their metropolis, Schechem, who saw that he had honored the Jews, so they determined to profess themselves Jews. Josephus rather declares them "apostates (*apostaton*) of the Jewish nation" (11.340). "If anyone were accused by those of Jerusalem of having eaten things common, or of having broken the Sabbath, or of any other crime of the like nature, he fled away to the Schechemites..." (11.346–47).

The second story: Antiochus IV Epiphanes of Syria took Jerusalem and installed a garrison of Macedonians, but impious and wicked Jews also lived there, according to Josephus, who caused their co-citizens much suffering (Antiquities 12.246, 252; narrative time: second century BCE). Antiochus built an idol altar on God's altar and offered swine, forbidding Jews to circumcise their sons, which many obeyed (12.253–55). When Samaritans witnessed this suffering, they denied they were Jews, but rather claimed to be a colony of Medes and Persians, with which Josephus agrees (12.257). Samaritans say rather that they choose to live according to the customs of the Greeks (12.263). In this context Josephus begins narrating the revolt of Mattathias the Maccabee against the Syrians (12.265).

In Josephus's narrative time, the conflicts between Judeans and Samaritans are centuries old, going back to Alexander the Great and Antiochus. The Judeans' neighbors, the Samaritans, were occasionally their cultural/religious/political antagonists, viewed by some as "apostates." When Judeans from Jerusalem had violated key identity symbols/commandments (not keeping kosher, violating the Sabbath, or obeying Antiochus's order not to circumcise their sons), some of them fled for safety to Samaria.[10]

We are neither arguing that Josephus's description is objective and historical nor that he correctly describes all Jews and all Samaritans.[11] Since Josephus was himself Judean, however, it is plausible that historically, some Judeans in the first century CE felt the way he did about Samaritans and that the conflict Josephus describes also reflects historical tensions within Judea and Jerusalem. As such, we are not arguing that Jesus' position on these issues was unique; on the contrary, he addressed contemporary ethnic negotiations in a colonial setting where diverse Judeans constructed Jewish identity in diverse ways.

Conflicts between Jesus and some other Jews occur along these fault lines: some fellow Jews criticize his eating habits (Mark 2:15-17, 18-20; 7:18-19; Q/Luke 7:22, 34; 10:8; 13:28), and others dispute the meaning and practice of the holy Sabbath (Mark 2:23-28; 3:1-6; 7:1-2; 12:13; Q/Luke 7:30; 11:39-44; Gospel of Thomas 39 [Greek text], 89, 102). Though the Gospels never narrate conflicts about circumcision, the other two customs/laws (kosher and the Sabbath) are not simply traditional religious rituals; rather, they are symbolic boundary markers between Judeans and foreigners/outsiders, powerful dividing lines between constructed ethnicities. By walking across the border into Samaria (Luke 9:51-55), healing a Samaritan leper (Luke 17:11-16), and narrating the parable of the Good Samaritan (Luke 10:25-29, judged authentic by almost all scholars), Jesus would generate a powerful response, as Josephus insists, in some Judean audiences.

After specifying these conflicts, two clarifications remain: 1) to articulate how we understand these conflicts theoretically and 2) to make clear that the tensions outlined are not between Jesus the Christian and other Jews. Jonathan Z. Smith is helpful in this regard. He provides two models of social change, refusing to value only one of them.[12] "Order can

---

10 See also Josephus, War 2.232-46; Antiquities 18.30; 20.118; compare Matthew 10:5; Acts 1:8; 8:25; John 4:4-30.

11 Josephus is not always consistent (see Antiquities 2.290), but before and after the time of Jesus, he repeatedly narrates political and military conflict between Jerusalem and Samaria-Sebaste, precisely the social context that we are describing. See e.g., Antiquities 11.84-116; 12.156; 13.74-79; 18.29-30; 20.118-36 (compare War 2.232-46).

12 J.Z. Smith, *Map Is Not Territory: Studies in the History of Religions* (Leiden: Brill, 1978), 129-46, cited by David Rhoads, *Reading Mark: Engaging the Gospel* (Minneapolis: Fortress, 2004).

be creative or oppressive. The transgression of order can be creative or destructive. Yet the two options represent such fundamentally different worldviews that 'to change stance is to totally alter one's symbols and to inhabit a different world.'"[13] Jesus' proclamation of the reign of God by both word and deed, for example, by crossing the ethnic boundary into Samaria, created a new world; his words and deeds did not leave Judean institutions as they were.

As Jewish, Jesus advocated a new order that he also practiced. Actually, he claimed to be practicing the order of God's creation, which is multiethnic. This is such a powerful term that it needs definition. Contemporary Judaisms were multiethnic, in the sense that many Jews in different geographical locations, in Rome, North Africa, Greece, Syria, and Persia, for example, as well as in Judea lived orthopraxic lives. When Jesus the Jew crossed the boundary into Samaria, and when he told the parable of the Good Samaritan, he was "multiethnic" without orthopraxy.[14] The Samaritan in Jesus' parable loved God and loved his neighbor as himself (Luke 10:27 and 37, citing Deuteronomy 6:4 and Leviticus 19:18) as a Samaritan,[15] which as Josephus, himself a Judean, defined their practice, did not involve keeping kosher or resting on the holy Sabbath.

Contemporary discussions of ethnicity insist that ethnic identities are negotiated, particularly when difference is encountered in a colonial context. Such encounters evoke discursive justification of particular cultural practices, which is why many, probably most contemporary students of ethnicity deny that any static list of ethnic characteristics is adequate.[16] Interpreting Judea in the first century CE, it would be inadequate to list kosher, Sabbath, and circumcision as religious laws that distinguish Judeans from other ethnicities; such a list has no single *sine qua non* that defines a particular ethnic group. Ethnic difference is malleable, even mutable. In the texts quoted above, we hear Judean ethnic identities being constructed and contested by diverse colonized Judeans.

---

13 Rhoads, *Reading Mark*, 164, quoting J.Z. Smith, *Map Is Not Territory*.
14 Again, this was not unique. See e.g., 1 Maccabees 1:43, 52; 2 Maccabees 4:13–17; as well as Josephus, Antiquities 11.346–47 and 12.246, 252, cited above.
15 In general, colonizing Greeks (Antiochus IV Epiphanes) demanded identity of religious practice, that Judeans eat pork sacrificed to Zeus (see 2 Maccabees 6–7), but colonizing Romans allowed diversity in practice. Compare the contrast between Greeks and Romans by A. Wallace-Hadrill, *Rome's Cultural Revolution* (Cambridge: Cambridge University, 2010), 33–35. Given this distinction, the colonized Jewish Jesus' parable and multiethnic practice is Roman, not Hellenistic.
16 Barreto, *Ethnic Negotiations*, 23, 39, 44.

We focus on a particular example of a Judean ethnic boundary construction in the citations given above, circumcision. Shaye Cohen with many contemporary scholars argues that there was no single, objective definition of Jewishness in the ancient world, that Jewish identities were "subjective . . . , constructed by the individual him/herself, other Jews, other gentiles, and the state."[17] There was no evidence that individual Jews were easily recognizable in antiquity: neither somatic difference, clothing, ritual participation, nor circumcision were reliable ethnic markers. "How then, did you know a Jew in antiquity when you saw one? The answer is that you did not. But you could make reasonably plausible inferences from what you saw."[18]

Cohen's conclusion is one-sided, inquiring primarily about Jewish ethnic symbols, not also about the power of Greco-Roman institutions on the other side of the ethnic boundary, that is, the social power of those symbolic institutions to include individuals and ethnic groups or to exclude them. In the contemporary West, a Conservative or Reformed Jewish male may be relatively invisible; in ancient Greco-Roman gymnasia, an orthopraxic Jewish male was publicly visible. One of the core symbols of Greco-Roman culture was the gymnasium, where Greek men exercised nude, and Roman men and women bathed nude.[19] Romans discovered concrete, and one of the key symbols of ancient Roman culture that remains until the present day are aqueducts that they constructed to bring water from some source to their cities, in which they constructed fountains and baths. Gymnasia were core cultural symbols of colonizing Greeks and Romans by which they distinguished between civilized and barbarian, between those who bathed nude and those who did not. Circumcised Jewish men—in Jerusalem,[20] Antioch, Alexandria, or Rome—faced a defining choice whether to participate in Greco-Roman culture or not when they decided whether or not to bathe nude, whether or not to join the "civilized." "In those days out of Israel came

---

17 S. Cohen, *The Beginning of Jewishness: Boundaries, Varieties, Uncertainties* (Berkeley: University of California, 2001), 3.
18 Cohen, *Jewishness*, 67, quoted by Barreto, *Ethnic Negotiations*, 17.
19 Garrett G. Fagan, *Bathing in Public in the Roman World* (Ann Arbor: University of Michigan, 1999). Wallace-Hadrill, *Rome's Cultural Revolution*, 169–90.
20 See Monika Bernett, "Space and Interaction: Narrative and Representation of Power under the Herodians," in *Contested Spaces: Houses and Temples in Roman Antiquity and the New Testament*, D.L. Balch and A. Weissenrieder, eds. WUNT 285 (Tübingen: Mohr Siebeck, 2012), 289–97, citing Josephus, War 1.401-25; Ant. 15.266-388; 16.143-44 on Herod's building program, including aqueducts and gymnasia. Herod dramatically changed the architecture of Judea immediately before and during Jesus' lifetime.

sons, transgressors of the law, and they persuaded many. . . . And they built a gymnasium in Hierosolyma [Jerusalem] according to the precepts of the nations, and they fashioned foreskins for themselves and apostatized from the holy covenant. . . ." (1 Maccabees 1:11–15 NETS; compare 2 Maccabees 4:9, 12). The choice was not merely philosophical or rational, and the consequences were not only individual. For Jews it was both religious and cultural. The choice for Jewish individuals or communities was a bodily decision, a choice of the gut, not merely of the mind.

In a gymnasium Jewish men were clearly visible, different. If they bathed nude, their circumcision was ridiculed by the "civilized" and their nudity forcefully challenged by traditional compatriots. In a core institution of Greco-Roman culture, virtually a *sine qua non*, the gymnasium, Jewish men were visible and exposed in a non-traditional way. Cohen incorrectly asserts that Judaism moved from an ethnic, geographically defined people to a cultural, religiously defined one. Those who circumcised their sons and rejected nudity in gymnasia/baths had to construct an identity visibly separate from "civilized" Greco-Roman culture and its symbols. What should be clear from this consideration of circumcision is that Jesus proposes a way of being multiethnic without imposing orthopraxy on other ethnic groups. In crossing the ethnic border with Samaritans, he confronts critical symbolic boundary markers and advocates for a radical shift in worldview.

As to the second necessary clarification, that this conflict was not between Jesus the Christian and the Jews, J.Z. Smith explains, all institutions, including religious ones, face social change, face the alternatives of order or transgression of order. Contemporary religious institutions, Jewish, Christian, Muslim, or Buddhist, have been hearing persuasive feminist critics for two centuries. Our contemporary churches, synagogues, mosques, and more have more recently begun facing gay and lesbian critique of traditionally homophobic practices. Such critique or change evokes conflict and reinterpretation of scripture, e.g., in 2009, the Evangelical Lutheran Church in America voted to permit those bishops and synods that choose to do so to ordain qualified gay and lesbian persons as pastors, with institutional conflict before and after the decision. In this example, there is a radical change in the interpretations and praxes of the denominational group (a transgression of previously established order), but in transgressing the old order we are not suggesting that those bishops and synods that choose to ordain qualified gay and lesbian persons now represent a separate religious social order.

In a similar vein, Jesus was a prophetic critic within Judaism, not unique, which we have mentioned above and now illustrate both by Jeremiah and by the founder and first leader of Hasidism in Eastern Europe, the Ba'al Shem Tov (1700–1760, "master of the good name"). First, Jeremiah (3:16) makes the astounding assertion, "the ark of the covenant of the Lord . . . shall not come to mind, or be remembered, or missed; nor shall another one be made." The ark, a portable shrine in the wilderness, signifying God's divine presence (Exodus 25:10–15), which contained the two tablets of laws from Sinai (Deutoronomy 10:2, 5), which David brought to Jerusalem, signifying the unity of the Northern and Southern kingdoms (2 Samuel 6), and which Solomon placed in the Holy of Holies in the new temple (1 Kings 8:4–7), that ark shall not be remembered! Even more surprising, "it shall no longer be said, 'As the Lord lives who brought the people of Israel up out of the land of Egypt,' but 'as the Lord lives who brought out and led the . . . house of Israel out of the land of the north' . . ." (Jeremiah 23:7–8) Israel will not speak of the Exodus from Egypt, but rather of a new Exodus from Babylon! Jeremiah the prophet is encouraging significant change in how to celebrate and where to experience the presence of God. Our colleague at PLTS/GTU, Prof. Steed Davidson, tells us that these verses in Jeremiah are probably from later redactors, but in a sense, that makes them even more remarkable. Not the original, creative prophet himself, but later scribes in Israel, the later institution, is making radical adjustments, changes.

The Ba'al Shem Tov repelled some other Jews by his activity as a miracle worker. There was a bitter struggle in Lithuania, led by Elijah ben Solomon Zalman of Vilna, who opposed Hasidic "ecstasy, visions, and miracles, their dangerous lies and idolatrous worship." In the 1770s and 1780s there were bans (harem) against Hasidism. Hasids and their opponents denounced each other to authorities, which led to arrests.[21] Hasidism, now the most important form of religious Judaism in Europe, North America, and Israel, was bitterly opposed when first introduced.

Jeremiah, Jesus, and the Ba'al Shem Tov illustrate the alternatives of order or transgression of order within Judaism. It is not anti-Jewish to observe that Jesus transgressed traditional order in Judea in the first century, no more than it is to observe that Jeremiah offended many in Israel in the sixth century BCE, and that the Ba'al Shem Tov transgressed

---

21 "Israel ben Eliezer Ba'al Shem Tov," *Encyclopedia Judaica* 9 (1971), 1049–48, and "Hasidism," *Encyclopedia Judaica* 7 (1971), 1290ff.

traditional Jewish order in Eastern Europe in the eighteenth century, although unlike the other two, Jesus failed to persuade many other Jews that this new order was a good development.

Theological/Ethical Consequences of Jesus' Emphasis on Creation: Modification of the Greek Political Friendship Ethic, a Transformation That Leans into the Future (Ted Peters)

Later Christian theologians realized that Jesus' form of multiethnicity implies a different political friendship ethic than the Greek Aristotle's. Here we depend on an Argentine theologian, Nancy Bedford,[22] and have space to emphasize only one point. Aristotle, the Greek philosopher, claimed (Nic. Eth. 8.8) that friendship exists only between persons who are equal and similar. The ethic we have identified in Jesus' preaching and acts, especially with regard to ethnic boundary crossing as a disjunctive force in conceptualizing Judean ethnic boundaries, flies in the face of this necessity of similarity.

As a theological/ethical theme, this is not new and is addressed at various points in the tradition. The Latin Ambrose, for instance, later suggested (De officiis ministrorum 3.22.135)[23] the possibility of mutuality and friendship between persons whose social location is very different, because both are friends of the same God, who manifested her love in the incarnation. Ted Peters helps us gain a distinctive foothold within this theological approach that hearkens back to the connection between ethics and creation theology we have found in Jesus' preaching and acts.

Peters, like the wisdom approach to Jesus' creation theology, encourages us to think about theology and the doctrine of creation epigenetically and not archonically. It is a call to take seriously the continuing process of creation and the place of eschatological consummation as continuous with the evolving and emerging transformations of natural and human history. Borrowing the term prolepsis from Wolfhart Pannenberg, Peters uses it to emphasize the ontological heft of the future, of anticipation, for understanding the meaning of the present and the past. This future, which he sometimes calls *venturum* or ethically, the Life of Beatitude,

---

22 Nancy Bedford, "La Amistad y la eferescencia teológica," in *La Porfía de la Resurrección: Essayos desde el Feminismo Teológico Latinoamericano* FTL 30 (Buenos Aires: Kairós, 2008), chap. 10. She cites David Konstan, "Problems in the History of Christian Friendship," *JECS* 4 (1993): 87–113.

23 Bedford, "Amistad," 192–95.

breaks into our present life imbuing it with the anticipated meaning of the coming Kingdom of God.[24]

> We have observed above that new wholes transform past parts. Integration into new, more comprehensive unities preserves while renewing what came before. This holistic complexification process is nonlinear. Adding a new whole changes an entire situation in a significant way. The possibility of transformative effect renders redemption possible. Now, suppose we apply this to eschatology and then to creation? God's eschatological redemption will so reconfigure all that had been past that it might as well be a new creation or, perhaps more accurately, the completion of the creation already begun. Does this mean that eschatological omega takes ontological priority over what happened at the beginning? I believe it does.[25]

While Peters has done a tremendous amount of work with regard to the implications that such a proleptic theology would have for the interaction of theology and natural science, especially with the diverse array of issues arising from evolution, stem cell research, and astrobiology, there is also an undeniable realization of the ethical implications of his theological outlook. Perhaps this is most clear in his arguments for proleptic dignity. He argues that human dignity must stand at the center of our value system, but that we have forgotten its proleptic and relational features, instead reifying it as an inherent attribute of personhood. Peters urges us to remember that, phenomenologically speaking, dignity is first conferred and then claimed: we treat the other as valuable, which allows her to claim value for herself. Theologically, this conferral of dignity is ultimately rooted in God. God treats each of us with dignity, allowing us to treat others with that dignity first conferred upon us, something very akin to Ambrose as cited above.

We have to understand, though, that Peters takes us a decisive step further than Ambrose in this argument. Ambrose's theological revision of Aristotelian friendship ethics is essentially archonic. Peters' process of conferral is proleptic, and he contrasts it with inherent dignity insofar as his approach is eschatological.[26] The inherent dignity of persons stems

---

24 See Ted Peters, *Anticipating Omega: Science, Faith, and Our Ultimate Future* (Vandenhoeck & Ruprecht: Göttingen, 2006), 24–27, and Peters, *GOD—The World's Future*, 319–21.
25 Peters, *Anticipating Omega*, 25.
26 Peters, *Anticipating Omega*, 185.

from the anticipation of God's saving activity: dignity is not archonically an innate part of our created being but a retroactively (or epigenetically innate) value realized through our anticipated unity with the divine life. Conferring dignity in our relations with others proleptically advents the hope for our future final dignity in relation to God.[27] By connecting human dignity to prolepsis, living out the value of human dignity is our way of participating in the transformation of our world into God's kingdom. Peters makes very explicit how the ways in which we ethically confer dignity have real ontological effect in terms of the Kingdom of God. By systematically applying prolepsis as a principle to traditional theological loci, Peters is highlighting for our world today the connection between eschatology, creation theology, and ethics we have argued is modeled in Jesus' preaching and acts.

Notably, the ethical impetus here implied is no easy task. It involves entering into the contested space of forming ethnic identity. Moreover, in a Christian context it requires, as Bedford appropriately cautions, that we must enter into this space well aware of how power or prestige, or both, effect the formation of dignity or friendship, e.g., between pastor and parishioner, between professor and student, or between those with or without computers. Bedford emphasizes the transformations, modifications, changes, and mixing (*mezclar*)[28] that can and do occur between friends whose social locations differ. This is true, both of conversations between individual friends in different social locations, and of conversations between diverse ethnic groups with differing customs and values.

Such transformation, such "mixing," is not only individual, but also occurs between ethnic/cultural/religious groups.[29] One of the convincing theses of Andrew Wallace-Hadrill's extraordinary new book, *Rome's Cultural Revolution,* is that Greek and Roman cultures/societies intermingled in Italy for three centuries (the first two centuries BCE and the first CE). Colonization was not one-way.

Gosden's idea of a "middle ground," in which cultures stand in dialectic with one another, provides a way out. If we focus on the reciprocity of the process whereby the colonial power not only provides powerful

---

27 Ibid., 178–187.
28 Bedford, "Amistad," 189-91, 196-97.
29 For Greek opposition to and Roman support for ethnic "mixing,"—a generalization with exceptions—see David L. Balch, "Jesus as Founder of the Church in Luke-Acts," in *Contextualizing Acts: Lukan Narrative and Greco-Roman Discourse,* Todd Penner and C. Vander Stichele, eds. (Atlanta: Scholars and Brill, 2003), 167–73.

new cultural models to the colonized, but in turn takes to itself cultural models from the colonized (enough to refer to the spread of tea and curry in colonial Britain, and the fashions of oriental art and religion), we can allow that Roman conquest of Greece led not to fusion but reciprocal exchange. The cultures do not fuse..., but enter into a vigorous and continuous process of dialogue with one another. Romans can "hellenise" (speak Greek, imitate Greek culture), without becoming less Roman.... Reciprocally, the Greeks under Roman rule define their own identity more sharply by paideia even as they become Roman in other ways....[30]

This theoretical approach would surely be productive in interpreting the interaction of Jewish, Christian, and Roman cultures in the centuries before Constantine, or in understanding the dialogues between North American colonizing and Latin American colonized "Christian" cultures.[31]

Here we emphasize that Jesus' crossing the border into Samaria intensified a dialogue or dialectic between Jewish and Greco-Roman religion and culture that still continues.[32] Dialogue with different others, whether individual or religious/political, generates transformation, change, "mixing." Such change/mixing in political contexts often involves tragedy; nevertheless, in this dialogue both partners, each with their own past, constructed histories, lean into the future as they are transformed and transform others. Jesus taught and lived a dynamic form of Judaism that was colonized by Rome, not in the era of the earlier Greek imperial rule of Alexander and his successors. Jesus the Jewish, wise prophet was in dialogue with others, including a Syrophoenecian woman, and according to literary tradition (John 4), a Samaritan woman.

---

30 Wallace-Hadrill, *Rome's Cultural Revolution*, 23–24.
31 For official Lutheran and Reformed church documents protesting the political ethics of North America, which generate hunger, unemployment, homelessness, and death in South America, see René Krüger, ed., *Life in All Fullness: Latin American Protestant Churches Facing Neoliberal Globalization* (Buenos Aires: ISEDET, 2007). For biblical hermeneutics supporting these South American ecclesial statements that call for dialogue with North America, see Rubén Dri, "*Las Iglesias, el capitalismo y el ideario socialista,*" in *Teología de la Liberación y los Derechos Humanos: Por un nuevo cielo y un nuevo mundo*, Arturo Blatezky, ed. (Buenos Aires: Movimiento Ecuménico por los Derechos Humanos, 2011), 263–79. For an Argentine Lutheran theological critique of globalization, see Guillermo Hansen, *En las fisuras: esbozos luteranos para neustro tiempo* (Buenos Aires: Iglesia Evangélica Luterana Unida, 2010); Hansen is now a professor of theology at Luther Seminary, St. Paul.
32 See Luke T. Johnson, *Among the Gentiles: Greco-Roman Religion and Christianity* (New Haven: Yale University, 2009).

One critical point remains: to refuse such dialogue, to close our individual persons or our religious/economic/political cultures and communities off against diverse others would be to reject Jesus' initiative. In the past, when Lutheran theologians in Germany turned against Jews, our mothers in the faith, and legitimated the murder of six million in the Holocaust, that was both a heinous crime against human rights and also a sacrilegious offense by those who claimed the name of "Christian," who claimed to be followers of Jesus who crossed ethnic and religious boundaries into Samaria.[33] When Roman Catholic bishops in Argentina legitimated the military dictator Jorge Rafael Videla (1976–1983), as he "disappeared" 30,000 mostly young Argentine "Marxist" students, literally throwing a generation of Argentine youth into the Pacific Ocean in the Cold War between capitalists and "communists,"[34] that was a crime against human rights and a heinous sacrilege against the Creator God who revealed herself in Jesus, the Jew of Nazareth, who engaged in dialogue with religious and ethnic others, with Samaritans. In the present, when North American churches close themselves off against dialogue with Latin American churches and culture, that isolation is also counter to Jesus' own interethnic dialogue between Judeans and Samaritans. Moreover, just as Jesus' interethnic dialogue was steeped in protological and eschatological commitments, we must, as with Peters, realize the proleptic ramifications of closing ourselves to diverse others: as we cease to confer dignity in refusing interethnic dialogue, we stymie the adventing of the kingdom of God.[35]

---

33 See Susannah Heschel, *The Aryan Jesus: Christian Theologians and the Bible in Nazi Germany* (Princeton: Princeton University, 2008); S. Heschel, "Historiography of Antisemitism versus Anti-Judaism: A Response to Robert Morgan," *JSNT* 33, no. 3 (2011): 257–79. A few protested publicly, e.g., Dietrich Bonhoeffer.

34 Rubén Dri, *La hegemonía de los cruzados: La iglesia católica y la dictadura militar* (Buenos Aires: Biblos, 2011). Carlos Mugica (1930–1974), a well-known priest, protested, and in the same era in El Salvador, so did Bishop Oscar Romero (1977–1980); both were martyred. See Nancy E. Bedford, *Jesus Christus und das Gekreuzigte Volk: Christologie der Nachfolge und des Martyriums bei Jon Sobrino* CRM 15 (Aachen: Augustinus, 1995). Perhaps the most courageous protest in Buenos Aires was by Rabbi Marshall Meyer.

35 David Balch thanks Pacific Lutheran Theological Seminary (PLTS) for a sabbatical and Texas Christian University for an emeritus grant that supported writing his portion of this essay. Balch thanks his hosts at ISEDET in Buenos Aires, especially Rector José David Rodriguez and René Krüger, Professor of New Testament.

"Happily Ever After"

An Approach for Novice Readers of Revelation

Wayne C. Kannaday

Over the years Ted Peters has been fond of quoting Anselm's definition of theology as "faith seeking understanding."[1] While this definition adequately captures the essential work of generic theology, it falls short in my mind of conveying the effectual work of the Christian version of the discipline. Christian theology by its nature is communal, which requires that enlightened believers share with others their understanding of transformative truth.[2]

Without bearing such witness, Christian scholars lapse into Gnostic heresy, reserving their "secret knowledge" for an instructed intellectual elite and restricting the potential benefit of what theological truth they may discern to inform or to enhance the faith of the Christian masses or the perspectives and attitudes of the pluralistic culture. Thus, where such understanding might breed ecumenical dialogue, in its place abides denominational and sectarian suspicion. Where we Christians might come together around shared scriptures and doctrines to address concerns of social justice and global sustainability, we find ourselves polarized. Instead of confronting the demons of our day, we find ourselves demonizing one another, producing the ecclesiastical version of the quagmire that haunts contemporary American politics.

---

[1] See Ted Peters, *Futures Human and Divine* (Atlanta: John Knox Press, 1978), 150; idem, *GOD—the World's Future: Systematic Theology for a Postmodern Era* (Minneapolis: Fortress Press, 1992), 28.

[2] These are, I believe, points with which Ted Peters would concur. See his discussion of "ecumenic pluralism" in idem, *GOD—The World's Future*, 334–56.

To the extent this is true, there has come to exist a sizable chasm between the enlightened theologian in the tower and the ill-informed believer on the streets. Perhaps nowhere is this hermeneutical epidemic more widespread and apparent than in the interpretation of John's apocalypse.

Elaine Pagels has called Revelation the strangest and most controversial book in the Bible.[3] John J. Collins begins his opus, *The Apocalyptic Imagination*, by acknowledging a paradox that plagues modern readers of apocalyptic literature. He juxtaposes Ernst Käsemann's pronouncement that "apocalyptic was the mother of all Christian theology" with Klaus Koch's declaration that modern scholars in the face of apocalyptic literature find it *ratlos*, "perplexing, stupefying, even embarrassing."[4] Christopher Rowland notes that although historical scholarship has succeeded in taming the mystical magniloquence of the Apocalypse, it has done so "at the expense of drifting the book into the hands of those who use it, in their own form of historical reconstruction, to delineate the calendar of Doomsday."[5] More simply put, in the words of Mark Twain, history has shown that recent predictions about the demise of this world "have been greatly exaggerated." Consider these brief examples:[6]

- The Seventh Day Adventist followers of William Miller continue to wait for the termination of the terra firma that he first anticipated in 1843, and then recalculated for 1844.
- Pat Robertson failed both in his bid for the presidency and his pronouncement that the world would end in 1982 in a global Armageddon.
- In the 1970s, the *New York Times* identified Hal Lindsey as "The Jeremiah of Today"; his best-selling *The Late Great*

---

3 Elaine Pagels, *Revelations: Visions, Prophecy, and Politics in the Book of Revelation* (New York: Penguin, 2012), 1.
4 John J. Collins, *The Apocalyptic Imagination: An Introduction to Jewish Apocalyptic Literature*, 2nd ed. (Grand Rapids, Michigan: Wm. B. Eerdmans Publishing Co., 1998), 1.
5 Christopher Rowland, "Preface," in *Studies in the Book of the Revelation*, Steve Moyise, ed. (Edinburgh and New York: T&T Clark, 2001), ix.
6 Details and sources for these and other instances of apocalyptic predictions and millennial cults may be found in Martha Himmelfarb, *The Apocalypse: A Brief History* (Oxford: Wiley-Blackwell, 2010), 137–60; Eugen Weber, *Apocalypses: Prophecies, Cults, and Millennial Beliefs through the Ages* (Cambridge, MA: Harvard University Press, 1999), 193–222; and Bart Ehrman, *Jesus: Apocalyptic Prophet of the New Millennium* (Oxford: Oxford University Press, 1999), 3–19.

Planet Earth announced that the cosmic countdown had begun with the creation of the state of Israel in 1948, which meant that all would end by 1988.[7]

- Having missed the mark on that one, Lindsey more recently has offered thirteen reasons the world will end in 2013, hedging his bets by explaining that what he means is wrapped up in the concept of TEOTWAWKI, "the end of the world as we know it."
- Proponents of the Y2K theory thought that the advent of the new millennium would mark the end, prompting some to party like it was 1999.
- Some contemporary purveyors of the Mayan calendar interpreted its ending to signal the end of all time, thus leaving us with the symmetrical 12-21-12 as the appropriately binary end of all things.
- Anyone who drove American highways during 2011 encountered billboards paid for by the ministry of Family Radio host Harold Camping, whose numerological interpretation of biblical quotations led him to herald May 21, 2011, as "Judgment Day."

As of this writing, none of these predictions has come to pass. Of this, history has left no doubt.

Yet, my contention is not that the calculus has been in error or that the cipher has not been properly decoded. Rather, such readings are destined to be out-of-bounds because their interpreters are asking the wrong questions, playing the wrong game, operating under false premises. The proponents of each of these prognostications—and the plethora more these serve to represent—err not because they did not properly do the math but because they did not previously study with Ted Peters.

It was Peters who first tutored me in the formerly forbidding concepts of eschatology, apocalyptic, and prolepsis that, in turn, paved the way for me to evolve into a mindful, mature exegete. In an effort, then, to pay forward my debt, what I propose to offer in this essay is a primer for those who have previously found Revelation too alien, too disturbing, or too overwhelming to explore.

---

7   Hal Lindsey, *The Late Great Planet Earth* (Grand Rapids, Michigan: Zondervan, 1970).

To be sure, Revelation does include a number of alien, disturbing, and overwhelming features. It comes to us from a foreign language (Greek), an ancient time (late first century CE), and a distant land (Patmos, a Greek island in the Aegean Sea). Its imagery draws from a diversity of cultures—Palestine, Hellenism, the Roman Empire—and a wide body of literature, including the Hebrew Scriptures, Ancient Greek mythology, Platonic philosophy, Pseudepigrapha, and Christian oral and written traditions. It belongs to a genre of writings called apocalypses that are among the most misunderstood in the biblical corpus.[8] Naturally, then, there is much that is strange about this book.

Still, however, at its core Revelation may be read at a level that is both basic and yet, no pun intended, revealing. In order to enable such a reading, I offer here three principles.[9] First, do not fail to see the forest for the trees; the devil is in the details. Second, understand that Revelation belongs to the literary genre of apocalypse, and therefore, its purpose is not prediction but proclamation. Third, as contemporary readers, let us draw on our experience of fairy tales to better understand this otherwise alien genre and its "happily ever after" message. Allow me to elaborate on each of these principles.

Don't Miss the Forest for the Trees; the Devil Is in the Details

What I mean about not seeing the forest for the trees is the failure of some readers to recognize that the book consists not of a series of revelations but of a single revelation with a central focal point: Jesus. The book itself clearly tells us this:

Ἀποκάλυψις Ἰησοῦ Χριστοῦ ἣν ἔδωκεν αὐτῷ ὁ θεὸς δεῖξαι τοῖς δούλοις αὐτοῦ ἃ δεῖ γενέσθαι ἐν τάχει, καὶ ἐσήμανεν

---

8 For the scholarly definition of the genre "apocalypse," see John J. Collins, *Apocalyptic Imagination*, 5. For the fuller discussion on the cluster of traits that distinguish apocalypse, see J.J. Collins, ed., *Semeia 14: Apocalypse: The Morphology of a Genre* (Missoula MT: Scholars Press, 1979).

9 What I offer here is not a comprehensive way to organize the book but some guidelines for approaching it initially. A survey of the numerous commentaries on the Revelation will reveal as many outlines. One of the simpler yet useful models is that of David Barr, who sees the Revelation as consisting of three distinct stories within a common frame: (1) Jesus encounters a majestic human figure; (2) John ascends to the throne room of God; and (3) the seer watches a holy war play out between the forces of good and evil. See David L. Barr, "The Story John Told: Reading Revelation for Its Plot," in *Reading the Book of Revelation: A Resource for Students*, David L. Barr, ed. (Atlanta: Society of Biblical Literature, 2003), 11–23.

ἀποστείλας διὰ τοῦ ἀγγέλου αὐτοῦ τῷ δούλῳ αὐτοῦ Ἰωάννῃ, ὃς ἐμαρτύρησεν τὸν λόγον τοῦ θεοῦ καὶ τὴν μαρτυρίαν Ἰησοῦ Χριστοῦ ὅσα εἶδεν (Revelation 1:1-2 NA).

A revelation of Jesus Christ that God gave to him to show to his servants what must inevitably transpire shortly, which he transmitted by sending his herald to his servant John, who in turn bore witness to the word of God and the witness of Jesus Christ, whatsoever he saw (Revelation 1:1-2, my translation).

Grammatically, the title of John's Apocalypse is singular, not plural. Moreover, the Greek phrase Ἀποκάλυψις Ἰησοῦ Χριστοῦ indicates that Jesus is not only the source of the revelation but also its content.[10] In the words of Elizabeth Schüssler Fiorenza, "the title of the Apocalypse describes the book's contents as well as the authority behind its chain of communication."[11] From the beginning, therefore, the reader is informed that the cohesive theme of what is about to be revealed is Jesus Christ; everything else, however bold and colorful it may be, serves as mere backdrop.

Like finding Waldo in those entertaining children's books, readers are to make sense of the authentic message of the Revelation by locating at the core of the book Jesus the Christ. Trying to detect purposeful and exact meaning in every number, symbol, and image of the book becomes an overwhelming—and failing—proposition. The devil thus proves to be in the details because the details are not the focus of the work. The trees are there to constitute the forest that serves as an apocalyptic landscape, the landscape into which Jesus appears in various guises: Son of Man (Revelation 1:12-20; 14:14), Lion of Judah (5:5), the Worthy Lamb (6:6; 14:1), endangered infant (12:5), warrior on a white horse leading the heavenly host into cosmic conflict (19:11-16), grape harvester (14:15-16), bridegroom (21:2, 9), the root of David (22:16) and the coming Alpha and Omega (22:12-13, 20), to name a choice few.

---

10 The Greek phrase can be interpreted to mean either that Jesus was the source of the revelation or its content. Although scholars have sometimes been divided on this, for readers who follow the narrative flow of the Apocalypse it becomes difficult to deny that Jesus stands as the central character of the book. For support of this view, see Gilbert Desrosiers, *An Introduction to Revelation* (London and New York: Continuum, 2000), 11. For support of the contrary view that Jesus is chiefly the source of the Revelation, see Mitchell G. Reddish, *Revelation* (Macon, GA: Smyth and Helwys, 2001), 32.

11 Elizabeth Schüssler Fiorenza, "The Words of Prophecy: Reading the Apocalypse Theologically," in *Studies in the Book of the Revelation*, Steve Moyise, ed. (Edinburgh and New York: T&T Clark, 2001), 3.

Not seeing the forest for the trees, then, results when interpreters restrict their vision too narrowly, most often by explaining an ancient image in light of a contemporary phenomenon. One of the most blatant instances of this for me appears in *The Late Great Planet Earth* when Hal Lindsey asserts that the description of the locusts in Revelation 9:7–10 is best explained as an attack helicopter.[12]

Two observations may help prevent readers from falling prey to such literal and anachronistic exegesis. First of all, a strict literalistic reading of the Revelation cannot survive scrutiny. The case for this could be made in any number of ways, but perhaps no plainer evidence need be adduced than the opening of the sixth seal (6:12–17). With the breaking of this seal, a celestial drama unfolds that includes the sun turning black, the moon turning blood red, and the stars of the sky falling to the earth. Now imagine that scene. Were the sun to grow dark, not only would the moon have no color but the earth would reach absolute zero in a matter of minutes. Or if even one star fell to earth, the earth itself would be incinerated long before the two collided. Yet, two verses later we are told that myriad rich and powerful political and military leaders flee to hide among the boulders and caves of the mountain in order to escape this catastrophe. But what caves? What mountains? What humans would survive? If the stars fell to the earth the planet would cease to be, incinerated in a kind of cosmic cremation. Clearly, opening the sixth seal is not offering us a literal description of a step in some eschatological timeline. The imagery is meant to arouse not delineate, evoke not measure.[13]

Moreover, the text itself frequently instructs its readers on how to read (and not to read) the text. The author himself alerts his readers when there is a code word to be decrypted. Perhaps the most famous instance of this involves the mark of the beast described in 13:8. "This calls for wisdom," the writer beckons. "Let anyone with understanding calculate the number of the beast, for it is the number of a person. Its number

---

12 Hal Lindsey, *There's a New World Coming*, updated ed. (Eugene, Oregon: Harvest House, 1984), 7.

13 In the words of Adela Collins, "The Apocalypse is as evocative as it is expressive. Not only does it display attitudes and feelings; it also elicits them." See her rich discussion in Adela Yarbro Collins, *Crisis and Catharsis: The Power of the Apocalypse* (Philadelphia: Westminster Press, 1984), 141–52. In contrast, for a conservative evangelical's attempt (futile in my mind) to make literal sense of the events described in the opening of the sixth seal, see John Walvrood, *The Revelation of Jesus Christ* (Chicago: Moody Press, 1966), 135–38.

is six-hundred-sixty-six" (Revelation 13:8).[14] Scholarly consensus generally regards this as a cryptic reference to Nero, but understanding what the reference to Nero means invites a wider range of commentary.[15]

Another example of this occurs in Revelation 17:9. Here the writer again calls for wisdom, for discernment is necessary in order to recognize that the Great Whore of Babylon who sits on seven hills is indeed "the great city that rules over the kings of the earth" (17:18). The reference to ancient Rome is hard to miss—if, as the seer invokes, one has ears to hear.

Mitchell Reddish offers readers wise words of exegetical guidance. When approaching Revelation, he says, to "literalize" is to trivialize.[16]

The Purpose of an Apocalypse Is to Proclaim, Not Predict

A second error that untutored readers of Revelation commonly commit consists of failing to understand that the purpose of Revelation is not prediction but proclamation. This is, at its most basic, the product of "genre confusion." Most often this mistake results from the failure to distinguish apocalypse from "prophecy." Reading Revelation as a blueprint for the end of time is as misguided as basing doomsday on the Mayan calendar. Neither document was directly addressed to our age. Although people of faith may look to scripture to speak anew to every age, it constitutes arrogance to consider that the Bible is speaking new to any age.[17] The power of canonical writings from any religion is that whatev-

---

14　Textual critics have reported that some manuscripts read 616 rather than 666. Metzger notes that this could have been intentional since the difference in the Latin and Hebrew spellings of Nero Caesar could account for the difference. See Bruce Metzger, *A Textual Commentary on the Greek New Testament*, 2nd ed. (New York: American Bible Society, 1994), 676.

15　For a brief but thorough discussion of the phenomenon of gematria and how its application to 666 produces reference to Nero as well as possible connections with Caligula, the Babylonian Nimrod, and others, see J. Massynberde Ford, *Revelation*, The Anchor Bible, vol. XXXVIII (Garden City, New York: Doubleday, 1975), 225-28.

16　Reddish, *Revelation*, 31.

17　Let me be clear here. By "anew" I mean "fresh and timely"; by "new" I mean "novel" or "original." My point is that the Scriptures address each age with a message that is both consistent over time but alive, afresh, and timely for each age. They do not, however, suddenly disclose a message that was formerly hidden, previously irrelevant, and now, suddenly and currently disclosed (if interpreters got the code figured out). Peters supports this idea when he speaks of, on the one hand, the hermeneutical question that calls theologians to reinterpret the Bible in light of a new situation, but he also acknowledges that some aspects of the faith cannot be translated or replaced. "What permits the gospel to ride out the centuries, traveling from one age to another and one language to another is not its translatability. It is the protean power of its symbols to emit new meaning in new contexts." Ted Peters, *GOD—The World's Future*, 13-14.

er truth they possess lingers across time and space, and above history and culture. Belief that these writings have lain dormant, encrypted, and irrelevant for 2,000 years only to address at last our contemporary age is rooted in a school of hermeneutics that, from the perspective of historical exegesis, resides far outside the mainstream, and that, from the perspective of faith, denies the inspiration of the Holy Spirit as the source for divine truth. The Church declared Gnosticism a heresy long ago, and for good reason.

In all fairness, however, those who treat Revelation as a book of prophecy can locate apparent vindication in the text. "Blessed is the one who reads aloud the words of the prophecy, and blessed are those who hear and keep what is written in it; for the time is near" (Rev 1:3). The confusion is born out of misunderstanding the biblical term "prophecy."[18] In his classic work on the subject, Abraham Heschel described prophets not as divine soothsayers but as covenant advocates.[19] They serve, like committed attorneys, as God's spokespersons to every audience—from regular crowd to regal king—interpreting and applying divine law and covenant to the questions and crises of their day. Their divine announcements of judgment, therefore, are not rooted in reading the stars but in recognizing the consequences of human actions. As Heschel says, they see the present with the 20-20 vision of divine insight. The inevitability of their oracles of doom is conditional upon present trends continuing. Yet, one of the major themes of the prophets was also repentance. Regularly, the prophets called for behavioral changes that would in turn avert any impending disaster. Prophets address those for whom it is not too late. Doom may lay on the horizon, but it has not yet come.

Not so for apocalyptic writers. Authors of apocalypses do not address a penultimate state; theirs is a time too late for dire warnings, penitent transformation, or even last minute escape. Whatever disaster prophets may have warned about has come to pass by the time apocalyptic authors apply stylus to papyrus. Apocalypses are born in the midst of crisis: the enemy has won, disaster has struck, and the atmosphere

---

18 For useful guides to the prophetic writings in addition to Heschel below, see Walter Brueggemann, *The Prophetic Imagination*, 2nd ed. (Minneapolis: Fortress Press, 2001); and David L. Petersen, ed. "Prophecy in Israel," *Issues in Religion and Theology* 10, Philadelphia: Fortress Press, 1987).
19 Abraham Heschel, *The Prophets* (Peabody, Massachusetts: Hendrickson, 1962), 3-26.

is thick with despair because evil has won the day.[20] Thus, apocalyptic authors do not attempt to predict "the end of the world as they know it" precisely because the end has already come. It is not near; it is finished. There is nothing new to be tried, nothing else to be done. At least not by mortals. The present is over; all that remains is God's future.[21]

Think of Revelation as a Fairy Tale

G.K. Chesterton is credited with declaring, "Fairy tales are more than true; not because they tell us that dragons exist, but because they tell us that dragons can be beaten."[22] To the extent that Chesterton was right about the effective truth of fairy tales, his maxim may prove useful in helping us contemporary readers discern the functional message of John's Revelation.

Recall for example the magnificent children's story from C.S. Lewis, *The Lion, the Witch, and the Wardrobe*.[23] The story begins with young Lucy climbing through a wardrobe into a parallel land known as Narnia. Almost immediately she meets the faun Tumnus, who explains to her that Narnians live under a curse cast by the evil White Witch, whereby it is always winter but Christmas never comes. Heroic figures who have attempted to defeat the witch in order to counteract her spell have been turned to stone. What little hope remains rests in an ancient tale that one day two kings and two queens would come from another world, take their seats upon the four thrones of Cair Paravel, and usher in a new golden age of Narnia.

---

20 Adela Collins characterizes this apocalyptic dynamic as the unbearable tension between what is and what ought to be. See again Adela Yarbro Collins, *Crisis and Catharsis*, 141–61. Ted Peters describes it as "future consciousness," i.e., dissatisfaction with the present state of affairs if it is believed that the future can be better. See Peters, *Futures: Human and Divine*, 68.

21 Brian Blount states that apocalypses implore people to act in the present in a way that agrees with its understanding of the future. In every case it means choosing sides. The apocalypse calls for people to understand and join God's side. See Brian Blount, *Revelation: A Commentary* (Louisville, Kentucky: Westminster John Knox, 2009), 20.

22 Although attributed to Chesterton, the saying in this form appears in the epigraph of Neil Gaiman, Coraline (New York: HarperCollins, 2002). Chesterton at one point declares, "Fairy tales do not give a children his first idea of bogey. What fairy tales give the child is his first clear idea of the possible defeat of bogey." G.K. Chesterton, *Tremendous Trifles* (New York: Dodd, Mead, and Co., 1909), 130.

23 C.S. Lewis, *The Lion, The Witch, and the Wardrobe*, volume I of *The Chronicles of Narnia* (New York: Macmillan, 1950). Barbara Rossing also adduces *The Chronicles of Narnia* in her analysis of Revelation and her compelling arguments in exposing the rapture. See Barbara Rossing, *The Rapture Exposed* (New York: Basic Books, 2004), 8–10.

Notice the apocalyptic elements in the story. In Narnia, evil reigns. Despair hangs over the land like a shroud. The White Witch rules with ruthless terror and heartless ego, and the native heroes are helpless to do anything about it. Only a power from beyond, we are told, can do something to snatch victory from the jaws of defeat. There is no prophetic message here: no oracle of judgment with a repentance escape clause. This is apocalypse.

The comparison works in reverse, as well. Consider elements of the fairy tale located in the Apocalypse. The narrator enters a highly stylized but boldly imaginative throne room (recognizing that most ancients would never have seen an actual throne room). He finds himself in an alternate reality where creatures of all kinds—including a lion—talk.[24] Evil is embodied in the form of a dragon (Revelation 12:1-18), beasts (13:1), and a woman clad as a harlot who holds sway over all the kings of the earth. There are heroes that strive and fail (e.g., the martyrs of the fifth seal in 6:9-11; the two witnesses of 11:1-10). There is a cosmic final conflict, Armageddon (16:16). And the story climaxes with the heroic and victorious prince making all things new and wedding the "bride adorned for her husband" (21:1-22:7). How can one summarize the final two chapters of Revelation any better than "and they live happily ever after"?

---

[24] Recall that the "Christ figure" in *The Chronicles of Narnia* appears in the form of the talking lion, Aslan.

An Author-Character Match Made in Heaven

Ted Peters and Leona Foxx

Jan-Olav Henriksen

Theology as Relevant for the Interpretation of Experience, Reaching Out to a Wider Public

It is not so rare that theological scholars write about novels they have read in order to analyze them and make points that can illustrate and deepen their concerns. Many do, in different camps of theology. But not many write such books themselves. Even fewer write mystery books. And one may ask, with good reason: should *writing* novels or mystery books be the concern of a theological scholar and teacher? Ted Peters apparently thinks it should. And there may be far more justification for entering into the practice of writing such books than what may appear at first sight. In one of his most recent publications, Peters introduces his readers to inner-city Chicago pastor Leona Foxx, former CIA operative. In Foxx, he has found an outlet for creativity, for reflection, and for commenting on recent developments and trends in American public and political life. The book in question, about which this article is going to reflect, is *For God and Country: A Leona Foxx Suspense Thriller.*[1]

During the last years, it has become increasingly clear to me that the experiential dimension of theology needs to come more into focus if Christian theology (and therefore also Lutheran theology) is to have a viable future. The emphasis on doctrine seems, at least in the Nordic

---

1 Ted Peters, *For God and Country: A Leona Foxx Suspense Thriller* (Berkeley: Ted Peters Publishing, 2013). I have used the Kindle edition.

countries, to have led to a perception of theology as something that is remote from ordinary peoples' lives, and to be mostly about "theoretical things." If one is to counter and correct this wrong-headed perception of theology, theologians need to reaffirm an understanding of theology as the interpretation of all aspects of human experience, as well as seeing it as a practice that can also open up new experiences of life to people, using the biblical sources and the Christian tradition.[2] After all, experiences are what shapes and forms us as human beings, far more than what we read in books or watch on the television. And it is good Lutheran theology to affirm the life of experience as the counterpart to our interpretation of Scripture and doctrine. Such an understanding presents theologians with a challenge: how can we relate the contents of Christian faith to the lives of ordinary people and what they experience? This is not a new task, of course, but one that faces every preacher in the preparation of every Sunday sermon. To link life and theology is what this is all about. It is against this backdrop that we may read Ted Peters' story about Leona Foxx.

Furthermore, most people do not read theology any more. Many read fiction, though. A visit to an airport will convince you that the most read literature in the world that people read apart from their studies is what you may find in the bookstores in these places. And even though you may also find non-fiction there, it is a likely assumption that most people who buy something in an airport do not buy non-fiction books—and surely not *theology*. So why not enter into the field of what people are actually buying if you have a message you think it is important for them to receive? From the point of view of wanting to communicate on recent social and political topics, as well as central theological ones, the decision to write a suspense thriller appears as an obvious strategy to adopt. By writing a mystery novel called *For God and Country*, Ted Peters can play on American patriotism, and serve a meal of mystery, theology, and political commentary that allows you to sit with a page-turner during your flight. You actually get more than you expected. For a theological reader, or for someone engaged in church life, there are also many small descriptions that will make you smile with recognition and think, He got that right! In short, Foxx helps Ted Peters to find a new audience that can read about the life of quite ordinary Christian people who are

---

2   I argue more extensively for this approach to theology in Jan-Olav Henriksen, *Life, Love and Hope: God and Human Experience* (Grand Rapids, Michigan: Wm. B. Eerdmans Publishing Co., 2014).

engaged in big-time operations to save lives and make sure politics is not shaped by anti-Muslim sentiments.

Life and Theology in Leona Foxx: Dealing with the Basic Ambiguities of Life[3]

By choosing Foxx and her life as the center of the novel, Peters can develop his main character in a way that captures many of the ambiguities that conscious and conscientious people have to live with and deal with. Her main way of dealing with her challenges is by employing the resources of the Christian tradition. Foxx appears as a person who wanted to make a clean break with her past, which she found devastating and contrary to all her ethical intuitions and perceptions. The story suggests that she has had some type of breakdown on the personal level after being held captive in Iran and that her decision to leave the CIA is related to her attempt to make a new life on a new basis. And contrary to many other thriller heroes, Foxx is depicted as a person who is vulnerable, who is struggling, and who turns to her friends in times of need. She does not hide herself from her friends by trying to appear as perfect and invulnerable. One of her friends, Angie, reminds her of this time and process of recovering, and of how her life is one in which things may not be one of perfect harmony and easy solutions. Furthermore, she sees Foxx's decision to go to seminary as a way to cope with tensions and fragmentation, and as what started her process of re-integration. In her response to this reminder, Foxx says something about the importance of both friendship and Scripture: "Angie, I could not have done without you during my recovery. You were so present for me. I treasure all those days when you would read me a poem or a passage from Scripture. You helped me put my mind back together with my heart. I owe you my present life, Angie." In other ways, Peters here suggests that going to seminary may be a way of finding a path to more fullness and integrity in life.

To live with heart and mind as one is Foxx's task, one that she finds hard to solve. Foxx's time as an agent in the CIA and what she experienced during captivity in Iran, has forced her to change not only her course of life, but also to view some of the activities that her own country was involved in there with new eyes. She says: "When I left the

---

3 My repeated use of the notion "ambiguities of life" in this article is inspired by Tillich's development of these in his *Systematic Theology*, vol. 3 (Chicago: University of Chicago Press, 1976).

agency, I turned in everything and made a clean break. I have no relation whatsoever to the CIA or its mission. I went to seminary in Berkeley. Got a divinity education. And now I'm serving as pastor here in Chicago. I am doing everything in my power to forget or, if I have to, deny what happened when I was serving the insatiable lusts of the Whore of Babylon." We note that the institution she attends for her transition period is the one where Ted Peters teaches. So already, there is a hint that there may be some relation between the two of them.

Foxx leaves one institution for another. The CIA is exchanged for the Lutheran church. A context of war, violence, and corporate greed (as hinted at in the description of the CIA's and the Government's subcontractors) is substituted with a church context where inner-city problems, but also Sunday services, the visiting of the sick, and the consolation of those who have lost someone are in focus. But as the story progresses, it becomes apparent that this is not a clean break, and that one cannot perceive Foxx's new life as one in which she has gone from darkness to light. Her story follows her, and soon she has to realize that her own experiences in the Middle East are linked to what happens in downtown Chicago. There is violence in her neighborhood in Chicago, and there are tensions in her inner life as well that make it clear that to be simultaneously a sinner and a righteous person (*simul iustus et peccator*) is a description that fits not only Foxx's inner life, but also to some extent can be used to describe what she experiences in her own context in Chicago. Her vision of a clean cut becomes increasingly more a perception of the deep ambiguities of life. Some of the ambiguities and tensions that she experiences are voiced in conversations with friends and colleagues. As the story develops, she is given a bodyguard with CIA affiliation; the following quote is an extract from one of their conversations:

> [Graham:] "Do you believe that by quitting the CIA you're completely disconnected from what it did, or does? Are you innocent now as a pastor, whereas guys like me still in the service are marching under orders from Satan?"
>
> [Leona:] "No. I don't believe that I'm innocent. Nor are you Satanic. But there's no way I can become disconnected. I'm connected, whether I like it or not. I'm connected like every citizen of this nation or of any nation in this world. We all share in the violence at home as well as abroad. When I try to extend a helping hand, I'm fully aware that I have blood

on that hand. It may be invisible blood, but it's blood all the same.

By presenting reflections in this way, Peters can address the illusion that evil is only elsewhere, and that what happens in other parts of the world is something that Americans can dissociate themselves from. Sin and evil is in us and around us, no matter where we go. But so is grace, and chances for goodness, although only accessible in glimpses and fragments. Foxx describes her own ministry in a rather nuanced and realistic manner: "The work of a pastor is small, fragmentary at best. I no longer work out of a grand vision of collecting food to prevent starvation, or peace on earth, or universal justice, or saving the planet from climate change, or whatever. Rather, I work day by day to share just one little crumb of grace—just one eye-blink of love—with people whose lives are painful, brutish, and short. I have to leave the rest up to God, if there can be a God with this kind of world. I can't lift a single brick to build even a step on the porch of God's kingdom."

There is one important implication or underlying condition to this way of reasoning about human experience that Peters brings very clearly to the fore in his story about Foxx: All the world is relevant to theology. Theology is not only about the inner life of a church. Christians should not, and cannot, only relate to other Christians as their relevant audience. In Foxx's case, this is shown in how she relates to both Jews and Muslims. One of her most important counselors is a Jewish rabbi she met during her time in seminary. Furthermore, Foxx's practice also makes apparent that patriotism and the relation to one's country easily can become a form of idolatry that excludes others from the universal care and concern of God. Several places in the book, a critical attitude towards American patriotism is articulated. As an outsider to that society, I find it refreshing to see this critique of a phenomenon that has developed substantially towards the negative after 9/11 2001. Peters is able to show that for Christians something is prior to and more important than one's country when it comes to alliances and priorities.

The way Foxx is described is refreshing and in many ways may appear as contrary to how people think a pastor should be: one who is pious, has good answers to everything, and knows how to find a solution to the moral dilemmas of human life. Although Foxx has tried to leave some of her own moral problems behind her by ending the affair with her former lover (who is the President of the United States, a turn in the book that I have to admit I find is somewhat over the top), her present everyday life still offers her enough struggles and challenges.

Foxx deals with her struggles in two main ways: By speaking with her friends, and in prayer. There is much wisdom and realism in describing a pastor in this way: Pastors are ordinary people. They struggle with much the same as the rest of us. They need good relations to others in order to cope with all that is in front of them. And Foxx's ordinary way of living and acting is also one that shows how important it is to be authentic in front of God, especially when we lament and find that life is hard. She is thereby depicted as a hero who is not perfect, but who is human and trying to be honest in all she does. In one of her prayers, which addresses the problem of evil in language that may have many well-churched Christians raise their eyebrows, she says:

> God, you have got such a fucked up world. Why did you put me here like a pincushion to feel every prick of its pain? Yes, I want to love your world as much as you do. But goddammit, it's hard. I'd like to ask the Holy Spirit for the wisdom and strength to trust in what I cannot see. But goddammit, I'm too pissed off to think it's worthwhile. I hope your grace covers me. Amen.

Peters shows us that these can be the words of a Lutheran pastor—and convinces us that this is even a likely way for her to articulate herself when things get hard. Furthermore, in the way both her conversations and prayers are presented, we meet a person who is actively engaged in reflecting on what life contains, and on what this means for her calling and for her spiritual life. Thus, Foxx tries actively and constantly to bring life and faith together. She does this by facing head on the ambiguities of life that make it impossible for her to look at what she experiences in black and white. At one point she has to kill an intruder in order to save a friend's life. She reflects on these events later:

> Could the killing be justified? She talked it through with God in a walking prayer. Suppose I had not answered the phone? Suppose I had kept on jumping rope and simply listened to the phone message after everything was over? Perhaps then, Lars would be dead. No, that won't work…. This is getting me nowhere. Lars lives, that's what's important. Right? Amen? So many questions about what might have happened had Leona refused to take action. But Leona had acted. And now

history could not be written any other way. Innocence was not an option.

During the course of the story, we see how the external action and the internal struggles are two sides of the same coin in Foxx's life. One cannot separate oneself from the life, the history, and the community of which one is a part. Her ministry is her way of dealing with the ambiguities of life—not a way to get rid of them. In one of her prayers, she comes very close to interpreting her experiences in light of Luther's doctrine of the hidden God:

> Leona sought solace in sleep. But it did not come easily. She offered an audible prayer to God, an anguished prayer in which she told God both sides of her story. "Come on, God, iron out the wrinkles. Why do I have to have such a tortured soul? Why can't you deliver me some internal peace? I've lived up to my side of our bargain. I'm now an ordained pastor. I'm now a shepherd guarding your flock. Why do you call me—literally call me—to blast someone's brains out? Why can't my little church be the city built on a hill, the beacon of light showing the world the path toward godliness and community and peace? For Moses, you led the people of Israel with a mighty arm and an outstretched hand. For me, you're holding your providential hand behind your back. Why? All I can do is give you my 'whys,' God. Amen." She gained little comfort from this. Her eyes remained wide.

There could be a lot more to say about what Peters helps us see through the eyes of Foxx: American politics, the still prevalent racism in Chicago, or what other scholars in the field, like for example, Jeffrey Stout, have pointed to in his analysis of how corporate power shapes part of American politics both domestic and abroad.[4] American politics should, according to Foxx, be decided by something other than what can increase the value of Texarab oil stock. No doubt, she is Ted Peters' voice on these matters. More recently, she also voices some of the concerns that Peters shares with her when it comes to science and religion in her blog on *Huffington Post*.[5]

---

4 See J. Stout, *Blessed Are the Organized* (Princeton: Princeton University Press, 2012).
5 See http://www.huffingtonpost.com/leona-foxx/. I think many will find what she / he writes there a valuable addition to what is otherwise voiced as religious contributions in the US public sphere.

Conclusion

From the above, it should be apparent that I commend Ted Peters for his choice of protagonist for a suspense thriller. The main reason is that she appears as a credible witness to what is means to be a Christian today: Christians are not perfect, but they live by resources in Scripture and theology that help them deal with, accept, and come to terms with the ambiguities of life, even when "the wrinkles cannot be ironed out." Foxx is also an exciting alternative to the all-too-sweet or all-too-harmonious picture of who Christians are or should be that we find elsewhere in literature or movies that try to make the Christian message available to a wider audience. I think Peters has found a better, more reliable witness, than many of these, to what a Christian life is or may be today. And finally, this may have to do with the fact that Foxx's theology is sound and dynamic, like any viable Lutheran theology should be.

The Theology of the Cross and Cultural Analysis

Ted Peters

Ordinarily, when we think of the cross of Jesus Christ we think of soteriology, of the work of salvation. This is fitting. Yet, in recent years, I have increasingly seen the value of teasing out the revelatory power of the cross. The cross reveals. The cross reveals something about the God of grace, to be sure, but my attention has been given more to what the cross reveals about the human condition. Who we are as human creatures becomes illuminated in the light of the cross.

What the cross reveals is that we human beings are killers. We kill one another and, in turn, we would even kill God if we could get our hands on God. One way to read the Gospel of John is this way: the light shone in the darkness, and the power of darkness rose up to snuff out the light.

In addition to exposing the fact that we are killers, the cross helps reveal that we lie about it. We deny the truth that we are violent. We pretend to be good even while we are pursuing evil. We try to hide our violent propensities under a layer of lies, excuses, rationalizations, and self-justifications. The cross shines a light into our darkness that exposes our lies, but we turn our back to the cross so that we can preserve enough darkness to keep the truth hidden. This is the human condition, at least as I am gradually discerning it.

Here is what I am discerning: human nature includes a strong dose of self-justification. We daily draw lines between good and evil, and we place ourselves on the good side. We might behave differently if we could hear the message: God has justified us by grace through faith, so we don't need to self-justify any more. In his *Festschrift* chapter, "Justification, Self-Justification, and Forgiveness: Ted Peters on Sin and Its Overcoming," Derek Nelson puts it this way: "Peters pairs his understanding of sin-as-self-justification with a rich notion of divine grace, and faith therein, that can actually speak to the depths of sin. Sin is bad enough that we cannot save ourselves from it. We need another. We need Jesus."[1] Yes, we need Jesus in order to learn that our justification is a gift of a gracious God, not the product of our own self-justification.

Eden and Self-Justification

I find that by interpreting the Adam and Eve story in light of the cross we gain further insight into just who we creatures are in relationship to our Creator. Like Adam and Eve, each of us individually and our social institutions collectively engage daily in an identifiable practice: we draw a line between good and evil and we place ourselves on the good side of the line. The knowledge of good and evil that Eve and then Adam gained after conversation with the serpent has become a human delusion. We constantly identify with what is good because deep down we think—rightly or wrongly—that the good is eternal. The principles of justice and goodness and righteousness establish the eternal structure of the universe, right? Well, we seem to work with an intuition that this is the case. So, if we can remain on the good side of every line we draw, then we fool ourselves into thinking that eternal goodness belongs to us.

The cross reveals that this is folly. Here's why it is folly: When we draw a line between good and evil and place ourselves on the good side, God moves over to the evil side. This line we draw places ourselves on the opposite side from God. To be with God eternally, we need to cross the line to the evil side where God is to be found.

Paul writes "For our sake he made him [Christ] to be sin who knew no sin, so that in him we might become the righteousness of God" (δικαιοσύνη θεοῦ) (2 Corinthians 5:21). We find the cross of Christ on the evil side of the lines we draw. We find the cross of Christ where we find the victims of someone's self-justification, self-righteousness, and violence against those judged to be sinful. The righteousness of God (δικαιοσύνη θεοῦ) is not found on our side of the lines we draw; rather, it is found on the side of those we victimize out of our uncontrollable passion to be right, to be strong, to be eternal.

This phrase, δικαιοσύνη θεοῦ, could be translated "God's justification." In Christ God justifies us. To get straight on this point, we need

---

[1] Nelson, 173.

to move over to the evil side of each line we draw in order to see God's justifying work in action.

This is what I learn from Martin Luther's *theology of the cross*. The basic task of the theology of the cross is to reveal something about God's grace that we do not ordinarily see. If in our daily life we want to see ourselves on the good side of every line we draw, we will miss seeing God in Christ on the other side. The theology of the cross tells us: look on the evil side of our lines. Where you find sin, suffering, and death, there you will find God in Christ reconciling the world. There, on the evil side of our line, we discern Paul's point in 2 Corinthians 5:19: "in Christ God was reconciling the world to himself, not counting their trespasses against them, and entrusting the message of reconciliation to us."

Self-Justification and Scapegoating

I employ the term *self-justification* to refer to placing ourselves on the good side of the lines we draw. Sometimes we place someone else on the evil side of that line, and we treat that person or group or minority or enemy as a scapegoat. Because the scapegoat is evil, we tell ourselves, then to heap violence on the head of the scapegoat insures the fact that we are doing good. We only curse our rivals in gossip in the name of what is just, decent, and right. When we fight or send our armies to fight for us, we only kill in the name of justice, not injustice. Those who suffer our gossip or our killing I wish to call the *scapegoat*. We justify victimizing the scapegoated enemy because we are fighting for freedom or justice or something else that we judge to be good. The problem with the human condition as revealed in the cross is this: we kill and we justify our killing, both figuratively in gossip and literally in war.

Jesus in his teachings tries to guide us by telling us to avoid drawing those lines, to avoid rendering judgments against others. "Why do you see the speck in your neighbor's eye, but do not notice the log in your own eye?" (Matthew 7:3). If we avoid drawing lines between ourselves and others, suddenly we have no more enemies. "You have heard that it was said, 'You shall love your neighbor and hate your enemy.' But I say to you, Love your enemies and pray for those who persecute you" (Matthew 5:43–44). For those of us who insist on self-justifying, insist on drawing lines and judging our enemies, Jesus offers a label: *hypocrite*. "Woe to you, scribes and Pharisees, hypocrites! For you are like whitewashed tombs, which on the outside look beautiful, but inside they are full of the bones of the dead and of all kinds of filth" (Matthew 23:27). Even though we may think of ourselves as eternally good, we are akin to the rotting filth of disguised death.

These are Jesus' teachings. What about Jesus' cross? The cross carries the same message as the teachings, but the cross functions symbolically. Symbols reveal ourselves to ourselves. We have just seen how the line between good and evil places the self-justifying person on the good side and the scapegoat on the evil side. But, the symbol of the cross reveals more about how you and I engage in self-justification and scapegoating.

Just as Jesus was mocked, we mock the scapegoat through cursing. Cursing is the language that surfaces when we are drawing the line between us and them. In the class struggle, the upper class curses the lower class. Brazilian educator Paulo Freire provides examples. "For the oppressors . . . it is always the oppressed (whom they obviously never call 'the oppressed' but—depending on whether they are fellow countrymen or not 'those people' or 'the blind and envious masses' or 'savages' or 'natives' or 'subversives') who are disaffected, who are 'violent', 'barbaric,' 'wicked,' or 'ferocious' when they react to the violence of the oppressors."[2] This vilified scapegoat—the underclass—is visible to those prophetic eyes among us who complain that the human race is constantly given over to dividing between we vs. they, us vs. them, insiders vs. outsiders, good guys vs. bad guys. Critical consciousness born of honest observation can, in principle, make this scapegoat mechanism visible, with or without the cross.

Yet, there is another kind of scapegoat which is more difficult to expose. This second kind of scapegoat is found with us on the good side of the line. We victimize this scapegoat, to be sure, but our victimization takes a different form. We make the scapegoat on the good side of the line sacred. Then we rally all our friends around this sacred goat to create community. We still sacrifice the good scapegoat in the act of self-justification, to be sure, but our violence is hidden from our own eyes. Whereas our sacrifice of the scapegoat on the enemy side of the line is visible, our sacrifice of the scapegoat on the friendly side of the line is invisible. It is invisible because we lie to ourselves. It must remain invisible, or we could not in good conscience live with ourselves.

There is only one form of self-justification, but it takes two forms of scapegoats: the visible and the invisible. We try to distance ourselves

---

[2] Paulo Friere, *Pedagogy of the Oppressed*, Myra Bergman Ramos, trans. (New York: Seabury Press, 1968), 41.

from the visible scapegoat, dehumanizing our enemy through cursing. We draw a line between good and evil, and we place the enemy on the evil side. We treat the invisible scapegoat differently. Here, when we draw the line between good and evil, we place the invisible scapegoat on the good side of the line.

The scapegoat binds and blinds. It binds us together in community while blinding us to the scapegoat mechanism. The binding power of the scapegoat is vividly illustrated with the decision to crucify Jesus. This decision united two rival powers, Rome and Jerusalem. "That same day Herod and Pilate became friends with each other; before this they had been enemies" (Luke 23:12). The invisible power of the sacrificed scapegoat is that it brings us together; it unites us in community.

In the New Testament, Jesus appears as the final scapegoat. With God, the scapegoat mechanism does not work. The theology of the cross includes a divine judgment against the human practice of self-justification and scapegoating. This is the way I interpret Jesus as the high priest of Melchizedek. "Unlike the other high priests, he has no need to offer sacrifices day after day, first for his own sins, and then for those of the people; this he did once for all when he offered himself" (Hebrews 7:27). Jesus' sacrifice is a once and for all sacrifice. No more sacrifices! One way to read the book of Hebrews is to discern this message: because of the death of Jesus Christ God is saying to us, *no more scapegoats!*

However, self-justification and scapegoating is ubiquitous in human community. Each community executes the scapegoat mechanism in its own way. In the United States, the soldier functions as the prime invisible scapegoat. The soldier is one of us. The soldier dies just like our enemy dies, to be sure, but the death of the invisible scapegoat sanctifies our community. Not only does the hero's self-sacrifice unite us, it also makes us holy. Our land becomes sacred ground. In the American self-understanding, the soldier is the perpetual scapegoat from generation to generation, blinding Americans while binding us together.

Keeping the Scapegoat Invisible by Stealing Christian Symbols

We can begin to discern just how the sacrificed invisible scapegoat makes America holy if we attend to the way U.S. presidents handle civic liturgies on festival days such as Independence Day, Memorial Day, Veterans Day, as well as military funerals. At one such civic liturgy honoring U.S. soldiers on Memorial Day 2011, President Barack Obama linked today's warriors into a chain with our first patriots in the Revolutionary War of 1776, and he linked this chain with God's holy word.

> What binds this chain together across the generations, this chain of honor and sacrifice, is not only a common cause—our country's cause—but also a spirit captured in a Book of Isaiah, a familiar verse, mailed to me by the Gold Star parents of 2nd Lieutenant Mike McGahan. "When I heard the voice of the Lord saying, 'Whom shall I send? And who will go for us?' And I said, 'Here I am. Send me!'"[3]

The Bible is a powerful symbol in North America, and the president's speech writers know this. The mere allusion to Holy Scriptures in a political speech connotes sacred presence, blessing, and reverence. But, note the overt symbol theft. The call of God to the prophet has become transmogrified into the call of America to the soldier. Whereas the ancient Hebrew prophet answered God's call to deliver the divine word, America's soldier answers the same divine call to enter into combat. To fight for America is a holy calling, says the president.

The ascending rhetorical crescendo ritually recalled the sacrifices that founded this president's nation. Patriotic sacrifice stands on the same level as religious sacrifice. Or, perhaps more precisely, patriotism becomes the spiritual bond.

> That's what we memorialize today. That spirit that says, send me, no matter the mission. Send me, no matter the risk. Send me, no matter how great the sacrifice I am called to make. The patriots we memorialize today sacrificed not only all they had but all they would ever know. They gave of themselves until they had nothing more to give. It's natural, when we lose someone we care about, to ask why it had to be them. Why my son, why my sister, why my friend, why not me? . . . We remember that the blessings we enjoy as Americans came at a dear cost; that our very presence here today, as free people in a free society, bears testimony to their enduring legacy.[4]

---

3 http://www.whitehouse.gov/the-press-office/2011/05/30/remarks-president-memorial-day-service.
4 http://www.whitehouse.gov/the-press-office/2011/05/30/remarks-president-memorial-day-service.

To sacrifice for America's freedom is to offer the ultimate sacrifice. There is none higher. And we today—those of us who are Americans—enjoy the blessings of the salvation wrought by our soldier's sacrificial blood. America is sacred because the soldiers' blood sanctifies this land.

The Theology of the Cross must say "no" to this. The revelatory power of the cross, I think, desacralizes the invisible scapegoat. "Christ became a scapegoat in order to desacralize those who came before him and to prevent those who come after him from being sacralized," observes scapegoat theorist René Girard.[5] The New Testament memory of Jesus dismantles any community oriented around the sacred; it does so by exposing the ugly truth regarding how this or any community is established or sustained. The death of Jesus makes visible what had been invisible. The death of Jesus shocks us with truth, with revelatory truth. One of the clear messages of the New Testament that becomes habitually garbled, muddied, and twisted in modern civic and moral rhetoric is this: *No more scapegoats!*

What is so difficult for the theologian of the cross is to untie the knots of political rhetoric so that the cross can do its job of revealing the self-justification, hypocrisy, and exploitation of the invisible scapegoat. The redemptive power of death expressed in today's patriotism represents a symbolic theft, the theft by the state of what was once a Christian symbol, the cross. There is power in Christ's death on the cross. There is power in the death of the Christian martyr willing to die innocently as did his or her Lord. Now I ask: is this redemptive power transferrable to the secular soldier? By no means. Should a prophet dare to suggest that this is all a lie, we can safely predict the equivalent of another crucifixion. Recall Jesus' words in Luke 4:24: "Verily I say unto you, No prophet is accepted in his own country" (KJV).

The revelatory power of the cross could shine a light into the darkness of American solidarity. But any would-be prophet who wishes to shine the light of the cross onto the plight of the US soldier should be careful. To accuse American society of creating a secular sacred on the

---

5   René Girard, *The One by Whom Scandal Comes*, M.B. DeBevoise, trans. (East Lansing, Michigan: Michigan State University Press, 2014), 44. I have benefitted significantly from the analysis of the scapegoat in the insightful scholarship of Girard. However, Girard does not distinguish as I do between the visible and invisible scapegoats. His analysis shows masterfully how the social lie binds and blinds due to the invisible scapegoat. But he does not sufficiently show the connection with the visible enemy and the cursing, which accompany national self-justification.

THE THEOLOGY OF THE CROSS AND CULTURAL ANALYSIS

tomb of our fallen hero—the hero whom we scapegoat—will unavoidably face a violent backlash. When the truth begins to bleed through into our awareness, the social group reacts defensively. The social fabric must be defended against the terror precipitated by a revelation of the truth. This defensive denial may take the form of repudiating the prophet, or it may take the form of turning the invisible scapegoat into a visible scapegoat.

The latter—turning the invisible scapegoat into a visible scapegoat—is what happened in the United States during the war in Vietnam. America's military action in Southeast Asia was a travesty by any measure, reaping far more human suffering and misery than could be tolerated by the American psyche. Americans had become so accustomed to drawing a line between good and evil and placing themselves on the good side of the line that revelations about what was happening in Vietnam became intolerable. The mechanism of distancing clicked in. In order to ease the nation's conscience, the U.S. soldier was transformed from an invisible to a visible scapegoat. The evils perpetrated by America could be blamed on the U.S. soldier. Conscripted into the Army at age eighteen, the twenty-year-old soldier returned to his homeland in disgrace. No honored place in the Memorial Day parades for a Vietnam vet!

Because the self-justification mechanism of American self-understanding had become dismantled, the line between good and evil was redrawn to place the soldier on the other side. "Baby killers . . . murderers . . . butchers. . ." became the curse returning veterans of the Vietnam war had to hear in their homeland. Lt. Colonel Dave Grossman says Vietnam vets "were rejected by girlfriends, spit on, and accused by strangers and finally dared not even admit to close friends that they were veterans. . . . They denied their experiences and buried their pain and grieving beneath a shell . . . Vietnam vets endured an absolutely unprecedented degree of societal condemnation."[6] The social soul of America began to fissure, but the fissuring could be stopped by turning the previously invisible scapegoat into a visible one. If today's twenty-first century soldier avoids reading history books, he or she may be unaware of the fragility of the laud the military receives from presidential speeches. Warning: at any moment appellations of heroism could turn into condemnatory curses.

Uncovering or exposing the scapegoat mechanism is one of the valuable revelations performed by the theology of the cross. But, it is just as dangerous for us today as it was for Jesus. To disturb this sacri-

---

6 Dave Grossman, *On Killing* (New York: Little Brown and Co., 1995, 2009), 291–92.

ficial mechanism with prophetic criticism is to precipitate a protective reaction, to precipitate our getting cursed. Cursing the critic sustains community oriented around the holy, around the scapegoated victim.

Scapegoating blinds while it binds. The prophet or social critic wants to reveal what is beneath the social lie so that society can repent, but the threat of such a revelation terrifies us because it portends a loss of communal unity. "One of the insidious characteristics of structural injustice (structural sin) . . . is its tendency to remain invisible to those not suffering from it. If we do not see the structural injustice in which we live, we cannot repent of it. Failing to renounce it, we remain captive to it," says Cynthia Moe-Lobeda.[7] However, despite the prophetic impulse of Moe-Lobeda, the sad news about the human condition is this: Once the scapegoat is revealed, the social soul will panic and redirect its self-justificatory venom toward another victim. In the twenty-first century we have buried our invisible scapegoat beneath multiple layers of self-justification: national security, liberation, freedom, and, of course, heroism. Should a prophet or social critic try to expose what lies beneath these layers, he or she can only expect to release a new barrage of cursing.

"Scapegoating is one of the deepest structures of human sin, built into our religion and politics. It is demonic because it is endlessly flexible in its choice of victims and because it can truly deliver the good that it advertises. Satan can cast out Satan, and is the more powerful for it," writes S. Mark Heim.[8] We victimize others in the name of the good. Because we believe we are doing good, the evil we do becomes invisible to us. Our virtues reap as much violence as our vices. The pursuit of justice is just as deadly as the pursuit of injustice. The human race is badly in need of grace, in need of God's justification (δικαιοσύνη θεοῦ).

A Theology for the Victims of Scapegoating

Christian compassion should be directed first toward the victims of the human scapegoating mechanism, not at those who gain from self-justification. "To preach the gospel today means confronting the world with the reality of Christian freedom," writes James Cone. "It means telling black people that their slavery has come to an end, and telling whites to

---

7 Cynthia Moe-Lobeda, *Resisting Structural Evil: Love as Ecological-Economic Vocation* (Minneapolis: Fortress Press, 2013), 61.
8 S. Mark Heim, "Saved by What Shouldn't Happen," *Cross Examinations: Readings on the Meaning of the Cross Today*, Marit Trelstad, ed. (Minneapolis: Augsburg, 2006), 217.

let go of the chains.... The church not only proclaims the good news of freedom, it actively shares in the liberation struggle."⁹

This concern for the victim has led liberation theologians to propound a guiding principle, the *preferential option for the poor*. If we start with the cross, we start with the poor, the marginalized, the sick, the lame, the outcast, and those who are imprisoned. If Philip Melanchthon were among us today, he might join the choir of liberation theologians to sing: "God loves most those who are needy, troubled, poor, and lowly."[10] This includes those who are cursed.

For nearly three millennia now, the caste or *varna* system in India has systematically scapegoated lower caste persons and especially outcastes. Moses Penumaka's heart has been triggered by compassion for the victims of this long and still oppressive tradition. Penumaka has affiliated himself with the *dalit* school of theology, a school which keeps focus on the victims. In his *Festschrift* chapter, "The Poetry of Gurram Joshua, GOD—the World's Future, and Their Implications for *Dalit* Theology," Penumaka writes: "From the dalit perspective, their suffering is their actual reality, and that reality, in which each of them finds inner strength, gives them hope for liberation. In these perspectives, the suffering reality becomes a liberating reality. In other words their suffering becomes central to the Godhead not detached or indifferent ... When we look to God as the world's future, the suffering reality of creation's history is remembered through the cross, through the painful experience of the victims in the past. God experiences this pain, and so God too remembers it."[11]

This draws us to a second dimension of the theology of the cross, namely, in the cross God absorbs the sufferings not only of Jesus but of the world. I credit Reformed theologian of hope Jürgen Moltmann for lifting up this dimension of Luther's theology of the cross in his important book of 1973, *The Crucified God*. Moltmann recognizes the first and revelatory role of the cross for Luther. "Just as man misuses his works to justify himself, so too he misuses the knowledge of God to serve his hubris ... the knowledge of God in the suffering and death of Christ takes this perverse situation of man seriously. It is not an ascending, exalting

---

9 James H. Cone, *A Black Theology of Liberation* (Philadelphia and New York: J. B. Lippincott, 1970), 231.
10 Philip Melanchthon, *Loci Communes* in *Library of Christian Classics*, XIX (Louisville: Westminster/John Knox Press, 1969), 116.
11 Penumaka, 194.

knowledge, but a descending, convincing knowledge."[12] This leads to our de-divinization. "Luther reverses this [Theology of Glory] approach and sees in the cross God's descent to the level of our sinful nature and our death, not so that man is divinized, but so that he is de-divinized and given a new humanity in the community of the crucified Christ."[13]

In the above discussion of self-justification and scapegoating, we described the revelatory role played by the theology of the cross. What Moltmann adds—an addition consistent with Luther yet underdeveloped in Luther—is the real presence of God in the suffering and abandonment and death in the cross. "When the crucified Jesus is called the 'image of the invisible God', the meaning is that *this* is God, and God is like *this*.... The Christ event on the cross is a God event."[14] In sum, the trinitarian God is fully present in the cross, and this means that the divine life is affected by the suffering of Jesus and the suffering of the world.

When creatures suffer, God suffers. One need not join the Whiteheadian school of process panentheism to learn this point. Nor need one study at the feet of the open-theists now holding forth within American Evangelicalism. I would rather join the new school of trinitarian theology—which includes Moltmann along with Karl Barth, Karl Rahner, Catherine Mowry LaCugna, and Wolfhart Pannenberg—developing during the final half of the twentieth century. The new trinitarians make the case that, in the incarnation of the second person of the Trinity, the entire Godhead experiences the alienation and suffering of the world. What happens in time becomes constitutive of God's eternity.

The suffering of the world becomes God's suffering. This is what the cross both effects and reveals according to the new trinitarianism.[15] Does God the Father suffer? Is this a form of patripassianism? No, but it is a form of theopassianism. "Jesus' death cannot be understood 'as the death of God' but only as death *in* God," says Moltmann.[16]

Moltmann is much more timid than Luther himself was. For the sixteenth century Reformer, God actually dies. "If it cannot be said that God dies for us, but only a man, we are lost." He continues to endorse phrases

---

12 Jürgen Moltmann, *The Crucified God*, R.A. Wilson and John Bowden, trans. (New York: Harper, 1973), 211.
13 Ibid., 213.
14 Ibid., 205, Moltmann's italics.
15 See, Ted Peters, *God as Trinity: Relationality and Temporality in Divine Life* (Louisville, Kentucky: Westminster John Knox Press, 1993).
16 Moltmann, *Crucified God*, 207.

such as "God's dying, God's martyrdom, God's blood, and God's death."[17] Because it is the second person of the Trinity for whom death comes, we probably should apply the term *theopassianism* rather than *patripassianism*. Regardless of what we call it, the suffering and dying in the world becomes in Christ the experience of the divine life.

One item of theological impact of this rendering of the Theology of the Cross is that, by taking the "slings and arrows" of human suffering and death into the divine life, God confers dignity on all of us who suffer and die. What we deem the sacrifice of Christ is, among other things, a divine conferral of human dignity. We are the end or goal of Christ's saving work.

Conferring Dignity

When translated into the concerns of our liberation theologians, this becomes an affirmation that the suffering of the dalit people and other marginalized peoples is felt by God, experienced by God, and owned by God. The dalits are not left alone in their plight.

When it comes to developing an ethic of political action and cultural transformation, one way I wish to depict the Christian ministry is to describe it as the conferral of dignity. I like to use the term *dignity* as Immanuel Kant did: to treat a person with dignity is to treat him or her as a moral end and not merely as a means to some further end. "Act in such a way that you always treat humanity, whether in your own person or in the person of any other, never simply as a means, but always at the same time as an end."[18] In the incarnation in Jesus Christ, God conferred dignity on us humans as well as on the entire creation. We enjoy dignity because of this divine conferral. Our ministry consists in large part in the expanding of dignity conferral to any and all who could benefit from it. The act of love includes the conferral of dignity, of treating a person as

---

17 Luther cited by the *Formula of Concord: Solid Declaration, Article VIII: Person of Christ* in *The Book of Concord: The Confessions of the Evangelical Lutheran Church,* Robert Kolb and Timothy J. Wengert, eds. (Minneapolis: Fortress, 2000), 624. Pannenberg does not side with Luther here. "On the cross the Son of God certainly died and not just the humanity that he assumed. Nevertheless, the Son suffered death in his human reality and not in respect of his deity." *Systematic Theology 3 vol.,* Geoffrey W. Bromiley, trans. (Grand Rapids, Michigan: Wm. B. Eerdmans, 1991–1997), 2:388. Still, for Pannenberg, the empathetic love of the Father for the Son's suffering causes pain for the Father. This brings Pannenberg closer to patripassianism than either Luther or Moltmann.

18 Immanuel Kant, *Groundwork of the Metaphysic of Morals,* H.J. Paton, trans. (New York: Harper, 1948), 96.

an end and not merely a means. It would seem to me that dignity conferral would best describe the mission of the Christian church in India as well as the mission of dalit leaders aimed at themselves and their wider dalit community.

When interpreting the ethnic border crossing exercised by the historical Jesus, David Balch and Adam Pryor see Jesus as conferring dignity. In their *Festschrift* chapter, "Jesus' Creation Theology and Multiethnic Practice," Balch and Pryor connect with my work in proleptic ethics at this point. "Phenomenologically speaking, dignity is first conferred and then claimed: we treat the other as valuable which allows her to claim value for herself. Theologically, this conferral of dignity is ultimately rooted in God. God treats each of us with dignity, allowing us to treat others with that dignity first conferred upon us."[19] The Jesus they describe is a propleticist, because the crossing of ethnic boundaries anticipates the eschatological unity of the coming Kingdom of God. If you and I fail to embody this multiethnic agenda, we could actually stymie God's work in the human world. "Just as Jesus' interethnic dialogue was steeped in protological and eschatological commitments, we must, as with Peters, realize the proleptic ramifications of closing ourselves to diverse others: as we cease to confer dignity in refusing interethnic dialogue, we stymie the adventing of the Kingdom of God."[20] I like this verbatizing of the noun "advent." We who confer dignity on behalf of God's eschatological conferral of dignity are "adventing" the kingdom of God. Nice.

Adventing the Kingdom of God in the Book of Revelation

New Testament scholar Wayne Kannaday takes up the matter of adventing the kingdom of God by counseling us on how to read the Bible's final book, the Apocalypse of John. Kannaday offers three principles for a healthy reading. "First, do not fail to see the forest for the trees; the devil is in the details. Second, understand that Revelation belongs to the literary genre of apocalypse, and therefore its purpose is not prediction but proclamation. Third, as contemporary readers, let us draw on our experience of fairy tales to better understand this otherwise alien genre and its *happily ever after* message."[21]

---

19 Balch and Pryor, 206.
20 Balch and Pryor, 209.
21 Kannaday, 213.

I must think deeply about Kannaday's second principle: the purpose of this apocalypse is "not prediction but proclamation." Frankly, treating the Book of Revelation as prediction plays a big role in my retroactive ontology. Of course, by prediction I do not mean anything like Hal Lindsey's *Late Great Planet Earth* or what we find in pre-millennialism. Yet, the Book of Revelation along with Jesus' promise of an imminent Kingdom of God and Paul's promise of a new creation orient my faith toward the future. I believe the biblical proclamation is this: we should trust God for the future. So, if we would remove the prediction entirely from John's apocalypse, my boat would drift in uncertain waters.

In particular, I rely heavily on the climactic welcoming of the New Jerusalem. "And I heard a loud voice from the throne saying, 'See, the home of God is among mortals. He will dwell with them; they will be his peoples, and God himself will be with them; he will wipe every tear from their eyes. Death will be no more; mourning and crying and pain will be no more, for the first things have passed away.' And the one who was seated on the throne said, 'See, I am making all things new.' Also he said, 'Write this, for these words are trustworthy and true.' Then he said to me, 'It is done! I am the Alpha and the Omega, the beginning and the end. To the thirsty I will give water as a gift from the spring of the water of life. Those who conquer will inherit these things, and I will be their God and they will be my children.'" (Rev 21:3–7).

Now, I do not treat this highly symbolic language univocally, to be sure. Yet, in this symbolic speech the proclamation is still relatively clear to me: God promises salvation in the form of a new creation in which past sufferings will be healed, permanently healed. Now, either this is true or not. Either this will be shown to be true, or not. If it is true, then at the advent of the new creation we will retroactively confirm the veracity and legitimacy of today's trust in our God's promises.

If the devil is in the details, I can do without the details of each passage or allusion in the Book of Revelation. Nevertheless, it is my hope that a new creation is coming, that God will keep the promise made when raising Jesus from the dead on the first Easter. Beyond the darkness of the apocalypse, I still expect the dawn of a new and eternal day.

Leona Foxx

Since the time of my stint as a parish pastor on the south side of Chicago, I have harbored the plan to write a fictional account of a Lutheran pastor struggling with both gospel and service. I flew a number of kites over the years, but they all seemed to tumble to the ground. Now, finally, in 2013 the kite actually flew. Look up in the sky and you'll see the glide of my new heroine, Leona Foxx.

The first in a series of what I hope will be five suspense thrillers, *For God and Country: A Leona Foxx Mystery,* is now published and available at Amazon along with Barnes and Noble in both paperback and ebook form. Leona Foxx leads a double life. On the one hand, she's a disillusioned CIA operative suffering from moral injury, a form of PTSD I deal with at length in my book, *Sin Boldly! Justifying Faith for Fragile and Broken Souls* (Fortress, 2015). She has a broken soul. Yet, she also serves as a faithful pastor in a difficult inner city parish setting. Although devoted to her pastoral ministry, Leona is unwillingly called back into espionage. Her skills as a defender of America against threats both foreign and domestic conflict with her conscience, a conscience shaped by her faith and her compassion for both friends and enemies.

Leona is a deliberate amalgam of at least three persons I know. One is me. Another is a woman pastor whose heart I admire and whose selfless dedication to preaching the gospel and loving her people is nothing short of supererogatory. The third is the CIA agent whose traumatizing experience of moral injury while in an Iranian prison marks the threshold Leona must cross to attain some level of sanity and personal integration.

In this the first of the five-part series, Pastor Leona uncovers a terrorist plot hatched by American mercenaries who intend to blame Iran. She divests her clerical collar to pack her .45 Kimber Super Match II and rallies a counter-terrorist alliance of professional crime fighters with black gang members. The story climaxes with an attempted assassination of the US president, a thwarted helicopter attack at the 85th floor of the John Hancock Building. This climactic scene takes place right next door to the condo of Martin and Harriet Marty, friends in real life who are safely out of harm's way when the action gets frightening in the novel. Whew! That was a close call!

In his review of the book here titled, "An Author-Character Match Made in Heaven: Ted Peters and Leona Foxx," Jan-Olav Henriksen comments: Leona "appears as a credible witness to what it means to be a Christian today: Christians are not perfect, but they live by resources in Scripture and theology that help them deal with, accept, and come to terms with the ambiguities of life, even when 'the wrinkles cannot be ironed out.' Leona is also an exciting alternative to the all-too-sweet or all-too-harmonious picture of who Christians are or should be that we find elsewhere in literature or movies that try to make the Christian message available to a wider audience."[22]

The Boy Scouts of America have long enticed boys-becoming-men to earn an award called "God and Country." The specifically Lutheran form of this award is written in Latin, *Pro Deo et Patria* (Both God and country demand allegiance). The question Leona must face is this: Is it possible to worship both? In Matthew 6:24, it is written, "No one can serve two masters; for a slave will either hate the one and love the other, or be devoted to the one and despise the other." In *For God and Country*, Leona puts these words of Jesus to the test.

Concluding Prayer

In his review Henrikson picks up on one of Leona's prayers. This prayer summarizes many prayers I have presented before the throne of grace over the years.

> God, you have got such a fucked up world. Why did you put me here like a pincushion to feel every prick of its pain? Yes, I want to love your world as much as you do. But goddammit, it's hard. I'd like to ask the Holy Spirit for the wisdom and strength to trust in what I cannot see. But goddammit, I'm too pissed off to think it's worthwhile. I hope your grace covers me. Amen.[23]

When a theologian of the cross tries to be both realistic and faithful, this is about the best we can expect.

---

22 Henriksen, 227.
23 Henriksen, 225.

THE EVOLUTION CONTROVERSY

Encountering Evolution

Ted Peters on Darwin and Christian Theology

Martinez Hewlett

It was November 2001, just a few short weeks after 9/11. We were all attending the American Academy of Religion meeting in Denver, Colorado. The events of that fall weighed heavily on everyone. Ted Peters sat with me in the restaurant of the Adams Mark Hotel to talk about a research program he called Theodicy, Evolution, and Genocide (TEG). While the attacks in New York, Washington, D.C., and Pennsylvania formed a backdrop to this discussion, the precipitating issue was a seminar that Peters had just heard by Richard Dawkins at UC Berkeley. The prominent evolutionary biologist, whom Peters would later dub an "evangelical atheist," was speaking about the genetic reductionism that had become his hallmark with books such as *The Selfish Gene*[1] and *The Blind Watchmaker*.[2] In Peters' report of this lecture to me, he said that Dawkins argued the following premise: given the comparison of the relatedness of DNA sequences of two populations, it could be predicted whether or not one group would commit genocide against the other.

Peters' immediate reaction as a theologian was revulsion. How could this be reflective of the real nature of humans, created in the image of God? His second reaction was more interesting. What if there is some sense in which Dawkins is correct? What if the evolutionary model of Darwin is actually predictive of behavior in some way? What would this mean for our theological understanding of *imago Dei* and, indeed, of all creation?

---

1 Richard Dawkins, *The Selfish Gene* (Oxford: Oxford University Press, 1976).
2 Richard Dawkins, *The Blind Watchmaker* (New York: W.W. Norton, 1986).

A New Research Program

It was this second reaction that led to his suggestion of the establishment of a research group consisting of scientists, philosophers, and theologians dedicated to asking questions about biological evolution and human nature. Thus arose the Theodicy, Evolution, and Genocide (TEG) program. The initial team consisted of Peters and myself as Principal Investigators along with Bob Russell and Carol Jacobson as Senior Research Scholars. We had a starting group of graduate students that included Gaymon Bennett, Nathan Hallanger, Mary Anne Cooney, and Joshua Moritz.

Very early on in the program, we created a vision document with the following statement:

> The task of TEG is to analyze and compare competing explanations of this tension—the tension between committing genocide and revulsion against genocide—within human behavior to reach a sixfold goal: (1) to define the phenomenon of genocide; (2) to identify the most adequate scientific explanations, if any; (3) to bring to bear philosophical schools of thought which depict the primordial human experience of moral responsibility; (4) to expand or provide theological descriptions and explanations according to Christian understandings of sin, evil, and suffering; (5) to provide ethical insights into human nature that would inform public policy in anticipation of future possible outbreaks of mass murder; and (6) to analyze the theodicy problem in light of evolutionary biology and in light of large scale human suffering at the hands of state supported genocide or mass murder.[3]

Although by the end of the program we had not nearly achieved these lofty goals, we did make some significant forays into the issues we raised. We developed a number of sessions on genocide at various Center for Theology and the Natural Sciences (CTNS) conferences. There were two separate Graduate Theological Union (GTU) courses that stemmed from the work of the program. We officially culminated the program with the publication of a set of papers in an edited volume entitled *The Evolution of Evil*.[4]

---

[3] Ted Peters and Martinez Hewlett, "Theodicy, Evolution, and Genocide," unpublished document, n.d.

[4] Gaymon Bennett, Martinez Hewlett, Ted Peters, and Robert John Russell, *The Evolution of Evil* (Göttingen, Germany: Vandenhoeck & Ruprecht, 2008).

It was this program, however, that led to a collaboration between Peters and me, examining the nature of the conversation between science and religion that has existed since the publication of Darwin's monumental work. It is that collaboration upon which I will focus for the remainder of this chapter.

Encountering Biological Evolution

From the outset, it was essential that we had a clear understanding of biological evolution and its implications for human behavior. This meant examining the details of evolutionary theory as well as critiquing the fields of sociobiology and its more recent offshoot, evolutionary psychology. Inevitably, this landed us in the controversy, the so-called "war," between science and religion that has taken place since the late nineteenth century.

We initially insisted that this presumed war existed only in the current day between the extremes: the conservative Christian biblical literalists on the one hand, and those in the scientific community committed to materialism and atheism as philosophical and theological positions respectively. As such, we felt that we had no scholarly place in this discussion. In addition, it seemed to us that the issue had been settled by court decisions related to the teaching of evolution in public schools in Arkansas and Louisiana.[5] As it turns out, this analysis was quite superficial.

Shortly after the beginning of the TEG Program, Peters was asked by Abingdon Press if he would be interested in writing a book on the evolution controversy. Peters asked if I would join him as co-author, and we both met with Kathy Armisted, who would be our editor. The initial outline, research, and writing for this first book, a textbook formatted for a graduate level course, began in 2002 at my home in Taos, New Mexico, during the fall of that year. The resulting *Evolution from Creation to New Creation*[6] was published in November 2003.

---

5 For instance, the landmark 1987 Supreme Court ruling in the Edwards v. Aguillard decided that the "equal time" provision of a Louisiana statute amounted to a violation of the Establishment Clause of the U.S. Constitution. See the National Center for Science Education web site for a summary of this and other cases related to the teaching of evolution (http://ncse.com/taking-action/ten-major-court-cases-evolution-creationism, last accessed on 26 June 2013).

6 Ted Peters and Martinez Hewlett, *Evolution from Creation to New Creation: Conflict, Conversation, and Convergence* (Nashville, Tennessee: Abingdon Press, 2003).

The Divine Action Spectrum

We set ourselves to the task of reviewing all sides of the issues surrounding evolution and theology. This involved reading a number of key works by the most prominent spokespersons for their respective positions. It became clear that this could be expressed as a function of whether or not and to what degree direct Divine intervention was involved in the origin and complexity of life on our planet. We chose to represent this as a spectrum, from a completely interventionist view of God's actions to atheism:[7]

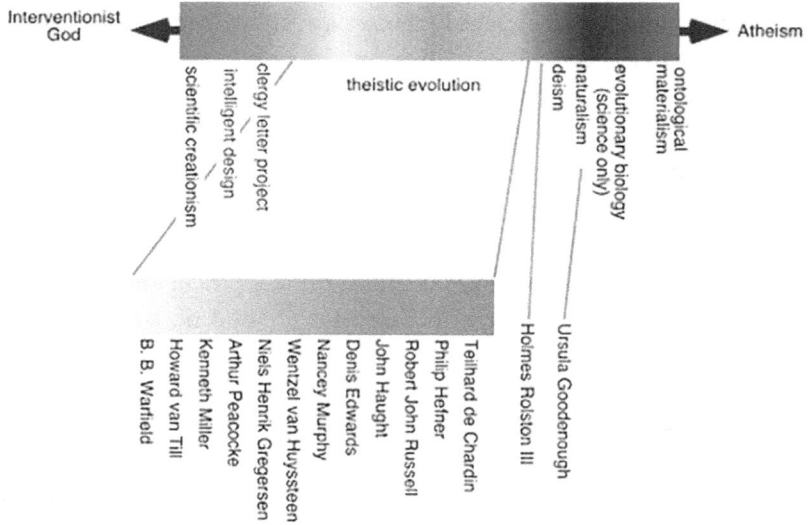

This spectrum not only helped to categorize the viewpoints we were analyzing, but also defined for us the broad range of positions in the middle, which included our own. We have claimed the term "theistic evolution" to identify this middle ground.[8] We have subsequently defended this as the most reasonable position to be taken that honors both the scientific enterprise as well as the theological reflection on that enterprise.

Our definition of theistic evolution can be stated as the following set of four positions:

---

7   This is a recent version of this spectrum. The original can be found in *Evolution from Creation to New Creation*.

8   Peters recounts that the term was initially used in a pejorative manner during an interaction with a group of scientific creationists, who, at one point, fired at him the accusation: "It's you theistic evolutionists who are the problem."

1. We accept the neo-Darwinian model as the best current theoretical explanation for numerous observations in biology. In this, we are looking at the science of evolution, rather than the philosophical "shrink wrapping." I'll say more about this below.
2. We argue for a Thomistic understanding of causes. That is, the proper role of science is the investigation of secondary causation. God, on the other hand, operates as though God's actions were a primary cause. We are clear in this that God is not to be seen as an actual cause in the world.
3. The self-defined role of science as we know the activity does not involve purpose. Science as it is currently practiced is blind to teleology.
4. Our theological reflection, however, leads us to conclude that God does indeed have a purpose for the natural world. This is an eschatological statement that has no impact on the scientific venture.

A Visit to the Battlements

Needless to say, we were met with scorn by the very extremes whose verbal cannonades make the press reports of the "war" imagery so vivid. We were determined to cover as sympathetically as we could all of the arguments being made, especially those with which we could not agree. To this end, Peters proposed a fact-finding trip early in our work to the Institute for Creation Research (ICR). At the time, ICR was located in Santee, California, in the foothills east of San Diego.[9]

My initial reaction was to decline this interaction. My reasoning was that I did not want to get into a fight with anyone. I felt that, as a scientist, I would have a hard time refraining from confrontation. Peters wisely insisted that this was the very reason I needed to go on this trip. How could I write and lecture effectively about all sides of the argument without hearing from the proponents themselves?

The trip from Taos to Santee actually involved a stopover in Berkeley. There, the night before our meetings at ICR, we all met at Peters' now famous condominium on Virginia Street. The theme was to calm Dr. Hewlett down. To this end, we watched the film, *Inherit the Wind*, ac-

---

9   In 2007, Institute for Creation Research relocated to Dallas, Texas.

companied by a very nice lecture by Nate Hallanger on the history of creationism in the United States. This was followed by a frank discussion of what might be my concerns. By the next morning I was ready, and we all boarded a flight for San Diego.

Our visit began with lunch at a nearby restaurant, attended by the late co-founders of the Institute, Henry Morris and Duane Gish, along with Henry's son John, the current president of ICR. I learned that Gish and I had a common scientific history, in that he had trained as a virologist at UC Berkeley.[10] We followed this with a tour of the research facilities of the Institute, and ended with a walk through the Museum of Creation and Earth History.

I said very little during the early part of the visit. After the sessions of the previous evening, I really wanted to listen and not to indulge in my internal critique. However, I did ask two questions, one of Gish and one of John Morris. I learned that these scientists were not actually biblical literalists in the absolute sense of the phrase, but rather were committed believers trying desperately (and, in my opinion, unsuccessfully) to reconcile their faith in Scripture with their scientific training.[11]

In fact, we did not pay a visit to the battlements on the other side. Our reading of and listening to Richard Dawkins, Daniel Dennett, Edward Wilson, and others was, we felt, fairly complete to allow us to analyze their positions. As far as the broad middle ground in this discussion, the field of theistic evolution, we were immersed within its sheltered, non-violent confines from the outset and were quite frankly speaking from this position.[12]

Our most cogent disagreement with the evangelical atheists, represented for us by the spectrum from Thomas Huxley to Richard Dawkins, has to do with what Peters described as the "shrink wrap" placed over

---

10 Additionally, there is a distant familial connection. My sister-in-law's sister is married to one of Dr. Gish's nephews.

11 I asked Duane Gish about the verse in the Old Testament regarding the sun stopping in the sky (Joshua 10:13). He said that this did not actually happen. While visiting the museum, in the room devoted to the Third Day of Creation, I asked John Morris when the ferns (non-seed bearing plants) were created (Genesis 1:9–13). His answer was that by "plants," the Bible meant all kinds of plants, even though Scripture refers specifically to "seed-bearing plants."

12 The warfare or conflict model for the extremes in this discussion has been most clearly defined in the typologies of Ian Barbour [Barbour, *Religion in an Age of Science* (San Francisco: HarperSan Francisco, 1990)] and John Haught [J. Haught, *Science and Religion: From Conflict to Conversation* (Mahwah, New Jersey: Paulist Press, 1995)]. Our position broadly encompasses their other three typologies: contrast, contact, and conversation (to use Haught's terminology).

the scientific model that Darwin has so powerfully constructed. Almost immediately upon publication of *Origin of Species*,[13] Charles Darwin received a letter from the eminent Victorian biologist, Thomas Huxley. Of course, Huxley was familiar with the broad outlines of the model. However, the publication of the book presented the data that Huxley needed not only to accept the model, but also to become its most vocal champion.

The problem was, and still remains, the degree to which the science of biological evolution is made the basis of social, philosophical, and even theological positions. From that November day in 1859 to the present, many assume that to accept the scientific model is to also accept the social implications first described by Herbert Spencer and given voice today in areas such as sociobiology and evolutionary psychology. A significant number of scientists believe that biological evolution necessarily precludes any kind of belief in God. These are the ideological shrink wrappings that seem to precipitate such strong reactions, especially within the more conservative sections of the religious spectrum.

In order to describe our approach to uncovering the exciting and productive science implicit in biological evolution, we need to drill down beneath these overlays. To that end, we devised another metaphor, this time using the image of oil exploration and recovery:[14]

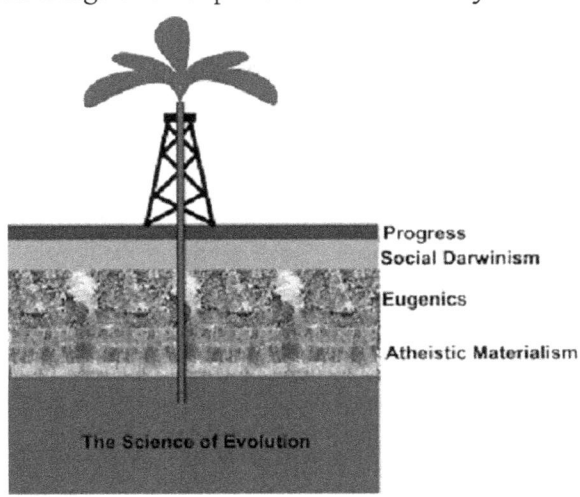

---

13 Charles Darwin, *On the Origin of Species by Means of Natural Selection*, 1st ed., (London: John Murray, 1859).
14 In fact, this image is from our second book: Ted Peters and Martinez Hewlett, *Can You Believe in God and Evolution? A Guide for the Perplexed* (Nashville, Tennessee: Abingdon Press, 2008), discussed in the next section.

We included in this image the "geological" layers of progress, social Darwinism, eugenics, and atheistic materialism. Each of these plays a significant role in the development of the anti-evolution positions espoused by the so-called "creationists,"[15] as well as the counter-reaction of the evangelical atheists. And, most important, none of these movements has anything to do with the actual utility of the scientific model itself.

The development of our view of theistic evolution is therefore a reaction to both sides in this non-existent war.

The Controversy for the Non-Academic

Our first book for Abingdon was crafted as a scholarly work, suitable as a text for graduate or seminary students. There was also a clear need for a book that could be read by those most immediately affected by this discussion: teachers, parents, and the confused faithful in the pews.[16] As a result, we agreed to write a second book on this subject: *Can You Believe in God and Evolution? A Guide for the Perplexed*.[17]

In this book, we re-tell our arguments for theistic evolution with the aim of giving high school teachers and parents solid footing for championing the best science education for our children. Here, the intent was more narration than scholarly discourse. For instance, we begin the book recounting anecdotes of our own experiences from interactions with students we have counseled.

Like the earlier book, however, we attempt to cover all sides of the issue, focusing on their arguments and on our counter-arguments. In the end, we make the case that our students deserve the very best science to prepare them for the challenges of our technological age. But they also need not be indoctrinated into the philosophical positions that either side of this artificial battle. They can, if they choose, have a religious

---

15 I place the term "creationist" in quotes here to indicate the positions of organizations such as the ICR. In fact, the evangelical atheists consider anyone with a belief in a Creator God as a creationist, by definition, especially those of us who are theistic evolutionists. In order to not be given this label, one would have to accept both the science of evolution as well as the philosophy of atheistic materialism.

16 To be honest, my wife, Gail Hewlett, had been lobbying for this kind of book from the outset. While she appreciates the scholarly effort we put into this project, she was also keenly aware that what we had to say should be cast in a framework that was accessible to those without advanced degrees in science, philosophy, and theology. She was right!

17 Peters and Hewlett, 2008, with apologies to Maimonides.

life along with their scientific career, contrary to what Richard Dawkins holds to be the only possibility.[18]

A Tribute to Our Sponsor

Well, Darwin didn't actually sponsor our work, but his brilliance certainly was our inspiration. To that end, we proposed and wrote a third book for Abingdon, as our contribution to the year of celebration marking 2009 as the 200th birthday of Darwin and the 150th anniversary of the publication of *Origin of Species*.[19] This gave us both the chance to read once again Darwin's great work, this time with an eye towards critical commentary. We also took the opportunity to tackle another monumental volume, Stephen Jay Gould's *The Structure of Evolutionary Theory*, his final contribution to the field he loved so dearly.[20]

We included in the book a CD-ROM containing the complete text of the 6th and final edition of *Origin of Species*.[21] This is an interactive disk that allows the reader to navigate through the text in response to certain "frequently asked questions" that we posed, such as "What does Darwin say about 'design'?" or "Does Darwin appeal to secondary causation as an explanation?"

We considered the Year of Darwin to be the culmination of this phase of our scholarly interaction. We had said all that we felt was necessary from the standpoint of champions of theistic evolution. This is not to say that the issue has been put to rest, or that intelligent design, the current favorite of the anti-Darwin faction, is not still debated. It is just that Peters and Hewlett needed to move on.

What Next?

Indeed, with Peters' fertile scholarly drive at work, there is never a break in stride, moving from one research program to the next. So it is that I happily signed on for the next excellent adventure. We are currently embarked on an edited volume, edited by Peters, with the working title of *Outer Space for the Inner Soul: Astrotheology Meets Extrater-*

---

18 Richard Dawkins, *The God Delusion,* reprint ed. (New York: Mariner Books, 2008).
19 Ted Peters and Martinez Hewlett, *Theological and Scientific Commentary on Darwin's* Origin of Species, (Nashville, Tennessee: Abingdon Press, 2008).
20 Stephen Jay Gould, *The Structure of Evolutionary Theory* (Cambridge, Massachusetts: Belknap Press of Harvard University Press, 2002).
21 This final edition was published by John Murray in 1872. All six of the editions were written and edited by Darwin.

restrial Life.[22] This project has been a long-standing interest for Peters, and our current discussions of it were precipitated by our involvement in a meeting in 2008 sponsored by the Astrobiology Program at the University of Arizona.[23]

After that? I envision a series of programs extending well into our truly "old age." I would be delighted to be discussing and writing about science and theology with Peters as long as we can both bring minds to the contest and fingers to keyboards.

---

22 Ted Peters' collaborators, at this writing, include Bob Russell, Joshua Moritz, Margaret Race, Mark Graves, in addition to myself. The manuscript is currently in process.
23 Papers from this conference were published in the book, *Encountering Life in the Universe,* Chris Impey, Anna Spitz, and William Stoeger, eds. (Tucson: University of Arizona Press, 2013).

Human Origins

Present, Past, and Future

Ronald Cole-Turner

It is hard to find a theologian who engages the challenges of our day more seriously or courageously than Ted Peters. With energy and boldness, he takes up the most provocative developments in science and technology and invites readers to reflect with him on everything from genetics and stem cell ethics to the possibility that we may soon discover proof of life beyond our little planet. At the same time, he addresses core Christian doctrines such as Trinity, incarnation, and most of all, eschatology.

What makes his engagement with science and technology so fruitful is that he consistently asks how the latest technical developments affect these core Christian beliefs. He does this in a refreshingly open-minded way and with a willingness to rethink theology to its roots. On top of that, what I like most is that he uses everyday language and writes with his own distinctive flare.

Here I take up a theme raised in Peters' reflections on evolution and Christianity. His work, whether written alone or in collaboration with Martinez Hewlett, is mostly focused on the broad implications of evolution for Christian faith. He nicely covers such topics as evolution and purpose, design, divine action, and theodicy. In this essay, I build on these writings but point our attention specifically to questions about human origins. In particular I want to focus on some unexpected theological challenges arising from scientific work related to human origins and only recently published, mostly since 2010.

To begin, let us note what Peters and Hewlett say about human origins at the conclusion of their book, *Evolution from Creation to New Creation*. Quite rightly they object to the use of any science, including evolutionary biology, to support elitist or racist views of human life. They suggest that "the common descent of humanity emphasizes the unity of our species."[1] They add this warning: "...we reject the use of the evolutionary model to separate us, one from another."[2]

Earlier in this book, they discuss the views of creationists such as Ken Ham. Peters and Hewlett appear to agree with the creationists on one key point. They write: "Essential to Christian anthropology is the oneness of the human race with Adam and with Christ, the second Adam. In Adam, we all die. In Christ, we are all made alive. Jesus Christ is the image of God *(imago Dei)* in incarnate form, an image in which we all share. Racial divisions simply cannot be considered fundamental, from a theological point of view; and the creationists argue this point with considerable passion."[3] In other words, they all seem to agree (as I also agree) with the core principle of human unity in Christ, the sort of unity that rules out any notion of racial division.

But on another point, Peters and Hewlett clearly disagree with the creationists. They protest against Ham's claim that evolutionary biology supports racism. They especially do not like the way these creationists seize the non-racial moral high ground for themselves and then claim that only creationists can occupy this ground. Peters and Hewlett target the creationists' claim that evolution is implicitly and necessarily racist. Not surprisingly, Peters and Hewlett think this is unfair, objecting to the idea "that evolutionary biologists must be racists and creationists egalitarians...." Then they add this: "To draw the picture this way would be a distortion."[4]

Why do they call this a distortion? Because the evolutionary biologists actually agree on this point with creationists and with Christians in general. Human beings are all fully members of one species or one race. We are all from one original population. We may not all come from just one primal pair (Adam and Eve), but we do come from only one population that is small enough and recent enough to offer the same level of

---

1 Ted Peters and Martinez Hewlett, *Evolution from Creation to New Creation: Conflict, Conversation, and Convergence* (Nashville: Abingdon Press, 2003), 168.
2 Ibid., 169.
3 Ibid., 88.
4 Ibid.

assurance of species unity. Until recently, I said pretty much the same thing. And when Peters and Hewlett wrote it, most experts in human origins would agree with this point of view. Science offered support for human unity, not human division.

Whenever I bring up such questions in the seminary classroom, I am aware of student fears. I tell them that it is true that science does not support the idea of a literal Adam and Eve, so if they need that belief to support their traditional view of a fall into original sin, they are going to have some trouble with science. But I quickly try to reassure them of the idea of human species unity in terms of scientific support. According to the sciences of human origins, all humans have one recent common origin.

At least that is what I used to say. Now I have to qualify what I say in light of recent findings that add new complexity to the story of human origins and to very notion of human unity. Human beings living today do have somewhat different origins. Some of us, it turns out, are the result of interbreeding with other forms of humanity, such as Neandertals. Put simply, I have Neandertals in my family tree. Their DNA is in my body.

I taught this material again in 2013. To make sure that the students were clear about what is now at stake, I did something I have never done before. I showed a video featuring a white supremacist. I warned students in advance about what was coming and gave them permission to leave the room if they did not want to see it. My point was that the latest research on interbreeding is already being given a racist interpretation. Minus the vitriol, it goes roughly like this. Europeans and Asians are descended in part from Neandertals. And since Neandertals had large brains, the progeny of this interbreeding, according to this video, are superior to others. Once I had the students' attention, I tried to argue that this new science is theologically challenging, but it does not support racism.

Genetics and Human Species Complexity

The new findings are possible because of some remarkable technological advances in genetics. This field got a major boost in the 1990s through the Human Genome Project. At that time, Ted Peters led a group of us in a three-year research program at the Center for Theology and the Natural Sciences. Our research focused on philosophical and religious implications of the federally funded project to map and sequence the entire human genome. The project was expected to take several years and cost more than $3 billion.

No one expected then that today, just twenty years later, the cost of sequencing a complete human genome would drop to about $1,000 and the time would be measured in a few hours. These advances in gene sequencing affect not just medicine and biomedical research, but also the study of human origins, where its effect has been startling, even revolutionary. Today we have multiple human genomes sampled from many living human beings representatively selected from around the globe. We have complete genomes of some plants and many animals, some of them long extinct. Computers can scan genomes to look for broad similarities and subtle differences.

All this bears directly on questions of human origins. Mostly through the work of a team led by Svante Pääbo, researchers have learned to extract DNA fragments from fossils dating back tens of thousands of years and reconstruct them into reliable sequence information. So now we have not just contemporary human genomes but also the Neandertal genome.[5] This work also revealed something quite surprising. Samples first thought to be somewhat unusual Neandertal remains turned out to be something clearly different, a previously unknown type of humans called the Denisovans, named for the central Asian cave where they were found.[6]

Today we have the Denisovan and the Neandertal genome at a quality of sequence information equal to what we have for any living human being. This allows detailed comparisons between living humans from various parts of the world with Neandertals and Denisovans. Not surprisingly, we are remarkably similar genetically. We share some 97% of our DNA with chimpanzees, so it is not unexpected that we share much more than that with Neandertals and Denisovans.

What is surprising is that in terms of sharing genes with Neandertals and Denisovans, some human beings living today share more than others. Those with ancestry from sub-Saharan Africa share fewer genes with Neanderthals than those whose ancestry lies in Europe, Asia, or the Americas. Humans whose ancestors are from the islands south and east

---

5   R.E. Green, J. Krause, A.W. Briggs, et al, "A Draft Sequence of the Neandertal Genome," *Science* 7 vol. 328, no. 5979 (May 2010): 710–22, DOI: 10.1126/science.1188021.

6   D. Reich, N. Patterson, M. Kircher, et al, "Denisova Admixture and the First Modern Human Dispersals into Southeast Asia and Oceania," *The American Journal of Human Genetics* 89, no. 4 (07 Oct 2011): 516–28.

of Asia, along with aboriginal Australians, share more genes with Denisovans than the rest of us do.

Why do different human groups today have different levels of shared Neandertal and Denisovan genes? There are at least two ways to explain the differences. The first explanation points out that when *Homo sapiens* left Africa sometime within the past 100,000 years, the ones who left came from northeast Africa, roughly where Egypt is today. Compared to the humans living further south, those living in northeast Africa were already slightly different genetically, with a somewhat higher proportion of DNA shared with Neandertals. In other words, the sharing goes back to a period of common ancestry, when lineages leading to Neandertals and *Homo sapiens* diverged, somewhere on the order of 500,000 years ago.

The second explanation is that after some *Homo sapiens* left Africa less than 100,000 years ago, they encountered Neandertals. The two groups were remarkably similar. Their lines had only diverged some 500,000 years earlier, not enough time for great changes but plenty of time for DNA mutations to accumulate. Genes in Neandertals and genes in *Homo sapiens* were still largely the same in sequence and function. But they carried tiny differences in the form of mutations, tell-tale markers of a time of divergence. According to the second explanation, these Neandertal-specific DNA sequences were passed to some *Homo sapiens* through interbreeding that occurred less than 100,000 years ago, after the time of divergence and after *Homo sapiens* had left Africa. Something similar appears to have happened when a few of these *Homo sapiens* made their way south and east. They encountered Denisovans, and to this day their descendants carry the molecular evidence of those encounters.

Which explanation is correct? The best evidence supports the second explanation. A 2012 analysis strongly suggests that some of the DNA from Neandertals only entered the *Homo sapiens* population after this group had left Africa. The date of the "introgression," or "gene flow," is now placed between 37,000 and 86,000 years and most likely occurred between 47,000 and 65,000 years ago.[7]

The date is significant for two reasons. First, it is pretty strong evidence in favor of the second explanation of differences in the amount of Neandertal DNA found among humans today. If these Neandertal-spe-

---

[7] Sriram Sankararaman, Nick Patterson, Heng Li, Svante Pääbo, David Reich, and Joshua M. Akey, "The Date of Interbreeding between Neandertals and Modern Humans," *PLoS Genetics* 8, no. 10 (04 Oct 2012): e1002947; DOI: 10.1371/journal.pgen.1002947.

cific sequences have only been in humans for less than 86,000 years at the most, then they must have entered by interbreeding rather than by common ancestry. Second, the date also offers hints of where the interbreeding may have occurred. It seems to have been early in the period of *Homo sapiens*'s migration into Eurasia, which suggests that it occurred in the Middle East.

Do these Neandertal gene variants affect those of us who have them? At least in one regard, the answer appears to be "yes." According to a 2011 study, human immune systems today have the benefit of some of the immune capacity acquired by Neandertals during the time of divergence. The idea is that when *Homo sapiens* left Africa less than 100,000 years ago, their immune systems were not ready for the challenges of life in colder, more varied climates. But the Neandertals had lived in Eurasia successfully for more than 200,000 years. Their immune systems were adapted, and they passed these genetic modifications to *Homo sapiens*. Today, those who carry these Neandertal genes show evidence of what researchers call the "selected introgression of functionally advantageous genes."[8] On the whole, Neandertal genes contribute only about one to four percent to modern humans. But when it comes to certain humanity genes, in some modern humans *more than half* of these genes come from Neandertals.

Another unexpected finding is that recent interbreeding is not limited to Eurasia around 50,000 years ago. It seems that interbreeding also occurred in sub-Saharan Africa. No Neandertals lived there, at least as far as we know. In fact, nothing is known about other types of humans who may have lived there at the time the interbreeding is thought to have happened. But gene sequences distinctively present in today's human populations in these areas suggest a history of interbreeding similar to what occurred in Eurasia.[9]

All this points toward a fundamentally new view of recent human origins. Until just a few years ago, most experts thought that at some point between 100,000 and 200,000 years ago, *Homo sapiens* evolved in

---

8 Laurent Abi-Rached, Matthew J. Jobin, Subhash Kulkarni, et al, "The Shaping of Modern Human Immune Systems by Multiregional Admixture with Archaic Humans." *Science* 334, no. 6052 (07 October 2011): 89–94.

9 Michael F. Hammer, August E. Woerner, Fernando L. Mendez, Joseph C. Watkins, and Jeffrey D. Wall, "Genetic Evidence for Archaic Admixture in Africa," *Proceedings of the National Academy of Sciences* 108, no. 37 (13 September 2011): 15123–28; DOI: 10.1073/pnas.1109300108.

Africa. They migrated to every part of that continent and to Europe and Asia, replacing any other types of humans that they encountered. The Neandertals simply disappeared, dying out due to hunger or violent encounters. The same fate met any other similar forms of humans that may have existed at the time. As far as we are concerned, they just do not matter except as intellectual curiosities.

That is the old view. Now we are faced with an entirely new possibility. Yes, *Homo sapiens* evolved in Africa more than 100,000 years ago and migrated. They came into existence as a new and distinct lineage, one that looked very much like we do and led directly to us. As these new humans followed earlier migration pathways throughout Africa and into Asia and Europe, they encountered other forms of humanity and interbred occasionally with them in ways that leave lasting effects to this day. The proof of interbreeding comes from the careful analysis of human global genetic variation in comparison with DNA from extinct forms of humanity. This technology was not possible until about 2010. More evidence and more arguments will surely be presented in the years ahead. But for now, the story of the human species just got a whole lot more complicated.

Human Unity and Human Uniqueness

According to Ernst Mayr's classic definition, species are "groups of actually or potentially interbreeding natural populations, which are reproductively isolated from other such groups."[10] If the new humans that left Africa less than 100,000 years ago interbred with Neandertals and Denisovans, are all these human types members of one species? To answer yes stretches our usual view of our species, to say the least. Answering no suggests that some humans are hybrids, the products of inter-species mating, something we know is possible but is seen as an exception to Mayr's definition.

If the science here is an open question, the theology is even more uncertain. If Neandertals are seen as members of the human species, do we see them as bearers of the image of God? Is their humanity assumed in the incarnation? With a reasonable degree of certainty, we must now say that Jesus of Nazareth, like humans today of his particular ancestry, carried genes inherited from his distant Neandertal ancestors. Are they included in the incarnation?

---

10 Ernst Mayr, *Systematics and the Origin of Species* (New York: Columbia University Press, 1942), 120.

And it is not just the Neandertal question that we face here. The new picture arising from the most recent work in human origins suggests that the human family tree is not a tree at all. It is more like a tangled vine, with moments when lineages diverge and then converge. In times of divergence, separated breeding communities respond to environmental challenges and climate oscillations that are now seen as playing a key role in human selection within small, isolated populations.[11] These isolated populations then converge and interbreed again, only to diverge and converge in new ways and in response to new situations. In this new perspective, which is still more conjecture than conclusion, our interbreeding with Neandertals is part of a wider pattern, not an isolated event.

In recent decades, those who study human origins have argued the merits of two alternative views. One view is that today's humans descended from *Homo erectus*, which spread throughout Africa and Eurasia, changing over hundreds of thousands of years by adapting to regional environments and to climate fluctuations. Although spread across thousands of miles, these humans remained in occasional contact through migrations, enough so that they can be seen as one species with regional differences. As they evolved, they became the globally diverse, modern human species that we know today.

The other view is that our form of humanity arose in Africa less than 200,000 years ago. They spread throughout Africa and then made their way to Asia and Europe, starting about 80,000 years ago. Eventually these new humans completely replaced all other forms of humans, such as Neandertals. All human beings today are closely related members of this one, relatively young species, and human variations are the result of recent adaptations to local conditions, such as the amount of sunlight received.

Stated so simply, both views are partly right and partly wrong. *Homo erectus* did lead over hundreds of thousands of years to highly developed regional forms of humanity, such as Neandertals. These forms did not simply disappear, and interbreeding with them appears to explain some of the human diversity found even today. But it is also true that overwhelmingly, we human beings are all descendants of the relatively recent emergence of a new form of humanity that appeared in Africa and then spread throughout the globe, interbreeding but largely displacing other forms of humanity.

---

11 J.R. Stewart and C.B. Stringer, "Human Evolution out of Africa: The Role of Refugia and Climate Change," *Science 16, vol.* 335, no. 6074 (16 March 2012): 1317-21, DOI: 10.1126/science.1215627.

One key implication is that we now must see these other forms of humanity, such as Neandertals, as remarkably like us. The earliest cave art in western Europe goes back to more than 40,000 years ago, back to the very time when Neandertals were encountering their new neighbors.[12] Just who made this early art is not completely clear. Did Neandertals have the ability to communicate in complex or symbolic ways? Perhaps we will never know, but most current research suggests that they were not so different from us.

All this raises new questions for theology. In a time when human uniqueness seems less clearly supported by scientific evidence than we once thought, theology's challenge is to restate what it means by "image of God." The new problem today is not so much what that term means but to whom it applies. Drawing from Peters' future-oriented theology, we can say that all the forms of humanity in the past and in the present (including us) are not yet in the image of God but are on our way toward that image. Christ is the only full or perfect image of God, and by incarnation Christ brings together all the strands of our evolutionary past into one still-emergent species.

This approach will not satisfy those who hope to reconcile current science with an historic fall. For some traditional Christians, this event in human history is needed to make sense of the redemption offered in Christ. Without the fall of Adam and Eve, they argue, there is no need for redemption through Jesus Christ. But for many Christians today, the growing evidence from the sciences of human origins undermines any thought of a literal human fall into sin. Not only is there no historic pair, there is no longer any simple lineage or line of descent in which such an event might have occurred. One way to preserve a high view of incarnation in light of this problem is to reclaim the idea that Christ would have become incarnate even if Adam and Eve had not sinned, or even if they never existed in the form of a distinct lineage. From Irenaeus in the second century to medieval Franciscans, from Friedrich Schleiermacher to Karl Barth and Karl Rahner, great Christian theologians have argued for what is called a *supralapsarian* view, claiming that the redemptive

---

12 A.W.G. Pike, D.L. Hoffmann, M. García-Diez, et al, "U-series Dating of Paleolithic Art in 11 Caves in Spain," *Science* vol. 336, no. 6087 (15 June 2012): 1409-13, DOI: 10.1126/science.1219957.

purposes of God have more to do with the completion of creation than with a rescue from sin.[13]

Today there can be no authentic theological anthropology that does not take into account what we are learning from the sciences, including the dynamic and interdisciplinary scientific investigation into human origins. This field is only a hundred years old, and most of the key work has been accomplished in the past fifty years, especially in the last five to ten years. Theologians of an earlier age might be forgiven for ignoring this field, but we may not.

In addition to the theoretical challenges that come from findings in this field, there is the daunting practical challenge that theologians face in trying to keep up with new discoveries, shifting debates, and fresh questions. But if theology today is to make its own truly informed and contemporary contribution to that perennial question—what does it mean to be human?—it has little choice but to engage this field of inquiry as it is being set before us at an almost breathless pace in the science journals of our day. In that regard, Ted Peters is both a model and an inspiration.

Today more than ever before, we are just beginning to get a clear picture of how we came into existence as human beings. It is a long, slow, complex process, full of diverging and converging lineages that defy any linear view of our origins. There were no great evolutionary leaps to humanity and no great cultural leaps to modernity. Of course it is true that we stand out today as an oddity among creatures. But when seen against the backdrop of all our ancestors, we are hardly unique or markedly different. What sets us off more than anything from other living species or from our distant ancestors is our technology. Just as the use of stone tools once helped to make us human in the first place, so now the use of our tools seems poised to make us something beyond our present form of human life.

---

13 Ronald Cole-Turner, "Incarnation Deep and Wide: A Response to Niels Gregersen," *Theology and Science* vol. 11, no. 4, (17 Dec 2013): 424–35; DOI: 10.1080/14746700.2013.836886.

Sacramental Evolution

Emerging into the *Imago Dei*

Peter M.J. Hess

> "Through him all things were made,
> and without him nothing was made that was made....
> And the Word became flesh and dwelt among us."
> John 1:3, 14

God, Creation, and Sacramentality

The rating of a rock climb is generally determined by the difficulty of the "crux" move—the most difficult step confronting the climber on her or his route up the face. If the dialogue between religion and science over the last half century were portrayed as a climb, I believe the crux move would be the evolution of the human spirit.

We live in a very different world from that inhabited by the biblical writers and the theologians of the early church. The picture of a compact, young, finite, and static cosmos has given way incrementally (and sometimes traumatically[1]) to that of a universe understood as vast, ancient, dynamic, and evolving. An early stage in this cosmic reconstruction was the incremental assimilation of heliocentrism, of an atomic theory of matter, of deep geological time, and of a universe of myriad galaxies, and the recognition of the extinction and evolution of species. Genetics and DNA were gradually integrated into biology, and plate tectonics explained the dynamism of earth. Western science ultimately arrived at a unified account of the history of terrestrial biology, from the first eukaryotic cell to the bush of life bursting with branches,

---
1 Marjorie Nicolson, *The Breaking of the Circle* (New York: Columbia, 1960), 100–07.

of which primates form one branch and *Homo sapiens* one leaf, related to all others through their shared inheritance and common ecologies.[2] Relativity, quantum mechanics, and Big Bang cosmology have been recognized as presenting intriguing prospects for theologies of divine action.[3] And evolution as "God's way of working through nature" has been enthusiastically endorsed by most mainline Protestant, Catholic, and Jewish congregations.[4]

But the "crux" move in this climb into scientific post-modernity has not been made so easily by most religious communities, and by some, not at all. How can Christian theology integrate a naturalistic evolutionary account with questions in theological anthropology—questions about the nature of the soul, the nature of human personhood, and the doctrine of the *imago Dei*? How might we both affirm divine sovereignty and maintain the integrity of biological and genetic science?

The warrant for such an integration lies in the sacramental nature of Christianity. In its theology of creation—solidly rooted in Hebrew tradition—Christianity affirms not only the infinite transcendence of God, but also the divine immanence. To employ a panentheist model, the created universe unfolds within the all-encompassing matrix of the divine reality.[5] Because it exists within God, nature is capable of manifesting the divine through bread and wine, oil and water, fire and light—as we find expressed in scripture, in liturgy, and in theology.[6] Within this divine reality "nature" through its own integrity through evolution brings forth many wondrous forms, from the first eukaryotes to *Homo sapiens*.

Thus divine creativity operates through the secondary causes of a universe endowed with the integrity of internal unfolding. Science on its own is intrinsically incapable either of disproving or of discovering God, but a Christian believes God to be immanent in the processes that are

---

2 Richard Fortey, *Life: A Natural History of the First Four Billion Years of Life on Earth* (London: Vintage, 1999).
3 See the volumes in the series jointly published by the Vatican Observatory and the Center for Theology and the Natural Sciences, http://www.ctns.org/books.html.
4 See the many statements included in *Voices for Evolution*, http://ncse.com/media/voices/religion.
5 Philip C. Clayton, "Barbour's Panentheistic Metaphysic," in *Fifty Years in Science and Religion: Ian Barbour and His Legacy*, R. J. Russell, ed. (Aldershot, United Kingdom: Ashgate Publishing, 2004), 116.
6 See Linda Gibler, *From the Beginning to Baptism: Scientific and Sacred Stories of Water, Oil, and Fire* (Collegeville, Minnesota: Liturgical Press, 2010).

the subject of science.⁷ Therefore, science is complementary to theology in the great human enterprise of knowing, for in Ted Peters' words, "the tie between God and the scientists honors human genius for revealing the secrets of God's second book, the Book of Nature."⁸ A critical faculty, which recognizes all experience as being evolutionary or developmental in character, is essential to interpreting our changing knowledge through science. If we appreciate this—as did Newman with respect to doctrine more than a century ago⁹—we will understand why theological models are subject to periodic reinterpretation, and why this should pose no threat to the core of our faith tradition.

This is an exhilarating time to be rethinking theology. Daniel Dennett has asserted that the theory of evolution by natural selection is a universal acid that "eats through just about every traditional concept, and leaves in its wake a revolutionized world-view, with most of the old landmarks still recognizable, but transformed in fundamental ways."¹⁰ This is hardly news to a theologian familiar with how science works, and may indeed be considered salutary for the critical rethinking of religious concepts. A theology that is not challenged and transformed as the scientific culture changes around it, is not really a living theology at all, but only the fossilized relic of a once-living tradition.¹¹ John Haught welcomes the evolutionary perspective as "Darwin's gift to theology,"¹² and Józef Życiński notes that evolution forces the theologian to integrate religious belief into cosmic history, and offers a context for a doctrine of

---

7   Peter M.J. Hess, "Creation, Design, and Evolution: Can Science Discover or Eliminate God?" *The Journal of Law and Public Policy* (Minneapolis: University of St. Thomas Law School, 2010).
8   Ted Peters, "Playing God with Our Evolutionary Future," in *Evolutionary and Molecular Biology: Perspectives on Divine Action* (Vatican City: Vatican Observatory, 1998), 493. Along with Martinez Hewlett as co-author, Peters has published three works dealing directly with the evolution controversy: *Evolution: From Creation to New Creation* (Abingdon, 2003), which won the Templeton Book of Distinction Award in 2005; *Can You Believe in God and Evolution?* (Abingdon, 2006, Anniversary Edition 2009), which won the Templeton Book of Distinction Award in 2007; and *Theological and Scientific Commentary on Darwin's Origin of Species* (Nashville, Tennessee: Abingdon Press, 2008).
9   John Henry Cardinal Newman, *Essay on the Development of Christian Doctrine* (London: Longmans Green and Co., 1888).
10 Daniel C. Dennett, *Darwin's Dangerous Idea: Evolution and the Meanings of Life* (New York: Simon & Schuster, 1996), 63.
11 Max N. Wildiers, *The Theologian and His Universe: Theology and Cosmology from the Middle Ages to the Present* (New York: Seabury Press, 1982), 158-60.
12 John F. Haught, *God after Darwin: A Theology of Evolution*, 2nd ed. (Boulder, Colorado: Westview Press, 2008), 49-60; *Deeper than Darwin* (Boulder, Colorado: Westview Press, 2003), *passim*.

God as compassionate, suffering with, active in, and fully related to the world.[13]

Christianity has retained its essential sacramental orientation through centuries of changing explanatory frameworks of science. Pope Benedict XVI has said that "only in the mystery of the Word made Flesh does the mystery of man truly become clear."[14] In the Incarnation, God enters into an ancient and dynamic creation, communicating divine truth through the capacities of the human creature. We can express this truth in complementary ways. From the perspective of evolutionary biology or anthropology, *Homo sapiens* represents the most fully developed terrestrial manifestation of emerging primate rationality. From the theological perspective, humans as *imago Dei* embody the moral and spiritual response called forth by God from evolving creation. The Incarnation is the supreme expression of this response: in the person of Jesus, God took on the quarks of the Big Bang, the dust of supernovae explosions, the DNA of dinosaurs, and the long history of the primate genome. In an evolutionary paraphrase of St. Gregory of Nazianzus, God assumes creation by becoming incarnate at its heart in a human person, Jesus Christ.[15]

A sacramental perspective carries important implications for theologically understanding our evolving universe. The Hebrew account in Genesis declares that God saw the world as good, and the Christian tradition has always affirmed the goodness of creation against Gnostics or Manichean denunciations of the material world as evil. Karl Rahner noted the significance of this affirmation:

> The point at which God in a final self-communication irrevocably and definitively lays hold on the totality of the reality created by him is characterized not as spirit but as flesh. It is this which authorizes the Christian to integrate the history of salvation into the history of the cosmos.[16]

Indeed, in Catholic perspective, creation is necessarily the domain of God's redemptive work, capable of bearing the incarnation and of being transfigured in turn by that creation.

---

13 Discussed by Archbishop Józef Życiński in *God and Evolution: Fundamental Questions of Christian Evolutionism* (Washington, D.C.: The Catholic University of America Press, 2006), 181–94.
14 Pope Benedict XVI, *Address to Catholic Educators*, Catholic University of America, 17 April 2008.
15 Gregory of Nazianzus, "what is not assumed is not redeemed," from "To Cledonius the Priest against Apollinarius," in *Nicene and Post Nicene Fathers*, vol. 2, no. 7, 648.
16 Karl Rahner, *Hominization: The Evolutionary Origin of Man as a Theological Problem* (Freiburg: Herder, 1958; London: Burns & Oates, 1965), 55.

Evolution, the Soul, and "Original Sin"

One of the thorniest problems raised by evolution is the nature of the human person and the implications of an evolutionary account for the theology of "original sin."[17] Following the publication of Darwin's *The Descent of Man* in 1871, it became progressively more difficult to deny both the evolutionary history of *Homo sapiens* and the genealogical relationship between humans and other animals.

In 1950, in *Humani Generis*, Pope Pius XII cautiously endorsed evolution, including that of the human body, but he drew a protective belt around the soul, which he declared to be uniquely created by God.[18] To be sure, by definition, the purely spiritual lies rightly outside the province of science, but just what the parameters of the "soul" are is a profound question. Moreover, to seal off forever from scientific study the most interesting and important dimensions of what it means to be human seems both scientifically and theologically misguided. *Humani Generis* categorically ruled out "polygenism," the view that humans did not descend from a single pair:

> For the faithful cannot embrace that opinion which maintains that either after Adam there existed on this earth true men who did not take their origin through natural generation from him as from the first parent of all, or that Adam represents a certain number of first parents.[19]

The problem is that science has now shown that monogenism—in the sense of the descent of our entire species from one set of parents, Adam and Eve—is genetically impossible. Inbreeding reduces population viability because the resulting lack of genetic diversity makes the population more susceptible to disease and trauma. When a species falls below a certain threshold of breeding pairs, it reaches what is called a "genetic bottleneck," carrying the risk that the population will suffer irreversible genetic degradation.[20] The genetic evidence tells us that hu-

---

17 See: Gaymon Bennett, Martinez Hewlett, Ted Peters, and Robert John Russell, *The Evolution of Evil* (Göttingen: Vandenhoeck & Ruprecht, 2008).
18 Pope Pius XII, Encyclical Letter *Humani Generis* (Vatican City: Vatican, 1950), paragraph 36.
19 *Humani Generis*, paragraph 37.
20 The European bison, the cheetah, and the giant panda are all animals with very low heterzygosity, and thus are suffering severe bottlenecks. See Ridley, *Evolution* 3rd ed. (Malden, Massachusetts: Blackwell Publishing), 151–53; Menotti-Raymond and O'Brien, "Dating the Genetic Bottleneck of the African cheetah," *Proceedings of the National Academy of Sciences* 90, (1993): 3172–76.

mans appear not to have suffered any catastrophic bottlenecks within the last ten thousand years,[21] although the climatic results of Sumatra's Mt. Toba eruption were severe enough to reduce the population significantly.[22] It is estimated by some that the minimum population during the tens of thousands of years it took hominids to evolve into full human consciousness was between 3,000 and 10,000 breeding pairs.[23] All humans are descended from a population of ancestors, including "mitochondrial Eve" (who, however, never met or had children with "Y-chromosome Adam" as he lived 50,000–80,000 years later than she did).[24]

What does this genetic evidence imply about the story of Adam and Eve in Genesis? It implies that the author(s) of Genesis was employing richly symbolic theological language, as is true of the other cosmogonic stories in Genesis 1–11. "Adam" (*Ādām*, "dust, humankind") and "Eve" (*Hawwā*, "living one") do not denote individuals, but symbolize rather the whole human race. Their names may appropriately be applied to *Homo sapiens* as a whole as the species was evolving into rationality, moral consciousness, and spiritual sensitivity. In the story, the breathing of God produces a *nefesh hayya*, or "living being," but it seems pointless to pursue even a modified literal interpretation that seeks to map Genesis 1:26–28 or 2:7–25 onto a prehistoric infusion of souls into some tribe of suitably prepared hominids tens of thousands of years ago.[25] *Prima facie*, this would seem flatly to contradict *Humani generis*, and to reject established dogma about Original Sin as caused by Adam's and Eve's disobedience, and as transmitted to their descendants through the "car-

---

21 John Hawks et al, "Population Bottlenecks and Pleistocene Human Evolution," *Molecular Biology and Evolution* 17 (2000): 2–22; W.J. Xiong et al, "No Severe Bottleneck during Human Evolution: Evidence from Two Apolipoprotein C II Alleles," *American Journal of Human Genetics* 48, no. 2 (February 1991): 383–89.
22 Stanley H. Ambrose, "Late Pleistocene Human Population Bottlenecks, Volcanic Winter, and Differentiation of Modern Humans," *Journal of Human Evolution* 34, no. 6 (1998): 623–51.
23 Alec MacAndrew, "Misconceptions around Mitochondrial Eve: A Critique of Carl Wieland's AiG Article on Mitochondrial Eve," at http://www.evolutionpages.com/Mitochondrial%20Eve.htm.
24 Dennis R. Venema, "Genesis and the Genome: Genomics Evidence for Human-Ape Common Ancestry and Ancestral Hominid Population Sizes, *Perspectives on Science and Christian Faith*, 62, no. 3 (2010): 166–78.
25 As, for example in Nicanor Austriaco, O.P., "What Can Human Genomics Tells Us about Adam and Eve? A Catholic Perspective," in The Portsmouth Institute, *Modern Science, Ancient Faith: Portsmouth Review*, Conference Proceedings (Lanham, Maryland: Sheed & Ward, 2013).

nal begetting" frowned upon by Saint Augustine.[26] However, it is by no means evident that Augustine's is the only theologically viable model of original sin, and Jerry Korsmeyer, Ilia Delio, and numerous others have articulated models of original sin that are more reflective of what we know from science.[27]

How should we conceive theologically of the nature of the human person in light of evolution? Traditional dualist conceptions carry the usual problems of defining what the soul is and how it is connected to the body. Recent reconsiderations range from defenses of a modified dualism[28] or a dipolar monism[29] to various forms of non-reductive physicalism and philosophies of the soul as an emergent property of what is essentially a psychosomatic unity.[30] The Hebraic vision of the human as a psychosomatic unity created in the image of God was at the core of the earliest Christian theological anthropology. This was submerged by Platonic dualism in the Patristic era, although Thomistic metaphysics held for a closer relation between body and soul. Catholic theology since Vatican II has moved back in the direction of a Hebraic psychosomatic unity of the person,[31] a view supported by various theories of emergence.[32]

Homo sapiens is now understood as being intimately bound up with the universe, from the atoms or "star dust" that compose our matter and the genetic information that is our form, to the self-reflective awareness that drives us to try to understand ourselves, the universe, and God. Theology has been able to accommodate evolution of the human body from pre-human ancestors. Therefore, once we have accepted a symbol-

---

26 Allen and Hess, *Catholicism and Science*, 102.
27 Ilia Delio, *Christ in Evolution* (New York: Maryknoll, Orbis Books, 2008), 53–65; Jerry D. Korsmeyer, *Evolution and Eden: Balancing Original Sin and Contemporary Science* (New York: Paulist Press, 1998).
28 Philip A. Rolnick, *Person, Grace, and God* (Grand Rapids, Michigan: Wm. B. Eerdmans Publishing Co., 2007), 248–55.
29 Terence L. Nichols, *The Sacred Cosmos: Christian Faith and the Challenge of Naturalism* (Grand Rapids, Michigan: Brazos Press, 2005), 127, 153–81.
30 Warren S. Brown, et al., eds, *Whatever Happened to the Soul? Scientific and Theological Portraits of Human Nature* (Minneapolis: Fortress Press, 1998); Philip Clayton and Paul Davies, eds., *The Re-emergence of Emergence: The Emergentist Hypothesis from Science to Religion* (Oxford: Oxford University Press, 2006).
31 Karl Rahner, "Natural Science and Reasonable Faith," in Rahner, *Theological Investigations*, vol. 21, Hugh M. Riley, trans. (New York: Crossroad, 1988), 42. Citation from Mark F. Fischer, "Karl Rahner and the Immortality of the Soul," *The Saint Anselm Journal* 6, no. 1 (Fall 2008): 2.
32 Philip Clayton and Paul Davies, *The Re-emergence of Emergence: The Emergentist Hypothesis from Science to Religion* (London; New York: Oxford University Press, 2008).

ic, non-literalistic interpretation of the Genesis creation story, theology seen from a sacramental perspective should also be capable of accommodating evolution of the "soul," or of "soulishness," the moral and spiritual capacities that set our species apart. A theology in which God works in, with, and through creation can conceive of the soul as being transmitted integrally through the evolution of human physical nature and its increasing neural endowment, consistently with a Hebraic understanding of the person as a psychosomatic unity. This theology addresses a number of important theological problems:

(1) It preserves the sacramental idea of the universe as transfigured by God, and it rejects a Platonic dualism in which all and only human souls are "saved," a position that in itself renders unintelligible the Pauline notion that "all creation is groaning together" (Rom 8:22). "Salvation" involves the whole of creation, not merely human souls being somehow "raptured" out of bodies. As Ted Peters has written, "becoming human, in the last analysis, then, is not really a restoration to a prefallen state of grace that humans once possessed and then lost. It is not a return to the old creation. It is rather a future arrival for the first time. It is participation in the new creation."[33]

(2) It solves the problem of a radical and genetically unintelligible disjunction between pre-human hominids and *Homo sapiens*. Since all life on earth shares a common ancestry, and *Homo sapiens* represents the one twig on the great terrestrial bush of life that so far has evolved into rational self-awareness, it is impossible to draw a sharp dividing line between creatures that possess an immortal soul and those that do not. Depending on how we calculate it, humans share close to 98.4 percent of genes with chimpanzees,[34] and our basing ensoulment on whether or not an entity carries human DNA seems little more than genetic chauvinism. All beings are possessed of soul, at an intensity appropriate to their level of neural complexity. In the evolutionary model we avoid the irrational conundrum of having a generation of non-human parents giving birth to human children, or of one single breeding pair as progenitors of the entire human species.

---

33 Ted Peters, *GOD—The World's Future: Systematic Theology for a New Era* (Minneapolis: Fortress Press, 2000), 156.
34 The Chimpanzee Sequencing and Analysis Consortium, "Initial Sequence of the Chimpanzee Genome and Comparison with the Human Genome," *Nature,* vol. 437, (1 September 2005): 69–87, DOI: 10.1038/nature04072; http://www.genome.gov/Pages/Research/DIR/Chimp_Analysis.pdf.

(3) It makes sense of an ecological theology that regards all God's work as the subject of a new creation, including the whole spectrum of life from the evolution of the first self-replicating molecule to the evolution of rational life wherever suitable conditions are found in the universe. The human moral obligation to stewardship of creation takes on even greater urgency in light of anthropogenic climate change, habitat destruction, and the accelerating extinction of our fellow creatures that share in the *imago Dei*.

(4) It maintains the integrity of both scientific and theological perspectives on reality. Theology does not need to assert a soul infusion that is in principle undetectable by science, or an historical Fall of Adam and Eve, because there never was such an infusion or historical Fall. In evolutionary history in sacramental perspective, the soul evolves concomitantly with the capacities of the body, at a rate commensurate with it. Long ago Cardinal Ratzinger argued for an architectonic vision of truth rather than a simplistic biblical literalism.[35] If God works "in, with, and under" evolution, then biology, genetics, and neuroscience need not fear treading upon theological claims about personhood.

Imago Dei and the Range of Personhood

Related to the difficulty of justifying a sharp demarcation of immortally ensouled from non-ensouled primates is the problem of the range of manifestations of "personhood" within the human species. It is deceptively simple to look at "normal" human beings as carrying the *imago Dei*, and on that basis to ascribe to every human—and *only* to humans—an immortal soul. Some experts estimate that up to fifty percent of human conceptions result in miscarriage because the zygotes or embryos have a chromosomal abnormality incompatible with life, or because they are otherwise so genetically compromised that they cannot develop to mature gestation and a normal birth.[36] If immortal souls are imputed to these zygotes, fifty percent or more of humanity will never have lived conscious lives on earth, but rather will have entered immediately into

---

[35] Joseph Cardinal Ratzinger, *"In the Beginning . . .": A Catholic Understanding of the Story of Creation and the Fall*, Boniface Ramsey, O.P., trans. (Huntington, Indiana: Our Sunday Visitor Publishing, 1990), 18.

[36] D.K. Edmonds, K.S. Lindsay, J.F. Miller, E. Williamson, and P.J. Wood, "Early Embryonic Mortality in Women," *Fertility and Sterility* 38, no. 4 (1982): 447–53, PMID 7117572. One study testing hormones for ovulation and pregnancy found that 61.9 percent of conceptuses were lost prior to 12 weeks, and 91.7 percent of these losses occurred subclinically, without the knowledge of the once pregnant woman.

eternity without ever having been able to make any decisions at all, moral or otherwise. The eternal destiny of more than half of humanity will be independent of ethical decision making or moral life, and while we are not in any position to pass judgment on the status of these embryos, the implications of this disconnect are not insignificant.

The doctrines of both "soul" and *imago Dei* are complicated yet further by the twinning continuum. When a conception results in conjoined twins who are easily separable, or who have discrete brains, the theological conclusion appears to be straightforward: each twin is an ensouled person. The situation is more complicated with parasitic twins, however. When a twin embryo fails to separate fully, one embryo can cease to develop but remain as vestigial tissue attached to the otherwise healthy and fully formed twin. In the well-publicized case of Lakshmi Tatama (born in 2005) in Bihar State in India, Lakshmi's parasitic twin could not independently move the extra arms and legs that projected from Lakshmi's body, because the twin had no head or brain.[37] It could experience nothing, feel nothing, learn nothing, and make no moral or aesthetic judgments. Without a developed personality or conscious life, the personhood of Lakshmi's twin remained entirely and solely *in potentia,* and its eschatological state would presumably be independent of its truncated organic life. In contrast, like that of any other normal person, Lakshmi's eschatological state would presumably depend, at least in part, on her moral state during her life and at the time of her death.

On the extreme end of the twinning spectrum lies another perplexing phenomenon. "Tetragametic chimeras" carry the genetic contribution of four gametes (two eggs and two sperms) resulting from the fusion of two fertilized ova at the blastocyst stage.[38] Each ovum or population of cells in the developing blastocyst retains its own character, resulting in "mosaicism" or a mixture of tissues. One pair of gametes supplies the genetic information for part of the body, and the other pair supplies the information for the rest. Mosaicism might explain baffling phenomena such as gender dysphoria, in which an XY gametic pair forms the head, and an XX pair forms the genitalia. Most tetragametic chimeras appear outwardly normal, however, and have a unified psychological sense of self. Prior to the era of genetic testing, they would have gone through

---

[37] http://en.wikipedia.org/wiki/Lakshmi_Tatma.
[38] Claire Ainsworth, "The Stranger Within," *New Scientist* 180, no. 2421 (Nov 15, 2003): 34–37 (4).

life without ever knowing about their dual origin, and thinking of themselves only as "I," not as "we."

In the case of tetragametic chimeras, if we insist upon the doctrine of the infusion of an immortal soul at the moment of conception, do we end up theologically speaking with two souls living side-by-side in one body, one of them perhaps lying dormant for the entire life of that body? Or is the soul whose gametes did not supply the brain removed by God at the moment of fusion? Could we imagine two souls and thus two images *Dei* in one person? The case of the tetragametic chimera is one in which science compels us seriously to rethink our theological anthropology. Jose Mario Francisco has warned in another context that the term "soul" is too easily drawn into a radical dualism, and that it might be better simply to use the pronoun "I."[39] Considering the ancient religious and cultural valence of the term "soul," this proposal may not be realistic.

However, in light of the sacramental character of an evolving creation, perhaps we can rethink the whole concept of *imago Dei*. God has become incarnate within creation, illuminating it from within. The entire created order in this sense is in the image of God, and its many elements reflect that image with a degree of opacity or transparency commensurate with their degree of evolution toward moral responsiveness and spiritual sensitivity. Perhaps we should reckon personhood or ensoulment or reflection of the *imago Dei* as depending less on a presumed ontological state at the moment of conception than on how that image is developed throughout the life of the individual. Noreen Herzfeld has maintained that the capability of sustaining authentic relationships is a sounder criterion for what it means to mirror the image of God than is intelligence or some other genetic endowment.[40]

I make the case that consciousness of personal identity, the ability to sustain relationships, and the capacity for graced perfection should count for more toward determining the presence of the *imago Dei* than the number of fertilized ova at conception.[41] I would add to this Ted Peters' insight that there is a proleptic quality to the *imago Dei*: "Our created

---

39 Jose Mario C Francisco, "Too Much 'Soul': Points and Counterpoints from Culture, Theology, and Science," in *Science and Religion . . . and Culture in the Jesuit Tradition: Perspectives from East Asia* (Adelaide: Australian Theological Forum Press, 2006), 135–56.
40 Noreen Herzfeld, *In Our Image: Artificial Intelligence and the Human Spirit* (Minneapolis: Fortress Press, 2002), 94–95.
41 The author gratefully acknowledges the counsel of Patristic theologian Hamilton Hess, D.Phil., on., on this and other points.

humanity is our eschatological humanity. Who we are is determined by who we will be.... The *imago Dei* is the divine call forward, a call we hear now and respond to now, but a call that is drawing us toward transformation into a future reality."[42]

Conclusions

We began with the question of how Christianity can integrate theological anthropology with evolutionary theory. How can we remain faithful to our foundational beliefs while at the same time absorbing the reality that we inhabit an ancient, dynamic, and evolving universe? When we study the Christian worldview as it has unfolded over many centuries, we see that it has retained its integrity through countless changes in our understanding of how the world actually works. And however estranged they may sometimes appear to be today, faith in scientific reason lies on the same continuum as religious belief.[43] Theology and science are natural partners in an astonishing enterprise of knowing.

Reflection upon the sacramental character of an evolving creation can enrich our theological vocabulary by rendering it more responsive to our deepening knowledge of the universe we inhabit. For two millennia Christians expressed their theologies in the terms of the prevailing philosophical language and scientific models used to describe the natural world, whether Platonic or Aristotelian, Newtonian or Darwinian, pre-scientific or post-modern. As they have done in every revolution in worldview in the last twenty centuries, Christians in our century can make peace with new scientific perspectives. So long as our biblical interpretation, our doctrinal formulations, and our other foundational beliefs are not irrevocably wedded to one particular model of nature, there need be no conflict between scientific and religious worldviews. The sacramental perspective is consonant both with biblical revelation and theological tradition, and with a science that recognizes the limits of methodological naturalism.

For scientists the nature of the evolutionary universe is quite properly a puzzle to be unraveled by means of the scientific method.[44] For

---

42 Peters, *GOD—the World's Future*, 157.
43 Michael Heller, *Creative Tension: Essays on Science and Religion* (Philadelphia: Templeton Foundation Press, 2003), 161.
44 Francisco J. Ayala, "Darwin's Devolution: Design without Designer," in *Evolutionary and Molecular Biology: Scientific Perspectives on Divine Action*, Robert J. Russell et al, eds. (Vatican City and Berkeley: Vatican Observatory Publications, CTNS, 1998), 113.

theologians and religious believers the universe is both this and something infinitely greater: it is a mystery before which we fall silent. Pope John Paul II has noted that scientists are well aware that

> ... the search for truth, even when it concerns a finite reality of the world or of man, is never-ending, but always points beyond to something higher than the immediate object of study, to the questions which give access to mystery.[45]

Theology written from an evolutionary perspective, which takes seriously the antiquity of the world and its dynamic processes and its long ages of suffering, has an apophatic character—it has nothing to say when it confronts the blank wall of mystery. Christians believe God to be the author both of nature and of our act of knowing, and in Karl Rahner's words "in every act of knowing a person has an innate grasp of God, not as an object, but rather as a horizon of mystery."[46] I will give the final word to Pope John Paul II, who noted that since "the things of the earth and the concerns of faith derive from the same God," a vital interaction between science and theology "leads to a greater love for truth itself, and contributes to a more comprehensive understanding of the meaning of human life and of the purpose of God's creation."[47]

---

[45] Pope John Paul II, *Fides et Ratio*, paragraph 101. "I would urge them to continue their efforts without ever abandoning the sapiential horizon within which scientific and technological achievements are wedded to the philosophical and ethical values which are the distinctive and indelible mark of the human person."

[46] Anne M. Clifford, "Creation," in *Systematic Theology: Roman Catholic Perspectives*, vol. 1, Francis Schüssler Fiorenza and John P. Galvin, eds. (Minneapolis: Fortress Press, 1991), 236.

[47] Pope John Paul II, *Ex Corde Ecclesiae: Apostolic Constitution on Catholic Universities* (Vatican City: Vatican, 1990), 17, 20.

Animal Suffering, Animal Sin, Theistic Evolution, and the Problem of Evil

Joshua M. Moritz

It is a great pleasure and honor to celebrate the philosophical, theological thought of Ted Peters on the occasion of this *Festschrift* and to explore the impact and implications of his numerous contributions to the central questions arising from the interface of systematic theology and the natural sciences. Making a courageous, methodological commitment that "serious theology and honest science are compatible," Peters has never been one to flinch in the face of troubling theological difficulties posed by theories emerging from the realms of empirical discovery.[1] For many years Peters has examined the nature and origins of sin and evil, and their relationship to evolution and the biology of freedom.[2] One challenging theological area in particular in which I have had the great privilege of working with Peters throughout the years is with regard to the problem of how an affirmation of theistic evolution bears upon the question of God's goodness in creating and, in particular, why a perfectly benevolent God would choose to create biological life through a process where ruthless competition, pain, and suffering are central. Peters has always begun discussions in this area with the methodological assumption that a Darwinian model of evolution will, upon investigation, turn out to be compatible with both Christian anthropology and the Christian doctrine of creation. In this essay I will endeavor to follow Peters' lead

---

1 Ted Peters, "The Evolution of Evil" in *The Evolution of Evil*, G. Bennett, M.J. Hewlett, T. Peters, and R.J. Russell, eds. (Göttingen: Vandenhoeck and Ruprecht, 2008), 22.
2 Ted Peters, *Sin: Radical Evil in Soul and Society* (Grand Rapids, Michigan: Wm. B. Eerdmans Publishing Co., 1994); Ted Peters, *Playing God? Genetic Determinism and Human Freedom* (New York: Routledge, 2003).

and to embrace his theological intuitions about science in an exploration of the origins of sin and the problem of evolutionary evil as it concerns animal suffering. The question I raise here is "does an affirmation of theistic evolution, and the reality of animal suffering in evolutionary history, make the task of theodicy impossible?" To address this dilemma I will take on Peters' methodological assumptions regarding the compatibility of "honest science" with "serious theology." Drawing attention to an ancient Jewish insight that evil—as resistance to God's will that results in suffering—precedes the arrival of human beings and already has a firm foothold in the non-human, animal world long before humans are ever tempted to go astray, I will then show that this ancient Semitic understanding of the origins of sin and evil is conferred renewed relevance in light of the empirical reality of evolutionary continuity and the recent findings of cognitive ethology with regard to animal freedom and morality.

Animal Suffering and the Classical Christian Foundations of Evolutionary Theodicy

The sobering reality of animal suffering is nothing new, and from ancient times scores of sages and seers have reflected on the ill-fated fact that all is not perfect in the realm of nature. The pre-Socratic philosopher Heraclitus exclaimed that "struggle is the father of everything,"[3] and Aristotle observed the empirical reality of fierce competition between animals in nature.[4] In both Scripture and in the witness of the early Church Fathers animal suffering was ubiquitously perceived as a symptom of a much deeper cause, and such suffering in the world of nature was never thought to be part of God's original intention for creation. Suffering in nature was indeed understood to be a reflection of the *fallenness* of creation. Representative of the Eastern Christian and Syriac theological traditions, Bishop Theophilus of Antioch (b. 120) explains, "nothing was made evil by God, but all things good, yea, very good."[5]

---

3 Heraclitus of Ephesus (ca. 500 BCE) quoted in *The Fragments of the Work of Heraclitus of Ephesus on Nature,* trans. from the Greek text of Ingram Bywater by G.T.W. Patrick (Baltimore: N. Murray, 1889), fragment #62.
4 Aristotle, "The History of Animals" in *The Basic Works of Aristotle,* Richard McKeon, ed. (New York: Random House, 1941), 637–39, or Book IX, paragraphs 608b–609b.
5 Theophilus, "To Autolycus," in *The Ante-Nicene Fathers: The Writings of the Fathers Down to A.D. 325: Fathers of the Second Century - Hermas, Tatian, Theophilus, Athenagoras, Clement of Alexandria,* Alexander Roberts and Sir James Donaldson, eds. (New York: Cosimo, 2007), 1.4 and 2.4, 98.

Embracing the ancient Hebrew biblical tradition regarding the close relationship between humans and animals, Theophilus argues that God's original intent for human and animal creation was for peace and harmony to reign without inter-species bloodshed and violence. "The loss of animal life," for Theophilus, "is not an indigenous phenomenon of paradise. It is an example of evil." For him and for many of the early Church Fathers, predation and carnivorous bloodshed are contrary to God's divine law and are the result of sin.[6]

While all of the early Church Fathers agreed that there *was* a historical fall, there was not universal consensus on the *timing* of the fall, the *degree* of human and animal *perfection* before the fall, or the *extent* to which the human fall marred such initial goodness. Bishop Irenaeus of Lyons, for instance, believed that before the fall the primitive condition of human beings was one of innocence and childhood,[7] and was not perfect from the beginning.[8] Augustine and the Western theological tradition that followed his lead, however, held a different interpretive opinion. As is well known, Augustine argued that humans, animals, and the whole earth existed in a state of graced perfection before the fall. The effect of human sin was to introduce a cataclysmic cascade of tragedy, suffering, and evil into the hitherto perfect created realm.

Regarding the problem of suffering and evil, Augustine, writing against the Pelagians, introduced the principle *sub Deo justo, nemo miser nisii* (under a just God, no innocent suffers). His key concern here, however, was with the suffering of humans and not animals, and he was deploying this principle against his opponents to establish his doctrine of original sin. It is evident, said Augustine, that many infants suffer. Under a just God, therefore, these infants cannot be innocent. For Augustine this meant that these infants must have inherited guilt, as a result of Adam's original trespass (i.e., they bear original sin).[9] With regard to how the suffering of animals relates to the problem of a just God, Augustine says, we need not be concerned. For example, explains Augustine, "some try to extend this commandment ['Thou shall not kill'] even to wild and

---

6 Rick Rogers, *Theophilus of Antioch: The Life and Thought of a Second-Century Bishop* (Lanham, Maryland: Lexington Books, 2000), 58.
7 Irenaeus *Against Heresies*, 3.23.5. See also Osborn, *Irenaeus of Lyons*, 219.
8 Irenaeus, *Against Heresies*, 4.38
9 Augustine, *Against Julian*, 3.3 and 3.5; for a discussion, see Peter Harrison, "Animal Souls, Metempsychosis, and Theodicy in Seventeenth-Century English Thought," *Journal of the History of Philosophy* 31, no. 4 (October 1993): 523.

domestic animals and maintain that it is wrong to kill any of them. Why not extend it to plants? . . . Hence, putting aside these ravings . . . we do not understand this phrase to apply to bushes, because they have no sensation, nor to the unreasoning animals...because they are not partners with us in the faculty of reason."[10] Since animals—excluded by their irrational nature—are not included within the moral community of humans, the suffering of animals, in Augustine's view, is of little or no account to humans. He observed that although we can perceive by their cries that animals die in pain, we make little of this since the beast, lacking a rational soul, is not related to us by a common nature.[11] Grounding his understanding of animals and their suffering in Stoic philosophy, rather than in the teachings of the Old Testament or even the New Testament, Augustine's theology offers few direct resources for addressing the modern question of why God allows non-human animals to suffer.[12]

The Cartesian Solution to the Problem of Animal Suffering and Its Theological Detractors

Many generations later, however, Augustine's principle *sub Deo justo, nemo miser nisii* (under a just God, no innocent suffers) provided the point of departure for many subsequent discussions of theodicy as it relates to animal suffering. For example, in the 1600s the Cartesians were partly driven by the theological concern for innocent animal suffering and the implied question of theodicy as they inherited the dilemma from the Augustinian tradition.[13] The French philosopher and theologian, Nicolas Malebranche (1638–1715), a prominent early disciple of Descartes, makes this Augustinian theological concern explicit. Malebranche argues against the common theological opinion—that animals have souls and mental awareness—as giving rise to consequences directly opposite to what we are taught by faith: "Now they [animals] never sinned,

---

10 Augustine quoted in Paul Waldau, *The Specter of Speciesism: Buddhist and Christian Views of Animals*, American Academy of Religion Academy Series (Oxford: Oxford University Press, 2002), 191.
11 Augustine, *De Moribus Manichæorum*, 2.17.59; John Passmore, "The Treatment of Animals," *Journal of the History of Ideas* 36 (April–June 1975): 197.
12 For a discussion of Augustine's dependence on Stoic philosophy for these views, see Passmore, "The Treatment of Animals," 198. Augustine likewise adopts the Stoic position that all non-rational things exist for the sake or utility of the rational, namely, human beings. Augustine, *83 Different Questions,* Question 30.
13 See Peter Harrison, "Animal Souls, Metempsychosis, and Theodicy in Seventeenth-Century English Thought," *Journal of the History of Philosophy* 31, no. 4 (October 1993): 523.

or made ill use of their liberty, since they have none: Therefore God is unjust, in punishing them, and making them miserable; and unequally miserable, since they are equally innocent." Malebranche goes on to argue that "if God renders justice to all his creatures, then animals must be incapable of suffering, for they have neither committed wrong, nor have they the opportunity for compensation in a future life." If innocent animals do not feel pain, then God's goodness and justice, at least in that regard, can be upheld.[14]

Those who were dissatisfied with the Cartesian mechanistic redefinition of animals as unconscious (and thus not suffering) *beast-machines,* focused on the eschatological side of the Augustinian theodicy equation and argued for the final redemption of animals and ultimate transformation of their suffering. The Scholastics of the seventeenth and eighteenth centuries continued to maintain the reality of animal souls and the fact of animal suffering against the Cartesians.[15] The Puritans—including John Milton and Richard Overton—likewise held that animals had souls, that they should be treated with compassion. As a result, they passed the first modern laws for the protection of animals.[16] Overton indeed declared that "all other creatures as well as man shall be raised and delivered from death at the resurrection."[17] George Fox and the Quakers, along with Bishop Joseph Butler and the Anglicans, agreed and together with John Wesley and the Methodists bore the standard of the biblically inspired vision of the final restoration of the non-human animal creation, proclaiming the ultimate salvation and resurrection of animals.[18] In arguing for a final redemption of animals and the transformation of their suffering, these Christian thinkers were indeed following in the line of a long and distinguished theological pedigree that includes John Calvin,

---

14 Nicolas Malebranche quoted in Harrison, "Animal Souls," 523.
15 Robin Attfield, *The Ethics of Environmental Concern*, 2nd ed. (Athens, Georgia, and London: University of Georgia Press, 1991), 38.
16 Richard D. Ryder, *Animal Revolution: Changing Attitudes towards Speciesism*, rev. and updated ed. (Oxford and New York: Berg, 2000), 49.
17 Richard Overton, *Man's Mortality* (1643), quoted in Preece and Fraser, "The Status of Animals in Biblical and Christian Thought: A Study in Colliding Values," *Society and Animals* 8, no. 1 (2000): 257.
18 John Wesley, "The General Deliverance," in *Animals and Christianity: A Book of Readings*, Andrew Linzey and Tom Regan, eds. (London: SPCK, 1989), 100–103; Ryder, *Animal Revolution*, 55.

Martin Luther, Bonaventure, John of the Cross, John Chrysostom, Basil of Caesarea, Irenaeus, Theophilus of Antioch, and numerous others.[19]

An Ancient Jewish Post-Darwinian Response to the Problem of Animal Suffering

While the idea that nature is red in tooth and claw preceded the scientific work of Charles Darwin, with Darwin's publication of *On the Origin of Species,* the character and extent of animal suffering, both in the present and throughout biological history, came into full focus. Meditating upon the "brutal inefficiency" of evolution by natural selection, Charles Darwin lamented to his friend Joseph Hooker, "What a book a devil's chaplain might write on the clumsy, wasteful, blundering, low and horribly cruel works of Nature!"[20] Many standard accounts of Darwinian evolution emphasize the central role of death, extinction, pain, selfishness, and competition as being entailed in the *very process* by which organisms are created. In so far as these are essential to the mechanism of natural selection, and God uses evolution through natural selection to create life, then God is ultimately accountable for such pain and suffering that results.[21] Others have pointed out, though, that *in scientific principle,* death, competition, suffering, and extinction are not the *driving forces* of natural selection, but rather, are a *consequence* of limited resources and the contingencies of the natural world.[22] This scientific point is helpful in many ways and in fact removes the empirical burden of guilt for animal suffering from natural selection—and thus also from any God who would choose to create through natural selection. If it is indeed the empirical case that pain and suffering are not entailed in the process of natural

---

19 John of the Cross, for example, says Christ in his incarnation and resurrection clothed both humans and animals with beauty and dignity. St. John of the Cross, "Beautifying the Creatures," in *Animals and Christianity: A Book of Readings,* 93. For a discussion of the early church views, see Richard Sorabji, *Animal Minds and Human Morals: The Origins of the Western Debate* (Ithaca, NY: Cornell University Press, 1995), 199. See also Joshua M. Moritz, "Martin Luther and the Medieval Saints among the Animals," *Dialog: A Journal of Theology* 51, no. 1 (March 2012).
20 Richard Dawkins, *A Devil's Chaplain: Reflections on Hope, Lies, Science, and Love,* (New York: Houghton Mifflin, 2003), 11.
21 Michael Ruse, *Can a Darwinian Be a Christian?: The Relationship between Science and Religion* (Cambridge: Cambridge University Press, 2001), 131.
22 Jeffrey Schloss, "Evolution, Creation, and the Sting of Death: A Response to John Laing, Part I" *Biologos,* http://biologos.org/blog/evolution-creation-and-the-sting-of-death-part-1; Joshua M. Moritz, "Evolutionary Evil and Dawkins' Black Box: Changing the Parameters of the Problem," in *The Evolution of Evil,* G. Bennett, M.J. Hewlett, T. Peters, and R.J. Russell, eds. (Göttingen: Vandenhoeck and Ruprecht, 2008).

selection, then the *philosophical-theoretical* necessity of evolutionary evil would be gone from the font of life's creativity. However, we would still be faced with the *fact* of so much pain and suffering within and throughout the history of nature.

Confronted with the universal *fact* of evolutionary evils without any *systemic necessity* for them, we must again ask *Unde Malum*—from where or what source does evil arise? Stemming from Augustine's initial response, a traditional solution to the moral and human aspect of this dilemma has centered on some form of the *free will theodicy*: as human beings exercise their free will and choose to reject God, moral evil enters into the human world resulting in a tragic cascade of calamitous consequences. The free will theodicy seeks to ground its theological logic in the existence of a type of "universal contingent," described by Robert John Russell as events or circumstances, which while not necessary in themselves, give rise to conditions that are presently unavoidable—i.e., humans could have originally freely chosen to obey God's commandment, but that original choice is now no longer up to us. However, if the theistic evolution scenario for the origin of animals is true, then how does animal death and suffering enter into this theological picture—especially if such suffering and death were occurring long before humans ever showed up?

To address this theological question at the core of the problem of evolution and animal suffering, I would like to draw attention to a few important details of the Genesis 3 narrative that are in danger of being overlooked in the contemporary discussion. In the third chapter of Genesis we find a description of a *non-human animal* that possesses intelligence, rationality, language, moral discernment, and death-awareness—namely, the serpent.[23] It is clear the Genesis 3 author considered the serpent to be a clever representative from the animal world and not a fallen angel. Old Testament exegete John Sailhamer explains that "it should not be overlooked that the serpent is said to be one of the 'wild animals' (*hayyat hassadeh*) that the Lord God had made (cf. 1:25; 2:19)."[24] The purpose of this statement, argues Bible scholar Otto Procksch, is to

---

23 The word for serpent (*nachash*) comes from a root that means "to learn by experience, or diligently observe the signs of the world." The serpent is called (*awram*)—subtle, shrewd, clever, wise, sensible, prudent, practical. *Awram* is etymologically related to *awrar*—a curse which stems from the breaking of covenant.

24 John H. Sailhamer, *Genesis*, vol. 2 of *The Expositor's Bible Commentary*, Frank E. Gaebelein, ed. (Grand Rapids, Michigan: Zondervan, 1990), 50.

exclude the notion that the serpent was a supernatural being. "The serpent" explains Old Testament scholar Benno Jacob, "is none other than a serpent."[25] I thus suggest that we resist reading back into the Genesis text the deutero-canonical *Wisdom of Solomon*'s interpretation of the serpent as Satan, and instead take the language of the Genesis 3 narrative at face value (i.e., we resist reading it *symbolically* or *allegorically*). The serpent who is described as the "cleverest of the animals" is, in the Genesis 3 story, depicted as the intellectual equal of the human pair. The serpent has an understanding of God's commandments and knows the consequences of breaking them. If the description of the serpent is taken at face value, he is clearly an example of an animal who is intentionally rebelling against the express will of God.

Interestingly, through introducing the serpent, the author of Genesis acknowledges that there was disobedience (or sin) present within the animal world *before* humans disobeyed God. From the "moral" disposition and questioning of the prudence of God's commandments posed by the "wisest" or "cleverest of the animals," it is evident that the Genesis 3 text discerns a *pre-human rebellion* against God within the animal creation—an insurgence that had arisen through the primeval disobedient actions of non-human animals.[26] Within the world of the narrative described in Genesis 3, there is thus *a non-human animal "Fall" which happens before the "Fall."*[27] In other words, the fallenness of creation is assumed by the author of Genesis and the onus of this primordial fall lies with pre-human animals.[28] Scripture presents the fallenness of the animal creation as a given, and we need not speculate on how or when this hap-

---

25 Benno Jacob, *Genesis: The First Book of the Bible*, aug. ed. (Jersey City, New Jersey: Ktav Publishing House, 2007), 102.
26 See my discussion of animal morality in Joshua M. Moritz, "Chosen from among the Animals: The End of Human Uniqueness and the Election of the Image of God," Ph.D. dissertation (Berkeley: GTU, 2011), chap. 7. For a discussion of animal morality and immorality within scripture, see Joshua M. Moritz, "Animals and the Image of God in the Bible and Beyond," *Dialog* 48, no. 2 (2009).
27 For the implications of this animal "Fall before the Fall" for the evolutionary theodicy problem, see Joshua M. Moritz, "Evolutionary Evil and Dawkins' Black Box: Changing the Parameters of the Problem," in *The Evolution of Evil*, G. Bennett, M.J. Hewlett, T. Peters, and R.J. Russell, ed. (Göttingen: Vandenhoeck and Ruprecht, 2008).
28 This is much closer to Irenaeus's understanding of the Fall than Augustine's. See Robert F. Brown, "On the Necessary Imperfection of Creation: Irenaeus' *Adversus Haereses* IV, 38." *Scottish Journal of Theology* 28, no. 1 (1975): 17–25. This pre-human understanding of the Fall, likewise addresses "the problem of the Fall without the Fall" as detailed by Robert J. Russell, *Cosmology from Alpha to Omega: The Creative Mutual Interaction of Theology and Science* (Minneapolis: Fortress Press, 2008), 10–11.

pened any more than the author of Genesis 3 does. Nor is the concept of animal rebellion an isolated incident found in Genesis 3 alone. As the Genesis story unfolds we see that God holds "all flesh" or "all living creatures" (Hebrew, *kol basar*[29]) accountable—at least to some degree—for the actions whereby they stray from God's primeval purposes for a peaceable creation. God judges both humans *and animals* for their bloodthirsty behavior.

> Now the earth was corrupt in God's sight, and the earth was filled with violence. And God saw the earth, and behold, it was corrupt; for all animals and humans had corrupted their way upon the earth. And God said to Noah, "I have determined to make an end to all humans and animals; for the earth is filled with violence through them" (Gen 6:11–14).

The Flood in Genesis is thus as much a punishment for the wayward ways of animals as for those of humans. In a similar manner, "at Mount Sinai, animals as well as humans are threatened with punishment should they touch the mountain." While earlier Mesopotamian legal codes exact no such punishment, for the Hebrews, an ox that gores and kills a human is to be held capitally guilty.[30] In a similar fashion, animals are to fast and to put on sackcloth and ashes with the rest of the repenting Ninevites in Jonah, lest they be destroyed by God's judgment upon the city.[31] The Hebrew Bible clearly reflects a theological zoology in which animals posses the capacity to obey and stray from the will of God. Both the doctrine of reward and punishment and retributive justice are extended to beasts as well as to men. Scripture does not spare animals from responsibility for their deeds.[32]

While the biblical notion of animal sin may sound a bit odd, archaic, or overly romantic to our modern ears, this was an understanding that continued to hold sway in the early church and was quite common among the Church Fathers. Theophilus of Antioch, for example, believed that animals are guilty of sin just as humans are. He points out that the original God-intended diet for both humans and animals was vegetari-

---

[29] The Hebrew word *Basar* refers to all living things other than plants, i.e., animals and humans.
[30] Elijah Judah Schochet, *Animal Life in Jewish Tradition: Attitudes and Relationships* (New York: Ktav Publishing House, 1984), 54.
[31] See Dan Cohn-Sherbok and Andrew Linzey, *After Noah: Animals and the Liberation of Theology* (London: Mowbray, 1997), 26.
[32] Schochet, *Animal Life in Jewish Tradition*, 54.

an,[33] and he sees the consumption of a fellow creature's flesh—in both humans and animals—as harming the weak and transgressing God's precepts. While some animals, explains Theophilus, "keep the law of God and eat the seeds of the earth" and thus adhere to their "original goodness," others such as "the great fish and carnivorous birds" are like "robbers, murderers, and the godless" devouring "those weaker than themselves."[34]

According to a straightforward or a narrative reading of the Genesis 3 text, the humans who were taken or selected by God and put in the garden in Eden (Gen 2:15) lived in a world that was already impacted by sin and death.[35] Given Scripture's portrayal of a *pre-human animal fall* we might wonder what relevance (if any) this has for the contemporary theodicy question as it relates to the problem of evolutionary suffering and evil. At this point an evolutionary understanding of creation actually helps us to make more sense of traditional understandings of Scripture (affirming the true capacity for disobedience in animals) than a modern so-called "traditional account" where humans are held up as being uniquely conscious, rational, linguistic, etc. and are the sole creatures with the capacity to intentionally respond to the will of God. If evolutionary biologists (and in particular cognitive ethologists) are right, then it

---

33 "He appointed from the first that humans should find nourishment from the fruits of the earth, and from seeds, and herbs, and acorns, having at the same time appointed that the animals be of habits similar to human's, that they also might eat of the seeds of the earth." Theophilus "To Autolycus" 2:18, 101-102.

34 Theophilus in Robert M. Grant, *Early Christians and Animals* (New York: Routledge, 1999), 75.

35 In Genesis 2:15, where God "took man and put him in the Garden of Eden," an uncommon term for "put" (*wayyannihehu*) is used that is elsewhere reserved for two specific purposes: "God's 'rest' or 'safety,' which he gives to man in the land (e.g., Genesis 19:16; Deuteronomy 3:20; 12:10; 25:19), and the 'dedication' of something in the presence of the Lord (Exodus 16:33-34; Leviticus 16:23; Numbers 17:4; Deuteronomy 26:4, 10)." Both nuances of this term may be understood to lie behind the author's use in Gen 2:15—"Man was 'put' into the garden where he could 'rest' and be 'safe,' and man was 'put' into the garden 'in God's presence' where he could have fellowship with God" (3:8). Sailhamer, *The Expositor's Bible Commentary*, 45. The conversation between God and the humans and the subsequent conversation between the humans and the serpent seems to presuppose a human awareness of death. Death-awareness appears to have been required in order for the first humans to comprehend the consequences of disobedience. Otherwise the humans would not have been able to understand God's warning, "you will surely die," (Genesis 2:17) or the serpent's questioning of God's admonition along with the serpent's counter assurance, "You will not surely die" (Genesis 3:4). From the context in which the first commandment was given, we may surmise that there was at least some knowledge of death *before* the humans disobeyed.

is not possible to exclude the phenomena of "consciousness, choice, deliberation, planning, intentions, and other mental processes" in animals from scientific consideration.[36] A wealth of empirical evidence has uncovered that numerous animal groups share the type of higher cognitive and communicative capacities that were once thought to be uniquely human. Beyond this, researchers have observed that "complex cognitive abilities evolved multiple times in distantly related species with vastly different brain structures in order to solve similar socioecological problems."[37] In-depth scientific studies on animal cognition have likewise underscored the vital role of rational deliberation, choice, and freedom in much non-human animal behavior.[38] Since the evolution of nervous systems, brains, sentience, and higher cognitive behaviors have been found to evolve convergently in a number of distantly related groups, some biologists have even argued that the emergence of human-like intelligence "must be an evolutionary inevitability."[39] Given the ubiquity of evolutionary convergence in the area of cognition it is thus not surprising to find that all intelligences "tend towards a similar end point."[40]

In addition to the scientific evidence for higher cognitive capacities among animals it is clear that through active niche construction and social learning, *non-human animals* "not only shape the nature of their world, but also in part determine the selection pressures to which they and their descendants are exposed."[41] In this way the behavioral decisions, environmental alterations—whether physical, social, or nutritional—and subjective choices of animals "play a major role in in-

---

36 Marc Bekoff, Colin Allen, and Gordon Burghardt, *The Cognitive Animal: Empirical and Theoretical Perspectives on Animal Cognition* (Cambridge, Massachusetts: MIT Press, 2002), xi.

37 Shigeru Watanabe and Ludwig Huber, "Animal logics: Decisions in the Absence of Human Language," *Animal Cognition* 9, no. 4 (October 2006): 241. Berkeley?

38 See Marc Bekoff, Colin Allen, Gordon Burghardt, eds., *The Cognitive Animal: Empirical and Theoretical Perspectives on Animal Cognition* (Cambridge, MA: MIT Press, 2002); Susan Hurley and Matthew Nudds, eds., *Rational Animals?* (New York: Oxford UP, 2006); and José Luis Bermúdez, *Thinking without Words* (New York: Oxford University Press, 2003).

39 Simon Conway Morris, "Evolution and the Inevitability of Intelligent Life," in *The Cambridge Companion to Science and Religion*, Peter Harrison, ed. (Cambridge: Cambridge University Press, 2010), 155.

40 Simon Conway Morris, "Evolution and Convergence: Some Wider Considerations," in *The Deep Structure of Biology: Is Convergence Sufficiently Ubiquitous to Give a Directional Signal?* (West Conshohocken, Pennsylvania: Templeton Press, 2008), 58.

41 Rachel L. Day, Kevin N. Laland, and John Odling-Smee, "Rethinking Adaptation: The Niche-Construction Perspective," *Perspectives in Biology and Medicine* 46, no. 1 (Winter 2003): 81.

troducing evolutionary change."[42] Evolutionary biologist Patrick Bateson elaborates specifically on how such evolutionary change takes place:

> If a population of animals should change their habits (no doubt often on account of changes in their surroundings such as food supply, breeding sites, etc. but also sometimes due to their exploratory curiosity discovering new ways of life, such as new sources of food or new methods of exploitation) then, sooner or later, variations in the gene complex will turn up in the population to produce small alterations in the animal's structure which will make them more efficient in relation to their new behavioral pattern.[43]

Within the current understanding of evolutionary biology, the biblical notion of a *pre-human fall*—where animals have actively or intentionally resisted the will of God for creation—becomes far more plausible than in a non-Darwinian account of creation that stresses the radical biological and behavioral uniqueness of human beings. In a Darwinian approach to evolution focusing on the dynamics of niche selection, non-human animals have an active rather than a passive part in their own evolutionary creation, and their choices, though perhaps not as self-conscious or culpable as those of humans, are theologically significant insofar as they influence the degree and specific types of evolutionary suffering that are brought into existence through such choices. The behavioral habits and choices of animals serve as a significant universal contingent in evolutionary history and such animal choices affect the actual occurrence of evolutionary evils by playing a central role in determining many of the specific forms in which instances of suffering are historically embodied.[44] "As life grew more complex and evolved more capacities, the greater capacities brought more evil into the world."[45] In this way the existence of evolutionary evil is directly related to an organism's capacity to choose different pathways of action which in turn may affect the actual course of evolutionary suffering.

---

42 Patrick Bateson, "The Active Role of Behavior in Evolution," *Biology and Philosophy* 19 (2004): 283–98.
43 Patrick Bateson, "The Active Role of Behavior in Evolution," in *Evolutionary Processes and Metaphors,* M.W. Ho and S.W. Fox, eds. (London: John Wiley and Sons, 1988), 196.
44 For examples, see Moritz, "Evolutionary Evil."
45 Patricia Williams, "How Evil Entered the World: An Exploration through Deep Time," in *The Evolution of Evil,* G. Bennett, M.J. Hewlett, T. Peters, and R.J. Russell, eds. (Göttingen: Vandenhoeck and Ruprecht, 2008).

In Darwin's own view, morality—like all biological traits and behaviors—is seen as a spectrum, rather than as a singularly unique phenomenon that appears *de novo* with anatomically and behaviorally modern *Homo sapiens*. Darwin's argument for rooting moral judgment and behavior in the evolved emotional brain found some converts, but many in his own day remained unconvinced. While even the natural theologians of the time could accept a certain degree of rationality among the non-human animals, hardly anyone—including some of Darwin's staunchest supporters—would cede morality to non-human animals. Much recent empirical evidence, however, substantiates Darwin's original intuitions on this point (which in turn were largely indebted to David Hume's conception of moral theory).[46] A number of contemporary researchers have argued that given the understanding (taken from Virtue Theoretical and Humean moral theory) that "moral cognition comprises any cognitive act that is related to helping us ascertain and act on what we should do" we may go on to acknowledge that "non-human animals (for example, primates and other social animals) might also engage in robust moral reasoning."[47]

To take seriously the emerging scientific notion of morality as existing across a spectrum of life forms opens up the theological possibility of what I have elsewhere referred to as a *Free Creatures Defense* to the problem of evolutionary evil. In the *Free Creatures Defense,* God has created a truly good world ("very good," in fact) where freedom and the capacity to directly respond to God's will are not solely the possession of one creaturely kind, but of many. Here the Creator is concerned not only with the moral development of human beings, but with that of all creatures who have at least some capacity to heed God's purposes. This is a view that has very deep roots in the scriptural and theological traditions and one that has an increasing amount support from data of the natural sciences. In my own philosophical and theological assessment, this world of *many free creatures* is truly a *better world* than "the best of all possible worlds" which contains only *one free creature* who can regard or disregard to the voice of its Creator. It is a world in which God's plans and purposes are not wrapped up in prerogatives and problems of one unique type of crea-

---

46 See Robert J. Richards, *Darwin and the Emergence of Evolutionary Theories of Mind and Behavior* (Chicago: University of Chicago Press, 1987), 207-08.

47 William D. Casebeer, "Moral Cognition and Its Neural Constituents," *Nature Reviews Neuroscience* 4 (October 2003), 842. See also Marc Bekoff, "Wild Justice, Cooperation, and Fair Play: Minding Manners, Being Nice, and Feeling Good," in *The Origins and Nature of Sociality*, R. Sussman and A. Chapman, eds. (Chicago: Aldine, 2004), 53-79.

ture, but are instead akin to convergent endpoints of evolution that a spectrum of animal species can and will reach.

Conclusion

In this chapter I have followed Peters' methodological intuitions concerning the relationship between theology and science as I have approached the theological problem of animal suffering as witnessed throughout the evolutionary history of life's creation. I have found that Peters' intuitions have borne much conceptual fruit—for even as Darwin's theory of evolution *via* natural selection has posed the problem of theodicy in its most profoundly potent form, Darwin's other insights regarding the common ancestry and radical continuity of all life contain the seeds of a scientifically informed theological response to the evolutionary theodicy dilemma. If the nature of biological life—including the vast diversity of traits and behaviors—is that of a spectrum, then there is ultimately no sharp biological dividing line between moral evil and natural evil. Theologically then, one may see the fallenness of creation as reaching all the way back to the first inklings of animal consciousness, freedom, and self-awareness—and, as a consequence, moral culpability can likewise be envisioned as existing in a variety of gradations along this spectrum. This evolutionary shift in perspective regarding the gradual nature of evil's emergence through the actions and intentions of "free creatures" (who increasingly possess greater levels of freedom as life's evolutionary history unfolds) echoes the fundamental insight of the story of the rebellious non-human animal serpent in Genesis 3. Evil—as resistance to God's will that results in suffering—precedes the arrival of human beings and it already has a firm foothold in the non-human animal world long before humans are ever tempted to go astray. As it stands, the world of human and non-human animals still abounds with ample evidence of both suffering and joy, evil and good. In this way our world appears to be structured so that the individual lives, and evolutionary destinies of countless creatures and their lineages are profoundly balanced on the edge of decision. Indeed, it would seem that such a balance is precisely what is required if all God's creatures are to be called and coaxed to freely respond to their Creator in obedience, faith, and love.

Evolution, Theodicy, and New Creation

Ted Peters

In his *Festschrift* chapter, "Encountering Evolution: Ted Peters on Darwin and Christian Theology," Martinez Hewlett tells the story of our Berkeley research group affectionately known back then as "Theodicy, Evolution, and Genocide," or TEG. Our basic question was this: should we blame God because Darwinian evolution requires such a long relentless battle for survival replete with violence, bloodshed, suffering, death, and extinction? Nature, said Alfred Lord Tennyson, is blood "red in tooth and claw." Nature kills, and it kills mercilessly. How could a Christian speak of this natural world as graced by the love of God? We stayed awake nights wrestling with this variant on the theodicy problem.

The theodicy problem is the big problem for any theologian holding to the position we know as theistic evolution. What are the smaller problems? Hewlett and I put the following smaller question on top of our list: what the heck is going on in the evolution controversy? Why all the clamor and clang over Darwin? Who's fighting with whom about what? In order to understand empathetically, we packed up our TEG scholars and flew to San Diego to interview creationists at the Institute for Creation Research. We invited Intelligent Design advocates to Berkeley to present their case. We grilled those who identify as theistic evolutionists. We identified and categorized and pigeon holed and packaged. Here's what we came up with.

Who's Fighting with Whom about What?

The evolution controversy may appear to be a war between science and religion. A closer look, however, will show that this is not the case. No one fighting in this war is opposed to science. Everyone loves science.

Even fundamentalist Christians and conservative Muslims love science. The war is actually being fought over what constitutes good science. Is Darwin's theory of evolution good science or not? That's the question asked by both established scientists as well as religious thinkers of all persuasions.

The first on a buffet of answers is: yes, Darwin's theory of evolution is good science, even great science! Darwin's theory is fertile, having spawned productive research from 1859 right down to the present day. This is the position universally assumed in evolutionary biology. Hewlett and I call it the science-alone position—that is, science without any attached ideological commitments. The reigning theory today is Neo-Darwinism, which combines Charles Darwin's original nineteenth-century concept of natural selection with the twentieth-century concept of genetic mutation to explain the development of new species over 3.8 billion years of life on Earth. Defenders of quality science education in the public schools most frequently embrace this "science alone" approach. This is Hewlett's confirmed conviction. He is, after all, a laboratory scientist.

The second answer is: yes, Darwin's theory of evolution is not only good science, it also provides philosophical grounds for materialism, naturalism, reductionism, and atheism. Hewlett and I call it materialist ideology. This materialist ideology includes repudiation of any divine influence on the course of evolutionary development.

The new breed of aggressive atheists now spreading like an ominous cloud is raining down invectives against religious believers, describing religious traditions as outdated, rigidly dogmatic, anti-science, homophobic, tribal, and violent. The atheistic troops arm themselves with evolutionary weapons, taking religion prisoner. The prison is evolutionary theory, according to which religion is described as a primitive survival mechanism—that is, religion is described as an early attempt to insure that human beings would make more babies and thereby contribute to the survival of the human species. This materialist ideology denies to religious believers what they themselves claim, namely, that believers are in tune with transcendent reality.

Curiously, our evolutionary atheists exempt themselves from their own theory. They do not reduce their own atheism to evolution's directive to make more babies; nor do they grant that atheism is a delusion flopped off on them by the selfish gene in the service of natural selection. One would expect that what is good for the goose should be good for the gander.

The third answer is given by the creationists: no, Darwin's theory of evolution is bad science. It is wrong. This position is self-named: creationism. Creationism denies the validity of Darwinian theory and complains that evolutionary thinking leads to moral degradation. Darwin's view is mistaken science because it fails to recognize that each species is distinct, having been created distinct at the beginning of the world. No evolution from one species to another has taken place. What counts as good science is the view that our Earth is young, say 10,000 years old. Therefore, it is misleading to say that species evolved over millions or billions of years. The human species is unique and was created especially by God. We do not have monkeys as uncles.

Bad science leads to bad ethics. Creationists remind us of the indisputable history of Social Darwinism and the Eugenics movement which led to justification of *laissez faire* capitalism, the involuntary sterilization of prisoners in American prisons, and the genocide perpetrated by German Nazis against physically disabled, mentally disabled, homosexuals, Gypsies, and Jews. This Darwinian influence is still at work today, trumpet creationists, subverting society by sponsoring divorce, homosexuality, and anarchy. Creationists strongly support racial equality, but they see support of LGBT rights as a threat to the divine order for creation.

It is important to distinguish two types of creationists, the biblical and the scientific. The biblical creationists appeal to the authority of the Bible—especially to the Genesis account of creation—to combat the rising influence of Darwinism in public education and the wider culture. The attack strategy of the biblical creationists is made clear by the Answers in Genesis website (https://answersingenesis.org/) and the Creation Museum in northern Kentucky on the outskirts of Cincinnati.

According to scientific creationists, we have a war of science against science. Science supports the creationist description of the natural world, they contend. They argue, for example, that the fossil record will contradict standard appeals to natural selection over long periods of time. Those known as young earth creationists (YECs) hold that our planet earth is less than ten thousand years old and, further, that all species of plants and animals were originally created by God in their present form. No speciation has occurred. Every species we see today was created according to its own "kind" at the beginning, a very recent beginning.

They deny macroevolution—that is, they deny that one species has evolved from prior species, although they affirm microevolution—that is, evolutionary change within a species. Key here is that creationists justify their arguments on scientific grounds, not by appeal to biblical authority.

A fourth answer is given by the school of Intelligent Design or ID: no, Darwinian theory is bad science because it relies on natural selection to explain speciation. Advocates of Intelligent Design sharply attack neo-Darwinian theory for overstating the role of natural selection in species evolution. ID argues that slow incremental changes due to genetic mutations are insufficient to explain the emergence of new and more complex biological systems. Many of the life forms that have evolved are irreducibly complex, and this counts as evidence that they have been intelligently designed. Who might that intelligent designer be? God? Well, ID advocates stop short of declaring God to exist; they plead agnosticism regarding the designer. Like the scientific creationists, ID combatants attack Darwinian theory with science. Unlike the scientific creationists, ID combatants admit that speciation has taken place in evolution, but they add that species evolution is due to an intelligent designer rather than blind natural selection. Despite this difference, it is not unusual to find soldiers in both the creationist and ID armies singing next to one another in church on Sunday.

In Turkey, conservative Muslims have watched the battle over Darwinian evolution carefully. Turkey's constitution, written in the 1920s, declares the public schools to be secular and even states flatly that Darwinian evolution must be taught. This angers anti-secular Muslims who want to see the Islamic worldview taught in the public schools. So, Islamic theologians and scientists borrow material developed by Christian creationists and Intelligent Design advocates. They Islamicize the arguments, and with such arguments they prosecute their own attack against the secular-Darwinian establishment.

The fifth answer is offered by the position we know as theistic evolution. Theistic evolutionists affirm the fertility and credibility of both the original Darwinian theory and Neo-Darwinism. What the Theistic Evolutionists add is this: God employs evolutionary processes over deep time to bring about the human race and perhaps even carry the natural world to a redemptive future. The theistic evolution battalion includes a variety of warriors. The minimalist theistic evolutionist respects the science and employs some form of the concept of *concursus* (concurrence) to harmonize the theological understanding of creation with this science. The maximalist theistic evolutionist reconstructs our entire worldview in terms of a long evolutionary process, drenched in temporality, moving progressively toward an eschatological fulfillment in our cosmic future. Most of today's theistic evolutionists find themselves somewhere between the minimalist and maximalist camps.

That a war is being fought over evolution is clear. However, because the actual points at issue deal specifically with the explanatory adequacy of natural selection, it would be misleading to simply dub this a war between science and religion. This became the theme of the many books and articles Hewlett and I co-authored.

Do We Share Sin with the Animals?

In his essay, "Human Origins: Present, Past, and Future," Ronald Cole-Turner reminds us of the responsibility of today's systematic theologian. "Today there can be no authentic theological anthropology that does not take into account what we are learning from the sciences, including the dynamic and interdisciplinary scientific investigation into human origins."[1] Not only origin but also evolutionary development must become constitutive of any theological treatment of the human condition.

One of my central concerns in constructing a theological anthropology that takes human origins and evolutionary development into account, as I already mentioned, is the theodicy problem. Have we human beings inherited from our pre-human evolutionary past a genetic or otherwise biological equivalent to original sin? The sociobiologists and evolutionary psychologists would say so. It certainly makes sense to me to understand that human proclivities to anxiety, self-preservation, survival, and violence are inclinations we share with the rest of the natural world. This would suggest, theologically, that the human race did not originate original sin. Rather, we inherited it.

This has become a major theme in the erudite research and writing of Joshua Moritz. We get a taste of his work in his *Festschrift* chapter, "Animal Suffering, Animal Sin, Theistic Evolution, and the Problem of Evil." On the surface, it appears that Moritz wants to deal with the simple question of timing. Did the fall into sin begin with the advent of *Homo*

---

1 Cole-Turner, 266.

sapiens? Or, did it precede our humanoid ancestors? If the latter, then it appears that both sin and death arrived on the earthly scene before Adam and Eve. "Within the current understanding of evolutionary biology, the biblical notion of a pre-human fall—where animals have actively or inentionally resisted the will of God for creation—becomes far more plausible than in a non-Darwinian account of creation that stresses the radical biological and behavioral uniqueness of human beings."[2] Moritz likes to mention that in the Eden story in Genesis 2–3, the serpent is already fallen into estrangement from God even before Eve engages in the fateful conversation about the forbidden fruit. Moritz concludes both biblically and Darwinically that the fall precedes Eden.

Yet, below the surface of this timing issue lies another one, namely, do we humans share our fallen condition with the rest of nature? The Darwinian worldview would say, yes indeed! "In a Darwinian approach to evolution focusing on the dynamics of niche selection, non-human animals have an active rather than passive part in their own evolutionary creation, and their choices, though perhaps not as self-conscious or culpable as those of humans, are theologically significant insofar as they influence the degree and specific types of evolutionary suffering that are brought into existence through such choices. . . . In this way the existence of evolutionary evil is directly related to an organism's capacity to choose different pathways of action which in turn may affect the actual course of evolutionary suffering."[3]

Now, we are going to dig a level still deeper. At level one, original sin originated in the biological kingdom prior to humans' arrival. At level two, we humans share our fallen condition with the rest of nature. Now, we are about to enter subterranean level three: pre-human nature fell because of choice. That's right: choice in the plant and animal kingdoms. "Freedom and the capacity to directly respond to God's will are not solely the possession of one creaturely kind, but of many. Here the Creator is concerned not only with the moral development of human beings, but with that of all creatures who have at least some capacity to heed God's purposes."[4]

One can hear echoes of the free-will-defense of God frequently used to resolve the theodicy question. The free will defense argument goes like this. Because God so desired creatures who would love God out of

---

2 Moritz, 291.
3 Moritz, 291.
4 Moritz, 292.

freedom, God created free creatures with the opportunity to accept or reject divine grace. God put the creation at risk for a fall into sin, suffering, and death because, on God's scale of values, free choice is more important. This is the path of argument the free-will-defense theodicy takes.

With this in mind, we can see Moritz's argument progressing: pre-human creatures must have enjoyed some level of free choice if the biological world is characterized by the struggle for existence and dog-eat-dog morality. "This is a view that has very deep roots in the scriptural and theological traditions and one that has an increasing amount of support from data of the natural sciences. In my own philosophical and theological assessment this world of many free creatures is truly a better world than 'the best of all possible worlds' which contains only one free creature who can regard or disregard the voice of its Creator. It is a world in which God's plans and purposes are not wrapped up in prerogatives and problems of one unique type of creature, but are instead akin to convergent endpoints of evolution that a spectrum of animal species can and will reach."[5] In short, if one connects sin with freedom, then both sin and freedom are spread throughout the natural domain and not limited merely to the human situation.

According to Moritz's constructive theological move, "the fallenness of creation" reaches "all the way back to the first inklings of animal consciousness, freedom, and self-awareness—and, as a consequence, moral culpability can likewise be envisioned as existing in a variety of gradations along this spectrum. This evolutionary shift in perspective regarding the gradual nature of evil's emergence through the actions and intentions of 'free creatures' (who increasingly possess greater levels of freedom as life's evolutionary history unfolds) echoes the fundamental insight of the story of the rebellious non-human animal serpent in Genesis 3. "Evil—as resistance to God's will that results in suffering—precedes the arrival of human beings, and it already has a firm foothold in the non-human animal world long before humans are ever tempted to go astray."[6]

Moritz exhibits not only creativity but courage in venturing forth this brave hypothesis. Where I can heartily agree with Moritz is on this point: the human condition shares most, if not all, its fundamental char-

---

5   Moritz, 292-3
6   Moritz, 293.

acteristics with the rest of the natural world. Evil, suffering, death, and such we share with at least the animals if not the plants as well. God's promised salvation in the new creation applies to the length and breadth and depth of the entire created order, not merely to humans.

However, where I am slow to agree with Moritz is that this requires attributing to pre-human organisms choice and the moral responsibility for the fall that hinges on choice. I am not a pupil in the free-will-defense school, so I do not rest my case for our fallen condition on choice, whether it be the choice of an animal or a human. It seems to me that our inherited sin—original sin?—comes to us in the form of bondage, not freedom. Christian freedom consists in liberation from this bondage, not the opportunity to choose this bondage. If I am reluctant to attribute a Pelagian-style freedom to Adam and Eve, then I am equally reluctant to attribute it to chimpanzees, spiders, and eukaryotes.

In, With, and Under

In recent decades, I have observed an increase in the number of theistic evolutionists who are embracing compatibilism—that is, they assert that natural processes are compatible with divine action. Benjamin Warfield at Princeton a century ago called this position: *concursus*. Warfield contended that a concursus or cooperative synergy between natural processes and divine action has brought the human race into existence according to God's intentions. He advocated divine intention without divine intervention. Contemporary theistic evolutionists follow Warfield and are showing a clear preference for Lutheran sacramental vocabulary: in, with, and under. Just as the body and blood of our Lord is in, with, and under the bread and the wine in the Lord's Supper, so also God's continuing creative activity works in, with, and under evolutionary processes.

Peter M.J. Hess offers his support for theistic evolution elsewhere in this volume. "A theology in which God works in, with, and through creation can conceive of the soul as being transmitted integrally through the evolution of human physical nature and its increasing neural endowment, consistently with a Hebraic understanding of the person as a psychosomatic unity. This theology addresses a number of important theological problems: (1) It preserves the sacramental idea of the universe as transfigured by God, and it rejects a Platonic dualism in which all and only human souls are saved, a position that in itself renders unintelligible the Pauline notion that 'all creation is groaning together' (Romans 8:22)." Hess adds, "Reflection upon the sacramental character of an evolving creation can enrich our theological vocabulary by rendering it more responsive to our deepening knowledge of the universe we inhabit."[7]

I have joined the in-with-and-under school of theistic evolution. Even though I embrace the *concursus* concept to describe God's creative work through biological evolution, I do not go as far as Peter Hess in adopting a sacramental view of creation. I affirm *creatio ex nihilo*, creation out of nothing, right along with *creatio continua*, continuing creation; a corollary of *creatio ex nihilo* is that the material world is not made of the same stuff as God. The creation is loved by its Creator God, to be sure, but in itself the creation is not sacred. God is actively present in, with, and under the creation, to be sure, but this does not render the creation sacramental in character. I believe we should love God's creation, to be sure, but we do not need to treat the creation sacramentally to warrant our loving it.

Conclusion: Theodicy and Resurrection

I do not believe we can resolve the theodicy problem by appeal to ingenious philosophical logic. Nor can we resolve it by appeal to free will on the part of our ancestors, whether in Eden or prior to Eden. The resolution can be found only in the future, the eschatological future.

Just as God raised the crucified Jesus on the first Easter, God will raise this creation up into the new creation. Or, to say it another way, in the new creation the present creation will finally warrant God saying, "Behold, it is very good."

If I recall correctly, I began to think this way after reading a powerful chapter in Jürgen Moltmann's book, *Hope and Planning*. "Jesus' resurrection is the answer to the cry of the forsaken and the glorious beginning of the resolution of the question of theodicy in the world. The cross of Jesus has lasting meaning only as the conquered, dark past which is on its way towards a glorious future." Moltmann then draws upon what Lutheran's commonly call the "happy exchange" or "the communication of attributes," wherein God takes on our death and we take on God's life. "God is no longer the defendant in the human question of theodicy; rather, the answer is found in this question itself. The cross of Christ then becomes

---

[7] Hess, 278.

the Christian theodicy—a self-justification of God in which judgment and damnation are taken up by God himself, so that man may live."[8] In the cross, God takes on the sin, evil, suffering, and extinction of life which all of nature has endured on this planet since the evolutionary process began. God is not the perpetrator of suffering. Rather, God is the victim of suffering. With all the decayed organisms who had to die to make the petroleum we put in our cars as gasoline, God felt with them their suffering and endured with them their death. "God is no longer the defendant in the human question of theodicy," Moltmann rightly emphasizes.

By raising the crucified one on the first Easter Sunday, God makes a promise to creatures within this creation: the past will not be the future. The future will be different. The extinction of life in death will not be the final chapter written in creation's story. We have a new creation to look forward to. And, I will add, the advent of the new creation will constitute God's final act in creating the present creation. The new creation will be the fulfillment of God's present ongoing creative activity. The new creation will retroactively define and redeem all that has happened in the past. The eschatological future will be a consummate future.

---

8 Jürgen Moltmann, *Hope and Planning*, trans. Margaret Clarkson (New York: Harper & Row, 1971), 43.

ASTROTHEOLOGY & ETHICS, BOTH HERE AND BEYOND

Stem Cells in Wonderland?

Proleptic Ethics and Stem Cell Research

Karen Lebacqz

Ted Peters has long advocated "proleptic ethics," defined as working creatively in the present in light of a projected vision of a redeemed future.[1] With other scholars, Peters distinguishes two ways of looking at the future: *futurum* is the future that would be a continuation of the present reality, but *adventus* is a vision of a radically different future brought about by God.[2] This radically different future—imaginatively presented in the book of Revelation, for example—includes divinely established justice, abundance of joy, openness to all, and the elimination of pain. "It will be a new creation," says Peters.[3] Proleptic ethics seeks to envision this new creation and open ourselves to working toward it. Put another way, we are beholden not to the *old* Adam but to the *new* one. We do our ethics by asking: what is the future promised to us by God, and how can we move from here to there? In that process, we must think creatively, rather than conforming ourselves to a set of laws or commandments. Because God's promise is one of abundance, justice, and love, the core of proleptic ethics is beneficence—the bringing about of goodness.

Part of that envisioned new creation might be regenerative medicine. In its special report on "The Future of Medicine," *Scientific American* hails stem cells and other technologies that will usher in this new era of medicine.[4] The vision is indeed one of "adventus" rather than "futurum": no longer would cancer be treated with surgery, radiation, and

---

1 Ted Peters, *Playing God? Genetic Determinism and Human Freedom* (New York: Routledge, 1997), 161.
2 Ibid., 174. Peters acknowledges his debt to Letty Russell here.
3 Ibid.
4 "Special Report: The Future of Medicine," *Scientific American,* April 2013, 48–57.

chemotherapy, but bodies would be coaxed to heal themselves and to reject cancer cells without such interventions. An important part of regenerative medicine is the promise of stem cells for regenerating tissue and helping bodies repair themselves.

Peters and I served together on the first Ethics Advisory Board of the Geron Corporation, which pioneered in embryonic stem cell research.[5] We have attended international conferences on the subject. We have published our support for stem cell research, including embryonic stem cell research.[6] Indeed, Peters has written extensively on stem cell research, drawing from his proleptic ethics with its future orientation and emphasis on beneficence.[7] It seems appropriate, then, to honor Ted Peters' many achievements with some reflections on stem cell ethics.

Alice in the Wonderland of Stem Cells

In this arena, I think there are lessons we can learn from Lewis Carroll's delightful children's story, *Alice's Adventures in Wonderland*.[8] Alice falls down a rabbit hole and finds herself in a long, dark corridor. There are many doors leading off the corridor, but they are all locked. On a small table, Alice finds a tiny, golden key. Eventually, she discovers a tiny door to which the key fits. Opening the door and bending down to look through it, she can see a magical garden. Alice wants to get into that garden! But she is too big; she cannot fit through the door. Replacing the key on the table, she spies a bottle that says "drink me," and so she does. Magically, she shrinks down to the right size to fit through the door—but, alas—having shrunk, she can no longer reach the table to get the key!

Thus begins a series of adventures in which Alice eats and drinks various concoctions, growing smaller and then larger, all in an effort to find a way through the door into the magical, beautiful garden. Strange happenings surround her efforts. She nearly drowns in a pool of her own tears, encounters some very bizarre animals, and has various adventures that are odd, to say the least. The hallway dissolves and Alice finds her-

---

5 I served as the first chair of the Ethics Advisory Board of Geron Corporation, which sponsored James Thomson's ground-breaking work on human embryonic stem cells.
6 See Ted Peters, Karen Lebacqz, and Gaymon Bennett, *Sacred Cells? Why Christians Should Support Stem Cell Research* (New York: Rowman and Littlefield, 2008).
7 Ted Peters, *The Stem Cell Debate* (Minneapolis: Fortress Press, 2007); Peters, Lebacqz and Bennett, *Sacred Cells?*
8 Lewis Carroll, *Alice's Adventures in Wonderland*, from *The Annotated Alice: Alice's Adventures in Wonderland* and *Through the Looking Glass*, introduction by Martin Gardner (New York: Bramhall House, 1960).

self in a different garden filled with talking caterpillars, hostile pigeons, footmen shaped like fish, mad hatters, and other unusual creatures. Many frustrating adventures later, Alice finds herself once again in the original hallway leading to the magical garden. Holding the key and cleverly manipulating her size, she opens the door and enters the garden, only to find it—rather literally—a house of cards! The red roses are really white roses painted red, the king and queen and soldiers and gardeners are all playing cards, the croquet mallets are infuriating flamingoes, and the croquet balls are hedgehogs who keep unrolling themselves and crawling off to other parts of the garden. What looks beautiful and inviting turns out to be filled with additional bizarre creatures and adventures.

Thinking back on the years since 1998 when James Thomson first announced the derivation and cultivation of lines of human embryonic stem cells, and the Geron Ethics Advisory Board scrambled to find appropriate guidelines for stem cell research, I suggest that we can learn from Alice's adventures. Regenerative medicine is our vision of a beautiful garden—a place where bodies heal themselves, where illnesses no longer take such a toll on us and treatments are no longer as burdensome as our current chemotherapies and many other treatments are. Peters' proleptic ethics draws us toward regenerative medicine. It is the "redeemed future" of wholeness and completion—or, at least, so it seems! We want to be in that garden. We thought stem cells would be the golden key that would open the door. But we have had our political battles and our disappointments along the way, and it is not clear if we can we get to the "right size" to walk through that door into the garden. Like Alice, we may have to swallow some mysterious concoctions in order to enter the garden. Like Alice, we may not be able to go there directly.

Indeed, just like Alice, I think we began our approach the wrong way. In her eagerness to enter the garden, Alice put the key back on the table and *then* drank the bottle that reduced her size. Without the key, she could not open the door! We have done something akin to Alice. From the beginning, I always thought that a day would come when we would be able to derive pluripotent human stem cells without destroying embryos. Early in the stem cell saga, I asked a scientist why we could not remove one cell—one blastomere—from the inner cell mass of the blastocyst and derive stem cells from that. Today, that would be possible; at the time, it was not. Still, the possibility of deriving stem cells by cloning or by reprogramming somatic cells seemed almost inevitable. It therefore has always frustrated me that so much of the debate about stem cell research has been locked into controversy about the moral status of embryos and whether it is acceptable to destroy them. The assumption seems to be that if we did not have to destroy embryos, there would be *no* ethical issues surrounding stem cell research. Even as recently as fall 2012, when Professor Shinya Yamanaka was chosen to receive the Nobel Prize for his work on induced pluripotent stem cells (iPS), the report of the Witherspoon Council at Princeton University maintains that the destruction of embryos is the single, most important ethical question about derivation and use of stem cells.[9] Like others in the debate, the Council seems ready to assume that if embryos did not have to be destroyed, there would be *no ethical issues* around the derivation and use of stem cells.[10] Induced pluripotent stem cells would then be the "key" that unlocks the door to our beautiful garden of regenerative medicine while avoiding ethical controversy.

I disagree. No matter what the derivation of stem cells, a number of important ethical issues remain surrounding stem cell technology and its uses and implications. Proper attention to the ethical principles, I propose, is the key to opening the door to regenerative medicine.[11] The change from embryonic stem cells to induced pluripotent stem cells is akin to Alice's change of *size.* But without the key, being the right size is not sufficient, as Alice learned. As compelling as is our vision of regenerative medicine, in our rush to get into that garden, we will make a huge mistake if we forget the key. And just like Alice, even in the garden there may be strange "creatures" to confront—unresolved ethical problems that continue to swirl in the stem cell arena.

Three principles are well established now in the arena of medical ethics. They are: (1) respect for autonomy or for the self-determination of patients and research subjects; (2) beneficence (doing good) and its

---

9 The Witherspoon Council on Ethics and the Integrity of Science, *The New Atlantis*, 37, Fall 2012.

10 Of course, as Insoo Hyun has pointed out, human embryonic stem cells remain the "gold standard" against which other pluripotent stem cells will be measured. Thus, even with new approaches to the derivation of stem cells, we can never fully avoid some of the intractable ethical questions that have plagued human embryonic stem cell research. See Insoo Hyun, "Stem Cells from Skin Cells: The Ethical Questions," *Hastings Center Report* 38, no.1 (2008): 20–22; also Insoo Hyun, "The Caravan of Stem Cell Science," http://churchandstate.org.uk/2011/03/prof-insoo-hyun-the-caravan-of-stem-cell-science/.

11 I served on the United States National Commission for the Protection of Human Subjects of Biomedical and Behavioral Research. That Commission set standards for research on human subjects that utilizes any federal funding in the U.S.

companion principle, non-maleficence (avoiding harm); and (3) justice, or fairness in the distribution of burdens and benefits.[12] All three principles are applicable to stem cell research and practices. Some current practices violate one or more of these principles.

International Stem Cell Tourism and Nonmaleficence

For example, clinics around the world now advertise directly to consumers via the internet, inviting patients to travel to other countries for stem cell infusions that are termed treatments.[13] When traditional medicine has not given people satisfactory outcomes, they can now travel huge distances—and pay huge prices—for these advertised interventions. Darren Lau and colleagues studied 19 websites advertising in North America and claiming the use of stem cells as treatment for various diseases.[14] Many advertised treatments for neurologic disorders such as multiple sclerosis, Parkinson's disease, and spinal cord injury.[15] Others advertised treatments for cardiovascular disease. Of the websites studied, three-quarters did not mention any risks of the procedures. The sites give the impression that procedures are safe and effective for a broad range of diseases. However, for many of these diseases— e.g., for Parkinson's or Alzheimer's—there are few if any clinical studies to support claims of efficacy. Procedures are being advertised as "treatments" without evidence to show that they are efficacious. They may not be: Christine Murray and her colleagues note that clinics commonly use bone marrow stem cells for stem cell infusions and that bone marrow stem cells have not been shown to be effective for diseases other than blood diseases. [16]

---

12 Tom L. Beauchamp and James F. Childress, *Principles of Biomedical Ethics*, 5th ed. (New York: Oxford Univeristy Press, 2001).

13 In December 2012, I attended the BIT 5th Annual Congress of Regenerative Medicine and Stem Cell in Guangzhou, China. Knowing that I was going to China, I looked up "stem cells, China" on the internet, hoping to learn something about the status of stem cell research in China. Instead, what I found was precisely such advertisements.

14 Darren Lau, Ubaka Ogbogu, Benjamin Taylor, Tania Stafinski, Devidas Menon, and Timothy Caulfield, "Stem Cell Clinics Online: The Direct-to-Consumer Portrayal of Stem Cell Medicine," *Cell Stem Cell* 3, (December 4, 2008): 591–594.

15 StemCellChina.com, for example, advertises many case studies of patients who have had various stem cell "therapies," claiming success in cases ranging from ALS to epilepsy to Huntington's disease to Multiple Sclerosis, and many more. Because StemCellChina is an English language website, most of the patients whose stories I read are from the United States or Canada.

16 Christine Murray, Sir Ian Wilmut, Anja Van De Stolpe, and Bernard Roelen, *Stem Cell Scientific Facts and Fiction* (Amsterdam: Elsevier, Inc., 2011), 226.

Moreover, in clinical studies of some conditions, such as AHSCT (autologous hematopoetic stem cell transplantation) adjunct therapies such as chemotherapy have been part of the protocol in successful trials, but clinics advertising directly to consumers often do not include such adjunct therapies. Lau concludes that "...the treatments offered on stem cell websites are generally unsupported by the clinical evidence."[17] Failure to gain clinical support for procedures is troubling ethically for a number of reasons.

First, patients may not be benefitted. This violates the ethical principle of beneficence (doing good) that undergirds proleptic ethics. Patients are being offered procedures that are claimed as "treatments" but that have little evidence of benefit.

Worse yet, patients may actually be harmed by such procedures. Murray offers a case study that is instructive. A patient in the Netherlands had experienced a blockage in a vessel in her spinal cord and had been paralyzed from the chest down. Over time, with traditional therapy, she had regained a little use of her legs. Hoping to regain all her mobility, she travelled abroad for a stem cell procedure. Following the procedure, she lost what little use of her legs she had previously regained. Not only was she not benefitted; she was harmed. Thus, it is clear that at least some international stem cell tourism not only violates the ethical principle of beneficence but also the principle of non-maleficence—"*Primum, non nocere*" (first, do no harm).

The need for clinical trials in order to establish safety and efficacy raises additional ethical issues. Bernard Lo and Lindsay Parham suggest that requirements for "proof of principle" in clinical trials should be stricter if cells have been manipulated extensively in vitro or have been derived from pluripotent stem cells (and this would include iPS cells).[18] They note, for instance, that in older clinical trials where fetal dopaminergic cells localized to the correct target area of the brain, engrafted, and functioned to produce the intended neurotransmitters; nonetheless appropriately regulated physiological function was not achieved. Furthermore, about 15 percent of subjects developed disabling dyskinesias. Thus, the fact that cells migrate to the appropriate area and perform the expected function once in that area does not ensure that the outcome will be what we wish or that no harm will be done. What should be

---

17 Lau, 593.

18 Bernard Lo and Lindsay Parham, "Ethical Issues in Stem Cell Research," *Endocrinology Review* 30, no. 3 (May 2009): 204–213.

the standards for safety or efficacy? How do we set the boundaries for what constitutes acceptable "harm" and sufficient "benefit" to proceed to larger trials or to "treatment"?

Autonomy and Informed Consent

If we do have clinical trials, of course, we face the ethical issue of the "therapeutic misconception." Subjects in clinical trials always hope that *they* will benefit, even though the purpose of Phase I trials is to assess safety rather than efficacy. I have had occasion to review the protocol for one clinical trial using human embryonic stem cells and I found the protocol very careful in its language: subjects were told over and over that the purpose of the trial was to assess safety, not to treat their disease; further, they were cautioned that there was no guarantee that they would experience any benefits. In my view, the protocol was a model of carefulness. Nonetheless, carefulness in a consent form does not prevent prospective subjects from hoping for benefits and such hope may diminish their ability to assess risks adequately and hence, to give a truly informed and valid consent.

This brings us to the second ethical principle—indeed, the one that is often listed first: "respect for autonomy," which gives rise to the requirement of informed or valid consent. Since the time of the Nuremburg Code, informed consent has been regarded as an indispensable requirement for research with human subjects.[19] We usually think of informed consent as requiring knowledge of any *risks* involved in the procedure for withdrawing cells and any *benefits* that might be obtained from the research. But informed consent might also require knowledge of the *purposes* of research—is it for infertility treatments, for example, or for basic science, or does it have commercial possibilities or prospects? Should people who donate somatic cells for iPS stem cell research be informed of the purposes of the research? Should they be allowed to give consent for research geared toward *some* purposes but withhold it for others?

In the case of stem cell tourism, patients who travel long distances for stem cell procedures are no doubt asked to sign consent forms for the procedure. In some countries, the consent process is carefully regulated. However, in others it is not, and patients may be signing forms that

---

19 The Nuremberg Code states: "the voluntary consent of the human subject is absolutely essential." The focus on *voluntariness* has since been modified to become a focus on *informed* consent. In my view, this is a mistake.

fail to disclose risks, overemphasize benefits, do not explain procedures carefully, or are written in languages that the patient cannot read or understand. They may not be told, for instance, of the *source* of stem cells to be injected; they may not be told of the *risks* of procedures such as lumbar puncture (commonly used for injection of stem cells); and—most important in my view—they may not be told that there are *no clinical studies* to support the use of stem cells for their particular disorder. This constitutes a deceptive practice that undermines the validity of consent and does not respect the patient's right of self-determination.

The International Society for Stem Cell Research has promulgated a handbook for patients suggesting a number of important questions to ask of any proffered stem cell "treatment," including whether there have been any clinical trials that have demonstrated the safety and efficacy of the procedure proposed.[20] However, patients are not likely to have read these guidelines. Indeed, patients going abroad for stem cell treatments, although they may be wealthy, may nonetheless be a vulnerable population. They would not likely consider such a course of action unless conventional treatments were failing them. They may be desperate. To take advantage of people's desperation is to exploit them. Exploitation is a fundamental form of disrespect and of injustice. Ethical principles such as respect for autonomy must be scrutinized carefully as we move toward new stem cell interventions.

Xenotransplantation and Cross-Species Genetics

Yet another crucial issue is the mixing of human and animal tissues or the injecting of stem cells from other species into humans. In Egypt a few years ago, I met a researcher who claimed to have great success in producing cures for patients by injecting stem cells derived not from human but from *other* species. However, he presented no scientific evidence there to support his claims of success from such xenotransplants. This experience suggests two other ethical questions for me. First, how is "success" defined? In the early days of in vitro fertilization, clinics often claimed "success" rates of 25 percent or more. By that, they meant that a *pregnancy* was achieved in 25 percent of patients. But many of those pregnancies did not come to term and hence, did not result in live births. From the perspective of hopeful patients wanting to become parents,

---

20 www.isscr.org/home/publications/patient-handbook. See their various guidelines as well.

this would hardly be a "success." Thus, the claims of success were deceptive. What are the standards for success in stem cell research and how is success to be defined? These are crucial ethical questions that remain even as stem cell science switches from embryo or adult stem cells to induced pluripotent stem cells.

The second ethical question raised by my encounter in Egypt has to do with the mixing of species itself. Some religions have a deep resistance to the mixing of species and many people feel a moral repugnance to such intermixing of tissues from different species. They might have strong moral objections to xenotransplants, even if these transplants could be shown successful by accepted standards.[21] Leon Kass argues that our felt moral repugnance is morally significant.[22] While I have criticisms of Kass's position, I do take seriously that there are species boundary issues that have never been resolved on an international level and that may be particularly problematic for people from some religious traditions. Is it sufficient to inform patients of the source of stem cells—the use of other animal species? Are there any species that should be ruled out? This is a vast area of unresolved ethical issues in stem cell research.

Justice in Regenerative Medicine

Finally, stem cell practices can raise some very difficult questions regarding the third principle: justice. I have already mentioned one of these—the problem of exploitation of vulnerable people. But there are others. For example, if a patient is injured by a stem cell injection, who will bear the costs of treatment for that injury? Some patients may return home to countries where universal health care is assured, but others will return to places such as the United States where there is no guarantee of universal health care coverage and where patients might have to pay the costs of follow-up care. There is no time here to rehearse all of the very contentious issues that justice concerns would evoke. However, we can say at least this much: stem cell tourism is obviously for the wealthy or for those who can afford the cost of travel, of staying abroad for a period of time, and the clinic costs, not to mention the possible follow-up costs. Lau and colleagues found that the average advertised cost of a course of treatment was over $20,000.[23] If stem cell procedures are available only

---

21 I wrote an essay on this for the Islamic Organization of Medical Science conference in Egypt in 2007.
22 Leon Kass, "The Wisdom of Repugnance," *The New Republic*, 2 June 1997: 17–26.
23 This may be Canadian rather than U.S. dollars, but it is a lot of money in either case.

to the rich, serious questions of justice arise. Indeed, every country that invests public funds in stem cell research is making justice decisions about balancing needs for basic health care against the promises of exotic technologies.[24]

Because I have a life-long passion for justice, I think there is another justice issue that has received little attention: What diseases should be the targets of the first experiments in humans using new sources of stem cells? (Adult stem cells have been used in bone marrow transplants for many years, but to date there are only a few experiments approved using ES cells and none that I know of yet using iPS or other stem cells.) Should the choice of target diseases be left to the private arena, where financial concerns will dominate decisions? Should we target diseases where treatment would offer better *quality* of life—e.g., macular degeneration—or diseases where treatment would *lengthen* life, with all the attendant population issues?[25] What does justice require in the larger scheme of efforts to improve and prolong human life and in the face of the great disparities among nations and populations? These issues are so huge and so intransigent that they may never be solved, but they are ethical issues that should concern us all.

Finally, of course, there is the question of patents for stem cell research and interventions. In this arena, what should be permitted to be patented? Should stem cells themselves receive patents, or only the processes by which they are derived? Do patents really promote public policy interests, or only private financial interests? Should patents be combined with mandatory licensing agreements, so that if a patent holder is not utilizing the patent for commercial purposes, someone else has a right to try to do so? All of these and many more ethical issues that time does not permit are still before us as stem cell science progresses.

---

24 This also raises a very important question about the relationship between public funding and moral policy-making. Both in the NBAC review of stem cell research and in the recent Report of the Witherspoon Council, the claim is made that refusing federal funding is not equivalent to making something illegal. That is certainly correct. However, the refusal of federal funding does make a statement; it implies that the research is either unethical or undesirable or both. While the Witherspoon Council argues that the lack of federal funding for research in the United States did not hamper stem cell research, I am inclined to agree with those who think it did. Where we put our money is a statement of where our values lie.

25 I have written briefly on this question and have presented a paper on it to the Pacific Coast Theological Society in April 2013.

Conclusion

At the end of *Alice's Adventures in Wonderland,* we discover that Alice has been dreaming. There was no rabbit hole, no golden key, no beautiful garden, nor any strange creatures. It has all been a dream. We might be tempted to think that this is a cautionary tale, then, pointing us away from our dreams of regenerative medicine. But at the very end of the book, in an often forgotten passage, after Alice has awakened from her dream, her older sister sits and wonders about Alice's wonderland. "[S]he sat on, with closed eyes, and half believed herself in Wonderland, though she knew she had but to open them again, and all would change to dull reality...," writes Carroll. Will we wake up some day and find that our adventures with stem cells are all a dream and there is no Wonderland but only the "dull reality" of everyday medicine? Or is it important to hold onto that dream—that proleptic vision of a world of regenerative medicine? Is there a way to get from our "dull reality" to Wonderland? If there is, I argue, we must respect our ethical principles even as we close our eyes and dream.

The Dialogue between Worlds

Ted Peters' Proleptic, Planetary Ethic

Whitney Bauman

When theologian Ted Peters was faced with the false choice of the world of science and modernity or religion and superstition, as most of us are at some point in the Western world, he said, "No thanks!" Throughout the twentieth century religion has been pushed to the margins of life in contemporary American culture: from the expulsion of theology from public universities, to the ever-growing scientism of the revolutions in genetics and neuroscience, to the increasing globalization of cultures that has led to the relativizing of multiple religious beliefs, more and more the intellectual space of religion has been pushed into the private or personal realms. Some count this as "progress" while others see this as the clear decline of a moral, just, and all around better world. Unlike many of his colleagues, even those in the academy, Peters has consistently refused to make this false choice between some form of atheistic materialism (science) and otherworldly theism (religion). Through his scholarship, teaching, and work at the Center for Theology and the Natural Sciences, Pacific Lutheran Theological Seminary, and the Graduate Theological Union, he has consistently held these two realms together. This dialogical nature has also influenced his environmental ethic—which he taught in the Energy and Resources Department at the University of California—and is the subject of this chapter.

Rather than provide a complete intellectual history of Peters' thinking on the environment (something which I am not equipped to do), I will attempt to couch his environmental ethic in terms of the spatial turn in religion that has taken place in the twentieth century. Given his Tillichian and Pannenbergian influenced theology, (and therefore Heidegerrian influenced theology), Peters' understanding of time and creation is best understood in spatial terms. As such, the worlds of the past and the present are transformed by the possibility of a pregnant transcendent future: the arrow of time is constantly reaching back for the past and present in moments of prolepsis. Such a spatial understanding of the coming of the kingdom or a new creation flies in the face of much contemporary environmentalism which has opted for scientific materialism—an affirmation of the present and past as what is possible—and understands religion as (at best) a tool for motivating some towards environmental action. In outlining the dialogical nature of Peters' environmental ethic, I will first outline what I take to be his understanding of the current, fallen creation. I will then outline the role of human beings within that creation. From here I will examine how his eschatological (proleptic) creation offers us an environmental ethic that deals with the uncertainties and ambiguities of a postmodern, globalizing, and forever changing planet. Such an ethic is not one based upon a past paradise or a clinging to present understandings of "place" or wholeness, but rather is an ethic that looks toward the redemption of a planetary future in possibilities that are not yet known. Finally, I will end this essay with a brief dialogue between Peters' theistic, proleptic ethic and my own agnostic, planetary ethic. Such a dialogue suggests that one is not required to reject religion in order to be pluralistic, nor is one required to reject pluralism in order to be devoted to his/her own tradition.

The Becoming Creation

In *Anticipating Omega*, and in other places, Peters makes clear that value, meaning, and ethics are proleptic in nature.[1] In other words, the meaning of creation lies in the continuing, becoming process and ultimately in its End (Omega) and not in its Origin (Alpha). Such an ontology is one that, similar to process and other postmodern thought, rejects foundationalism that is based upon origins. Peters is not the type of theologian that would look to a prelapsarian creation for an understanding of what is good, right, or ethical in terms of human-human and human-nature relations. Rather, he looks toward the peaceable kingdom or future visions of God's promised "world to come." He writes, "We

---

1 See, e.g., Ted Peters, *Anticipating Omega: Science, Faith, and Our Ultimate Future* (Gottingen, Germany: Vandenhoeck and Ruprecht, 2006), 177ff. Cf. Ted Peters, *GOD— The World's Future: Systematic Theology for a Postmodern Era* (Minneapolis: Fortress Press, 1992), 358.

should orient ethical action around our eschatological vision of a justly ordered creation at peace; and we should take action to transform present destructive trends into constructive attempts at transformation."[2] Lest one think Peters is an idealist, his transcendent, proleptic ethics is based upon and acts within the lived historical past of all creation. In other words, this is not some type of vision of the future that is apocalyptic or escapist, but rather one that is always breaking in to the present history providing possibilities for transformation.

Another very important component of his understanding of creation is, of course, God. God is the future that breaks in and transforms present creation. God's love is that which guides creation toward New Creation. However, just as one cannot look to past nature to dictate the right and wrong way to go about living, so one cannot anticipate fully what the coming creation will, in fact, be. Following Tillich's Protestant Principle, and ultimately the iconoclasm that defines the spirit of the Reformation, Peters agrees that "God cannot be captured, contained, or constrained by human thought, ritual, or political institution."[3] Thus the task of developing a proleptic, planetary ethic for Peters starts with projecting and imagining what this new future is going to look like and working toward that projection, even though that projection is only an imaginative best guess at what God has in store for creation.

Peters' understanding of creation and hope for the future has much in common with postmodern understandings of epistemology/ontology. In other words, whether it is the critique of ultimate origins or final ends (e.g., Michel Foucault), the deconstruction of the link between our thoughts, ideas, and words and some ultimate reality (e.g., Jacques Derrida), or critiques of the understanding of what is natural based upon some sort of materialism (e.g., Donna Haraway), Peters finds a host of dialogue partners in postmodern discourse. The hierarchies critiqued by feminism, the critiques of economism coming from post-colonial and liberation thought, and even the heterosexism critiqued by queer theorists are all based upon a type of epistemic limitation and uncertainty that Peters' proleptic understanding of creation would support. Furthermore, his understanding of the role of humanity is largely in dialogue with these types of postmodern discourses, with a few differences that emerge from his robust theism.

---

2   Peters, *Anticipating Omega*, 186.
3   Ibid., 198.

The Becoming Human

> "Human Becoming" expresses the idea that we are *always in process*, we are a becoming, and being human means that the journey is the reality—there may well be no *final* destination.[4]

Peters' understanding of humans, like that of Hefner, is also based upon the notion of humans evolving with the rest of the planetary community. In other words, Peters largely agrees with critiques of anthropocentrism and other anthropologies that suggest humans are somehow above and beyond the rest of the planetary community and with the type of individualism that places human dignity in original essences. His non-origin-based-essentialist-idea of human becoming would also find many dialogue partners with non-essentialist postmodern thinkers. However, Peters does offer a form of proleptic essence for humans and humanity in general. In other words, he parts ways with Hefner's suggestion that there may be no final destination.

Though he critiques the types of understandings of essential humanity based upon the original Adam and Eve narrative or the *imago*, or any other sort of inherentism,[5] he does understand universal human dignity as proleptic. He writes, "Human dignity belongs at the center of our value system; and we should understand dignity as first conferred, then inherent."[6] In other words, dignity, much like the human person, is relational through and through.[7] The relational self is related to and with other humans and the rest of the planetary community past, present, and future. Ultimately, of course, this relational self is related to the Trinitarian God (Peters follows Jürgen Moltmann and others here). It is founded in God's promise of the kingdom to come and is in this regard different from a theology such as Hefner's (and my own). Regardless, Peters' theological anthropology does represent a significant and in many ways post-modern reworking of autonomy, individualism, and freedom in terms of the planetary common good.

Following closely the work of Robert Bellah, Peters argues that freedom has become reduced to autonomy with the public/private divide in the west, leading to two different meanings of autonomy. He argues that

---

4 Philip Hefner, *Technology and Human Becoming* (Minneapolis: Fortress Press, 2003), 5.
5 Peters, *GOD—The World's Future*, 371.
6 Peters, *Anticipating Omega*, 178.
7 Ibid., 183.

this dual understanding of individual autonomy has created "utilitarian individualism appropriate in the economic and occupational spheres and an expressive individualism appropriate to the private life."[8] He goes on to write that "when translated into political action, the best we can do is have people band together who share the same personal preference, that is, produce self-interest lobbies."[9] In other words, the faulty response to the erosion of a common good in the postmodern era has been a form of parochialism that we might refer to as identity politics in the public sphere and fundamentalism in the religious sphere. As such, there is no global common entity or planetary entity to resist the multinational corporations who long ago outstripped the laws and mores of nation-states. Instead, Peters suggests, we are left with the techno-secular mythology which basically means we are left to the reconstruction of the earth brought about by market forces. Techno-reason has no end in itself and thus market capitalism drives it. The end result, as Peters points out following Lyotard, "is Auschwitz . . . and Auschwitz symbolizes the dead end of technical reason."[10]

Peters echoes here the problem of technology that was pointed out by Heidegger and also the Frankfurt School in various ways. On the one hand, technology founded in market ideologies (the space of secularism in the West) turns the rest of the planet into "standing reserve."[11] The problem is that such an understanding of technology also begins to turn humans into standing reserve: techno-reason kills the very possibility of reason by turning reasonable bodies into market goods.[12] The Band-Aid solution to this problem is typically the "stop-sign" ethics that Peters critiques for being based upon a faulty assumption of what is "natural"

---

8 Ted Peters, *Science, Theology, and Ethics* (Aldershot, United Kingdom: Ashgate, 2003), 256.
9 Ibid.
10 Ted Peters, "Techno-Secularism, Religion, and the Created Co-Creator," in *Zygon* 40, no. 4 (December 2005): 855.
11 Martin Heidegger, *The Question Concerning Technology and Other Essays* (New York: Harper, 1977).
12 See, e.g., Max Horkheimer and Theodor Adorno, *Dialectic of Enlightenment* (Palo Alto, CA: Stanford University Press, 2007), 2: "What human beings seek to learn from nature is how to use it to dominate wholly both it and human beings. Nothing else counts. Ruthless toward itself, the Enlightenment has eradicated the last remnant of its own self-awareness. Only thought which does violence to itself is hard enough to shatter myths."

and what is "human enhanced."[13] Such an anthropology, Peters argues, is anthropocentric for many reasons not the least of which is that it tries to separate humans out from the rest of creation and the coming of God's kingdom. In place of this type of stop-sign ethics, Peters proposes his proleptic planetary ethics, to which I now turn.

A Proleptic, Planetary Ethic

Perhaps the best articulation of how Peters' proleptic, planetary ethic functions is found in his 1980 engagement with the thought of the futurists. In that book, he articulates seven calamities of the contemporary era and then argues that they can only be challenged with faith in the God of the future. Such faith is not blind and certain, and certainly not the same as believing in overall progress. Peters writes:

> Progress is understood as some impersonal principle or force impelling the world in growth or advancement toward some as yet undefined goal. God, on the other hand, is a person with a will and a specific purpose for human history; he acts and reacts in the course of events to accomplish his ends. Progress is not automatic. It is not guaranteed. What is guaranteed is that after all is said and done, God's will will be done. The ultimate or final future is in his hands. God is the power of the future.[14]

In other words, and in relationship to doomsday environmental prophesies both then and now, Peters argues that we need faith in God (as future power of transformation) in order to continue to work towards a "better" tomorrow rather than throw up our hands in despair, give in to some naïve notion that "everything will be alright," or even give into some form of individual hedonism since everything is going to be gone regardless of what we do. Such a faith is indeed the opposite of certainty. We really don't know what the future will hold, something which many scientific and environmental projections deny, but we have faith that what we do now will make some sort of difference. Granted, the power of the future and the unfolding of the future is entirely in God's hands,

---

13 Ted Peters, "Should We Patent God's Creation?" in *Dialog: A Journal of Theology* 35, no. 2 (1996): 120–22. On "stop-sign" ethics, compare Peters, "Proleptic Ethics vs. Stop Sign Ethics: Theology and the Future of Genetics," in *Journal of Lutheran Ethics* (February 2008): 42ff.

14 Peters, *Fear, Faith, and the Future: Affirming Christian Hope in the Face of Doomsday Prophecies* (Minneapolis: Augsburg Publishing House, 1980), 22–23.

according to Peters, but belief in this God as the future is the way that Christians are able to face the future and act, instead of cowering from the future in fear. Peters goes on to articulate a theology of proleptic eschatology as a way of facing the world's social and environmental dilemmas.

He argues that too many churches have developed survival, ideal/utopic, or muddle-through theologies and that the proper response ought to be a proleptic eschatological theology. Such a theology is more than survival and accepting the "end of the world," for, according to Peters, the entire creation is the recipient of God's promise and love. It is also not reliant upon trust in some sort of utopic vision that will emerge out of current science and technology (like the ideal/utopic theology). Finally, it is not the "business as usual" theology (such as the muddle-through theology) Peters critiques. Rather, it is about imagining what the final vision of God's world might look like and developing strategies that enable humanity to reach toward those visions.[15]

It cannot be stressed enough that this proleptic model for ethics that starts with theologically imagining God as future transformation breaking into the present moment, is meant for the entire planet. It is not just for humans and about humans. It may be up to humans to act toward this future on this planet, but it also recognizes that humans are not in control of the destiny of anything. In other words, the God as future model also bucks notions of progress that suggest human mastery is capable of transforming the planet. It keeps a certain amount of humility in the process of co-creating future worlds to live toward and provides spaces for all species and life past, present, and future. Again, as Peters notes,

> We need to view ourselves wholistically. Sometimes this is taken to mean bringing together the body, mind, and spirit of the individual. This is fine. But there is more. We need to view ourselves as part of the whole process of nature, the whole history of God with his creation. We are not alone. As we care for our natural world and as we love one another we proleptically anticipate the unity of the whole of reality yet to arrive in its fullness.[16]

Such words are as important today as they were in 1980. Having said that, I would like to offer some constructive, concluding comments on

---

15 Peters, *Fear, Faith, and the Future*, 25–32.
16 Peters, *Fear, Faith, and the Future*, 120.

Peters' work; these are constructive engagements between his proleptic ethics and my own thinking about planetary ethics.

Finding Common Grounds: An Open-Ended Planetary Future

At the heart of Peters' theology and his understanding of becoming creation is a radical focus on the future. This is evident in just about everything Peters writes, and his works on "the environment" are no different. It is this futurity that filters into my own viable, agnostic, planetary theology.[17]

Such a theology argues that the becoming creation is only viable, or living, when human knowing admits its limitations at the "edges" of our thinking. In other words, our thinking opens onto the rest of the planetary community when we realize that it shades off into uncertainty in the past and the future. We exist in-between, in this ever-evolving planetary community. Thinking that holds onto strong foundations in the past or future reifies creation into its own image and thus fosters much violence toward the planetary community.

In terms of Peters' focus on an eschatological ethic, I am in total agreement. Such an ethic is a very useful tool in combatting imperialisms of all kinds, whether those are divinely ordained relationships in the past, distinctions of what is "natural" or "unnatural" in the present, or misplaced certainty in the future progress of modern science.

In terms of the location of that futurity, Peters and I would probably disagree. For Peters (and Pannenberg), God-as-future is a transcendent reality. For me (and others), this type of futurity may also be too certain, even with our epistemic limitations. The question is (following Karen Barad's work here),[18] do we follow Heisenberg or do we follow Bohr? Heisenberg's uncertainty principle is a problem of epistemology but admits that there is a fixed and certain reality regardless of our ability to grasp that reality. From this position, it seems that ultimately there is a Right and a Wrong. Peters would fall into this in terms of his understanding of God as a transcendent future reality. If we follow Bohr's

---

17 See, e.g., Whitney Bauman, *Theology Creation and Environmental Ethics* (New York: Routledge, 2009) and Whitney Bauman, *Religion and Ecology: Developing a Planetary Ethic* (New York: Columbia University Press, 2014).

18 Karen Barad, *Meeting the Universe Halfway: Quantum Physics and the Engagement of Matter and Meaning* (Durham, North Carolina: Duke University Press, 2007), 97ff.

understanding of complementarity, which I do, then reality is indeterminate. As a result, our very constructions shape reality, and reality can become in many different ways; no one way is certain or correct. This latter position would place the future possibility of becoming life in emergent, possible "lines of flight."[19] In other words, my understanding of futurity is emergent rather than transcendent. It is that which is the ground of possible becomings.[20]

On this difference of the location of future possibilities, I think Peters and I can agree to disagree and still get along just fine in terms of dialogue about what we ought to do. However, there is one other difference that may point to a larger chasm between our ways of thinking. Though to a large degree Peters' proleptic theology is planetary and compatible with the evolutionary sciences (and he articulates a theistic evolution in many places),[21] humans do remain reified as humans in the future. Human dignity, even though relational and conferred, is God's special promise to humanity and leads to some questions in my mind when it comes to imagining the future of the planetary community.

Does this doctrine of eschatological dignity prevent humans in the near future from evolving with other creatures and technologies in some form of trans-humanism? On the one hand, Peters appears to dislike trans-humanism and remains a purist when it comes to the preservation of human dignity. On the other hand, he seems to support research into transgenics (even though his support comes with ethical criteria for doing so). If our job as ethical beings is to help to articulate and imagine the possible future, then by what criteria does Peters maintain a strict species boundary line around humans and their special dignity? I am not suggesting the eradication of humanity, but I am suggesting that evolving beyond our humanity is at least a likely scenario and would lead to ethical considerations different than would imagining humanity as a distinct and special species eternally.

---

19 Gilles Deleuze and Felix Guattari, *A Thousand Plateaus: Capitalism and Schizophrenia* (Minneapolis: University of Minnesota Press, 1987).
20 The literature on emergence theory is vast, but for a good analysis of the type of emergent freedom that I am articulating, see James Haag, *Emergent Freedom: Naturalizing Free Will* (Göttingen: Vandenhoeck and Ruprecht, 2008).
21 See, e.g., Ted Peters and Martinez Hewlett, *Evolution from Creation to New Creation: Conflict, Conversation, and Convergence* (Nashville, Tennessee: Abingdon Press, 2003), 115ff.

Conclusion

Of course, this very tension ties back into the location of God and faith in the revelation of God found in the Bible. Peters does, after all, remain a Christian theologian. What is important here is that Peters chooses (as much as that is possible in an interrelated world of evolving relations into which we all are born through no effort of our own) his theological commitments and treats them as such: choices. They are not meant as eternal foundations to be accepted by all, but they are his epistemic choices and what he believes to be an accurate interpretation of the Christian promise of new life. In other words, he recognizes that he is *response-able* and thus he can dialogue with agnostic people like me, just as much as he can dialogue with new agers, members of MUFON (Mutual UFO Network), creation scientists, and others with whom he holds radically different beliefs. This spirit of dialogue and mutuality serves as a model and invitation for an ever-increasingly globalized, postmodern world fraught with all types of environmental and social problems. Such creative, mutual interactions may just create the very dynamic tensions that will lead us toward a better future than we can possibly imagine from the present moment.[22]

---

22 Robert John Russell, *Cosmology from Alpha to Omega: The Creative Mutual Interaction of Theology and Science* (Minneapolis: Fortress Press, 2008).

Flying Saucers— No Laughing Matter!

Ted Peters and Astrotheology

Albert A. Harrison

On January 14, 1878, John Martin, a Texas farmer, reported seeing a large circular object flying overhead that he described as resembling a "saucer."[1] This label would remain dormant until 1947, when flying near Mt. Rainier in Washington state, pilot Kenneth Arnold spotted nine glittering crescents, flying at unheard-of speeds just a few miles away.[2] By chance a newspaper reporter rediscovered the term "flying saucers" in his description of Arnold's sighting. Many other reports immediately followed Arnold's and they continue today. In July 2014, the National UFO Reporting Center received 1,049 reports.[3] At that time and now, people wonder what has been seen. Perhaps some sort of natural phenomenon or illusion? Secret U.S. or, heaven forbid, Soviet aircraft? Could they be spaceships from another planet? Three years after Arnold's report made the news fewer than five percent of people polled believed that UFOs were extraterrestrial spaceships. But by the end of the 1950s, the "extraterrestrial hypothesis" that flying saucers (now renamed Unidentified Flying Objects or UFOs) came from outer space took hold. Studies over the years show that between 30 and 60 percent of Americans believe that there is life out there, although not all respondents believe

---

1 John A. Keel, "The Flying Saucer Subculture," *Journal of Popular Culture* 8:4 (1975), 871-896.
2 Thomas E. Bullard, *The Myth and Mystery of UFOs* (Lawrence, Kansas: University of Kansas Press, 2010).
3 National UFO Reporting Center, www.ufocenter.com (accessed 24 August 2014).

that UFOs are alien spaceships that have reached Earth. A 2012 survey of 1,114 Americans found that 36 percent of the respondents believe that UFOs exist.[4] This equates to 80 million "believers." About 77 percent of this group thought that aliens had visited Earth. Another survey conducted that same year found that more United Kingdom citizens believe in extraterrestrial life (estimated thirty-three million) than believe in God (estimated twenty million).[5] Twenty percent of the UK respondents thought that UFOs have landed on Earth.

Also in 1947, German engineers and technicians were improving rockets at White Sands, New Mexico. Space travel, relegated to the lands of fantasy and science fiction, was making the transition to reality. By 1950 a massive campaign was underway to convince the American public that spaceflight was both feasible and desirable.[6] In 1957, the Soviet's orbiting of Sputnik, followed by a rapid succession of other firsts, stimulated America's space efforts and led to the creation of the National Air and Space Administration (NASA). The frantic program that placed astronauts on the moon obscured the space agency's other important activities, including research on life and its precursors elsewhere in the universe. Originally known as exobiology, by the mid-1990s NASA's program had morphed into astrobiology, the study of the origin, distribution, and future of life in the universe.[7] Its best known activity is the search for extraterrestrial intelligence, or SETI. Astronomers use radio telescopes to hunt for electromagnetic activity that is intelligently controlled and of extraterrestrial origin.[8]

Astrobiology and SETI seek scientific evidence to inform our thinking about three of the great questions of human existence: Where did we come from? Are we alone? What will become of us?[9] While it may seem like scanning the horizon for extraterrestrial spaceships and listening

---

[4] Jeff Pfeifer, "In Advance of 'Chasing UFOs' Series, NatGeo Releases Results of 'Aliens Among Us Survey,'" *Channel Guide Magazine* (2012), http://www.channelguidemagblog.com/index.php/2012/06/28/ngc-chasing-ufos/ (accessed 22 July 2014).

[5] Lee Spiegel, "More Believe in Aliens Than in God according to U.K. Survey," Huffington Post (8 October 2012).

[6] Howard E. McCurdy, *Space and the American Imagination* (Washington, D.C.: Smithsonian Institution Press, 1997).

[7] Steven J. Dick and James E. Strick, *The Living Universe: NASA and the Development of Astrobiology* (New Brunswick, New Jersey: Rutgers University Press, 2005).

[8] Frank Drake, "The Search for Extra-Terrestrial Intelligence," *Philosophical Transactions of the Royal Society A* 369 (2011): 633–641.

[9] David Des Marais, Joseph A. Nuth, III, et al., "The NASA Astrobiology Roadmap," *Astrobiology* 8, no. 4 (2008): 715–730.

for radio broadcasts originating in other solar systems are synergistic, nothing could be further from the truth.[10] To gain traction in the scientific community SETI had to distance itself from UFOlogy with its fantastic theories, immodest claims, reliance on magical thinking, and deficient reality testing.

Today UFOlogists contend that occupied extraterrestrial spaceships have reached Earth, that governments have retrieved crashed UFOs and cadavers, and that a massive conspiracy hides the fact that "contact" has already been made. Meanwhile, SETI self-identifies as a purely scientific effort. According to some SETI enthusiasts the discovery of extraterrestrial life would give lie to the biblical tale of creation and consign Christianity to the scrap heap of abandoned ideas.

Is there any room for serious theology here? The answer is a resounding "yes," and over the years many religious scholars have pondered the implications of the discovery of life beyond Earth. But it is Ted Peters who, under the organizing concept of astrotheology, has formalized, systematized, and integrated far ranging issues at the juncture of astrobiology and religion.

Astrotheology

Astrotheology is a form of systematic theology that addresses the roles of scripture, history, experience, and reason (including natural science) in human exploits in space. It is "that branch of theology which provides a critical analysis of contemporary space sciences combined with an explication of classic doctrines such as creation and Christology for the purpose of constructing a comprehensive and meaningful understanding of our human situation within an astonishingly immense cosmos."[11] At a minimum, astrotheology is a theology of space science. Astrotheologians look at astrobiology through the broader lens of culture as well as through the eyes of their profession.

A chief task of astrotheology is to keep discussions of space science honest. Peters has identified religious beliefs masquerading as science and reassigned misplaced scientific and religious beliefs to their ap-

---

10 Albert A. Harrison, "How SETI Succeeds in an Era of Pseudoscience and Alternative History," in *Civilizations Beyond Earth: Extraterrestrial Life and Society*, Douglas Vakoch and Albert A. Harrison, eds. (New York: Berghahn, 2011), 141–158.
11 Ted Peters, "Astrotheology," in *The Routledge Companion to Modern Christian Thought*, Chad Meister and James Beilby, ed. (London and New York: Routledge, 2011), 838–854, quote on 838.

propriate categories. A foe of both scientism and false idolatry, Peters has been merciless at unmasking ill-considered, if not fraudulent, ideas about alien intervention in human evolution and culture from antiquity through today. He questions the validity of skeptical arguments condemning UFOlogy, observing that, for example, UFOlogy does include legitimate scientists, that many people within UFOlogy are skeptical about their own field, and that they have good reason to be skeptical of the critics who are skeptical of them. He has interacted frequently and intensively with the astrobiology and UFOlogists communities, and sought to prepare scientists, theologians, and the public for the possible discovery of extraterrestrial life.

God's Chariots

Peters has written extensively on astrotheology, including several major, published works.[12] Although it does not cover all aspects of astrotheology, my favorite is *UFOs: God's Chariots? Spirituality, Ancient Aliens, and Religious Yearnings in the Age of Extraterrestrials*.[13] Developed over five decades, this book's central thesis is that religion and myth permeate thinking about extraterrestrial life. Contrary to public belief, atavistic religious needs—to grasp all that is and become oriented within the broadest reality, to find moral guidance, to maintain hope for the future, and to be forgiven for sins—remain in full force today. However, in our increasingly materialistic world so heavily dominated by science, satisfying these needs with traditional religious beliefs and rituals has become difficult. Embedded in a culture that discourages people from pinning their hopes on God, people turn to science and technology for comfort. Fascination with the prospects of interstellar spacecraft piloted by visitors from benevolent and wise extraterrestrial civilizations is one manifestation of this.

Religious themes appear openly, as in the case of UFO religions, or implicitly when anyone turns to advanced spacemen for answers to great existential questions, for succor and support, and for a brighter future. This is defective theology because an infinite, omniscient, eternal, transcendent, and forgiving supernatural God is abandoned for purely finite natural beings, which by virtue of their advanced technology, project

---

12 Ted Peters, *The Evolution of Terrestrial and Extraterrestrial Life: Where in the World Is God?* (Kitchener, Ontario: Pandora Press, 2008), 118.
13 Ted Peters, *UFOs: God's Chariots? Spiritualty, Ancient Aliens, and Religious Yearnings in the Age of Extraterrestrials* (Pompton Planes, New Jersey: New Page Books, 2014).

god-like qualities to us. Even researchers who study abductees' claims such as "I talked to God" are so focused on finding scientific explanations that they turn a blind eye to religion.

Alien Designs

As Alfred Kracher once remarked, "Until we meet real aliens we should take advantage of the aliens that live in our imagination."[14] These aliens are the products of ancient and modern culture, guesswork, and fantasy. Descriptions are highly anthropomorphic, in part because such interpretations are forced upon us by our cognitive frameworks and psychological processes, and in part because anthropomorphic interpretations create an illusion of familiarity, confer a false sense of control over encounters, and alleviate anxieties about the unknown.[15]

Peters discusses four human roles we assign to extraterrestrials, which appear in reports of encounters of aliens and, less blatantly, in some scholarly discussions of what extraterrestrials may be like. Interstellar Diplomats arrive with friendly greetings, warnings, and helpful advice. The prototype here is Klaatu, the interstellar statesman in the movie "The Day the Earth Stood Still," who arrived in the 1950s to warn us about the perils of nuclear warfare. The Research Scientist comes to study us, much like Charles Darwin traveled on the H.M.S. Beagle to take detailed notes on exotic lands. Human scientists are intensely interested in studying life. Might we not expect similar interests on the part of extraterrestrials? In UFO lore aliens dig up plants, kidnap dogs, sample food, and interact with people oftentimes in clumsy or inappropriate ways. Their brilliance in science and engineering is not matched in anthropology, sociology, and psychology. Celestial Saviors are benevolent entities with god-like powers, who we hope will give us philosophical and scientific insights, practical advice, and insight into the future. As false prophets, it is the Celestial Saviors that play the most prominent role in Peters' thinking.

The Hybridizers are the highly publicized "Little Greys" who kidnap, study, and try to impregnate women. Unlike the roles of emissaries, scientists, and missionaries, the role of the hybridizer is relatively new

---

14 Alfred Kracher, "Meta-Humans and Metanoia: The Moral Dimension of Extraterrestrials," *Zygon* 41, no. 2 (2006): 346.
15 Nicholas Epley, Adam Waytz, and John T. Cappioco, "On Seeing Human: A Three-Factor Theory of Anthropomorphism," *Psychological Bulletin* 114, no. 4 (2007): 864.

and less easily related to standard human activities. Their activities do not seem to be crimes of passion, as the aliens go about their business in cold, emotionally detached ways. However, we can find models in other terrestrial animals where guile and deceit between species contribute to reproductive success.[16] UFO sightings are just the latest installments of a long stream of reported contact with superior beings from the sky. This includes contacts with the angels and other heavenly beings reported in the Bible and later with spiritual masters from other planets.[17] In Western religions, especially, gods were seen as residing in the sky and flying objects were both signs of great power and portents of change. Since sky gods can fly through outer space and we cannot, they are more advanced and powerful than those of us stranded on planet Earth. By the early 1950s a number of "contactees" came forward, including George Adamski, Truman Bethurum, Orfeo Angulucci, Daniel Fry, George King, Howard Menger, and George Van Tassel who reported meeting heavenly beings as far back as the 1930s.[18] In most ways, it was difficult to distinguish them from other prophets, visionaries, and seers. Their accounts differed from those of earlier prophets mainly in that extraterrestrials are material beings that arrived by means of advanced technology rather than via astral projection, channeling, or some other spiritual means. Through public appearances and writings, these contactees spread and reinforced the notion that flying saucers were extraterrestrial spacecraft, and that their occupants were benevolent. In the 1950s a number of new religious movements began, some of which continue (with low enrollment) today.[19] Through sacrifice, prayer, devotion, and ritual, members of these flying saucer religions hope to be rescued before Armageddon or to achieve exalted status when loving extraterrestrials descend on Earth.

Approximately 25 years ago Alan Elms and I wrote that "One 'standard model' of the aliens whom we are most likely to contact" [not all ETI everywhere] "consists of benevolent scientists [that] beam forth endless insights in the physical and perhaps biological or social sciences for the benefit

---

16 Robert Trivers, *The Folly of Fools: The Logic of Deceit and Self Deception in Human Life* (New York: Basic Books, 2011).
17 James R. Lewis, "Introduction," in *Encyclopedic Sourcebook of UFO Religions*, James R. Lewis, ed. (Amherst, New York: Prometheus Books, 2003), 9–14.
18 Mikael Rothstein, "The Rise and Decline of the First Generation UFO Contactees," in *Encyclopedic Sourcebook of UFO Religions*, James R. Lewis, ed. (Amherst, New York: Prometheus Books, 2003), 43–62.
19 James R. Lewis, ed., *Encyclopedic Sourcebook of UFO Religions* (Amherst, New York: Prometheus Books, 2003).

of emerging civilizations such as ours."[20] Certainly, there are pessimistic expectations, but overall, optimism tends to prevail.[21] Much of my own research has been based on the assumption that we are more likely to contact a very old society than a very young society because an old society is more likely to overlap ours in time.[22] The question is do societies achieve great longevity by means of threat and force, or through democratic, peaceful and accommodative activities and (when necessary) defensive pacts? Over time, societies on Earth have accorded increasingly larger groups of people favored insider status; authoritarian governments are giving way to liberal democracies; democracies do not go to war with one another but rather enter into effective defensive pacts; and across many different timescales and locations, violence of all kinds, including warfare, is on the decline. To me, this suggests an edge for finding the "good guys" of the universe. But I do draw a distinction between God and ET.

> SETI is not to be confused with religion and myth, so any superficial similarities among extraterrestrial radio astronomers, God, ancient astronauts, and space brothers have to be taken with a huge grain of salt. God, if He exists, is supernatural. Extraterrestrials would be the product of biological evolution. God is everywhere; extraterrestrials may be scattered here and there throughout the universe. God is omniscient; extraterrestrials would have to use surveillance technology to watch over us. God is eternal; extraterrestrials may be very old, perhaps kept alive by advanced biotechnology or within the electronic circuits of robots and computers. ... Most importantly of all, for religious people, God is a given, but for scientists, extraterrestrials are hypothetical, at least pending empirical verification.[23]

In Peters' view, I just don't get it.

---

20 Albert A. Harrison and Alan C. Elms, "Psychology and the Search for Extraterrestrial Intelligence," *Behavioral Science* 35 (1990): 214.
21 Douglas A. Vakoch, ed., *Extraterrestrial Altruism: Evolution and Ethics in the Cosmos* (Berlin and Heidelberg: Springer Verlag, 2014).
22 Albert A. Harrison, "The Relative Stability of Belligerent and Peaceful Societies: Implications for SETI," *Acta Astronautica* 46, no. 10-12 (2000): 707-712; *Starstruck: Cosmic Visions in Science, Religion and Folklore* (London and New York: Berghahn Books); "Cosmic Evolution, Reciprocity, and Interstellar Tit for Tat," in *Extraterrestrial Altruism: Evolution and Ethics in the Cosmos* (Berlin and Heidelberg: Springer-Verlag, 2014), 3-25.
23 Albert A Harrison, *Starstruck: Cosmic Visions in Science, Religion and Folklore* (London and New York: Berghahn Books, 2007), 99.

The ETI Myth

According to Peters, despite fierce re-assurances to the contrary, even "scientific" discussions are suffused with religion and myth. Why do so many searchers assume that they will discover wise, benevolent, god-like beings living under utopian conditions, just itching to help us solve our problems? The ETI myth refers to widespread beliefs that extraterrestrial beings exist and that they are more advanced than we are.[24] Sometimes the myth includes trust in the evolutionary advance of intelligence and science, suggesting that the more highly evolved form could bring scientific salvation to planet Earth. There is no evidence for this belief, yet it structures our images of extraterrestrials and provides a major base for discussion. Implicit in this myth is the idea that science has the power to save the nations of our world from self-destruction by nuclear war or eco-disaster or related violence. When we look to extraterrestrial science for solutions to Earth's problems, we are relying on a doctrine of progress (because we expect their science to be more advanced than our science). This involves casting a blind eye to the reality that science creates as well as solves problems.

Are we positioning ourselves to become interstellar panhandlers? Ben Finney reminds us that when outsiders armed with advanced technology arrived at some isolated locations (such as Pacific islands) natives sometimes developed "cargo cults" based on beliefs that the gods could send modern technology and a cornucopia of goods by means of airplanes and ships.[25] (After all, they saw airplanes and ships deliver useful supplies to colonial masters and military troops stationed on their lands.) Cargo cults built artifacts (such as fake airplanes and radio stations made of wood, bamboo, and vines) and developed rituals intended to attract real planes bringing real cargo for their personal use. Cannot we be more resourceful than trying to bum freebies from ET?

Christianity in the Post Contact World

Eric Chaisson claims, SETI is "driven by a fierce anthropocentrism, an earnest desire to show that we do not depend on a Creator or intelligent designer."[26] Discovery of intelligent life elsewhere would constitute

---

24 Ted Peters, "Astrotheology and the ETI Myth," *Theology and Science* 7 (2009): 3–20.
25 Ben Finney, "The Impact of Contact," *Acta Astronautica* 31, no. 2 (1990): 117–121.
26 Eric Chaisson, *Cosmic Evolution: The Rise of Complexity in Nature* (Cambridge, Massachusetts: Harvard University Press, 2001), 39.

proof positive that intelligence is the result of purely natural rather than divine processes. Yet many leading theologians are highly receptive to the notion of extraterrestrial life and would view the discovery as further testimony to the greatness of God. Constance Bertka recently suggested that this battle consists largely of scientists announcing that the discovery of extraterrestrial life will be problematic for religion while theologians offer counterarguments.[27] We can supplement opinion with fact by considering Ted Peters and Julie Louise Froehlig's religious crisis survey.

Peters and Froehlig conducted an internet survey of 1,325 adherents to the world's established religious traditions (Roman Catholicism, mainline Protestantism, evangelical Protestantism, Orthodox Christianity, Mormonism, Islam, Judaism, and Buddhism) and nonbelievers. They found that 83 to 94 percent of the respondents (depending on religious affiliation) strongly disagreed with the statement "Official confirmation of the discovery of intelligent beings living on another planet would so undercut my beliefs that my beliefs would face a crisis." They were slightly less confident that their religious tradition would be unshaken, but still 67 percent of the Catholics, 73 percent of the evangelical Protestants, and 99 percent of the mainline Protestants disagreed strongly that the discovery would precipitate a crisis within their faiths. Intriguingly, respondents could see how such a discovery could cause a crisis within other people's religions. Agnostics and atheists were more likely to expect religious crises than were the members of the religious groups themselves. Will some religious people be troubled by the discovery of ETI? Probably, but the same will be true for some people from every other sociological category. There is plenty of room for future research.

Conclusion

Ted Peters' work in astrotheology has made important contributions to theology as we take one more step beyond geocentrism and broaden our perspective on a universe that is fourteen billion light years across. He has made significant progress at the juncture of theology and astrobiology, including acknowledging the unmentionable, that ever-present elephant in the living room, UFOs. Flying saucers are no laughing matter

---

[27] Constance M. Bertka, "Christianity's Response to the Discovery of Extraterrestrial Life: Insights from Science and Religion and the Sociology of Religion," *Astrobiology, History, and Society*, Douglas A. Vakoch, ed. (Berlin and Heidelberg: Springer Verlag, 2013).

because UFO lore shapes people's views of extraterrestrial life and will influence their reactions to an authenticated discovery. UFOs have been part of popular culture for almost seventy years. UFOlogy is the spider in the center of a web that attracts all sorts of paranormal ideas and conspiracy theories. Richard Dolan writes, "a proper study of UFOs is a revolutionary experience. It shatters the old belief systems and forces us to look at the world in a completely new way. Everything is affected: history, politics, economics, science, religion, culture, and our ultimate vision of who and what we are as human beings."[28] There is much wishful thinking about UFOs and perhaps most wishful of all is that better science education will somehow make UFOs go away.

We should not be surprised that so many people react with wonder, awe, and reverence to UFOnauts because they react to astronauts and cosmonauts pretty much the same way. Spaceflight, like the search for extraterrestrial life, is also suffused with religion and myth. Russian cosmists, for example, sought to gather up the dust of all past generations, resurrect them (by purely scientific means), and let them populate other planets where they would live forever in solidarity.[29] They also hoped that through space exploration and settlement they could achieve perfection and attain everlasting life. During the great race to the Moon, god-fearing American astronauts were pitted against godless cosmonauts.[30] Astronauts read scripture and took communion in space. Two Bibles that made bureaucratically perilous journeys may be found on the Moon. Today, astronaut religious activity is muted by the separation of church and state, but before departure, cosmonauts receive from Russian Orthodox priests, and carry religious scripture and icons on the International Space Station. Some astronauts and cosmonauts report transcendent experiences and their resulting recommendations (let's abolish war and protect Earth's fragile ecosystem) bear an eerie resemblance to the advice given to contactees. For space aficionados, outer space is a promised land, which offers life without limits and solutions to Earth's problems, as well as transcendent experiences and salvation. Typically, people involved in space exploration insist that they are scien-

---

28 Richard M. Dolan, *UFOs and the 21st Century Mind* (Rochester, New York: Richard Dolan Press, 2014), 2.
29 Albert A. Harrison, "Russian and American Cosmism: Religion, National Psyche, and Spaceflight," *Astropolitics: The International Journal of Space Politics & Policy* 11, no. 1–2 (2014): 25–44.
30 Albert A. Harrison, "Astrotheology and Spaceflight: Prophecy, Transcendence and Salvation on the High Frontier," *Science & Theology* 12, no. 1 (2014): 30–48.

tists and their work is not related to religion, but Roger Launius argues that it is precisely because spaceflight is religion that manned spaceflight continues despite tepid results.[31] For Peters and other astrotheologians, the sky is not the limit, and their work has just begun.

---

31 Roger D. Launius, "Escaping Earth: Human Spaceflight as Religion," *Astropolitics: The International Journal of Space Politics & Policy* 11, no. 1–2 (2013): 45–64.

Astrobiology, Theology, and Ethics

Brian Patrick Green

Through his work, Ted Peters has given us a unique permission to dream[1]—permission to dream about God's creation not only as it is right now on Earth, but also how it might be elsewhere in the universe both now and in the future. He has taken three of the grandest fields of human endeavor—astrobiology, theology, and ethics—and pioneered them into the new field of astrotheology.[2]

In this chapter I will present three areas in which Peters' work has motivated my own thinking. First, I want to consider the idea of convergent cultural, theological, and moral evolution between humans and other intelligent life-forms, terrestrial or otherwise. Second, I want to consider the possibilities for divergences between these two groups. Lastly, I want to consider some of the larger-scale evolutionary issues at play in this theorizing, consider a few scenarios, and suggest some directions for future inquiry.

Imagining the Other and Seeing Ourselves

Can we have any expectations of intelligent life-forms? First, we need to define what an "intelligent life form" is and to investigate whether we have any other data points for what intelligent life-forms look like. For the purposes of this essay I will define material intelligent life forms as "self-conscious, learning, tool-makers, and symbol-makers." Humans clearly fit; we

---

[1] Not only permission, but also something of a mandate: "I recommend the theological community begin a research program..." Ted Peters, "Detecting ET and the Implications for Life on Earth," *Theology and Science* 8 (2010): 124. I am pleased to oblige.
[2] Though as Peters notes, the term "astro-theology" originated in 1714 with Anglican clergyman William Derham. Ted Peters, "Astrotheology," in *The Routledge Companion to Modern Christian Thought*, Chad Meister and James Beilby, eds. (London: Routledge, 2013). Peters has also previously used the term "exotheology."

are self-conscious, and we need society in order to learn symbolic language and tool culture, especially during our long childhood development. These traits are necessary for society, culture, and technology.

What about other creatures on our planet? The great apes, elephants, some cetaceans, and magpies can all pass mirror-self-recognition tests.[3] Many of them (as well as some other creatures) are also swift learners and tool-makers and can even manipulate and communicate via symbols.[4] But none of them utilize these traits to the extent that humans do. They are semi-intelligent. We are more semi-intelligent.

Why is *the extent* of these traits so important? These traits make culture possible, and culture requires intelligence—it requires teachers and learners, as well as a means of communication between the two. Reliance on culture indicates an adaptable intelligence, one marked by communication and learning.

I think we can expect intelligent life forms of extraterrestrial origin also to be like us in these ways (provided they are not significantly more technologically self-modified than we are, i.e., they are not yet "post-aliens"). They will most likely be socio-cultural toolmakers with symbolic language, related bodily systems for manipulating tools and generating symbolic representations, long childhoods for teaching and learning, and so on. In short, there may only be one way to be an intelligent species.[5]

The idea of convergent biological evolution raises the question of convergent cultural evolution. Might there also only be one way to have

---

[3] See, for example, Gordon G. Gallup, "Chimpanzees: Self-Recognition," *Science* 169 (1970): 86–7; Karyl B. Swartz, Dena Sarauw, and Sian Evans, "Comparative Aspects of Mirror Self-Recognition in Great Apes," in *The Mentalities of Gorillas and Orangutans: Comparative Perspectives*, Sue Taylor Parker, Robert W. Mitchell, H. Lyn Miles, eds. (Cambridge: Cambridge University Press, 1999), 283–94; Diana Reiss and Lori Marino, "Mirror Self-Recognition in the Bottlenose Dolphin: A Case of Cognitive Convergence," *Proceedings of the National Academy of Sciences* 98 (May 1, 2001): 5937–42; Joshua M. Plotnik, Frans B.M. de Waal, and Diana Reiss, "Self-Recognition in an Asian Elephant," *Proceedings of the National Academy of Sciences* 103 (November 7, 2006): 17053–57; Helmut Prior, Ariane Schwarz, Onur Güntürkün, "Mirror-Induced Behavior in the Magpie (Pica pica): Evidence of Self-Recognition," *PLoS Biology* 6 (August 2008): e202.

[4] R. Allen Gardner and Beatrice T. Gardner, "Teaching Sign Language to a Chimpanzee," *Science* 165 (15 August 1969): 664–72; Gavin R. Hunt, "Manufacture and Use of Hook-Tools by New Caledonian Crows," *Nature* 379 (18 January 1996): 249–51.

[5] Simon Conway Morris describes this very well in his book, *Life's Solution: Inevitable Humans in a Lonely Universe* (New York: Cambridge University Press, 2003).

morality, or certain moral norms? Might the religions of other life-forms, terrestrial or otherwise, resemble human ones purely due to convergent evolution and the necessities built into creation from the beginning?

This raises the question of whether there could be multiple incarnations of Jesus in the universe.[6] I assert that multiple incarnations are likely to be found among extraterrestrial intelligent (ETI) civilizations *even if God did not exist*. Call them false-positive Jesus Christs, or even "false-messiahs."

In general, it should not surprise us that if at some point in the future we encountered ETIs with religion, we would see similarities. We should expect prophet traditions, mystical traditions, asceticism, avatars, god-kings, and the like. Assuming these ETIs are technologically comparable to us, they probably also have the scientific method, which means we will probably also share some metaphysical presuppositions with them. And if we have shared metaphysical presuppositions, then perhaps we will have religious similarities, even incarnating gods. Certainly on Earth the idea seems to have appeared multiple times, in various ways.

So are there multiple incarnations? If there are ETIs at all, then I think the answer will be yes. But beware the false-positives, and we may have no way of distinguishing true from false. Of further theological interest would be that multiple incarnations, true or false, could make Christianity more similar to Hinduism, where particular avatars gain the allegiances of devotees. Will Christians someday worship the incarnations of other worlds? And will it be right to do so? The speculation may never be answered, but I think it is worth trying to stretch our theology to see if it is steadfast, bends, or breaks.

On the larger ethical scale, I believe we can expect ETIs to be ethically similar to us.[7] This is both good and bad. Good because we will be comprehensible to each other. Bad because we may not treat each other well. Convergent evolution will be both our friend and foe if we meet ETIs. With all the good and evil that entails, they will be like us.

---

6   See, for example, Ted Peters, "The Implications of the Discovery of Extra-Terrestrial Life for Religion," *Philosophical Transactions of the Royal Society A* 369 (2011): 651–52, and Ted Peters, *The Evolution of Terrestrial and Extraterrestrial Life: Where in the World Is God?* Carl S. Helrich, ed. (Kitchener, Ontario: Pandora Press, 2008) 123–32, 163–64.

7   As Conway Morris notes in *Life's Solution*, 313, referencing G.K. Chesterton, "The Blue Cross," in *The Innocence of Father Brown* (London: Cassell, 1940) 22; also Robert John Russell, "What Are Extraterrestrials Really Like?" in *God for the 21st Century*, Russell Stannard, ed. (West Conshohocken, Pennsylvania: Templeton Press, 2000) 65–67; and Peters, "The Implications of the Discovery of Extra-Terrestrial Life for Religion," 649–51.

Imagining Ourselves and Seeing the Other

Except that they may no longer be like us. History has not yet ended. As Francis Fukuyama noted in *Our Posthuman Future*, his follow-up book to *The End of History and the Last Man*, political-economic history, which he predicted would "end" on democratic liberalism because that best suits human nature, might not "end" there because technology could change human nature.[8] And then history would be on the move again.

The contemporary tranhumanist/posthumanist/humanity+ movement seeks to improve human nature, enhancing us towards a nearly unimaginable future.[9] In its most conservative it seeks to use eugenic means to make humans smarter, healthier, stronger, and so on. In its most outlandish it seeks to upload humans into computerized immortality.

Some transhumanist ideas are not worthy of serious consideration, but others are very possible indeed. Humans are already being mechanically and electronically integrated with artifacts, for example, with implanted neural stimulators that can restore sight to the blind and move robotic arms by thought alone.[10] What are currently medical treatments for dire conditions could turn into piloting drones by thought, or connecting one's brain to a bat to experience bat-ness.[11] Rats have

---

8 Francis Fukuyama, *Our Posthuman Future: Consequences of the Biotechnology Revolution* (New York: Picador, 2002) and Francis Fukuyama, *The End of History and the Last Man* (New York: The Free Press, 1992).

9 Ted Peters has covered the intellectual territory on transhumanism as well: Ted Peters, *Anticipating Omega: Science, Faith, and Our Ultimate Future* (Göttingen: Vandenhoeck and Ruprecht, 2006) 106–53; Ted Peters, "Progress and Provolution: Will Transhumanism Leave Sin Behind?" in *Transhumanism and Transcendence: Christian Hope in an Age of Technological Enhancement*, Ronald Cole-Turner, ed. (Washington, DC: Georgetown University Press, 2011); and Ted Peters, "H-: Transhumanism and the Post-Human Future: Will Technological Progress Get us There?" *Metanexus* (September 1, 2011) http://www.metanexus.net/magazine/tabid/68/id/10546/Default.aspx (accessed March 28, 2013).

10 Eberhart Zrenner et al, "Subretinal Electronic Chips Allow Blind Patients to Read Letters and Combine Them to Words," *Proceedings of the Royal Society B* (3 November 2010) http://rspb.royalsocietypublishing.org/content/early/2010/11/01/rspb.2010.1747.full (accessed March 28, 2013), and Jennifer L. Collinger et al, "High-Performance Neuroprosthetic Control by an Individual with Tetraplegia," *The Lancet* 381 (16 February 2013): 557 – 64.

11 Thus answering Thomas Nagel's famous article asking "What Is It Like to Be a Bat?" *The Philosophical Review* 83 (October 1974): 435–50.

already had their brains linked to each other in this way.[12] The next step, I offer with only mild humor, will be undergrads.[13]

How will human nature change when we can command computers by thought alone and communicate with each other via telepathy? Previous generations have a hard enough time understanding youngsters now, with their texting and Twitter, just wait until *they* can't understand *their* children, with telepathy, telekinesis, and who-knows what.

All of this makes the future extremely unpredictable. By the time we are getting any distance into space we might be sending crews who are neurally integrated with each other and their onboard computers. And their onboard computers will likely be good approximations of artificial intelligences. This is a possible future, one that might occur if we let it.

Now imagine this strange human-crew-ship-entity encountering another intelligent species, one that has also technologically modified itself. Likely at some point in the past these two sides would have resembled each other and been comprehensible to humans of the early twenty-first century. But even the "humans" in this scenario are too alien to comprehend, much less the actual aliens. How can we envision the truly-alien when we cannot even envision ourselves in fifty or one hundred years?—assuming we still exist in fifty or one hundred years.

And this brings us to a few scenarios which I would like to propose as possible futures.

Where Act Becomes Being

It is a fundamental axiom of Catholic natural law that *agere sequitur esse*: action follows being. The identity of a thing will determine how it behaves. A rock will act like a rock. A sapling will act like a sapling. A human will act like a human.

Ontologically, action follows being. But epistemologically, we know being by its actions.[14] Thus, if the activity of something changes we may

---

12 Miguel Pais-Vieira, Mikhail Lebedev, Carolina Kunicki, Jing Wang, and Miguel A.L. Nicolelis, "A Brain-to-Brain Interface for Real-Time Sharing of Sensorimotor Information," *Scientific Reports* 3 (28 February 2013): article 1319, http://www.nature.com/srep/2013/130228/srep01319/pdf/srep01319.pdf (accessed March 28, 2013).

13 Indeed, shortly after writing this, a human brain-to-brain interface was done, though not undergrads. See Rajesh P.N. Rao et al, "A Direct Brain-to-Brain Interface in Humans," *PLOS One* 9 (5 November 2014): e111332.

14 This relates to Peters' excellent question "Where's 'Nature' in 'Natural Law'?" *Theology and Science* 7 (2009): 115–17. Natural science is a good place to turn for information for natural law.

well have to re-describe the identity of that thing. For example, a caterpillar may become a butterfly. The caterpillar contained an unrealized potency, a potency which later actualized, and if we did not expect such an occurrence we would have to alter our future expectations of such similar creatures. What we believed to be the identity of the creature would need to be updated.

But humans are particularly difficult to deal with for natural law, especially now that we are gaining the ability to actually manipulate our own human nature.[15] The first question is whether this transformation is more like that of a caterpillar to a butterfly—that humans always could do this but merely never expressed the potency (thus humans would be something like "the creature whose nature is to change its nature"), or whether this is more properly thought of as an act unnatural to humans, that it is not a proper potency being realized, but rather an improper expression of human nature's power being directed towards damaging itself rather than perfecting itself. And if this is a moral question for human self-manipulation, it also raises the question of the morality of evolution as a whole.

Evolution is that process by which efficient causes lead to changes in formal cause over time. In other words, actions change being. Like in virtue ethics, only across generations, actions become identity. Long ago some creatures evolved more towards eating meat and others more towards eating plants. Eventually some creatures became extremely specialized towards one side or the other. Biology in conjunction with behavior yielded permanent changes in both biology and behavior. And at this point we might ask ourselves: was this the right thing to do? Where is morality in all of this?

Because perhaps it is immoral to eat meat. Genesis 1–3 seems to imply that possibility since God explicitly tells Adam and Eve to eat of the fruit of the garden (except one). Eating of the fruit of the garden implies

---

15 As I have discussed previously: Brian Patrick Green, "Could Transhumanism Change Natural Law?" presented to the American Academy of Religion's Transhumanism and Religion Group at the national meeting in San Francisco, California, November 19–22, 2011; Brian Patrick Green, "The Human Future: Changing Human Nature and Changing Natural Law," presented to the 3rd annual Student Symposium on Science and Spirituality of the Zygon Center for Religion and Science, Chicago, Illinois, March 25, 2011; and Brian Patrick Green, "Transhumanism and Catholic Natural Law: Changing Human Nature and Changing Moral Norms," in *Religion and Transhumanism: The Unknown Future of Human Enhancement*, Calvin Mercer and Tracy J. Trothen, eds. (Santa Barbara, California: Praeger, 2015) 201–16.

eating of its excess, not its essential being. Eating an animal kills it. Eating a fruit just prevents another plant from growing; it does not harm the plant itself.

So has evolution forced us into immoral natures? And if so, do these natures need correction? And if our natures are morally flawed and need correction, should we do so? And—and this is a desperately dangerous "and"—should we also impose those moral understandings on other humans and creatures? Perhaps all carnivory on Earth ought to be stopped. Furthermore, if we adopt this ethic, then if or when we encounter extraterrestrial creatures, will we see fit to do the same to them? Even if they are intelligent and disagree with us? And if we do not choose this ethic, what if we encounter another intelligent species that has? And what if it thinks it ought to impose these morals upon us? Here we enter the realm of science fiction.

Artificial intelligence theorist Eliezer Yudkowsky once wrote a short story called "Three Worlds Collide" about just such a dangerous, first-contact encounter between three highly divergent intelligent species.[16] The first are humanity. The second are the "Babyeaters"—crystalline beings that eat the majority of their own offspring. The third are the "Superhappies"—blobs that reject permitting any form of pain and whose genetic and neural information are the same substance.[17] All three species immediately find the others intolerably defective, immoral, and dangerous.

The issue of "technological humanitarian intervention" becomes a moral question when confronted by the "defective" natures of other species. In "Three Worlds Collide," the natures and concomitant moralities of the ETIs in question are incompatible. The Superhappies, being the most powerful, demand to alter the natures of all three alien species, in order to make all acceptable to all. If the other species refuse, they will be destroyed.

---

16 Eliezer Yudkowsky, "Three Worlds Collide," *Less Wrong* website, http://lesswrong.com/lw/y4/three_worlds_collide_08/ (accessed 27 March 2013).

17 It should be mentioned that the Superhappies are the epitome of everything that transhumanism stands for: the unrestrained pursuit of happiness and unlimited control over the human body's information, both genetic and neural. This ultimate control over nature is, by the way, extremely dangerous. There is good reason that we cannot, simply by one thought, mutate the DNA in our cells. It would be suicide. God, as necessary Being-in-Itself, could do it, but humans, as contingent creatures, cannot. This is a very theologically relevant point for transhumanism.

Returning to the ideas of convergent and divergent evolution, in "Three Worlds Collide," the ETIs do manage to be significantly different from humanity, and furthermore, bent on doing good, become "alien enemies" of a particularly nefarious sort: Interstellar do-gooders—missionaries of the right and just—as they see it—empowered with advanced technology. Cultures on Earth are still experiencing this. And so they hate us for our lack of their morals.

Peters has discussed the "alien enemies" paradigm before, usually in conjunction with the benevolent "ETI myth," but—despite having written an entire book on sin[18]—I think he has perhaps not taken the potential "evilness" of the enemies seriously enough.[19] Whether do-gooders or cold-blooded killers, ETIs even slightly more advanced than we are—in other words with technology we can already envision today—could exterminate humanity before we even knew they existed. In the novel *The Killing Star*, by Charles Pellegrino and George Zebrowski, the authors create a story around the simple fact that any species capable of interstellar flight at relativistic speeds is also capable of destroying entire planetary ecosystems just by crashing a ship into a planet at relativistic speeds.[20] Such weapons are called "relativistic bombs." In fact, destroying a planetary ecosystem would actually only take half the energy of a successful interstellar flight because it would only have to accelerate towards the target, not accelerate and then slow down again. It is actually easier to devastate planets than to travel between them. And the weapon yield is limited only by the amount of energy the enemy is willing to put into it.

Furthermore, the authors propose a reason why the Fermi Paradox may be the case: all ETIs are hiding, trying to escape detection, lest they be targeted and destroyed. Like a sort of nightmarish galactic "Central Park" at night,[21] the only sounds ever heard are occasional pleas for help and death-screams, or perhaps a bumbling ignoramus, new to the neighborhood and thinking only the best of people, who just walks through whistling happily, not knowing what lies ahead. Likewise ETIs may have

---

18 Ted Peters, *Sin: Radical Evil in Soul and Society* (Grand Rapids, Michigan: Wm. B. Eerdmans Publishing Co., 1994).

19 Peters, "The Implications of the Discovery of Extra-Terrestrial Life for Religion," 648–51; even while discussing Stephen Hawking's warnings of "alien enemies" in "ET: Alien Enemy or Celestial Savior," *Theology and Science* 8 (2010): 245–46, the ETIs are less evil than possible.

20 Charles Pellegrino and George Zebrowski, *The Killing Star* (New York: Avon Books, 1995).

21 Ibid., 126–27.

the motivation to launch these attacks as well—because they know just as well that we might someday do the same to them. Any risk of extinction is too high. Therefore the logic is simply to strike first, following the old saying that it is better to "get them before they get you."

Of course, those searching for ETIs already know these things.[22] Luckily, ETIs must be godlike in both their technology and their morality—or at least so goes the myth.[23] "The Peters ETI Religious Crisis Survey" revealed this bias among non-religious participants, and it is an entirely unwarranted assumption.[24] Broadcasting our presence, then, might be a bad idea, but surely just listening could not be dangerous, right? Surely if the universe is a dangerous place, we ought to at least listen and learn about it, right?

Well, maybe not. Pellegrino and Zebrowski, as well as other researchers, have suggested that ETIs could also send malicious computer viruses through interstellar messaging,[25] even instructions to build an unfriendly artificial intelligence, or to build a universal replicator—a sort of ultimate 3D printer—as a "gift."[26] But this gift would be an interstellar Trojan Horse, perhaps generating dangerous products such as nanotechnological robots that would proceed to devour everything on the Earth; the "grey goo" or "global ecophagy" scenarios visited upon

---

22 For example, Seth D. Baum, Jacob D. Haqq-Misra, and Shawn D. Domagal-Goldman, "Would Contact with Extraterrestrials Benefit or Harm Humanity? A Scenario Analysis," *Acta Astronautica* 68 (2011): 2114–29.

23 The ETI myth has been a major interest of Peters; see Ted Peters, "Astrotheology and the ETI Myth," *Theology and Science* 7 (2009): 3–30; Ted Peters and Julie Froehlig, "The Peters ETI Religious Crisis Survey," *Counterbalance: New Views on Complex Issues* website, (2008), http://www.counterbalance.org/etsurv/fullr-frame.html (accessed March 28, 2013); Peters, "The Implications of the Discovery of Extra-Terrestrial Life for Religion," 648–51; Peters, "ET: Alien Enemy or Celestial Savior," 245–46; Peters, *The Evolution of Terrestrial and Extraterrestrial Life*, 101–32. See also Albert A. Harrison, "The ETI Myth: Idolatrous Fantasy or Plausible Inference?" *Theology and Science* 8 (2010): 51–68; and for the opposing myth, Christopher Partridge, "Alien Demonology: The Christian Roots of the Malevolent Extraterrestrial in UFO Religions and Abduction Spiritualities," *Religion* 34 (2004): 163–89.

24 Peters and Froehlig, "The Peters ETI Religious Crisis Survey," 13–14.

25 Pellegrino and Zebrowski, *The Killing Star*, 123–24; Baum et al, "Would Contact with Extraterrestrials Benefit or Harm Humanity?" section 6.2; and R.A. Carrigan, Jr., "Do Potential SETI Signals Need to Be Decontaminated?" *Acta Astronautica* 58 (2006): 112–17.

26 In light of this, a novel like Carl Sagan's *Contact* (New York: Simon and Schuster, 1985), where humans follow intricate ETI instructions to build a powerful machine, seem extremely naïve.

us just by listening to space.²⁷ Moreover, given that 3D printing technology is already progressing extremely quickly, maybe they wouldn't need to even send instructions to build the Trojan Horse. We can build it for them, and then the virus can just commandeer a few and set them to print replicators until they eat everything.

Perhaps we need not only to be quiet, but also to cover our ears.

It All Comes Back to (the Problem of) Evil

All these ideas for horrible outcomes raise, again, a theodicy problem for Christianity. "The Peters ETI Religious Crisis Survey" revealed that most religious believers did not feel that their faith would be personally threatened by the discovery of ETIs. After all, Christianity has already dealt with the discovery of one New World; what problem would a few more be? However, in the survey comments another possibility was suggested. *It depends on the kind of aliens.*²⁸

I agree. If the aliens are just regular folks like we are, then they present no difficulties for theology. But what if they are disturbingly different from us, or they are evangelical atheists, or they simply destroy us before we even get to say hello? Of course, if we are dead we cannot personally lose our faith, but the theodicy question would still stand even in the absence of humans to ask it: how could God permit such things? Would God permit the extermination of humanity by ETIs? God already has permitted the extermination, by *Homo sapiens*, of the Neanderthals, the Denisovans, and *Homo floresiensis*, barring the few that may have interbred. What are we to think of a God who would make a nature where such things can occur? How can we trust a Lord who has permitted and who will continue to permit such atrocities?²⁹

One traditional response to this argument was once offered to me by a Hasidic rabbi. If God does not exist, then such evils are not evil. They

---

27 K. Eric Drexler, *The Engines of Creation: The Coming Era of Nanotechnology* (New York: Anchor Press Doubleday, 1986) 172–73.

28 Peters and Froehlig, "The Peters ETI Religious Crisis Survey," Appendix 4, 65–101.

29 We might also note that if humans are the only intelligent species to have experienced a true Incarnation of God, this might "protect" us as bearers of the revelation of God, or it might not. Perhaps God would allow this revelation to go silent, by allowing us to be destroyed, thus leaving the universe forever in theological darkness. Or God could always raise up another species elsewhere to replace us. Relatedly, if there are multiple incarnations, that might make us less special and therefore less likely to receive special protection after all, if we go extinct, there will still be other incarnations to reveal God's presence to the universe.

can only be evil if God exists. This dissolves the problem, but still leaves God's character in question. Do we really just have to have faith, even in the face of such disturbing evidence of God's lack of interest in our temporal welfare? Yes. There are other ways to answer it, but they all just boil down to "yes." Jesus Christ makes a big difference, but in some ways, through his horrible death, he just re-emphasizes the "yes." We either accept that or we don't.

Many will not accept this answer. So I will offer one last thought before concluding. In the face of a universe that seems broken, and in the face of a lack of convincing evidence that, to quote Julian of Norwich "all shall be well," there is an understandable human drive to correct things on our own. Nature is broken. Human nature is broken. Both nature and human nature leave room for improvement, it seems, and we cannot sit idly by and live in that brokenness. If we have the power to act, and empowered by our technology we will, it seems by all that is right, that we should.

With that decision we have chosen the path of the knowledge of good and evil. What was once the exclusive province of nature we shall have stolen and bent to our will—or it will be bent to our will—technology and government willing. The universe must be corrected, and we are the only ones to do it. "You will be like gods," the snake promised. And to preserve our integrity, we must make the lie true.

To resist these interventions would be immoral. Or so it might seem.[30]

Conclusion

The intersection of astrobiology, theology, and ethics is fanciful intellectual territory. It is a land for dreamers. The questions raised are fascinating and difficult. But in the absence of any kind of evidence for non-terrestrial life we must ask ourselves, ultimately, what we can gain from it. The answer is that we gain our humanity. With difficult ideas we stretch our theological and ethical horizons. We strive for excellence. And we might even have practical benefits as well, though we may never know. What once seemed unimportant can suddenly become catastrophically important. Multiple incarnations? Currently irrelevant. If

---

[30] Karl Rahner addressed some of these issues with the neurotic pursuit of power over life and nature in two famous essays: "Experiment Man," *Theology Digest* 16 (1968): 61, and "The Problem of Genetic Manipulation," *Theological Investigations* 9 (1972): 205–22, as has Alasdair MacIntyre in "Seven Traits for the Future," *The Hastings Center Report* 9 (1 February 1979): 5–7.

we discover an ETI civilization that *has one*? Good thing to have thought about it first.

Then, until then, we search. We dream. We try to think the impossible. We sometimes succeed.

And that is something ETIs can do for us, whether they are angelic or demonic, and whether they really exist or not.

Terrestrial Ethics and Extraterrestrial Astrotheology

Ted Peters

During an office visit to one of my University of Chicago professors, Joe Sittler, I heard an idea that became cardinal for the way in which I ground ethics in theology. Sittler was waxing about Teilhard de Chardin and the implications of Teilhardian ethics for caring for our Earth. An ethic like Teilhard's would begin with a vision of a transformed future, said Joe.[1] Then, we would seek to fulfill this vision through our moral action.

I heard virtually the same thing from Carl Braaten at almost the same period in my studies. But, instead of Teilhard, Braaten was footnoting Wolfhart Pannenberg. Braaten's focus was on Pannenberg's concept of prolepsis: the pre-actualization of the future in the present. We begin with a vision of God's eschatological future, argued Braaten, and this vision lets loose the revolutionary impulse to transform present injustices accordingly.[2] With the help of Sittler and Braaten I began to formulate what would become my own version of proleptic ethics. What attracted me was the full integration of ethics with eschatology.

Immediately after departing graduate school I became a futurist and eco-ethicist. What I found in the World Future Society was a secular version of proleptic ethics. Futurists operated with what I identified as the u-d-c formula: understanding-decision-control. The first futurist task was to employ scientific methods to *understand* current trends and where they may be leading and to forecast alternative futures. The second task was to lay out the alternative futures before our moral conscience and ask us to *decide* which possible future to actualize. The third task was to

---

1   Joseph Sittler, *The Ecology of Faith* (Philadelphia: Muhlenberg Press, 1961).
2   Carl E. Braaten, *The Future of God* (New York: Harper, 1969).

initiate a plan of action. This action, believed the futurists, would give us *control* over our own destiny, perhaps even control over our future evolution. The idea of control seemed too promethean to me; yet, I resonated with the general structure of futurist ethics.[3]

Also important to me at that time was the presumption that only a planetary model for ethical deliberation would work. Whether we like it or not, the days of localism, parochialism, and even nationalism are over. At least, morally over. Decisions regarding our future must be worldwide decisions that lead to actions with impact on our entire terrestrial sphere. A single planetary society engaged in moral deliberation. Wow! I was drawn especially to this global dimension of futurist thinking.

My own contribution, I thought, would be to announce on the basis of the gospel that a better world is coming. I thought I could provide solid theological reasons for hope, for trusting that we would see revolution, transformation, and betterment in the future. Buckminster Fuller had challenged the world to choose between utopia and oblivion. It seemed to me that we should envision utopia and then formulate middle moral maxims for proleptic betterment of the world we live in. This seemed to me to mark a point of convergence between secular ethics and Christian ethics. An inspired Christian could and should contribute to the public square.

But, to my dismay, the futurists were as ignored as a belch in a crowded elevator. This was the early 1970s. Futurists forecasted that we would destroy our ozone layer leading to increased skin cancer, but our non-existent planetary society failed to make the decisions necessary to prevent destruction of the ozone layer by airborne pollutants. Futurists forecasted that 40 million people would die from AIDS, and 40 million people died from AIDS. Futurists forecasted that anthropogenic practices such as fossil fuel burning would lead to global warming; now we have a hotter planet. On the other side, futurists forecasted that population growth would lead to massive starvation, yet food production has kept pace. On it goes. In virtually no case has the world taken heed of futurist forecasts with sufficient seriousness to make the decisions required for responsible action. We just bumble along, flung from pillar to post. As of yet, no coordinated planetary society exists, and it's not likely to form, despite the gravity of issues raised by futurists.

---

3 See Ted Peters, *Futures—Human and Divine* (Louisville: Westminster John Knox Press, 1978); Ted Peters, *Fear, Faith, and the Future* (Minneapolis: Augsburg Publishing House, 1980).

Among those ignoring the futurists were the churches and their theologians. With few exceptions such as John Cobb and Jürgen Moltmann, concern for terrestrial life on a planetary scale could not make it on to theological agendas. Liberation theologians initially declared futurists to be representatives of the scientifically advanced first world and that their rejoinders against pollution would amount to one more first world blockage to third world industrial growth. Feminist theologians decried the futurists because the latter were yoked too closely to science and technology, and allegedly science and technology belong to the patriarchal modern world of dominance of men over women and humanity over nature. Christian theology should become advocacy theology, my colleagues argued. The idea of a single planetary society engaged in moral deliberation could not make it onto the theological radarscope.

Things changed with the nuclear spill at Chernobyl, Soviet Union, in 1987. Suddenly feminists began to think that they might have some responsibility for environmental protection and ecological ethics. Eco-feminism began to draw adherents. Within a few years, liberation theologians also converted to a form of environmentalism. But, to my dismay, a quarter century had been lost. The Christian voice could not be heard in the public silence regarding my original concern shared with Joe Sittler in the 1960s, care for the Earth.

Despite this disappointing history, I still affirm that the proleptic structure for ethical deliberation could work. By beginning with a vision of a better future—a vision guaranteed, so to speak, by God's eschatological promise of a coming kingdom or new creation—we begin with the mandate to make our present world a better place. The status quo is insufficient. Past precedents are insufficient. Orders of Creation or *Schöpfungsordnungen* are insufficient. A proleptic ethic by definition is revolutionary, transformatory, hopeful.

The task of proleptic ethics, I believe, is to devise middle axioms that connect the grand eschatological vision of a new creation with our quite human responsibilities in the present time. Middle axioms would be theological principles providing ethical support for scientific research, technological advance, political change, and cultural revolution. Theologically, we need to affirm that scientific and technological transformation actually participate in the renewing of our world in a way that is both human and divine. Yet, blanket baptism of anything and everything new would be imprudent, to say the least. Constructing such middle axioms requires wisdom and prudence, what the Aristotelian tradition knows as *phronesis* and hermeneutical philosophers know as *applicatio*. Such application incorporates the unavoidable ambiguity inherent in assessing the practical outcomes of speculative proposals. The task of the ethicist remains: face the ambiguities, invoke wisdom, think prudently, and render the best judgment that finite considerations can produce.

Whitney Bauman's Non-Eschatological Eco-Ethic

Whitney Bauman and I share a passion of eco-ethics and the urgent need for the human race to care for our Earth. However, in his *Festschrift* chapter, Bauman registers skepticism about the value of my proleptic approach. When I argue that God has promised us an eschatological transformation and a future new creation, he balks. Bauman fears this might actually close off the future, rather than open it up. Bauman fears a cloud of determinism will rain on our freedom parade.

Bauman wants a better future, to be sure; but it will be a future based on *futurum*, not *adventus*. The future of our terrestrial sphere will be the product of human decision and action, not augmented by a transcendent action that ends in the kingdom of God. Bauman prefers emergence over apocalypse.

"In terms of the location of that futurity, Peters and I would probably disagree," writes Bauman. "For Peters (and Pannenberg) God-as-future is a transcendent reality. For me (and others) this type of futurity may also be too certain, even with our epistemic limitations. . . . Reality is indeterminate. As a result, our very constructions shape reality and reality can become in many different ways, no one way is certain or correct. This latter position would place the future possibility of becoming life in emergent, possible, 'lines of flight.' In other words, my understanding of futurity is emergent rather than transcendent. It is that which is the ground of possible becomings."[4] Like many in the World Future Society, human destiny on our terrestrial sphere is in our own human hands. Tacitly, Bauman embraces the u-d-c formula. It's a good formula, but it lacks the underlying inspiration that the proleptic approach might provide.

In addition to his eco-ethical concern, Bauman fears that I might be too conservative in my approach to transhumanism. Bauman raises this challenge because part of my futurist vision includes affirmation of

---

4 Bauman, 326.

dignity for each and every human being. I project a vision of a future planetary society "organized socially so that dignity and freedom are respected and protected in every quarter."[5] But, such a goal might have to be surrendered if our future includes a post-human species, a species more intelligent than *Homo sapiens*. How could we continue to confer dignity on human persons when we will be surpassed by a supra-human intelligence? This is the problem Bauman insightfully raises. He fears that if I give too much quarter to human dignity that I might not be willing to hold out the welcome mat for our post-human descendants.

What are we talking about? "Transhumanism is the view that humans should (or should be permitted to) use technology to remake human nature," write Heidi Campbell and Mark Walker.[6] Through genetic technology, information technology, and nanotechnology transhumanists believe the possibility exists for us to greatly enhance the healthy life span of persons, increase intelligence, and make ourselves happier and more virtuous. The key is to recontextualize humanity in terms of technology. This leads to a vision of a posthuman future characterized by a merging of humanity with technology as the next stage of our human evolution. *Posthuman* refers to who our descendants might become if transhuman efforts achieve their goals.

Among other implications of the transhumanist scenario, we human beings will lose control as we cede authority to our supra-human, supra-intelligent cyborg children. "If some day we build machine brains that surpass human brains in general intelligence, then this new superintelligence could become very powerful," speculates Oxford's Nick Bostrom. "The fate of our species would depend on the actions of the machine superintelligence."[7]

My slowness to wrap my arms around the Promethean enthusiasm of the transhumanists is due to the need to keep ambiguity in mind. Theological anthropology is well aware of an item on which the transhumanists are incredibly naive, namely, advances in intelligence are not matched by advances in moral resolve. The *summum bonum* on the transhumanist list of values is intelligence. Yet, intelligence and its products such as scientific and technological advance can lead to increased evil.

---

5 Peters, *GOD—The World's Future*, 381.
6 Heidi Campbell and Mark Walker, "Religion and Transhumanism: Introducing a Conversation," *Journal of Evolution and Technology* 14, no. 2 (August 2005): 1.
7 Nick Bostrom, *Superintelligence: Paths, Dangers, Strategies* (Oxford: Oxford University Press, 2014), vii.

Even if it turns out to be technologically feasible to create a superintelligence, it has yet to be proven that this would be a good thing. The superintelligence might turn out to be super-evil. What transhumanism lacks, but needs, is a solidly grounded ethic that values what Christians value more than intelligence, namely, compassion. To have a better future, we need to enhance the heart much more than the brain.

Karen Lebacqz's Beneficence Bioethics

My approach to the ethics of transhumanism begins with a more comprehensive framework: how can genetic research and neuroscience along with advances in computer technology contribute to human betterment? I compare three scenarios: therapy, enhancement, and transhumanism. My own considered judgment is the following. Therapy or healing is incontrovertibly a divinely appointed ministry as well as a humane enterprise. Go for it! Enhancement is more complex, because enhancing some individuals at the expense of others raises justice concerns. Transhumanism can be dismissed because it is scientifically and philosophically unrealistic as well as theologically and ethically misdirected. It appears that this third dismissal is what bothers Whitney Bauman. But, it is not even on Karen Lebacqz's radar screen. Therapy and enhancement are.

As we see in her *Festschrift* chapter, "Stem Cells in Wonderland? Proleptic Ethics and Stem Cell Research," Lebacqz draws upon the now widely accepted bioethical principles: autonomy, nonmalificence, beneficence, and justice. Lebacqz is our champion of justice. "Because humans are created in the image of God and have equal dignity, justice requires equal treatment," says Lebacqz.[8] Because all of us share in the image of God, all of us require equal and fair treatment. The knight in shining armor coming to redress unfairness is Karen Lebacqz.

In public circles outside the church, Lebacqz's counsel on moral matters and women's equality is widely respected. Very widely respected. I respect especially her ability to transfer her ethical sophistication gained from within theological circles into secular, scientific, and public policy circles.

Justice is the prow of her ethical ship. She has written two books

---

8 Karen Lebacqz, "Justice and Biotechnology: Protestant Views," *The Routledge Companion to Religion and Science,* James W. Haag, Gregory R. Peterson, and Michael L. Spezio, eds. (London: Routledge, 2012), 452.

on justice. Lebacqz knows how to ferret out justice issues even when they are masked or hiding. Yet, she plays a card that occasionally trumps justice, namely, grace. Grace and mercy and restoration to unity add something more than what justice—at least justice understood as fairness—can deliver. When Lebacqz interprets Jesus' parable of the Prodigal Son, she recognizes that justice-as-fairness does not adequately describe the moral victory of that parable. Grace does. "In short, both sons have wronged their father, and both receive unmerited love."[9] Mercy trumps fairness.

What guides Lebacqz's astute moral judgment we might dub: *justice plus*. With this as background, I can report that in the preparation work we did for what became our co-authored book, *Sacred Cells? Why Christians Should Support Stem Cell Research,* it was Lebacqz who took the lead in developing the concept of beneficence. She preferred calling it "future wholeness." Because we could envision enhanced human wholeness, the potential benefit to human health and wellbeing warrants Christian support of stem cell research. If laboratory research leads to medical therapies and if human health improves, tomorrow's transformation will provide retroactive moral justification for investing in stem cells research today.

What outrages Lebacqz is that neither the churches nor the wider public can see that benevolence or future wholeness is an ethical issue. For whatever reason, scientists along with funders wish to narrow the scope of ethical thinking to one and only one issue, namely, the moral status of the early embryo. "The assumption seems to be that if we did not have to destroy embryos, there would be *no* ethical issues surrounding stem cell research. Even as recently as fall 2012, when Professor Shinya Yamanaka was chosen to receive the Nobel Prize for his work on induced pluripotent stem cells (iPS), the report of the Witherspoon Council at Princeton University maintains that the destruction of embryos is the single most important ethical question about derivation and use of stem cells. Like others in the debate, the Council seems ready to assume that if embryos did not have to be destroyed, there would be *no ethical issues* around the derivation and use of stem cells. Induced pluripotent stem cells would then be the 'key' that unlocks the door to our beautiful garden of regenerative medicine while avoiding ethical controversy."[10]

---

9 Karen Lebacqz, "Fair Shares: Is the Genome Project Just?" in *Genetics: Issues of Social Justice,* Ted Peters, ed., (Cleveland: Pilgrim Press, 1998), 101.

10 Lebacqz, 310.

If a Christian ethicist is going to make a contribution to the wider discussion of public policy, the first task is to get the right issues on the discussion table. Included in the method of correlation is getting the contemporary questions formulated properly so that the theological answers will fit. This seems so very difficult—frustratingly impossible!—in the case of the stem cell controversy.[11]

Astrotheology for Our Extraterrestrial Future

I've got space in my soul. This does not mean my soul is vacuous, containing empty space. Rather, it means that I am struck with awe and wonder at the immensity and magnificence of outer space. Outer space is lodged in my soul. This has led me to organize a group of Berkeley shipmates to crack a bottle of champagne on a new ship about to sail the intellectual seas: Astrotheology. Yes, we've christened her "Astrotheology." It combines *astro*, referring to the stars, with *theology* or reflection on God's relationship to the stars and to everything else in this vast universe.

Astrotheology is that branch of theology that provides a critical analysis of the contemporary space sciences combined with an explication of classic doctrines such as creation and Christology for the purpose of constructing a comprehensive and meaningful understanding of our human situation within an astonishingly immense cosmos. The scope of God's creative work includes, among other things, the origin and future of the universe as scientists picture it.

As the astrotheologian's ship sets sail it heads toward four ports, four tasks. First, today's theologian needs to reflect on the scope of creation and to settle the pesky issue of geocentrism. Or, to say it another way, we need to finish the Copernican revolution for people of faith. Second, the astrotheologian should set the parameters within which the ongoing debates over Christology (Person of Christ) and soteriology (Work of Christ) are carried on. Third, theologians should analyze and critique astrobiology and related sciences from within, exposing extra-scientific assumptions and interpreting the larger value of the scientific enterprise. The invisible religion of modern western society is functionally science and technology, and the theologian must critically integrate the scientific with the religious worldview. Fourth, theologians and religious intellectuals should cooperate with leaders of multiple re-

---

11 See Ted Peters, "The STAP Flap, the CIRM Squirm, and Lab Morality," *Theology and Science* 4 (Nov 2014).

ligious traditions and scientists to prepare the public for the eventuality of extraterrestrial contact. This fourth task is an ethical task; it involves formulating public policy regarding space exploration.

Albert Harrison Gets It!

Albert Harrison gets it. Oh, yes, I'm aware that he says, "In Peters' view, I just don't get it."[12] Just what is going on in his *Festschrift* chapter, "Flying Saucers—No Laughing Matter! Ted Peters and Astrotheology"?

When interpreting my work, Harrison gets what I am trying to say. "A chief task of astrotheology is to keep discussions of space science honest. Peters has identified religious beliefs masquerading as science and reassigned misplaced scientific and religious beliefs to their appropriate categories. A foe of both scientism and false idolatry, Peters has been merciless unmasking ill-considered if not fraudulent ideas about alien intervention in human evolution and culture from antiquity through today."[13] Harrison gets it because he is one of the rare social scientists who has placed himself both in the context of scientists with NASA and SETI and in the context of UFO experiencers and UFOlogists who study UFO experiencers. He sees the continuity between the two groups, even though these two groups seldom if ever attend the same barbecues. Harrison attends both barbecues. So, he gets it.

There was one moment in the past where I thought Harrison was not getting it. In one of his otherwise insightful books he wrote, "SETI is not to be confused with religion and myth, so any superficial similarities among extraterrestrial radio astronomers, God, ancient astronauts, and space brothers have to be taken with a huge grain of salt."[14] SETI is science, whereas religion and myth are something different, he was arguing. Why did I object to Harrison's expelling of SETI from the club of myth believers? It appeared to me that in some respects both SETI and UFOlogy believe the same myth about an alleged evolution of life on other planets that has led over time to superior science, technology, and morality. What both SETI and UFOlogy seem to be looking for is salvation from the skies, secular salvation courtesy of space beings who today replace the angels of yesterday. Instead of supernatural angels, this ETI myth affirms belief in highly evolved science and technology, and this

---

12 Harrison, 335.
13 Harrison, 330-1.
14 Albert A. Harrison, *Starstruck: Cosmic Visions in Science, Religion and Folklore* (London and New York: Berghahn Books, 2007), 99.

ETI myth is equally operative in both SETI and UFOlogy. In both cases, a non-supranatural religion had risen up to replace old fashioned, supranatural religion. It's still religion, but supranatural gods have been replaced by natural aliens. Yes, it appeared to me that we could locate myth right in the heart of science. Was Harrison resisting my analysis here?

A decade or so ago Harrison and I began to compare notes. He had worked with the assumption that to be religious is to believe in something supranatural. Once he bracketed this assumption, it became more clear just how SETI, UFOlogy, and our wider secular culture tries valiantly to substitute the natural for the supranatural even though traditional religious sensibilities continue to energize our hope for salvation. Recall the third port of call for the astrotheological ship, the critical examination of astrobiology and related sciences, including UFOlogy: "The invisible religion of modern western society is functionally science and technology, and the theologian must critically integrate the scientific with the religious worldview." Now, I wonder: does Harrison think Peters finally gets it?

Brian Green and Astroethics

In Brian Green's chapter, "Astrobiology, Theology, and Ethics," he recognizes the third port of call identified above.that the "invisible religion of modern western society is functionally science and technology, and the theologian must critically integrate the scientific with the religious worldview." It is one of the tasks of astrotheology to show how this is the case.

Another task is to address the question: if extraterrestrial civilizations exist on other planets, would we need multiple incarnations of the one divine Logos? Would the historical Christ on Earth suffice for the whole cosmos, or would God need an incarnation for each planet? Brian offers a fascinating observation. For a theologian to suggest multiple incarnations, Christianity would come to look a lot like Hinduism. "Of further theological interest would be that multiple incarnations, true or false, could make Christianity more similar to Hinduism, where particular avatars gain the allegiances of devotees."[15] Many Hindus incorporate Jesus into their list of Vishnu's avatars. Jesus is one avatar among many. If a Christian theologian would posit multiple incarnations on multiple

---

15 Green, 341.

planets, might this become a parallel move? What might this imply for the Christian theological enterprise? Should this encourage or discourage the multiple-incarnation hypothesis?

Let's turn from the incarnation issue to the role of myth within science. The ETI myth as I develop it sounds too optimistic to Green's ears. "Peters has discussed the alien enemies paradigm before, usually in conjunction with the benevolent ETI myth, but I think he has perhaps not taken the potential evilness of the enemies seriously enough. Whether do-gooders or cold-blooded killers, ETIs even slightly more advanced than we are—in other words, with technology we can already envision today—could exterminate humanity before we even knew they existed."[16] Obviously, Green does not believe the ETI myth. I'm glad. This opens the door to examining negative contact scenarios.

Green expands his speculation by imagining a scenario where we meet extraterrestrials who are the equivalent of our transhumanists. If the ETI myth exists, then aliens who have evolved longer than earthlings will be more advanced than earthlings. They may even have accomplished on their planets what transhumanists are planning for our planet. The aliens we meet might well be cyborgs or superintelligent machines, not flesh-and-blood humanoids like us. "Now imagine this strange human-crew-ship-entity encountering another intelligent species, one which has also technologically modified itself. Likely at some point in the past these two sides would have resembled each other and been comprehensible to humans of the year 2013. But even the 'humans' in this scenario are too alien to comprehend, much less the actual aliens. How can we envision the truly-alien when we cannot even envision ourselves in 50 or 100 years? Assuming we still exist in 50 or 100 years."[17] Despite Green's overt rejection of the ETI myth, he seems to be accepting a portion of the myth, namely, the idea that evolution on an off-Earth planet would follow our developmental path and, if longer than Earth, become our own future. I find this very unlikely, yet it is worth spinning out such speculative scenarios.

Green finally moves toward the theodicy problem, raised in a new form when speculating on the meeting of earthlings with spacelings. Suppose the transhumanists on Earth commit genocide against us *Homo sapiens*. Suppose something like this has already taken place on a more

---

16 Green, 346.
17 Green, 343.

highly evolved alien planet. "If the aliens are just regular folks like we are, then they present no difficulties for theology. But what if they are disturbingly different from us, or they are evangelical atheists, or they simply destroy us before we even get to say hello? Of course, if we are dead we cannot personally lose our faith, but the theodicy question would still stand even in the absence of humans to ask it—how could God permit such things? Would God permit the extermination of humanity by ETIs? God already has permitted the extermination of the Neanderthals, the Denisovans, and possibly *Homo floresiensis*, by *Homo sapiens*, barring the few that may have interbred. What are we to think of a God who would make a nature where such things can occur? How can we trust a Lord who has permitted and who will continue to permit such atrocities?"[18]

Green's scenario looks quite a bit different from the one projected by the ETI myth. Green's faith is not entrusted to science, whether terrestrial science or extraterrestrial science. Advanced science can kill in advanced ways. Green shocks the naive optimism of those whose tacit hope for salvation lies in the future of science. The God in whom Christians place their trust is a God of grace and promise, not genocide. Just what scenario might a believer in divine grace imagine for contact with brothers and sisters on exoplanets? That's on the agenda of the astrotheologian.

Conclusion

It has been a distinct honor to be invited to respond to the scholars writing in this *Festschrift*. For the leadership of volume editors Carol Jacobson and Adam Pryor and for the participation of all the other authors and support staff, I offer my gratitude.

In addition to the honor, this volume has provided an opportunity for debate. I am reminded of St. Paul in 1 Corinthians 13:12, "For now we see in a mirror, dimly." While we in this life still see in a mirror dimly, I recommend we adopt critical realism (CR). On the one hand, we will assume the reality of God. On the other hand, because we can see God only through a mirror dimly, we must construct our concepts of God with our human imaginations. These constructions are partial, distorted, malleable. For this reason, theological engagement and contention and debate must enter into our critical constructions. That is what we have been doing here in this *Festschrift*.

---

18 Green, 348.

I wish to thank the other *Festschrift* authors for both their analyses and criticisms. Curiously but not surprisingly, I could have criticized my work even more devastatingly. The soft punches I received here are the product of kindness. Thanks again.

Published Writings of Ted Peters

BOOKS, SINGLE AUTHOR:

Sin Boldly! Justifying Faith for Fragile and Broken Souls. Fortress Press, 2015.

The Evolution of Terrestrial and Extraterrestrial Life. Pandora Press, 2008. http://bookshop.pandorapress.com/book.php?id=6434

The Stem Cell Debate. Fortress Press, 2007.

Anticipating Omega. Vandenhoeck & Ruprecht, 2006.

Science, Theology, Ethics. Ashgate, 2003.

Playing God? Genetic Determinism and Human Freedom, Routledge, 1997. 2nd ed., 2002. Templeton Book of Distinction Award, 2003.

GOD—The World's Future: Systematic Theology for a Postmodern Era, Fortress Press, 1992; 2nd edition, 2000; 3rd edition, 2014.
    Korean, translation by Se-Hyoung Lee, *하나님—세계의미래* Concordia-Sa, Seoul, Korea, 2006. http://books.google.com/books?hl=en&id=plHN8u3sVXkC&dq=-god+the+worlds+future+ted+peters&printsec=frontcover&source=web&ots=eS-gixvvtw_&sig=pPehCUKdS12l5r5_cuQld-fKypE&sa=X&oi=book_result&resnum=7&ct=result#PPR13,M1

For the Love of Children: Genetic Technology and the Future of the Family. Westminster/ John Knox Press, 1996.

Sin: Radical Evil in Soul and Society. Wm. B. Eerdmans Publishing Co., 1994. http://www.eerdmans.com/shop/product_search_results.asp

GOD as Trinity: Relationality and Temporality in Divine Life. Westminster/John Knox Press, 1993.

The Cosmic Self: A Penetrating Look at Today's New Age Movements. Harper Collins, 1991.
    Portuguese, *O Eu Cosmico.*

Fear, Faith, and the Future. Augsburg, 1980.
    Finnish, *Uskallammeko Kohdata Tulevaisuuden.* Finland: Karas-Sana Oy, Lohja, 1981.

Futures: Human and Divine. John Knox Press, 1978.

UFOs—God's Chariots? Flying Saucers in Politics, Science and Religion. John Knox Press, 1977.
    Revised edition, 2014, with New Page Books, *UFOs: God's Chariots? Spirituality, Ancient Aliens, and Religious Yearnings in the Age of Extraterrestrials.*

BOOKS, CO-AUTHORED

with Karen Lebacqz and Gaymon Bennett, *Sacred Cells? Why Christians Should Support Stem Cell Research.* Roman and Littlefield, 2008.

with Martinez Hewlett, *Can You Believe in God and Evolution?* Abingdon, 2006.
    Anniversary Edition, 2009. Templeton Book of Distinction Award, 2007

with Martinez Hewlett, *Evolution: From Creation to New Creation*, Abingdon 2003. Templeton Book of Distinction Award, 2005.

with Martinez Hewlett, *Theological and Scientific Commentary on Darwin's Origin of Species.* Abingdon, 2008.

BOOKS, EDITED or CO-EDITED

with Derik Nelson and Joshua Moritz, *Theologians in Their Own Words.* Fortress Press, 2013.

with Gaymon Bennett, Martinez Hewlett, and Robert John Russell, *The Evolution of Evil.* Göttingen: Vandenhoeck & Ruprecht, 2008. Distributed by Eisenbrauns.

with Nathan Hallanger, *God's Action in Nature's World.* Aldershot, United Kingdom: Ashgate, 2006.

with Niels Henrik Gregersen, Bo Holm, and Peter Widman, *The Gift of Grace: The Future of Lutheran Theology.* Fortress Press, 2005.

with Muzafar Iqbal and Nomen Haq, *God, Life, and the Cosmos: Islamic and Christian Perspectives.* Ashgate 2002.
    Indonesian Bahassa, *Tuhan, Alam, Manusia: Perspektif Sains dan Agama.* Bandung: Logo Mizan Kronik, 2005.

with Robert John Russell and Michael Welker, *Resurrection: Theological and Scientific Assessments.* Wm. B. Eerdmans Publishing Co., 2002. http://www.eerdmans.com/shop/product_search_results.asp

with Gaymon Bennett and Kang Phee Seng. *Bridging Science and Religion.*
    English, SCM Press, 2002, and Fortress Press, 2003.

    Traditional Chinese,科學與宗教 Chung Hwa Book Company, Ltd., Hong Kong, 2003.

    Simplified Chinese,橋：科學與宗教China Social Sciences Press, Beijing, China, 2002.

Portuguese, *Construindo Pontes Entre a Ciência ea Religião*. Translated by Luis Carlos Borges. Supervised by Eduardo Cruz. Edicoes Loyola, Sao Paulo, Brazil, 2004.

German, *Brücken Bauen Naturwissenschaft und Religion*.Vandenhoeck & Ruprecht,Göttingen, Germany, 2006.

Indonesian Bahassa, *Menjembatani sains dan agama*. Forwards by Prof. Dr. H.M. Amim Abdullah and Pdt. Prof. E. Gerritt Singgih, Ph.D. Translated by Jessica Christiania Pattinasarany. Gunung Mulia in Jakarta, Indonesia, 2004.

Spanish, *Ciencia y religión en diálogo. Un puente en construcción* UPAEP in Pubela, Mexico, 2005.

Science and Theology: The New Consonance, editor & contributor, Westview Press, 1998

Korean translation by Heup Young Kim:
테드피터스편, 김흡영외역, 과학과종교: 새로운공명 (서울: 동연출판사, 2002)

Genetics: Issues of Social Justice, editor & contributor, Pilgrim, 1998.

Toward a Theology of Nature: Essays on Science and Faith, by Wolfhart Pannenberg, Introduction author and volume editor, Westminster/John Knox Press, 1993. Winner of Templeton Book Prize, 1995.

Cosmos as Creation: Theology and Science in Consonance, volume editor and contributor. Abingdon Press, 1989.

OTHER EDITING:

Editor, *Dialog: A Journal of Theology* (1993–2007).

Co-editor, *Theology and Science* (2000–Date)

Editor for "Science and Religion,"*Religion in Geschichte und Gegenwart*, Volumes IV–VIII, and for *Encyclopedia of Religion*, 2nd edition, 2005.

ARTICLES AND PAPERS (in chronological sequence):

1971

1. "Dead to Sin and Alive to God."*The Sermon Builder* (October 1971): 17–20.

1972

2. "The Atonement in Anselm and Luther,"*The Lutheran Quarterly*, XIV, no. 3 (August 1972): 301–14.
3. "You Play the Cop," *The Lutheran Standard* (September 19, 1972) 20.

1973

4. "Citizens of the World," *Pulpit Digest* (May–June, 1973) 45–47.
5. "Jesus' Resurrection: An Historical Event without Analogy," *Dialog*, XII, no. 2 (Spring 1973): 112–16.
6. "The Use of Analogy in Historical Method," *The Catholic Biblical Quarterly*, XXXV, no. 4 (Oct 1973): 475–82;paper read at SE/AAR, Emory University, Atlanta, March 16, 1973.

1974

7. "Chariots, UFOs, and the Mystery of God: The Science and Religion of Erich von Däniken," *The Christian Century*, XCI, no. 20 (May 22, 1974): 560–63. Papers read on this topic at annual meeting of the College Theology Society in Dayton, Ohio, June 1, 1974; at SE/AAR, Atlanta, March 22, 1975; and at the Symposium of the Mutual UFO Network, Ann Arbor, Michigan, June 12, 1976.
8. "Future Consciousness and the Need for Theology," *Dialog*, XIII, no. 4 (Autumn 1974): 251–57.
9. "The God of Our Future," funeral sermon, *Pulpit Digest* (Jan–Feb, 1974).
10. "Jesus' History and Our History." Trans. of *"Jesu Geschichte und Unsere Geschichte."* By WolfhartPannenberg. *Perspectives in Religious Studies*, 1, no. 2 (Fall 1974): 134–42.
11. "The Nature and Role of Presupposition: An Inquiry into Contemporary Hermeneutics."*International Philosophical Quarterly*, XIV, no. 2 (June 1974): 209–22; read at South Carolina Society for Philosophy, Wofford College, February 16, 1973.
12. "The Whirlwind as Yet Unnamed: Langdon Gilkey and Beyond."*The Journal of the American Academy of Religion*, XLII, no. 4 (December 1974): 699–709.

1975

13. "Chariots, UFOs, and Religious Needs." *Cross-Talk*, IV, no. 3 (Oct–Nov, 1975).
14. "Futures: Human and Divine." *The Lutheran Quarterly*, XXVII, no. 2 (May 1975): 112–24.
15. "Truth in History: Gadamer's Hermeneutics and Pannenberg's Apologetic Method." *The Journal of Religion*, 55, no. 1 (January 1975): 36–56.

1976

16. "Exo-Theology: Speculations on Extra-Terrestrial Life," read at annual meeting of the American Academy of Religion, St. Louis, October 30,1976.
17. "Future Consciousness and the Question of God," *Cross Currents*, 25, no. 4, 100th issue (Winter 1976):401–18.
18. "The Future of Liberal Education," presidential address, South Carolina Society for Philosophy, Furman University, February 6, 1976.
19. "Resurrection as Metaphor," SE/AAR, Vanderbilt University, March 1976.

20. "Values for a No-Growth Future," *Dialog*, XV, no. 4 (Autumn 1976): 179–86.

1977

21. "Femininity and the Future." *Lutheran Standard*, (March 1, 1977): 28f.
22. "Monotheism and Kingship in Ancient Memphis: A Study in Egyptian Mythology." *Perspectives in Religious Studies*, IV, no. 2 (Summer 1977): 160–73.
23. "*Sola Scriptura* and the Second Naiveté." *Dialog* XVI, no. 4 (Autumn 1977): 266–80.

1978

24. "Hermeneutical Truth and Theological Method." *Encounter*, 39, no. 2 (Spring 1978): 103–23.
25. "Metaphor and the Horizon of the Unsaid." *Philosophy and Phenomenological Research*, 38, no. 3 (March 1978): 355–70.
26. "Proleptic Ethics and the Eschatological Vision," read at College Theology Society Annual Meeting, Windsor, Ontario, June 1, 1978.
27. "The Religious Dimension to UFOs: A Case Study."*Cross Currents*, 27, no. 3 (Fall 1977): 261–78.
28. "UFOs and Modern Religion."*America*, 138, no. 14 (April 15, 1978): 306–08.
29. "The Messianic Banquet and World Hunger."*Religion in Life*, XLVII, no. 4 (Winter 1978): 497–508.

1979

30. "Faith's Focus: Its Formation and Reformation."*Bulletin of the American Protestant Hospital Association*, XLII, no. 1 (Spring 1979): 14ff.
31. "Fear, Faith, and the Future."*The Lutheran Standard*, (October 2, 1979): 4–7.
32. "The Religious Dimension to the UFO Phenomenon."*1979 MUFON UFO Symposium Proceedings*. San Francisco, July 7–8, 1979.

1980

33. "The Problem of Symbolic Reference." *Thomist*, XLIV, no. 1 (January 1980): 72–93.
34. "Thinking Globally, Acting Locally." Editorial, *Christian Century*, XCVII, no. 27 (August 27–September 3,1980): 813–14.
35. "The Future of Religion in a Post-Industrial Society."*The Futurist*, XIV, no. 5 (October 1980). This was a paper delivered to the First Global Conference on the Future at Toronto, July 20–24, 1980,and first published in the conference book, *Through the 80s: Thinking Globally, Acting Locally*, Frank Feather, ed. (Washington, DC: World Future Society, 1980), 285–91.
36. "The Future of Liberal Education." *Dialog*, XIX, no. 2 (Spring 1980): 123–26.

1981

37. "Future Consciousness and Ministry." *LCA Partners*, III, no. 4 (August 81): 15ff.

1982

38. "Nuclear Waste: The Ethics of Disposal." *The Christian Century*, 99, no. 8 (March 10, 1982): 271-73.
39. "Hermeneutics and Homiletics." *Dialog*, XXI, no. 2 (Spring 1982): 121-29.

1983

40. "Methode und System in der heutigen amerikanischen Theologie." *Kerygma und Dogma*, 29, no. 1 (January–March 1983): 2-46.
41. "Ethical Considerations Surrounding Nuclear Waste Repository Siting and Mitigation." In *Nuclear Waste: Socioeconomic Dimensions of Long-Term Storage*. Edited by Steve H. Murdock, F. Larry Leistritz, and Rita R. Hamm. Boulder: Westview Press, 1983, 41-56.
42. "Pluralism as a Theological Problem." *The Christian Century*, 100, no. 27 (September 28, 1983): 843-45.
43. "Lutheran Distinctiveness in Mission to a Pluralistic World." *Dialog*, 22, no. 4 (Fall 1983): 293-300.
44. "Post-Modern Religion." In *Currents in Theology and Mission*, 10, no. 5 (October 1983): 261-72; reprinted in *Update*, 8, no. 1 (March 1984): 16-30.

1984

45. "Futurologie." *Theologische Realenzyklopädie*, Band XI, 767-773.
46. "Theology in the Context of Transition from Modern to Postmodern Culture," read at "Paradigm Shifts in Buddhism and Christianity," the Second East-West Religions Encounter Conference, Honolulu, Hawaii, January 3-11, 1984.
47. "Cosmos and Creation." *Word and World*, 4, no. 4 (Fall 1984): 372-90.
48. "Creation, Consummation, and the Ethical Imagination." In *Cry of the Environment*. Edited by Philip N. Joranson and Ken Butigan. Sante Fe: Bear & Co., 1984, 401-29.

1985

49. "David Bohm, Postmodernism, and the Divine." *Zygon*, 20, no. 2 (June 1985): 193-217.
50. "On the New Christian Dogmatics." For "Theology Update," *Dialog*, 24, no. 2 (Spring 1985): 136-46.
51. "Toward Postmodern Theology," Parts I and II. For "Theology Update," *Dialog* 24, no. 3 (Summer 1985): 221-26 and 24, no. 4 (Fall 1985): 293-97.

1986

52. "Current Apocalypticism." *Resource* Cassette tape, Series 13, no. 8, Augsburg Publishing House (April 1986).
53. "What Is the Gospel?" *Perspectives in Religious Studies*, 13, no. 1 (Spring 1986): 21-43.

54. "Confessional Universalism and Inter-Religious Dialogue." For "Theology Update," *Dialog*, 25, no. 2 (Spring 1986): 145–49.
55. "Human Transformation: The New Age Anthropology." For "Theology Update," *Dialog*, 25, no. 3 (Summer 1986): 226–31.
56. "Images, Icons, and the Visual Arts."*Dialog*, 25, no. 4 (Fall 1986): 255–61.
57. "On Adding Divine Mothers to the Bible. "*Currents in Theology and Mission* 13, no. 5 (October 1986): 276–84.
58. "A Christian Theology of Interreligious Dialogue." *Christian Century*, 103, no. 30 (October 15, 1986): 883–85.

1987

59. "Toward 2010: Wholistic Agendas for Theology and Ministry."*Word and World*, 7, no. 2 (Spring 1987): 167–78.
60. "Trinity Talk," Parts I and II. For "Theology Update" column, *Dialog*, 26, no. 1 (Winter 1987): 44–48, and 26, no. 2 (Spring 1987): 133–38.
61. "The Real World Is the Yet-To-Be Whole World." *Dialog*, 26, no. 3 (Summer 1987): 167–74.
62. "David Tracy: Theologian to an Age of Pluralism."For "Theology Update" column *Dialog*, 26, no. 4 (Fall 1987): 298–305.
63. "On Creating the Cosmos."Paper delivered at a conference on "Probing the Interaction among Physics, Philosophy, and Theology." Sponsored by the Pontifical Academy of Sciences and the Vatican Observatory, Rome, September 21–26, 1987. Published as chapter 13 of *Physics, Philosophy, and Theology*. Edited by Robert J. Russell, William R. Stoeger, S.J., and George V. Coyne, S.J. (Vatican City: Vatican Observatory, and Notre Dame, Indiana: University of Notre Dame Press, 1988), 273–96.

1988

64. "Langdon Gilkey: Theologian to the Modern Mind." For "Theology Update" column, *Dialog* 27, no. 1 (Winter 1988): 55–62.
65. "McFague's Metaphors."For "Theology Update" column, *Dialog*, 27, no. 2 (Spring 1988): 131–40.
66. "Relationship, Women, and Theology." For "Theology Update" in *Dialog* 27, no. 3 (Summer 1988): 215–23.
67. "Pannenberg's Eschatological Ethics."In *The Theology of Wolfhart Pannenberg: Twelve American Critiques*, Edited by Carl Braaten and Philip Clayton (Minneapolis: Augsburg, 1988), 239–65.
68. "The Scientists among Us." *Lutheran Partners*, 4, no. 5 (September–October, 1988): 18–22.
69. "Discerning the Spirits of the New Age."*The Christian Century*, 105, no. 25 (August 31–September 7, 1988): 763–66.

70. "The New Age Is Here... and Everywhere." *The Lutheran*, 1, no. 16 (November 2, 1988): 9–11. Reprinted in *Canada Lutheran*, 5, no. 1 (January 1990): 12–14.

1989

71. "Reflections on Science as Vocation." In *The New Faith-Science Debate*. Edited by John M. Mangum. (Minneapolis: Fortress Press, 1989), 89–90.
72. "The Gospel and the New Age."*Dialog*, 28, no. 1 (Winter 1989): 18–29.
73. "The New Age Movement."*Adult Forum Studies*, Augsburg Fortress.
74. "Not in My Backyard! The Crisis in Waste Siting." *The Christian Century*, 106, no. 5 (February 15, 1989): 175–77; reprinted in *Readings for the 21st Century*, 2nd. ed. Edited by William Vesterman and Josh Ozersky. (Boston: Allyn and Bacon, 1994), 32–39.
75. "Matthew Fox and the Vatican Wolves." For "Theology Update," *Dialog*, 28, no. 2 (Spring 1989): 137–42.
76. "Role Models for Women Seminarians." Co-authored with Lora Gross, *Dialog*, 28, no. 2 (Spring 1989): 92–102.
77. "Voegelin for the Theologian." For "Theology Update," *Dialog* 28, no. 3 (Summer 1989): 210–22.
78. "Science and Religion: Toward a New Consonance." *Currents in Theology and Mission*, 16, no. 6 (December 1989): 417–24.

1990

79. "Heaven." In the *Mercer Dictionary of the Bible*. Edited by Watson E. Mills (Macon, Georgia: Mercer University Press, 1990).
80. "Sin, Sex, and Satan at the Bookstore." For "Theology Update," *Dialog* 29, no. 1 (Winter 1990): 42–51.
81. "The Theological Method of Schubert Ogden." For "Theology Update," *Dialog* 29, no. 2 (Spring 1990):125–34.
82. "John Cobb, Theologian in Process," Parts I and II. For "Theology Update," *Dialog* 29, no. 3 (Summer 1990):207–20, and 29, no. 4 (Fall 1990): 290–302. "The Systematic Theology of John Cobb." Paper for the Pacific Coast Theological Society, Berkeley, California, November 2–3, 1990.
83. "Evangelization within a Religiously Plural Society."Paper presented to The Academy for Evangelists, Luther Northwestern Theological Seminary, June 19, 1990. Published in *Journal of the Academy for Evangelism in Theological Education*, 5 (1990): 30–41.
84. "Genethics: Implications of the Human Genome Project." Co-authored with Ann Lammers. *The Christian Century*, 107, no. 27 (October 3, 1990): 868–72. This article received honorable mention by The Associated Church Press for in-depth coverage of a current issue. Reprinted in *The Borzoi College Reader*, Charles Muscatine and Marlene Griffith, eds. (New York: McGraw Hill, 1992) and in *Moral Issues and Christian Response*, 5th ed., Paul Jersild and

Dale Johnson, eds. (New York: Harcourt Brace Jovanovich, 1993). Reprinted in *CTNS Bulletin*, 11, no. 4 (Autumn 1991): 1–4.

85. "Hope and Eschatology: Response to John Polkinghorne." *CTNS Bulletin*, 10, no. 2 (Spring 1990): 27–29.

1991

86. "Scientific Research and the Christian Faith." In *Thought*, 66, no. 260 (March 1991): 75–94.
87. "Beyond the Genes: Epigenesis and God." In *CTNS Bulletin*, 11, no. 3 (Spring 1991): 34–35.
88. "Seeing No Evil: A Lutheran Minister Critiques the New Age." *Common Boundary*, 9, no. 6 (November 1991): 26–30; reprinted in *Areopagus*, 5, no. 4 (Trinity 1992): 33–36.
89. "Cosmic Consciousness on Campus." In *Entree*, 8, no. 1 (February 1991): 4–7.
90. "The Battle Over Trinitarian Language." For "Theology Update," *Dialog* 30, no. 1 (Winter 1991): 44–49.
91. "Identifying with the Gospel." In a thematic issue Peters helped edit on "Lutheran Identity in the 21st Century" for *Currents in Theology and Mission* 18, no. 1 (January–February, 1991): 38–44.
92. "*Urknallkosmologie und Gottes Schöpfungstätigkeit*" (Teil I). In *Glaube und Denken: Jahrbuch der KarlHeim-Gesellschaft*. Edited by Hans Schwarz. (Moers: Brendow Verlag, 1991) 4:145–163 and (Teil II) (1992) 5:25–42.
93. "Response to John Cobb." In *Dialog* 30, no. 2 (Summer 1991): 244–45.
94. "Resurrection or Reincarnation?" In *The Lutheran*, 4, no. 5 (April 3, 1991): 6–7.
95. "The Selling of Satan in Popular Literature." *The Christian Century*, 108, no. 14 (April 24, 1991): 458–62.
96. "Satan's Friends and Enemies." For "Theology Update," *Dialog*, 30, no. 3 (Fall 1991): 303–13.
97. "Wholeness in Salvation and Healing." In *Lutheran Quarterly*, 5, no. 3 (Autumn 1991): 297–314.

1992

98. "Sin, Satanism, and New Age Religion." In *Resource* Cassettes, Augsburg Fortress (January 1992).
99. "The Human Genome Initiative: What Questions Does It Raise for Theology and Ethics?" Co-authored with Robert John Russell. In *Midwest Medical Ethics*, 7, no. 3 (Summer 1991): 12–17; reprinted in *Genetic Engineering: A Documentary History*, Thomas Shannon, ed. (Greenwood, 1997).
100. "Atonement and the Final Scapegoat." In *Perspectives in Religious Studies*, 19, no. 2 (Summer 1992): 151–81.

101. "Moltmann and the Way of the Trinity." For "Theology Update," *Dialog*, 31, no. 4 (Autumn 1992): 272-79.

1993

102. "The Dimensions of God's Life." In *The Christian Century*, 110, no. 1 (January 6-13, 1993): 24-25.
103. "Culture Wars: Should Lutherans *Volunteer* or Be Conscripted?" For "Theology Update," *Dialog*, 32, no. 1 (Winter 1993): 37-52.
104. "Spiritual Autobiography."Delivered to the Pacific Coast Theological Society, Berkeley, California, April 2, 1993.
105. Channeling in the New Age, "Response to Claire Graham." In *Areopagus*, 6, no. 1 (Easter 1993), 25-26.
106. "Genes, Creation, and Co-Creation." In *CTNS Bulletin*, 13, no. 1 (Winter 1993): 23-27.
107. "The Trinity in and beyond Time." In *Quantum Cosmology and the Laws of Nature*. Edited by Robert John Russell, Nancey Murphy, and C.J. Isham.Vatican City: Vatican Observatory and Berkeley: The Center for Theology and the Natural Sciences, 1993. 263-91.Originally a paper for a conference on "Quantum Creation of the Universe and the Origin of the Laws of Nature."-Sponsored by the Vatican Observatory and the Center for Theology & the Natural Sciences, Rome, September 1991.
108. "Genome Project Forces New Look at Ethics." In *Forum for Applied Research and Public Policy*,8, no. 3 (Fall 1993): 5-13.
109. "Genes, Theology, and Ethics." *Science and Religion News*, 4, no. 3 (Fall 1993): 8.
110. "Resurrection: What Kind of Body?"*Ex Auditu*, 9 (1993): 57-76. Originally a paper delivered at the North Park Theological Seminary Symposium on the Theological Interpretation of Scripture, October 9, 1993.

1994

111. "On the Gay Gene: Back to Original Sin Again?" *Dialog*, 33, no. 1 (Winter 1994): 30-38. This essay won a prize in the 1994 John M. Templeton Foundation program of scholarly papers in Humility Theology.
112. "Intellectual Property and Human Dignity," Chap. 12 of *The Genetic Frontier: Ethics, Law, and Policy*, Mark S. Frankel and Albert H. Teich, eds. (Washington, D.C.: American Association for theAdvancement of Science Press, 1994), 215-24.
113. "Eschatological Sanctions and Christian Ethics." *Princeton Seminary Bulletin*, Supplementary Issue No. 3 (1994): 129-52. Originally a paper read at Princeton Theological Seminary Neuman Symposium on Biblical Interpretation, October 2,1993.
114. "Worship Wars: Battling on Four Fronts." In *Dialog*, 33, no. 3 (Summer 1994): 166-73.

115. "Satanism: Bunk or Blasphemy?" In *Theology Today*, 51, no. 3 (October 1994): 381–93.
116. "Designer Children: The Market World of Reproductive Choice." In *The Christian Century*, 111, no. 36 (December 14, 1994): 1193–96.

1995

117. "Isaac, Jesus, and Divine Sacrifice." In *Dialog*, 34, no. 1 (Winter 1995): 52–56.
118. "Exo-Theology: Speculations on Extra-Terrestrial Life." Chapter 8 in *The Gods Have Landed*. Edited by James R. Lewis. Albany: SUNY, 1995). Also published in *CTNS Bulletin*, 14, no. 3 (Summer 1994): 1–9.
119. "My Genes Made Me Do It!" In *The Lutheran*, 8, no. 3 (March 1995): 25–27.
120. "Still Becoming: A Theological Autobiography." In *Dialog*, 34, no. 2 (Spring 1995): 106–15.
121. "Build Schools." In *Dialog*, 34, no. 2 (Spring 1995): 141–42. Reprinted in *Lutheran Education*, 131, no. 4 (March/April 1996): 200.
122. "Revelation and Illumination." In *Journal of Religious Studies*, 19, no. 1–2 (1995): 1–26.
123. "The Physical Body of Immortality." In *CTNS Bulletin*, 15, no. 2 (Spring 1995): 1–20.
124. "Theology and Science: Where Are We?" For "Theology Update" in *Dialog*, 34, no. 4 (Fall 1995): 281–96; and *Zygon*, 31, no. 2 (June 1996): 323–43; see also no. 163 below.
125. "Playing God and Germline Intervention." In *Journal of Medicine and Philosophy*, 20, no. 4 (August 1995): 365–86.

1996

126. "Multiple Choice in Baby Making." In *Word and World*, XVI, no. 1 (Winter 1996): 11–23.
127. "Wolfhart Pannenberg." Chapter in *A New Handbook of Contemporary Theologians*. Edited by Donald W. Musser and Sam R. Marks. Nashville: Abingdon Press, 1996. 363–74.
128. "Patenting Life: Yes." In *First Things*, No. 63 (May 1996), 18–20.
129. "Should We Patent God's Creation?" For "Theology Update," *Dialog*, 35, no. 2 (Spring 1996): 117–32.
130. "The Good News of God's Grace." In *Radix*, 24, no. 1 (1996), 3.
131. "New Age Universalism and the Scandal of the Gospel." In *Radix*, 24:1 (1996) 8–11.
132. "Theology and the Natural Sciences." In *The Modern Theologians*. Edited by David F. Ford. Oxford: Basil Blackwell, revised edition, 1996, 649–688.
133. "Feminist and Catholic: The Family Ethics of Lisa Sowle Cahill." For "Theology Update," *Dialog*, 35, no. 4 (Fall 1996): 269–77.
134. "Dialogue *and* Mission." In *Dialog*, 35, no. 4 (Fall 1996): 303–04.

135. "In Search of the Perfect Child: Genetic Screening and Selective Abortion." In *The Christian Century*, 113, no. 31 (October 30, 1996): 1034–37.

1997

136. "Many Cultures, One Christ." In *Dialog*, 36, no. 1 (Winter 1997): 45–51.
137. "Clarity of the Part vs. Meaning of the Whole." Chap. 11 of *Beginning with the End: God, Science, and Wolfhart Pannenberg*. Edited by Carol Rausch Albright and Joel Haugen. LaSalle, Illinois: Open Court. Originally a paper delivered to the Chicago Center for Religion and Science, November 15–17, 1988.
138. "Does God Say No? Not Really." *San Jose Mercury News* (June 22, 1997): 6C.
139. "Two Thumbs Up, One Down." In *Dialog*, 36, no. 3 (Summer 1997): 229–31.
140. "Cloning Shock: A Theological Reaction." Chap. 2, *Human Cloning: Religious Responses*. Edited by Ronald Cole-Turner. Louisville: Westminster/John Knox Press, 1997, and in *CTNS Bulletin*, 17, no. 2 (Spring 1997): 1–9.
141. "Genetics and Genethics: Are We Playing God?" CTNS: http://www.ctns.org; PLTS: http://www.plts.edu.

1998

142. "Heaven's Gate and the Theology of Suicide." For "Theology Update," *Dialog*, 37, no. 1 (Winter 1998): 57–66.
143. Lenten Devotions for March 21–28, 1998, *The Nurturing Word*, published by Luther Seminary and PLTS.
144. "God Happens: The Timeliness of the Triune God." In *Christian Century*, 115, no. 10 (April 1, 1998): 342–44.
145. "The Systematic Theology of Wolfhart Pannenberg." For "Theology Update," *Dialog*, 37, no. 2 (Spring 1998): 123–33.
146. "The Dignity of the Child." In *Dialog*, 37, no. 3 (Summer 1998) 190–94.
147. "Co-Evolution: Pain or Promise?" Nobel Conference XXXIV, Gustavus College, October 6–7, 1998, forthcoming in *CTNS Bulletin*.
148. "Love and Dignity: Against Children Becoming Commodities." In *Genetic Testing and Screening*. Edited by Roger Willer. Division for Church in Society, Evangelical Lutheran Church in America. Minneapolis: Kirk House, 1998, 116–129.
149. "Revolution and Christian Hope: A Response to John Haught." Paper delivered at the CTNS J.K. Russell Research Conference, April 19, 1997. *CTNS Bulletin*, 18, no. 1 (Winter 1998): 22–25.
150. "Außerirdisches Wesen" (Extra Terrestrial Life), *Religion in Geschichteund Gegenwart*, 4th edition, Hans Dieter Betz et. al., eds. Tubingen: Mohr Siebeck, 1998; I: 995–996.
151. "Advances in Reproductive Technology: A Protestant Perspective." In *The Family Handbook*. Edited by Herbert Anderson, et.al. Louisville: Westminster/John Knox Press, 1998, 51–53.

152. "The Genetics-Theology Interface." In *Interface: A Forum for Theology in the World*. 1:2 (October 1998) 93–117.

1999

153. "Is Cloneliness Next To Godliness?" In *Word and World*, XIX:1 (Winter 1999) 92, 94.
154. "DNA and Dignity." In *Perspectives on Genetic Patenting: Religion, Science,and Industry in Dialogue*. Edited by Audrey Chapman. Washington: AAAS, 1999, 127–136.
155. "Research with Human Embryonic Stem Cells: Ethical Considerations."- Co-authored with Karen Lebacqz, Michael M. Mendiola, Ernle W.D. Young, and Laurie Zoloth *Hastings Center Report*, 29:2 (March–April 1999) 31–36. Reprinted in *The Stem Cell Controversy*. Edited by Michael Ruse and Christopher A. Pynes. Amherst, New York: Prometheus Books, 2006, 117–129.
156. "Playing God with Our Evolutionary Future." In *Evolutionary and Molecular Biology: Scientific Perspectives on Divine Action*. Edited by Francisco Ayala, Nancey Murphy, and Robert John Russell. Vatican City: Vatican Observatory Publications, and Berkeley: CTNS, 1998, 491–510.
157. "Creation," Segment 4. In *Christian Believer: Knowing God with Heart and Mind*, Videotape, Nashville: Abingdon Press, 1999.
158. "The Stem Cell Debate: Ethical Questions." *CTNS Bulletin* 19, no. 2 (Spring 1999): 3–10.
159. "Resurrection of the Very Embodied Soul." Paper for conference on "The Mind/Brain Problem: Scientific Perspectives on Divine Action." Sponsored by the Vatican Observatory and the Center for Theology and the Natural Sciences, Krakow, Poland, June 21–27, 1998. *Neuro Science and the Person*. Edited by Robert John Russell, Nancey Murphy, Theo Meyering, and Michael Arbib. Vatican City and Berkeley: Vatican Observatory and CTNS, 1999, 2000. 305–326.
160. "Our Genetic Future." In *God for the 21st Century*. Edited by Russell Stannard. Philadelphia: Templeton Foundation Press, 2000. 86–88.
161. "The Terror of Time." In *Dialog*, 39:1 (March 2000) 56–66.
162. "Sin, Scapegoating, and Justifying Faith." In *God, Evil, and Suffering: Essays in Honor of Paul Sponheim*. Edited by Terrence E. Fretheim and Curtis L. Thompson. *Word and World Supplement Series 4*. St. Paul: Luther Seminary, 2000. 62–74. Also in *Dialog*, 39, no. 2, Summer 2000.
164. "Theology and Science: Where Are We?" In *Evangelical Review of Theology*, 24, no. 2 (April 2000) 100–115; and *Uniting Church Studies*, 6, no. 1(March 2000) 39–67. Both in Australia; see no. 124 above.

2001

164. "Eschatology: Eternal Now or Cosmic Future?" *Zygon* 36:2 (June 2001) 349–356; and in *Religion in the New Millennium: Theology in the Spirit of Paul Tillich*.

Edited by Raymond F. Bulman and Frederick J. Parrella. Atlanta: Mercer, 2001, 319–327.Originally delivered to the North American Paul Tillich Society, New Harmony, Indiana,16–20 June 1999.

165. "Eschatology Full Strength." In *Dialog*, 40:2 (Summer 2001): 124–130.
166. "From Conflict to Consonance: Ending the Warfare Between Science and Faith." In *Currents in Theology and Mission*, 28, no. 3–4 (June/August 2001): 238–247.
167. "Theological Support of Stem Cell Research." Co-author Gaymon Bennett, *The Scientist* 15[17]:4 (4 September 2001).
168. "Encoding Altruism." In *Science and Spirit*, 12, no. 5 (September–October 2001): 23–27.
169. "Embryonic Stem Cells and the Theology of Dignity." In *The Human Embryonic Stem Cell Debate: Science, Ethics, and Public Policy*. Edited by Karen Lebacqz, Suzanne Holland, and Laurie Zoloth. Cambridge, Massachusetts: M.I.T. Press, 2001.
170. "The Science-Religion Dialogue: An Ecumenical Catalyst?" 22nd Paul Wattson Lecture, University of San Francisco, 29 January 2001.In *Dialog* 40, no. 3 (Fall 2001): 223–229.
171. "The Stem Cell Controversy." In *Dialog* 40, no. 4 (Winter 2001): 290–293.

2002

172. "Foreword."In *God, Life, Intelligence, and the Universe*. Edited by Hilary Regan. Adelaide, South Australia: Open Books, 2002. "Prefácio."In *Deus, Vida, Inteligencia e o Universo*. São Paulo, Brazil: Edições Loyola, 2007.
173. "Can Science Aid the Spirit in its Struggle with the Flesh?" In *CTNS Bulletin* 22, no. 3 (Summer 2002): 3–7.
174. "Writing in Science & Religion: Climbing Above the Plateau." In *CTNS Bulletin* 22, no. 4 (Fall 2002): 12–14.
175. "Cloning in the White House."With Gaymon Bennett. In *Dialog* 41, no. 3 (Fall 2002): 241–244.
176. "The Promise of Cosmic Peace."In *One Incarnate Truth*. Edited by Uwe Siemon-Netto. St. Louis: Concordia, 2002. 25–28.
177. "Grace, Doubt, and Evil: The Constructive Task of Reformation Theology." In *Dialog* 41, no. 4 (Winter 2002): 273–284.
178. "Ancient Faith and Modern Science." In *Omega: Indian Journal of Science and Religion* 1, no. 1 (December 2002): 9–35.

2003

179. "Embryonic Persons in the Cloning and Stem Cell Debates." In *Theology and Science*1, no. 1 (Spring 2003): 51–78.
180. "Why Should We Care about Cloning and Stem Cells?" In *Disciples World* 2, no. 3 (April 2003): 7.
181. "Genes/Genetics." In *A New Handbook of Christian Theology*. Edited by Donald W. Musser & Joseph L. Price. Rev. Ed. Nashville: Abingdon, 2003. 212–213.

182. "Freedom," 1:335–338."Genetic Determinism," 1:359. "Genetics," 1:362–370. "Human Genome Project," 1:419–426. "Playing God," 2:682. "Sin," 2:805–807. "UFO," 2:909–911. In *Encyclopedia of Science and Religion*. J. Wentzel Vrede van Huyssteen, Editor in Chief. New York: Macmillan/Thomson/Gale, 2003.

183. "Holy Therapy." In *Christian Century* 120, no. 16 (9 August 2003): 23–26.

184. "Genetic Technology and Christian Anthropology."In *Christian Anthropology and Biotechnological Progress: Conference Proceedings*, Orthodox Academy of Crete.Edited by Vassilis Gekas. Technical University of Crete, 2003. 13–28.

185. "A Plea for Beneficence in the Stem Cell and Cloning Debates." Co-authored with Gaymon Bennett. In*God and the Embryo: Religious Perspectives on the Debate over Stem Cells and Cloning*. Edited by Ronald Cole-Turner and Brent Waters. Washington: Georgetown University Press, 2003, 111–130.

186. "Protestantism and the Sciences." In *Blackwell's Companion to Protestantism*. Edited by Alister E.McGrath and Darren C. Marks. Oxford: Blackwell, 2004. 306–321.

187. "Eschatology."In *Essentials of Christian Theology*. Edited by William C. Placher. Louisville: Westminster John Knox Press, 2003. 347–365.

188. "Defining Human Life: Cloning, Embryos, and the Origins of Human Dignity."Co-authored with Gaymon Bennett. In *Beyond Determinism and Reductionism*. Edited by Mark L.Y. Chan and Roland Chia. Adelaide, Australia: ATF Press, 2003. 56–73.

189. "UFOs. Heaven's Gate, and the Theology of Suicide." In *Encyclopedic Sourcebook of UFO Religions*. Edited by James R. Lewis. Amherst New York: Prometheus Books, 2003, 239–260.

2004

190. "Is Our DNA Sacred?" In *Response*. Seattle Pacific University (Summer 2003) 10–13.

191. "Stem Cell Research and the Claim of the Other in the Human Subject." With Gaymon Bennett. In *Dialog* 43, no. 3 (Fall 2004): 184–204.

192. "Selfish Genes and Loving Persons."In *Fifty Years in Science and Religion: Ian G. Barbour and His Legacy*. Edited by Robert John Russell. Aldershot, United Kingdom: Ashgate, 2004. 191–212.

193. "New Age Movements." In *The Encyclopedia of Protestantism*. Edited by Hans J. Hillerbrand. 4 Volumes. London and New York: Routledge, 2004. III:1389–1391.

194. "Der *Dialog zwischen Schöpfungstheologie und Naturwissenschaften*." In *Religion in Geschichte und Gegenwart*. Edited by Hans Dieter Betz, Don S. Browning, Bernd Janowski, and Eberhard Jüngel. Tübingen: Mohr Siebeck, 2004. Band 7: 986–987.

195. "The Human Genome Project and the Future of Dignity."In *Das Gen als Mass aller Menschen: Menschenbilder im Zeitalter der Gene*. Volume 10 of *Darmstädter Theologische Beiträgezu Gegenwartsfragen*. Edited by Uwe Gerber and Hubert Meisinger. Frankfurt am Mein: Peter Lang, 2004. 255–268.

196. "*Naturwissenschaft und Religion. Ein wachsender Forschungsbereich.*" In *Verkündigung und Forschung.*49 Jahrgang (2–2004): 52–71.

2005

197. "Science and Religion: An Overview." In *Encyclopedia of Religion.* Lindsay Jones, Editor in Chief. 14 volumes: New York: Macmillan, 2nd ed., 2005. 12: 8180–8192.

198. "The Heart of the Reformation Faith." In *Dialog* 44, no. 1 (Spring 2005): 6–14. Revised lecture delivered at Seoul Theological University and Luther Theological University, Seoul, Korea, October 2004.

199. "Langdon Gilkey: *In Memoriam.*" In *Dialog* 44, no. 1 (Spring 2005): 69–80. In*Theology and Science* 3, no. 1 (April 2005): 221–236.

200. "UFO." In*Religion in Geschichte und Gegenwart.*Edited by Hans Dieter Betz, Don S. Browning, Bernd Janowski, and Eberhard Jüngel. Tübingen: Mohr Siebeck, 2005.

201. "Més enllà de l'embrió: El debat sobre les cél·lules mare." With Gaymon Bennett. In*Dialogal* 13 (Primavera 2005) 20–25 [www.dialogal.com].

202. "Dios Como El Futuro De La Creatividad Cosmica."In *Dios Y Las Cosmologias Moderna.*Edited by Francisco Jose Gil. Madrid: Biblioteca De Autores Cristianos, 2005, 177–200.

203. "Can the Body Heal the Spirit?"In *Spiritual Information: 100 Perspectives.* Edited by Charles L. Harper, Jr. Philadelphia: Templeton Foundation Press, 2005. 381–388. From"Holy Therapy" for *Christian Century,* 120:16 (9 August 2003) 23–26; #183 above.

204. "Techno-Secularism, Religion, and the Created Co-Creator." In*Zygon* 40, no. 4 (December 2005) 845–862.

205. "The Soul of Trans-Humanism." In*Dialog* 44, no. 4 (Winter 2005): 381–395.

206. "Intelligent Religion: Are Science and Faith Really Incompatible?" In *Sojourners*34, no. 11 (December 2005) 9. Republished in *Defining Moments: The Scopes "Monkey" Trial.* Omnigraphics, 2006.

207. "Dignity."In *Encyclopedia of Science, Technology, and Ethics.*Edited by Carl Mitcham. New York: Macmillan, Thomson, Gale, 2005, 2:528–530.

208. "Playing God."In *Encyclopedia of Science, Technology, and Ethics.*Edited by Carl Mitcham. New York: Macmillan, Thomson, Gale, 2005, 3:1424–1427. Revised 2013.

209. "Religion and Science from the Viewpoint of Western Scholarship." In *Religion and Science in the Context of Chinese Culture.* Edited by Chan Takkwong, Tsai Yi-Jia, and Frank Budenholzer. Adelaide, Australia: ATF Press, 2005, 7–18.

2006

210. "The Future of Resurrection."In *The Resurrection: John Dominic Crossan and N.T. Wright in Dialogue.* Edited by Robert Stewart. Minneapolis: Fortress, 2006, 149–170.

211. Westminster/John Knox Press, *Thoughtful Christian,* www.thoughtfulchristian.com 2006.

    "Stem Cell Research: Facts and Choices"

    "The Evolution Controversy," with Martinez Hewlett

    "How Do Christians Think about God?"

    "Why Do Christians Think of God as Trinity?"

    "What Happens When We Sin?"

    "Just How Does Jesus Save Us?"

    "Just What Is Our Soul?"

    "How Do Christians Think about Life beyond Death?"

212. "Stem Cells: Framing the Theological and Ethical Issues." In *KIATS Theological Journal,* Journal of the Korea Institute for Advanced Theological Studies, 11, no. 1 (Spring 2006): 6–26.

213. "Six Ways of Salvation: How Does Jesus Save?" In *Dialog,* 45, no. 3 (Fall 2006) 223–235.

214. "Why Darwin's Theory of Evolution Deserves Theological Support." With Martinez Hewlett. In *Theology and Science,* 4, no. 3 (July 2006) 171–182.

215. "Theology, Religion, and Intelligent Design." With Martinez Hewlett, Chapter 3 of *Not In Our Classrooms: Why Intelligent Design is Wrong for Our Schools.* Edited by Eugenie Scott and Glenn Branch. Boston: Beacon Press, 2007, 57–82.

216. "Contributions from Practical Theology and Ethics." For the *Oxford Handbook of Religion and Science.* Edited by Philip Clayton and Zachary Simpson. Oxford and New York: Oxford University Press, 2006, 372–387.

217. "The Return of the Chimera." In *Theology and Science* 4, no. 3 (November 2006): 247–260.

218. "Our Lutheran Future." In *Christus Lux* 1, no. 1 (Advent 2006) 5–21.

219. "Perfect Humans or Trans-Humans?" For St. Deiniol's Library research project. *Future Perfect? God, Medicine, and Human Identity.* Edited by Celia Deane-Drummond and Peter Manley Scott. London and New York: T & T Clark, 2006, 15–32.

2007

220. "Christian God-Talk While Listening to Atheists, Pluralists, and Muslims." In *Dialog* 46, no. 2 (Summer 2007): 84–103.

221. "A Theological Argument for Chimeras." In *Nature Reports Stem Cells:* http://www.nature.com/stemcells/2007/0706/070614/full/stemcells.2007.31.html

222. "Are We Playing God with Nano Enhancement?" In *Nanoethics: The Ethical and Social Implications of Nanotechnology.* Edited by Fritz Allhoff, Patrick Lin, James Moor, and John Weckert. New York: Wiley, 2007, chapter 4.3.

223. "Models of God." Paper delivered to the Mini-Conference on Models of God, American PhilosophicalAssociation Pacific Division, April 4–5, 2007.

Philosophia. (2007) 35:273–288Article 9066-8. (PHIA122). To be republished in a volume, *Models of God and Other Ultimate Realities,* Springer.

224. "Between the First and Second Comings." In *From Resurrection to Return: Perspectives from Theologyand Science on Christian Eschatology.* Edited by James Haire, Christine Ledger, and Stephen Picard. Adelaide: ATF Press, 2007, 95–111.

225. "Eschatology" video DIV in *Fundamentals of Christian Theology,* ELCA "Select Multimedia Resources" (2007) at Trinity Lutheran Seminary, 2199 E. Main St., Columbus Ohio 43209-2334.

226. "Re-Framing the Question: How Can We Construct a Theology of Religions?" In *Dialog* 46, no. 4 (Winter 2007): 322–334.

227. "Evolution, Evil, and the Theology of the Cross." In *Svensk Teologisk Kvartalskrif, ÅRGÅANG 83 (2007):* 98–120.

228. "Proleptic Ethics vs. Stop Sign Ethics: Theology and the Future of Genetics."*Svensk Teologisk Kvartalskrif, ÅRGÅANG 83 (2007)* 146–168; "Proleptic Ethics vs. Stop Sign Ethics: Theology and the Future of Genetics," *Journal of Lutheran Ethics* (on line journal: February 2008) http://archive.elca.org/jle/article.asp?k=775. Also, *Theological Foundations in an Age of Biological Intervention.* Edited by David C. Radtke. Minneapolis: Lutheran University Press, 2007, 82–115.

229. "Cells, Souls, and Dignity: A Theological Assessment." In *Boston College Law School Law and Religion Program,* "Matters of Life and Death: Selected Publications" (2006–2007), 15–36.

2008

230. "Stem Cells: A Moral Question?"In *The Lutheran* (January 2008) 17–18.

231. "Transhumanism and the Post-Human Future: Will Technological Progress Get Us There?" In *The Global Spiral* 9, no. 3 (June 2008). Republished in H+ *Transhumanism and Its Critics.* Edited by William Grassie and Gregory Hansell. Philadelphia: Metanexus Institute, 2011. #252. http://www.metanexus.net/magazine/tabid/68/id/10546/Default.aspx.

232. "Evangelical Atheism vs. the Grace of God." In *The Future of Atheism: Alister McGrath and Daniel Dennett in Dialogue.* Edited by Robert Stewart. Minneapolis: Fortress Press, 2008. Chapter 8.

233. "Genetic Science and the Frontiers of Ethics." In *Religion and Science: Pathways to Truth* (DVD). Hosted by Francis S. Collins. Wesley Ministry Network: www.Wesley Ministry Network.com.

234. "Anticipating Detection of Life in Space: AstroEthical Scenarios." In *Journal of Lutheran Ethics* (October 2008)http://archive.elca.org/jle/article.asp?k=814 .

235. with Julie Froehlig, *The Peters ETI Religious Crisis Survey.*http://www.counterbalance.org/etsurv/index-frame.html .

236. "Is ETI a Threat to Religion?" With Julie Froehlig. In *The MUFON UFO Journal* 485 (September 2008): 7–9.

237. "Religious Traditions and Genetic Enhancement." With Estuardo Aguilar-Cordova, Cromwell Crawford, and Karen Lebacqz. In *Altering Nature: Volume Two: Religion, Biotechnology, and Public Policy.* Edited by B. Andrew Lustig, Baruch A. Brody, and Gerald P. McKenny. Business Media B.V.: Springer Science, 2008, 109–159.

2009

238. "Astrotheology and the ETI Myth." In *Theology and Science* 7, no. 1 (February 2009): 3–30.

239. "From Easter to Parousia." In *Who Is Jesus Christ for Us Today* (*Festschrift* for Michael Welker). Edited by Andreas Schuele and Günther Thomas. Louisville, Kentucky: Westminster John Knox, 2009, 236–251.

240. "Atheist Stimulus and Faith Response." In *Trinity Seminary Review* 30, no. 2 (Summer/Fall 2009): 87–102.

241. "The Uses and Misuses of *Creation*." In *Lutheran Partners* (November/December 2009), http://www.elca.org/Growing-In-Faith/Vocation/Lutheran-Partners/Complete-Issue/091112/091112_04.aspx

242. "Afterword: Theological, Spiritual and Ethical Reflections on Radical Life Extension." In *Religion and the Implications of Radical Life Extension.* Edited by Derek Maher and Calvin Mercer. New York: Palgrave Macmillan, 2009, 155–168.

243. "Does Faith Contaminate Science? On the Appointment of Francis Collins." In *Theology and Science* 7, no. 4 (November 2009): 307–309.

244. "'Of Mice and Men': Making Babies from Stem Cells." In *Theology and Science* 7, no. 4 (November 2009): 311–315.

2010

245. "Is the Human Genome Sacred?" In *GenEthics and Religion.* Edited by G. Pfliederer, G. Brahier, and K. Lindpaintner. Basel: S. Karger Publishers, 2010: 108–117. http://content.karger.com/ProdukteDB/produkte.asp?Aktion=showproducts&searchWhat=books&ProduktNr=254162

246. "The Systematic Theologian at Work in an Atheistic Context." *Gudstankens aktualitet* [Festschrift for Peter Widmann]. Edited by Else Marie Wiberg Pedersen, Bo Kristian Holm, og Anders-Christian Jacobsen (Copenhagen: Forlaget ANIS, 2010), 55–76.

247. "Befriending Science." Patheos. (web only) http://www.patheos.com/Resources/Additional-Resources/Befriending-Science-Christian-Theologians-Respond?offset=5&max=1

248. "Is Craig Venter Playing God with Genetics and DNA?" In the *Journal of Cosmology* 8 (May 25, 2010) http://journalofcosmology.com/ArtificialLife108.html

249. "Constructing a Theology of Evolution: Building on John Haught." In *Zygon* 45, no. 4 (December 2010): 921–937.
250. "Can We Enhance the *Imago Dei*?" In *Human Identity at the Intersection of Science, Technology, and Religion*. Edited by Nancey Murphy and Christopher C. Knight. Aldershot, United Kingdom: Ashgate, 2010. Chapter 12, 215–238.

2011

251. "The Implications of the Discovery of Extra-Terrestrial Life for Religion." The Royal Society, *Philosophical Transactions A*, 369(1936) February 13, 2011: 644–655. http://rsta.royalsocietypublishing.org/content/369/1936.toc .
252. "Transhumanism and the Promethean Future: Will Technological Progress Get Us There?" *H+ Transhumanism and Its Critics*. Edited by Gregory R. Hansell and William Grassie. Philadelphia: Metanexus, 2011. Chapter 10, 147–175.
253. "Progress and Provolution: Will Transhumanism Leave Sin Behind?" in *Transhumanism and Transcendence*, ed. by Ronald Cole-Turner, Georgetown University Press, 63–86.
254. Ted Peters, et. al., "Book Symposium: *Sacred Cells? Why Christians Should Support Stem Cell Research*, in *Theology and Science*, 9:4 (November 2011) 451–465.
255. Devotions for December 11–17 in "There's a Voice in the Wilderness." Advent Devotional. St. Paul, Minnesota: Luther Seminary, 2011.
256. "Playing God? Genetic Determinism and Human Freedom."*Companion to the ISSRLibrary of Science and Religion,* ed. by Pranab K. Das II. Cambridge, United Kingdom: International Society for Science and Religion, 2011, 341–342.

2012

257. "The Problem of Suffering in Theistic Evolution," *Routledge Companion to Religion and Science*, edited by James Haag and Gregory Peterson. London and New York: Routledge, 2012, 270–282.
258. "What Is Sin?" (with Kristin Johnston Largen). *The Lutheran* 25:2 (February 2012): 18–19.
259. "Theology of Nature" in *Religion Past and Present: Encyclopedia of Theology and Religion,* ed. By Hans Dieter Betz, Don S. Browning, Bernd Janowski, and Eberhard Jűngel. Leiden and Boston: Brill, 2012, Volume 12: 651–652.
260. "Techno-Secularism, Religion, and the Created Co-Creator," *Virtual Zygon* (December 2012). See: 204. http://onlinelibrary.wiley.com/doi/10.1111/j.1467-9744.2005.00712.x/abstract .

2013

261. "Playing God," in *Encyclopedia of Science, Technology, and Ethics,* ed. by Carl Mitcham. New York: Macmillan, Thomson, Gale, 2005, 3:1424–1427. Revised 2013. See #208.
262. "Beatitudinal Eschatology: In Space or Time?" in *Churrasco: A Theological Feast in Honor of Vitor Westhelle,* ed. by Mary Philip, John Arthur Nunes, and Charles M. Colleier. Eugene, Oregon: Pickwick Publications, 2013, 29–37.

263. "E.O. Wilson's Conquest of Earth," *Theology and Science,* 11:2 (May 2013): 86–105.
264. "Would the Discovery of ETI Provoke a Religious Crisis?" in *Astrobiology, History, and Society,* edited by Douglas Vakoch. Springer: 341-355.
265. "Happy Danes and Deep Incarnation," *Dialog* 52:3 (Fall 2013): 248–254.
266. "Astrotheology" in *The Human Project in Science and Religion: Copenhagen University Discussions in Science and Religion, Volume II,* ed. by Anne L.C. Runehov and Charles Taliaferro. Copenhagen: University of Copenhagen, Faculty of Theology, 2013, 191–218.
267. "Astrotheology," Chapter 72 of *The Routledge Companion to Modern Christian Thought,* ed. Chad Meister and James Beilby. London and New York: Routledge, 2013, 838–853.
268. "Astroethics: Engaging Extraterrestrial Intelligent Life-Forms," *Encountering Life in the Universe.* Ed., Chris Impey, Anna Spitz, & William Stoeger. Tucson: Univ. Arizona Press, 2013, 200–221.
269. "Models of God" Chapter 5, in *Models of God and Alternative Ultimate Realities.* Ed. By Jeanine Diller and Asa Kasher. Heidelberg: Springer 2013, 43–61.
270. "The Higgs Boson: An Adventure in Critical Realism" (with Carl Peterson). *Theology and Science* 11, no. 3(2013) http://www.tandfonline.com/doi/pdf/10.1080/14746700.2013.809948#.UpVWD-7TklI.

2014

271. "In Memoriam: Ian Graeme Barbour (1923-2013)." *Journal of the American Academy of Religion.*82:2 (June 2014): 307–312. http://jaar.oxfordjournals.org/content/82/2/307.full.pdf?keytype=ref&ijkey=zvqicMweLCVaLS6
272. "Astrotheology: A Constructive Proposal," *Zygon* 49:2 (June 2014): 443–457.
273. "The Spirituality of Justification," *Dialog* 33:1 (Spring 2014): 58–68.
274. "The STAP Flap, the CIRM Squirm, and Lab Morality," *Theology and Science* 4 (November 2014)
275. "In Memoriam: Wolfhart Pannenberg (1928–2014), *Dialog* (Winter 2014).
276. "Does God Have a Plan for the Big History of the Cosmos?"*Theology and Science* 12:3 (August 2014) 1978: 200.
277. "Creation *ex amore*," Review of Ian A. McFarland's *From Nothing: A Theology of Creation* in *The Christian Century* 131:20 (October 1, 2014): 36–37.
278. "Science and Redemption: The Future of Creation," *The Science and Religion Dialogue: Past and Future,* ed. Michael Welker (Frankfurt am Main: Peter Lang, 2014), 93–106.

Index of Authors

A
Alison, James 172, 173
Ambrose 205, 206, 272
Anselm 88, 210, 273, 366
Aquinas 67, 122
Aristotle 195, 205, 281
Augustine 24, 56, 121, 122, 174, 273, 282, 283, 286, 287
Aune, Michael B. 3, 13, 81, 82, 83, 84, 85

B
Bailie, Gil 172, 173
Balch, David 4, 103, 195, 202, 207, 209, 240
Barbour, Ian G. 72, 87, 88, 252, 268, 378, 384
Barth, Karl 15, 45, 58, 163, 238, 265
Bataille, Georges 146, 148
Bateson, Patrick 291
Bedford, Nancy 205, 207, 209
Bennett, Gaymon 3, 28, 37, 85, 86, 171, 248, 271, 280, 285, 287, 291, 308, 365, 377, 378, 379
Bernett, Monika 202
Bernstein, Alan 117
Borges, Jorge Luis 144, 145, 150, 366
Bostrom, Nick 355
Braaten, Carl 104, 174, 351, 370
Brecht, Berthold 151
Butler, Joseph 284

C
Campbell, Heidi 355
Cardinal Ratzinger 275
Catherine of Sienna 128
Chesterton, G. K. 218, 341
Clayton, Philip 18, 73, 268, 273, 370, 380
Clement of Alexandria 124, 281
Cobb, John 353, 371, 372
Cohen, Shaye 202, 203
Cole-Turner, Ronald 4, 257, 266, 298, 342, 375, 378, 383
Collins, John J. 211, 213, 215, 218, 364, 381, 382

D
Dante 117, 118, 125, 389
Darwin, Charles 4, 76, 247, 249, 253, 255, 269, 271, 278, 285, 292, 293, 294, 295, 296, 332, 365, 380
Dawkins, Richard 14, 18, 70, 83, 84, 247, 252, 255, 285, 287
de Chardin, Teilhard 351
Deleuze, Gilles 30, 31, 48, 326
Delio, Ilia 273
Dennett, Daniel 252, 269, 381
Descartes 283
Dietrich, Gabriela 184, 185, 390

E
Eliade, Mercia 34, 181

F
Fagan, Garret C. 202
Fernyhough, Charles 170
Fiorenza, Elizabeth Schüssler 214, 279
Foucault, Michel 28, 30, 48, 51, 52, 54, 56, 57, 58, 148, 163, 320
Fox, George 284
Fuller, Buckminster 352

G
Gandhi, Mahatma 183, 184, 390
Giddens, Anthony 147, 148
Gilkey, Langdon 29, 35, 80, 168, 175, 176, 177, 367, 370, 379
Gish, Duane 252
Girard, Rene 172, 173, 234
Gould, Stephan Jay 255
Gregersen, Niels Henrick 3, 16, 25, 69, 72, 78, 87, 88, 89, 90, 91, 266, 365
Gregory of Nyssa 124

H
Haught, John 252, 269, 375, 383
Hawking, Stephen 87, 346
Heim, Mark 61, 112, 173, 236

Henriksen, Jan-Olav 4, 220, 221, 242
Heraclitus 281
Herzfeld, Noreen 277
Heschel, Abraham 209, 217
Hess, Peter M.J. 4, 267, 269, 273, 277, 301, 302
Hewlett, Martinez 4, 33, 171, 172, 247, 248, 249, 251, 253, 254, 255, 257, 258, 259, 269, 271, 280, 285, 287, 291, 294, 295, 298, 326, 365, 380
Hume, David 292
Huxley, Thomas 252, 253

I
Irenaeus 265, 282, 285, 287, 392

J
Jacob, Benno 287
Jacobson, Carol R. 9, 95

Johnson, Elizabeth 67
Josephus 199, 200, 201, 202, 390
Joshua, Gurram 4, 178, 180, 182, 183, 185, 186, 187, 188, 189, 191, 192, 193, 237

K
Kannaday, Wayne C. 4, 210, 240
Kant, Immanuel 31, 144, 239
Kierkegaard, Søren 70, 95, 151
Kitcher, Philip 75, 76
Kloppenborg-Verbin, John S. 196, 197
Koch, Klaus 211
Korsmeyer, Jerry 273

L
LaCugna, Catherine Mowry 67, 68, 238
Largen, Kristin Johnston 3, 111, 160, 383
Lindsey, Hal 211, 212, 215, 241
Lombard, Peter 122, 174
Luskin, Fred 169
Luther, Martin 27, 131, 132, 133, 134, 135, 136, 137, 138, 150, 160, 173, 174, 208, 226, 230, 237, 238, 239, 285, 366, 371, 375, 376, 379, 383, 389

M
Malebranche, Nicolas 283, 284
Milton, John 284
Moe-Lobeda, Cynthia 236

Moltmann, Jürgen 237, 238, 239, 302, 303, 321, 353, 373
Moritz, Joshua 5, 170, 248, 256, 280, 285, 287, 291, 298, 299, 300, 301, 365
Morris, Henry 252

N
Nagel, Thomas 90, 91, 342
Nelson, Derek R. 167

O
Origen 124
Otto, Rudolf 143, 144, 286
Overton, Richard 284

P
Pagels, Elain 211
Pannenberg, Wolfhart 16, 29, 32, 40, 42, 43, 44, 45, 46, 47, 48, 58, 59, 110, 127, 205, 238, 239, 325, 351, 354, 366, 367, 370, 374, 375, 384
Penumaka, Moses 4, 178, 237
Perdue, Leo 197
Peters, Ted 1, 2, 3, 4, 5, 7, 8, 9, 13, 14, 16, 17, 18, 19, 20, 24, 25, 26, 27, 28, 29, 30, 32, 33, 34, 35, 36, 37, 38, 39, 40, 41, 42, 43, 44, 47, 48, 49, 50, 51, 52, 53, 54, 55, 56, 59, 60, 65, 67, 69, 70, 71, 72, 73, 74, 75, 78, 79, 85, 86, 87, 88, 89, 91, 95, 96, 97, 99, 100, 101, 102, 103, 104, 105, 106, 107, 108, 109, 110, 111, 112, 113, 114, 116, 117, 123, 127, 138, 140, 141, 142, 143, 144, 147, 150, 152, 157, 162, 163, 167, 168, 169, 170, 171, 172, 173, 174, 175, 176, 177, 178, 179, 180, 181, 185, 194, 195, 196, 205, 206, 207, 209, 210, 212, 216, 218, 220, 221, 222, 223, 224, 225, 226, 227, 228, 238, 240, 242, 247, 248, 249, 250, 251, 252, 253, 254, 255, 256, 257, 258, 259, 265, 266, 269, 271, 274, 277, 278, 280, 281, 285, 287, 291, 293, 294, 307, 308, 309, 318, 319, 320, 321, 322, 323, 324, 325, 326, 327, 328, 330, 331, 332, 334, 335, 336, 338, 339, 341, 342, 343, 346, 347, 348, 351, 352, 354, 355, 357, 358, 359, 360, 361, 364, 372, 381, 383

Placher, William 66, 67, 173, 378
Pope John Paul II 279, 392
Pope Pius XII 271
Portmann, John 175
Procksch, Otto 286
Pryor, Adam 4, 9, 103, 152, 195, 240, 362

R
Rahner, Karl 102, 103, 163, 238, 265, 270, 273, 279, 349
Ratke, David 3, 25, 60, 92
Reddish, Mitchell 214, 216
Rorty, Richard 146
Rowland, Christopher 211
Russell, Robert John 3, 72, 88, 103, 105, 107, 109, 110, 157, 158, 159, 171, 248, 256, 268, 271, 278, 280, 285, 286, 287, 291, 307, 327, 341, 365, 370, 372, 373, 375, 376, 378

S
Sailhamer, John 286, 289
Schweitzer, Albert 143
Sittler, Joseph 32, 351, 353
Smith, Jonathan Z. 200
Sobrino, Jon 186, 209
Spencer, Herbert 253
Strohl, Jane E. 3, 129, 160

T
Thangaraj, Thomas 181, 182
Theophilus of Antioch 281, 282, 285, 288, 392
Tillich, Paul 20, 29, 34, 35, 39, 40, 51, 80, 81, 163, 176, 222, 320, 376, 377
Toulmin, Stephen 73
Tracy, David 80, 81, 82, 344, 370
Turner, Alice 4, 120, 257, 266, 298, 342, 375, 378, 383
Twain, Mark 211

V
van Huysteen, Wentzel 74
von Balthasar, Hans Urs 121, 127, 128

W
Walker, Mark 355
Wallace-Hadrill, Andrew 201, 202, 207, 208
Warfield, Benjamin 301
Weiss, Johannes 143
Wesley, John 284
Westhelle, Vitor 4, 140, 141, 142, 161, 162, 163, 164, 383
Whitehead, Alfred North 70, 110
Williams, Rowan 174, 175
Wilson, Edward 252

Index of Subjects

A
Abraham 62, 65, 113, 135, 217, 386
Acts 61, 64, 195, 198, 200, 207
Adam 1, 2, 4, 9, 115, 123, 133, 134, 135, 137, 152, 195, 229, 240, 258, 259, 265, 271, 272, 275, 282, 299, 301, 307, 321, 332, 344, 362, 387
advaitins 182
adventus 42, 112, 113, 114, 115, 307, 354
Alexander the Great 199
alien enemies 346, 361
alpha 153, 154
analysis 8, 20, 24, 29, 35, 36, 55, 85, 100, 101, 112, 125, 126, 134, 152, 167, 168, 172, 178, 180, 183, 197, 218, 226, 234, 249, 261, 263, 274, 326, 330, 358, 360
    downward analysis 100
    durative 101
    quantitative 100, 101
    upward analysis 99
Anglicans 284
animal suffering 281, 283, 284, 285, 286, 293
anthropocentrism 321, 335
anthropology 8, 35, 48, 258, 266, 268, 270, 273, 277, 278, 280, 298, 321, 323, 332, 355
    theological anthropology 8, 266, 268, 273, 277, 278, 298, 321
    Christian anthropology 258, 280, 378
Antichrist 132, 137
Antiochus IV 199, 201
anxiety 34, 147, 168, 298
apocalypse 136, 160, 211, 213, 216, 218, 219, 240, 241, 354
apocalyptic 129, 131, 137, 138, 147, 160, 161, 164, 198, 211, 212, 214, 217, 218, 219, 320
    apocalyptic literature 211
apokatastasis 111
Apostles' Creed 65, 66

apple tree 131, 132, 136, 139, 160, 161
arche 153
archonic 117, 206
Armageddon 147, 211, 219, 333
artificial intelligence 347
astrobiology 105, 206, 329, 330, 331, 336, 339, 349, 358, 360
astronauts 34, 329, 334, 337, 359
Astrotheology 5, 8, 255, 305, 328, 330, 335, 337, 339, 347, 351, 358, 359, 382, 384
Atheism 381
atheistic materialism 19, 254, 318
autochthony 182
autonomy 310, 313, 314, 321, 322, 356
avatars 341, 360

B
Ba'al Shem Tov 204
Baptism 126, 268
beatitude 54, 141
beneficence 356, 378
benevolent ETI myth 361

Big Bang 71, 154, 268, 270
bioethics 85, 356
biology of freedom 280
Bio-piety 182
blasphemy 169
boundary crossing 195, 205
Brahma 182

C
cargo cults 335
Cartesians 283, 284
caste system 182, 184, 185, 188
causal explanation 74, 89, 91
causation 90, 99, 100, 101, 157, 251, 255
centering 181
1 Corinthians 15 103, 114, 123
chosen people 63, 65

388

Christian
    Christian anthropology 258, 280, 378
    Christian discipleship 132
    Christian doctrine of creation 280
    Christian theology 15, 18, 23, 42, 46, 82, 121, 123, 147, 210, 211, 220, 268, 353
Christology 24, 25, 26, 27, 82, 330, 358
    actualization 24, 47, 82, 96, 107, 112, 154, 155, 156, 157, 159, 181, 194, 351
chronos 112, 143, 163
church 15, 20, 22, 25, 27, 64, 65, 66, 67, 85, 126, 131, 132, 137, 138, 140, 177, 178, 183, 186, 195, 208, 221, 223, 224, 226, 237, 240, 267, 285, 288, 297, 337, 356
    radically inclusive 65
    radically relational 65
circumcision 200, 201, 202, 203
classical electromagnetism 110
clinical studies 311, 312, 314
cognitive ethology 281
colonial 161, 194, 196, 200, 201, 207, 208, 320, 335
common sense 96, 153, 154
Communion 126
compatibilism 301
complementarity 13, 19, 326
concupiscence 168
concursus 298, 301, 302
conservatism 23, 82
contactees 333, 337
Cornelius 64
correlation 7, 20, 21, 24, 81, 82, 358
    method of correlation 7, 20, 21, 81, 358
cosmonauts 337
creation
    creation theology 4, 195, 196, 240
    new creation 8, 19, 34, 97, 152, 156, 157, 158, 159, 163, 164, 206, 241, 274, 275, 301, 302, 303, 307, 319, 353, 354
    prelapsarian 145, 319
creationism/ists 33, 249, 252, 296
    biblical creationists 296
    scientific creationists 250, 296, 297
Critical Deconstruction 53
Critical Realism 71, 72, 87, 88, 384

cross 4, 8, 22, 165, 173, 228, 234, 236, 239, 285, 314, 341, 367, 368, 381
cruelty 116, 169

D
dalit 180, 181, 185, 186, 187, 189, 191, 192, 193, 194, 237, 239, 240
Dante's *Inferno* 117
Darwinism 71, 254, 295, 296, 297
    Neo-Darwinism 295, 297
    Social Darwinism 296
Denisovans 260, 261, 263, 348, 362
determinism 96, 101, 102, 106, 154, 354
    absolute determinism 96, 106
    historical determinism 101
deutero-Isaiah 195, 196
Diet of Augsburg 130
dignity 20, 48, 164, 183, 185, 187, 191, 193, 195, 196, 206, 207, 209, 239, 240, 285, 321, 326, 355, 356
    eschatological dignity 48, 326
    human dignity 20, 183, 187, 191, 193, 195, 206, 207, 239, 321, 326, 355
dinosaurs 270
dipolar monism 273
divine creativity 268
divine intervention 301
DNA 247, 259, 260, 261, 263, 267, 270, 274, 345, 376, 378, 383
Docetism 186
doctrine 16, 27, 65, 66, 67, 68, 80, 97, 111, 112, 120, 123, 126, 127, 130, 132, 141, 160, 167, 168, 169, 171, 172, 173, 175, 176, 205, 220, 221, 226, 268, 269, 277, 280, 282, 288, 326, 335
Doomsday 211, 323
dualism 273, 274, 277, 301

E
Easter 97, 102, 103, 104, 107, 159, 172, 179, 194, 241, 302, 303, 373, 382
eco-feminism 353
ecological theology 275
El Salvador 209
embryonic stem cell research 308, 310
emergence 74, 264, 273, 290, 293, 297, 300, 326, 354
empirical 29, 30, 31, 35, 41, 43, 44, 47, 71, 78, 280, 281, 285, 290, 292, 334

389

enemy 62, 124, 128, 197, 217, 230, 231, 232, 234, 346
Enlightenment 46, 58, 67, 122, 322
environmental ethic 318, 319
environmentalism 319, 353
epigenetically 205, 207
Epiphanes of Syria 199
epistemology 57, 79, 320, 325
eschatological omega 157, 206
eschatology 3, 7, 93, 103, 104, 141, 142, 150, 161, 164, 372, 377, 378, 381, 384
  beatitudinal 141, 164, 384
  Christian eschatology 95, 162
  doctrine of eschatology 126
  temporal 45, 99, 127, 194, 349
eternal life 112, 126, 130
ethics 8, 29, 32, 36, 43, 54, 57, 103, 143, 185, 195, 197, 205, 206, 207, 208, 240, 257, 296, 307, 308, 309, 310, 312, 319, 320, 322, 323, 324, 325, 339, 344, 349, 351, 352, 353, 354, 356
  medical ethics 310
  planetary ethics 323, 325
  proleptic ethics 8, 32, 36, 43, 54, 103, 240, 307, 308, 309, 312, 320, 325, 351, 353
  stem cell ethics 257, 308
  stop-sign ethics 323
  Teilhardian ethics 351
ethnic difference 201
ethnic identity 207
ethnicity 63, 65, 201
eugenics 296
Eve 133, 134, 135, 137, 229, 258, 259, 265, 271, 272, 275, 299, 301, 321, 344
evil 5, 33, 168, 171, 172, 175, 219, 236, 248, 271, 280, 285, 287, 291, 293, 298, 300, 301, 346, 348, 364, 365, 372, 376, 377, 381
  evolutionary evil 281, 286, 291, 292, 299
  moral evil 171, 286, 293
  natural evil 171, 293
evolution 4, 5, 8, 33, 171, 172, 179, 245, 247, 248, 249, 250, 253, 254, 258, 264, 267, 268, 269, 270, 271, 272, 273, 280, 285, 287, 290, 291, 294, 298, 326, 331, 334, 335, 341, 344, 347, 355, 364, 365, 375, 380, 381, 383
  biological evolution 248, 249, 253, 302, 334, 340
  convergent evolution 341
  cultural evolution 340
  evolution controversy 4, 8, 245, 380
  theistic evolution 5, 280, 298, 383
  theory of evolution 269, 293, 295, 296
evolutionary
  evolutionary change 291, 297
  evolutionary evil 281, 286, 291, 292, 299
  evolutionary history 171, 179, 271, 275, 281, 291, 293, 300
  evolutionary theory 249, 278, 295
exegesis 161, 215, 217
exhaustive definite foreknowledge 97, 98, 100
experience 14, 17, 26, 30, 31, 35, 36, 40, 41, 46, 60, 67, 69, 70, 75, 76, 77, 80, 81, 102, 116, 126, 128, 131, 137, 144, 145, 147, 158, 171, 177, 179, 180, 181, 186, 188, 191, 193, 194, 204, 213, 221, 224, 237, 239, 240, 242, 248, 269, 276, 286, 313, 314, 330, 337, 342
explanation 7, 18, 66, 69, 70, 72, 73, 74, 75, 76, 77, 78, 84, 88, 89, 90, 91, 251, 255, 261
explanatory adequacy 19, 69, 70, 91, 298
extraterrestrial life 329, 330, 331, 336, 337

F

fairness 217, 311, 357
fairy tales 218
faith 13, 14, 17, 19, 20, 21, 22, 23, 24, 26, 39, 43, 44, 52, 53, 58, 68, 81, 85, 107, 132, 136, 137, 138, 142, 143, 161, 171, 173, 181, 183, 191, 198, 209, 210, 216, 217, 221, 225, 228, 229, 241, 242, 252, 257, 269, 278, 279, 283, 293, 323, 327, 348, 349, 358, 362
fall
  human fall 265, 282, 291, 299
fallenness of creation 281, 287, 293, 300
false idolatry 331, 359
feminism 320, 353

INDEX

fiction 145, 221, 329, 345
finite 43, 44, 47, 54, 69, 145, 146, 163, 169, 267, 279, 331, 354
first-order 50
Flying Saucers 5, 33, 328, 359, 365
foundationalism 319
Free Creatures Defense 292
freedom 37, 156, 280, 299, 307, 326, 364, 378, 383
    human freedom 37, 280, 307, 364, 383
    creaturely freedom 156
free-will-defense 299, 300, 301
fundamental theology 80
future
    proximate future 155, 158
    ultimate future 8, 96, 103, 104, 106, 152, 155, 158, 159
    consciousness 17, 37, 39, 41, 49, 50, 56, 86, 90, 181, 185, 186, 191, 218, 231, 272, 277, 290, 293, 300
future-giving 153, 154, 155
futurists 36, 38, 42, 323, 352, 353
futurity 153, 325, 326, 354
futurology 36, 39, 42
futurum 42, 112, 113, 114, 116, 307, 354

G
Gehenna 120
genesis 153, 154
Genesis 61, 65, 68, 96, 133, 195, 252, 270, 272, 274, 286, 287, 288, 289, 293, 296, 299, 300, 344
genetic mutation 295
genetics 7, 78, 257, 259, 275, 318
genocide 171, 247, 248, 294
genre confusion 216
geocentrism 336, 358
geo-piety 181
Gnostic 147, 210
gnosticism 173
God hypothesis 83
goodness 115, 169, 224, 229, 270, 280, 282, 284, 289, 307
gospel 15, 26, 64, 115, 116, 129, 130, 132, 136, 137, 138, 152, 183, 185, 187, 196, 216, 236, 241, 242, 352
grace 14, 15, 19, 20, 21, 24, 25, 26, 27, 57, 82, 84, 116, 117, 121, 125, 126, 128, 129, 132, 137, 150, 160, 161, 164, 167, 172, 173, 174, 175, 177, 178, 179, 194, 224, 225, 228, 229, 230, 236, 243, 274, 300, 357, 362
    God of grace 14, 19, 20, 24, 82, 84, 228, 362
grievance story 169
gymnasium 202, 203

H
Hasidism 204
heaven 65, 89, 96, 104, 112, 113, 114, 115, 116, 118, 119, 120, 122, 123, 126, 127, 130, 132, 133, 141, 160, 162, 167, 197, 328
hell 22, 79, 111, 112, 113, 114, 116, 117, 118, 120, 121, 122, 123, 124, 125, 126, 127, 128, 160
    depictions of hell 117, 118
    doctrine of hell 111
    end of 116, 117, 119, 120
Heraclitus 281
hermeneutics 32, 42, 73, 208, 217
heterosexism 320
Hinduism 180, 181, 182, 183, 187, 193, 341, 360
holism 60, 127
Holy Spirit 64, 65, 66, 92, 116, 194, 217, 225, 243
Homo sapiens 261, 262, 263, 268, 270, 271, 272, 273, 274, 292, 298, 348, 355, 361, 362
hospitality 60, 61, 65, 68, 92, 139
human behavior 173, 248, 249
human condition 172, 176, 180, 228, 230, 236, 298, 300
human genome 260
Humani Generis 271
human nature 168, 176, 177, 181, 228, 248, 299, 342, 343, 344, 349, 355
human origins 257, 258, 259, 260, 262, 264, 265, 266, 298
hypothetical consonance 71, 72

I
identity politics 322
imago Dei 4, 267, 275, 383
imitative desire 172
incarnation 26, 82, 97, 101, 104, 142, 179, 205, 238, 239, 257, 263, 265, 270, 285, 360, 361
indeterminism 108, 109, 157, 158

391

India 180, 183, 184, 185, 186, 187, 188, 189, 193, 194, 237, 240, 276
Indirect Apologetics 16
individualism 321, 322
    expressive individualism 322
    utilitarian individualism 322
infinite 140
inherentism 321
inscription 146, 147, 149
Intelligent Design 294, 297, 380
intelligent life-forms 339
interethnic dialogue 196, 209, 240
International Society for Stem Cell Research 314
Interpretation 220, 373
inter-species 263, 282
in vitro fertilization 314
Irenaeus of Lyons 282
Isaiah 126, 195, 196, 198, 233
Islam 336

J
Jeremiah 204, 211
Jerusalem 64, 198, 199, 200, 202, 203, 204, 232, 241
Jesus 4, 8, 14, 20, 23, 25, 26, 27, 39, 40, 41, 45, 46, 47, 63, 64, 65, 66, 82, 83, 84, 97, 101, 102, 103, 104, 111, 112, 113, 114, 115, 116, 118, 119, 120, 121, 122, 123, 125, 126, 127, 129, 130, 135, 138, 139, 143, 150, 159, 162, 173, 178, 179, 183, 185, 186, 187, 192, 193, 194, 195, 196, 197, 198, 199, 200, 201, 202, 203, 204, 205, 207, 208, 209, 211, 213, 214, 215, 228, 229, 230, 231, 232, 234, 235, 237, 238, 239, 240, 241, 243, 258, 263, 265, 270, 302, 341, 349, 357, 360, 367, 374, 380, 382
Jews 63, 64, 120, 137, 198, 199, 200, 201, 202, 203, 204, 205, 209, 224, 296
Jonah 62, 288
Judah 135, 214, 288
Judea 195, 196, 200, 201, 202, 204
Judeans 198, 199, 200, 201, 209
Judgment Day 212
justice 189, 190, 292, 315, 356, 357, 366
    social justice 357, 366
justification 8, 74, 81, 119, 168, 171, 173, 201, 220, 228, 229, 230, 231, 232, 234, 235, 236, 238, 296, 303, 357

K
kairos 38, 112, 150
Kannda Kaavyaalu 186
Kingdom of God 143, 195, 196, 197, 206, 207, 240, 241
knowledge 14, 37, 44, 46, 71, 74, 90, 98, 99, 100, 133, 143, 145, 146, 147, 148, 149, 151, 156, 163, 173, 179, 187, 191, 210, 229, 237, 238, 269, 275, 278, 289, 302, 313, 349
kosher 200, 201

L
Last Day 132, 138
laughter 122, 141, 146, 148
Leona Foxx 4, 220, 221, 222, 241, 242
liberation theology 179, 180, 185
liberation thought 320
Lutheran theology 25, 26, 365

M
marginalization 193
marriage 132, 134
Marthoma 183
materialist ideology 18, 19, 295
Matthew 113, 118, 120, 121, 129, 141, 150, 162, 197, 198, 200, 230, 231, 243, 262, 290, 371
maximalist 298
Memorial Day 232, 233, 235
memory 170, 234
mercy 54, 62, 63, 116, 126, 136, 162, 357
metaphysical realism 72
method 3, 20, 21, 56, 57, 59, 79, 81, 367, 368, 371
Methodists 284
methodology 81, 83, 85, 87, 89, 91
middle axiom 54
mimesis 172
minimalist 70, 297, 298
modernity 15, 21, 22, 23, 24, 32, 36, 37, 58, 59, 82, 145, 148, 266, 268, 318
monogenism 271
morality 144, 281, 287, 292, 300, 341, 344, 347, 359
moral responsiveness 277
multiethnic 201, 203, 240
multiple incarnations 341, 348, 360
multiplicity 61
Muslims 224, 295, 297, 380
    conservative Muslims 295, 297

INDEX

N
Naive World-Construction 53
NASA 329, 359
National UFO Reporting Center 328
naturalism 90, 91, 278, 295
natural science 17, 18, 206, 330
natural selection 74, 76, 89, 269, 285, 293, 295, 296, 297, 298
Neandertals 259, 260, 261, 262, 263, 264, 265
meo-orthodox theology 45
neo-orthodoxy 23, 82
neo-pragmatist 146
Newtonian mechanism 108
new trinitarianism 238
9/11 224, 247
Ninevah 62
non-maleficence 311, 312
non-origin-based 321

O
omega 60, 95, 97, 99, 100, 101, 102, 103, 104, 105, 107, 109, 126, 155, 158, 206, 214, 241, 287, 319, 320, 321, 327, 342, 364, 377
Onan 135
ontological indeterminism 109, 157
ontology 7, 95, 96, 97, 99, 100, 101, 102, 105, 106, 107, 108, 109, 110, 152, 154, 156, 157, 158, 159, 161, 185, 241, 319, 320
    ontology of freedom 99
    open ontology 108
    ordinary ontology 109
    proleptic eschatology 152, 164, 324
    retroactive ontology 3, 4, 7, 93, 105, 152, 157
orthopraxy 201, 203

P
panentheism 238
parables 119, 186
parochialism 322, 352
particularity 15, 24, 25, 26, 27, 82, 83, 84, 85
    Christian particularity 24, 85
    particularity of the Incarnation 26, 27, 83
    theology of particularity 15
patents 316
patriotism 221, 224, 233, 234

patripassianism 238, 239
person 14, 26, 52, 65, 67, 68, 82, 85, 117, 124, 129, 136, 146, 159, 168, 169, 170, 171, 174, 181, 184, 215, 222, 223, 225, 230, 231, 238, 239, 270, 271, 273, 274, 276, 277, 279, 301, 321, 323
Peter 4, 14, 25, 64, 65, 122, 137, 151, 174, 267, 269, 282, 283, 290, 301, 302, 365, 379, 380, 382, 384, 386
phenomenology 39, 181
philosophy 30, 52, 57, 282, 283, 291, 367, 368, 370, 374
    Platonic philosophy 213
    premodern philosophy 23, 53
physics 71, 73, 87, 89, 103, 109, 110
pluralism 17, 60, 61, 210, 319
polygenism 271
possibility 22, 31, 32, 34, 42, 44, 47, 48, 50, 51, 54, 55, 96, 99, 109, 112, 117, 120, 125, 138, 151, 158, 159, 181, 184, 186, 205, 206, 255, 257, 263, 292, 309, 319, 322, 326, 344, 348, 354, 355
post-colonial 161, 194, 320
Postcritical Reconstruction 53
posthuman 342, 355
postmodern 13, 17, 20, 22, 23, 49, 50, 56, 86, 145, 319, 320, 321, 322, 327
    holistic 17, 108, 127, 159, 163, 206
    pluralistic 17, 195, 210, 319
poverty 131, 180, 189, 192, 193
power 22, 54, 55, 56, 57, 58, 78, 86, 91, 98, 100, 101, 104, 113, 114, 116, 117, 118, 121, 122, 123, 124, 130, 134, 146, 147, 148, 157, 160, 164, 169, 170, 185, 193, 194, 198, 202, 207, 216, 219, 223, 226, 228, 232, 234, 323, 333, 335, 344, 349
    divine power 98, 100, 101, 157
praxis 180, 198
prayer 13, 80, 132, 137, 225, 226, 243, 333
prediction 213, 216, 240, 241
predispositional 109, 110
preferential option for the poor 185
presence 18, 27, 42, 81, 96, 132, 140, 143, 145, 146, 149, 150, 159, 162, 163, 164, 189, 190, 194, 204, 233, 238, 277, 289, 347, 348
pride 168, 189

process 28, 45, 125, 139, 155, 156, 170, 196, 205, 206, 207, 208, 222, 238, 256, 266, 280, 285, 298, 303, 307, 313, 319, 321, 324, 344
process theology 156
proclamation 15, 23, 64, 136, 201, 213, 216, 240, 241
progress 17, 72, 184, 254, 318, 323, 324, 325, 335, 336
prolepsis 32
proleptic ontology 185
prophecy 211, 214, 217, 337
prophet 160, 196, 204, 208, 233, 234, 235, 236, 341
protology 196, 197
psychosomatic unity 273, 274, 301
public policy 85, 248, 316, 356, 358, 359

Q
Quakers 284
quantum mechanics 107, 110, 158, 268
Qumran 196

R
racism 226, 258, 259
rebellion 287, 288
    pre-human rebellion 287
reconciliation 126, 127, 230
reconstruction 50, 52, 53, 55, 170, 211, 267, 322
recontextualization 13, 15, 20, 24
redemption 41, 84, 101, 127, 131, 135, 136, 139, 160, 186, 206, 265, 284, 319
reductionist materialism 90
regenerative medicine 309
relation 28, 32, 34, 36, 40, 42, 47, 48, 54, 56, 57, 59, 67, 71, 106, 109, 145, 180, 198, 207, 223, 224, 273, 291
Relational God 65
relationality 66, 67, 68, 92, 99
religion 29, 34, 36, 39, 53, 57, 62, 63, 69, 72, 78, 87, 88, 143, 144, 181, 184, 208, 216, 226, 236, 249, 267, 268, 294, 295, 298, 318, 319, 330, 331, 332, 334, 335, 336, 337, 338, 341, 358, 359, 360
    religious experience 144, 180
    religious literacy 61
repentance 129, 136, 183, 217, 219
representation 145, 146, 147, 149, 150

repristination 23, 82
resurrection 16, 26, 41, 46, 47, 66, 97, 101, 102, 103, 104, 111, 114, 115, 125, 126, 127, 130, 159, 178, 179, 194, 284, 285, 302
    final resurrection 97
    resurrection of Jesus 41, 46, 97, 101, 102, 103, 104, 111, 127, 159, 194
    resurrection of the cosmos 97
retribution 117, 118
retrieval 2, 13, 15, 19, 23, 24, 25, 26, 27, 81, 82, 83, 84, 170
Revelation 4, 44, 45, 46, 47, 58, 96, 160, 210, 211, 212, 213, 214, 215, 216, 217, 218, 219, 240, 241, 307, 374
Ruth 63

S
Sabbath 96, 199, 200, 201
sacramental perspective 270, 274, 275, 278
salvation 16, 34, 35, 36, 41, 47, 57, 102, 111, 112, 120, 121, 135, 136, 155, 160, 161, 173, 178, 186, 196, 228, 234, 241, 270, 284, 301, 335, 337, 359, 360, 362
    universal salvation 111, 112, 160
Samaria 195, 199, 200, 201, 208, 209
Samaritan 63, 200, 201, 208
Sanatana Dharma 181, 182
Sarah 62, 65, 135, 136
scapegoat 8, 169, 172, 230, 231, 232, 234, 235, 236
    invisible scapegoat 232, 234, 235, 236
    visible scapegoat 232, 235
Scholastics 284
science
    anti-science 148, 295
    research science 19
science-religion 69, 78
scientific materialism 319
scientific method 88, 89, 278, 341
scientific re-presentation 149
scientism 318, 331, 359
scripture 19, 45, 68, 203, 216, 268, 287, 330, 337
second-order observation 50
selfishness 38, 285

INDEX

self-justification 8, 171, 173, 228, 229, 230, 231, 232, 234, 235, 236, 238, 303
self-limiting 98, 99
semantic explanation 74, 78, 89, 91
semantic realism 72
semi-intelligent 340
serpent 133, 134, 229, 286, 287, 289, 293, 299, 300
SETI 329, 330, 334, 335, 347, 359, 360
Sheol 120
simul iustus et peccator 130, 223
sin 8, 57, 63, 116, 121, 126, 133, 134, 139, 167, 168, 169, 171, 172, 173, 174, 175, 176, 177, 229, 230, 236, 248, 259, 265, 266, 271, 273, 280, 281, 282, 287, 288, 289, 298, 299, 300, 301, 303, 346
   animal sin 288
   human sin 121, 171, 236, 282
   original sin 121, 133, 134, 139, 171, 259, 271, 273, 282, 298, 299, 301
social justice 21, 210
sociobiology 83, 249, 253
soldier 137, 232, 233, 234, 235
soteriology 161, 228, 358
soul 33, 61, 168, 255, 271, 273, 277, 280, 346, 364, 376, 379, 380
space 4, 140, 141, 142, 161, 202, 255, 329, 337, 338, 382, 384
species 76, 258, 259, 263, 264, 265, 266, 267, 271, 272, 274, 275, 282, 290, 293, 295, 296, 297, 300, 314, 315, 324, 326, 333, 340, 343, 345, 346, 348, 355, 361
specific intellectual 51, 52
spiritual sensitivity 272, 277
stem cells 8, 56, 85, 86, 307, 308, 309, 310, 311, 312, 313, 314, 315, 316, 317, 357
   embryonic stem cells 308, 309, 310, 313
   pluripotent stem cells 310, 312, 315, 357
   stem cell tourism 311
Stoic philosophy 283
Stoics 54, 55, 56
St. Thomas 183, 269
suffering 8, 78, 120, 122, 123, 126, 135, 138, 171, 178, 179, 181, 183, 186, 187, 191, 192, 193, 194, 199, 230, 235, 236, 237, 238, 239, 242, 248, 270, 271, 279, 280, 281, 282, 283, 284, 285, 286, 289, 291, 293, 294, 299, 300, 301, 303
superstition 318
supralapsarian 265
Swaraj 184
symbol 67, 126, 127, 188, 214, 231, 233, 234, 339
Systematic Theology 15, 20, 25, 29, 32, 60, 69, 81, 100, 127, 210, 222, 239, 274, 279, 319, 364, 371, 375

T
Tamar 135
Techno-reason 322
TEG 247, 248, 249, 294
teleology 251
Telugu poetry 183, 186, 187

TEOTWAWKI 212
Tetragametic chimeras 276
Thangaraj 181, 182
The Flood 288
theism 90, 97, 98, 99, 100, 101, 103, 104, 156, 157, 318, 320
   open theism 97, 98, 99, 100, 101, 104, 156, 157

theistic 8, 105, 108, 250, 252, 254, 255, 280, 281, 286, 294, 297, 298, 301, 302, 319, 326
theodicy 8, 248, 257, 281, 283, 284, 286, 287, 289, 293, 294, 298, 299, 300, 302, 303, 348, 361, 362
Theodicy, Evolution, and Genocide 247, 248, 294
theological method 20, 368, 371
theological principles 353
theology of the cross 4, 173, 228, 234, 239, 381
theopassianism 238, 239
Theophilus of Antioch 281, 282, 285, 288, 387
theoretical-explanatory realism 72, 73
therapeutic misconception 313
third-order 50
time 15, 110, 140, 141, 143, 161, 162, 163, 291, 343, 373, 376, 384
time symmetric 110

395

topos 143, 163
Tower of Babel 61, 145
transformation 19, 42, 103, 104, 152, 155, 164, 179, 180, 183, 185, 186, 194, 195, 207, 208, 217, 239, 278, 284, 320, 323, 324, 344, 352, 353, 354, 357
transhumanism 342, 345, 354, 356
transparency 86, 145, 277
Trinity 14, 65, 66, 67, 68, 92, 99, 127, 141, 142, 182, 238, 239, 257, 364, 370, 372, 373, 380, 381, 382
    economic Trinity 65
    immanent Trinity 66
triune relationality 99
twinning continuum 276

U
UFOlogy 330, 331, 337, 359, 360
UFOs 33, 34, 35, 36, 37, 56, 86, 181, 328, 329, 330, 331, 336, 337, 365, 367, 368, 378
universal intellectual 51, 52, 53
universalism 130
untouchability 184, 185, 188
untouchables 180, 181, 182, 188, 189, 190, 193, 194

V
Varnashrama Dharma 181, 182
venturum 113, 205
vocation 48, 132, 181

W
war 38, 175, 176, 213, 223, 230, 235, 249, 251, 254, 294, 295, 296, 298, 334, 335, 337
wisdom tradition 197
witness 16, 63, 67, 68, 84, 111, 123, 183, 194, 210, 214, 227, 242, 281
Worldview Construction 3, 13, 16

X
xenotransplants 314, 315